CHANGING

COURSE:

FISHING TRIPS
MERCHANT SHIPS
& NEW DIRECTIONS

BOB ADDEY

Dedication.

To Bethany, Isabelle and Elliott – this is how your grandparents met.

CONTENTS

PART FIVE - CHANGING COURSE

Preface

When I was a child I was given, as a gift, a bagatelle. A ball was fired by pulling a lever and then bounced from one pin to another until it landed in a scoring cup, or not depending on luck. As the game seemed to depend more on luck than skill I quickly abandoned it and never thought about it much until I looked back on life and felt that the game could be a useful analogy of life itself – we are propelled into the world and after an introductory period of parental guidance and care we bounce from pin to pin (influential people and experiences) making decisions that effect our future. Sometimes the decisions are right and sometimes wrong. Hopefully we end up with a happy and successful life. I was lucky in that the people that influenced me most offered not only guidance and advice that put me right when I could have been wrong, but also encouragement to take up opportunities that I may otherwise have missed, otherwise, like many less fortunate, the outcome could have been very different.

Many of these people are named in this book and I would like to apologise to those whose names I failed to remember. On the other hand some may have preferred that I had forgotten their names.

Particular thanks go to my sister's first husband, Jack Collins, who, along with my sister, took it upon themselves to offer a home to a homeless and aimless fourteen-year-old when they were barely out of their teens themselves. More than anything Jack provided a steadying hand, moral values and a work ethic. Further major influences were Peter Knox, an artist employed by the Seafarers' Education Service, who introduced me to a whole new interest, and Ron Fairfax, an inspirational teacher who encouraged me to open the door to education and a whole new career. I would also like to thank Mike Sterricker from Riverhead Books for his advice and guidance.

The book is primarily about my experiences at sea; experiences that helped shape me for the thirty-year career in education that followed. My thanks then to all my ex-shipmates for, while my main career may have been in education, at heart I was always, and always will be, a silly sailor.

Introduction

On a cold, wet morning in early January 1963, as the wind rattled the ratlines of the trawlers waiting for the tide, two fifteen-year-old schoolboys looked across St Andrews Dock towards the Hull trawler 'Lord Jellicoe'. The ship's lights lit up the deck and superstructure as the vessel prepared for sea.

One of the boys, me, was about to join the 'Lord Jellicoe' on my first trip to sea, the other lad, Ray Hawker, would follow to pursue his sea career later in the year. For now though it was just me, about to set out on a new life with some excitement, fear, and the thought of - what have I let myself in for?

The paddle steamer "Lincoln Castle" waiting at Victoria Pier to take passengers and cars from Hull to Newholland. The picture also shows Minerva Pier, the horse wash, and the Pilot Office.

PART ONE – HULL, HESSLE AND HALIFAX.

Chapter 1 . Anlaby Road

Kingston upon Hull, usually referred to as simply Hull, but locally known as 'ull, sits on the north bank of the Humber where the river Hull flows into the estuary. On the opposite bank is the county of Lincolnshire and at one time the only way to cross the estuary was by one of the ferries that ran from the pier in Hull. The ferries finished when the Humber Bridge opened in 1981 when only one ferry was left. I caught that ferry, along with my partner who would later become my wife and her two children, to leave Hull to start a new life in 1978.

My great, great grandfather, George Addey, had made the reverse journey from Lincolnshire to Hull, along with his partner and young children to start a new life in 1840, almost one hundred and forty years previously. His father, also called George, had been a solicitor in Epworth before shooting himself with a small pistol in 1830, five years after the death of his wife in 1825. George was only nineteen years old when his father took his own life but another local solicitor took young George on as an articled clerk. What happened next is unknown but George had been living in Winterton where he met his partner - they were never married - Louisa Atkinson, before moving to Hull to set up as a law stationer. George started a family tradition of calling the first-born male child John Thomas after George's two brothers and his grandfather. I don't think that George could have been aware of the innuendo involving the combination of these names, so his first son, John Thomas Atkinson Addey, a mariner turned coal merchant, called his first son John Thomas Addey, also a coal merchant, and he in turn called his first, John Thomas Henry Addey.

John Thomas Henry Addey was my father. Luckily I was the third son so I was named Robert. So although there was no euphemism for a penis involved in my name, an honour that was shared between my two elder brothers, there have been times when I've acted like one.

My father met my mother a couple of years before the outbreak of World War Two. My mother, Marjorie, was born in Cleethorpes to seafaring parents. Her father was a ship's steward who came from Cadenberge, Germany, and her mother, Edith Bailey, was a Bradford born stewardess on the Humber packets. My Father, John Thomas Henry Addey, was the only son of coal merchant John Thomas Addey and his wife Sarah Ann McDermott. My father always described his mother as having long curly, ginger-blonde hair and being very beautiful. John Thomas Henry also maintained that his mother was an actress and singer, noted for her fine singing voice. However, this information must have been passed down as Sarah Ann died on May 5th 1912, when John Thomas Henry was only seventeen months old, during an operation for cancer of the uterus. She was only thirty-four years old.

John Thomas continued to work as a coal merchant and did not remarry but foster parents with the name of Pennington brought up my dad. John Thomas Addey, my granddad, out-lived Sarah Ann by eighteen years. He died in 1930, in the hospital at 160 Beverley Road, the old Sculcoates Workhouse that had become known as the Beverley Road Institute in 1929, and what eventually became the Kingston General Hospital with the introduction of the NHS in 1948.

My grandfather on my mother's side also ended his life in what had been a workhouse. He had become naturalised British in 1911 but then the First World War with Germany broke out in 1914. This meant that in 1915 he had to register as an alien and report regularly to a police station in Hull. However, such was the bigotry and intensity of the anti-German feeling at that time, the family, then living in New Holland, suffered much verbal abuse and threats of violence as well as having the windows of their home broken. Eventually this became too much for my grandfather who had a mental breakdown and was committed to the mental health unit of what was then the Glanford Brigg (now known as Brigg) workhouse. The workhouse also became a hospital after the Local Government Act 1929 and this is where he died in 1939. I don't think he could face another war.

My dad first married in 1933 to a girl called Edna Dickerson and my older brother Malcolm Thomas was born in the same year. In 1935 my other brother, John Brian, was born. Tragedy struck when Edna died, aged only 24, on March 21st 1938. With two small children to look after my dad did not waste any time and on May 14th 1938 he married my mother at Hull Register office.

The couple met while Tom was singing with the Harry Gold band and Marjorie, working as a waitress in a café, was having a dalliance with the bandleader. Harry Gold had played with Joe Loss and several other bands prior to setting up his own band and touring the north of England in 1937 and 38. Later Harry was to become quite big in the jazz world, well as big as a five foot two saxophonist could be, as both an arranger and a performer with his later band known as Harry Gold and His Pieces of Eight.

My dad was a time served motor engineer but also aspired to a singing career. In 1939 Tom was appearing regularly at the Bridlington Spa. Tom Addey 'Sings Songs of Erin' was one billing in a show also featuring the young Vera Lynn. Then Hitler changed everything and another World War broke out. While this was the making of young Vera Lynn's career it was the end of Tom's. Soon he was called into the service of the RAF and sent down south to Middle Wallop to service Spitfires and keep them in the air during the Battle of Britain. Then my mother, still in Hull, got pregnant with my sister Denise and Tom was posted to Bridlington to work as an engineer on the Air Sea Rescue boats. This not only involved rescuing the living but also collecting the remains of the dead from the North Sea – something that stayed with him for the rest of his life.

After the war, Tom decided to set up in business. This consisted of a motor repair shop in Regent Street and a filling station and small shop at 241 Anlaby Road. The car repair workshop, which had its main entrance in Regent Street, could be accessed from a gate in the garden of the house. The family home, which consisted of a large kitchen where we spent most of our time and a sitting room, which we were not allowed to use except at Christmas or for special occasions on the ground floor, and bedrooms on the first floor, was accessed by a doorway next to the filling station. This is where I was born in 1947.

Apparently I was born with a caul, which was thought by seamen to be lucky and would prevent death by drowning. My mother wanted to keep the caul as a good luck charm (people put them into lockets when dried out) but it went missing, stolen by the midwife my mother claimed, as they were easy to sell to the fishermen on Hessle Road.

The filling station was in a line of shops between Regent Street and Bean Street; however the houses in these two streets were very different. Regent Street had larger houses that fronted the street with many having large rear gardens. Bean Street was largely made up of back-to-back terraces of very small houses but with a disproportional level of population. Both streets ran from Anlaby Road through to Hessle Road. Our house, which had been part of a row known as Adelaide Terrace when it was built around 1850, had originally been built as a large dwelling house but over the course of time the frontages of Adelaide Terrace had been converted into shops. Number 241 had in fact been a butcher's shop before becoming a petrol station. These were the days when there were a variety of shops like fishmongers, ironmongers, butchers and greengrocers so you had a good idea what you were eating before you ate it. The butchers for example would have lots of dead rabbits, still with fur and their heads in little tin buckets to catch the blood, hanging off their awnings. We didn't think 'Oh cute,' or feel sorry for them, we just felt that they would be yummy once made into a stew.

I remember that the shop on the corner of Bean Street was a Co-op that we used regularly, although many things including sweets were still rationed, as sugar rationing did not finish until 1953. I can still remember going to the sweet shop in Regent Street for a paper bag shaped like a cone filled with rainbow drops. To get to the sweet shop we had to pass a house with a porcelain dog in the window where I used to tell my mam was where my friend Wee Willie Winkie lived. He was my imaginary friend but because I didn't - not by choice - mix with other children, my mam indulged me this fantasy.

A couple of streets away, at the corner of Anlaby Road and the appropriately named Convent Lane, was a convent. My mam used to always hurry by the high walls that surrounded this building and would increase the speed, dragging me with her, if she saw a nun. She hated nuns. Apparently her mother had put her in a convent in Grimsby when she was a small child and the nuns had been very cruel to her. My mam said she thought this was because she was the only non-Catholic in the institution. She also said that she ran away from the convent on several occasions but each time her mother took her back for her to be punished by the nuns for running away. Eventually her mother got fed up of having to keep taking her daughter back to the convent and allowed her to stay in the family home with her brother. Some years later I asked her why her mother had treated her in this way and my mam simply said, "She didn't like me."

Mams in those days seemed to be able to make a joint of meat last for days, first as a roast, and then cold, then maybe a pie, and every home had a mincing machine so that nothing went to waste. Even the fat was saved in a bowl and served spread on bread with salt – delicious beef dripping. We also had some chickens for eggs and occasionally to eat. My mother was also an excellent baker. Her mother had been an apprentice time-served confectioner, and my treat was to 'lick the bowl out' with a wooden spoon after a cake had been mixed – very tasty even though it was just raw eggs, sugar, fat and flour.

These were also the days of strip washes, tin baths in front of the fire and coppers with a separate wringer for washing clothes. Bedrooms weren't heated and ice would form on the inside of the windows in winter and there were no duvets, just blankets with the addition of overcoats on top when it was really cold. Toilet paper was simply squares of the Hull Daily Mail dangling on string. Couple that with a weekly wash and the term 'skid marks' had different connotations to those caused by a braking, speeding motorist.

While we shared the large Victorian accommodation of 241 with an old lady and another family we had by far the largest portion of the building along with the large garden that led to my father's car repair garage. The filling station, which was part of my dad's business, consisted of two petrol pumps situated on the pavement in front of a small shop on the Anlaby Road frontage of the building. As this was a time when everyone smoked, the thought of petrol pumps on a busy pavement would today send any self-respecting 'health and safety' man diving for cover but no one cared then.

11

Access to the accommodation was by way of a doorway at the side of the filling station. Then down what seemed to me a very long and dark passageway into an even darker area, a stairwell with a staircase and doors to our rooms and, under the stairs, the cellar, where there were monsters! I never ventured into the cellar but my sister said one of my brothers spent a long time down there 'chopping wood'. I'm not sure but I always assumed that this was a euphemism.

Life really should have been very good. My dad employed two or three mechanics, we kept chickens in the garden, I had been born and all the family was back together. My eldest brother Malcolm (Thomas) was attending Kingston High School, my other brother (John) Brian, was attending the High School for Nautical Training and my sister Denise was at Bean Street where Brian had also attended before passing the scholarship to the Nautical School.

When I was five years old it was my turn to start at Bean Street and, having a sister six years older who returned home from school with horrific tales of school life although many of the complaints involved a certain George Collins - she was later to marry his brother Jack - who sat behind her and pulled her plaits, I knew this was not going to be an easy passage. Even though I didn't have plaits.

My main problem was that apart from my much older brothers and sisters, I had been brought up in almost complete isolation from other children. The consequence of this was that on my first day my mother had to drag me screaming into the school. I can still remember bracing my feet against the school steps as my mother pulled me towards the forbidding wooden doors. My first days were traumatic. I didn't even know how to use the school toilets as I had never used a urinal or a trough. I was used to lifting the lid of the toilet and that didn't go down too well with the girls. Soon, however, I settled in and enjoyed the company of the children in the school.

Malcolm's main interests at this time involved radio and electronics to the point that he, along with some school friends, built a radio station at home and started broadcasting. This of course was not legal but he got away with it and Malcolm was invited by the BBC to see how real radio stations operated. Malcolm, like the rest of us, left school at fifteen and did a variety of jobs before he was called up for National Service in the RAF. After leaving the RAF and working for the Ministry of Civil Aviation as a communications officer in Cheltenham he met his wife, Christa Guttmann, and they were married in 1955 and a few years later had a daughter Carmen. By then Malcolm and Christa had moved to London and Malcolm was working as a recording engineer for EMI at their Abbey Road studios. Malcolm worked on records for a number of household names of the late fifties and sixties including Cliff Richard and the Shadows -'Move It' and 'Apache', Johnny Kidd - 'Shakin' All Over', Helen Shapiro, Shirley Bassey, Adam Faith, and many others including the Beatles. He gained recognition as the engineer that produced 'Move it', recognised as Britain's first all-

British rock 'n' roll record, and also used his talent as a musician and his ability to read a score to do some composing and arranging.

Later, in 1968, Malcolm moved to New York where he still lives today with his partner since 1978, Charlotte Schroeder. Now in his eighties, Malcolm continues with his career and has been nominated for a Grammy Award several times.

About the same time as Malcolm joined the RAF, Brian left the Nautical School and signed on for seven years in the Royal Navy as a diver. During this service Brian was involved in the Suez Crisis. On leaving the Navy he worked on Hull tugs and then moved into engineering before starting up his own motor vehicle repair business. Brian was a talented table tennis and snooker player, as well as being an excellent roller skater, running a roller skating club in Hull, and becoming a club and mobile DJ. In later life he also took up flying as a hobby. Now in his eighties Brian continues with all of these activities and is also involved in community work. He still lives in Hull with his wife Jean Curtis who he married in 1971.

After joining the forces Malcolm and Brian only returned home during leave periods so I have little recollection of them during my first five years at 241 Anlaby Road. They were just mysterious bodies who turned up now and again, usually during the night when I was in bed, so most of the time it was just me, my sister and mam and dad.

I don't know quite when it all started to go wrong – but it did.

Above. Adelaide Terrace, between Regent Street and Bean Street on Anlaby Road. The Regent Service Station fronted 241 Anlaby Road in the middle of the block.

Right and below. The Regent Service Station.

(All the photographs on this page are reproduced with the kind permission of Paul Leslie Gibson, author of "The Anlaby Road" published by The Carnegie Heritage Action Team 2007)

Chapter 2. North Hull.

We got our first television in time for the Coronation in 1953 along with some memorabilia like specially pressed coins and a plastic golden coach. The television though was a big deal. Until buying this beast we had been content to listen to the Home Service on the radio so the addition of this new piece of furniture was a real novelty. And a piece of furniture was exactly what it was as the ten-inch screen and cathode ray tube was housed in a veneered wooden box. Later we even got a large magnifying glass to fit over the screen to try to make it look bigger. The grainy black and white picture was subject to constant tuning and knob twiddling by my dad to maintain some continuity, either visually or aurally and preferably both. All this for a very limited number of black and white programmes that closed down for an hour in the early evening and for good at about 10 o'clock.

The highlight of the week for a child in those early days was the Saturday edition of 'Muffin the Mule' - again not a euphemism - which featured a posh woman talking in a patronising way to a wooden puppet, which didn't speak and you could see all of the strings. On weekday afternoons there was a programme called 'Watch With Mother' which introduced characters like 'Rag, Tag and Bobtail', 'The Woodentops' (the star of this programme was the dog, Spotty), 'The Flowerpot Men', and 'Andy Pandy'. This latter programme, the flagship and most boring as I didn't understand innuendo, consisted of three puppets: a boy puppet, Andy, a girl puppet, Looby Loo and a teddy bear puppet called imaginatively, Teddy. Andy Pandy in his candy-striped onesie was the most camp puppet you could imagine, to the point that you expected Looby Loo to commit bestiality and elope with Teddy at the first opportunity.

People with upper class or middle class accents narrated all of these programmes. Working class people never seemed to be represented on TV unless they were actors or comedians pretending to be working class. This also applied to radio but at least on radio you didn't have to look at the announcers and presenters dressed in evening dress, but on TV even Fanny Craddock, a cook, wore a ball gown in the kitchen.

Radio was still the main home entertainment medium in those early days of television. The radio seemed to be on most of the time and the best programmes seemed to be on in the early evenings and on Sunday afternoons but these were mainly adult comedy programmes. For children there were programmes like 'Listen With Mother' - you can see where TV got its ideas from - and some serials and story sessions.

One of my favourite programmes was a children's music request programme on Saturday mornings where even though the music was requested you still heard the same tunes every week like: 'The Runaway Train', 'I Know an Old Lady Who Swallowed a Fly' and other gems by Burl Ives, 'I Tort I Taw a Puddy Tat' by Sylvester and Tweety Pie – my particular favourite, and many others. The programme was only spoiled when someone wrote in and asked for, 'The second movement from Mahler's Symphony No.1 in D Major, for my three-year-old daughter Alopecia Chlamydia,' or some such name.

Later in the fifties the programme that followed the children's requests was the 'Saturday Club' where generally second rate British singers copied the works of American rock'n' rollers. This was always regarded as second best and most young people preferred to listen to Radio Luxembourg in the evenings, even though the signal used to fade in and out. It wasn't until the pirate radio ships of the early 1960s forced the BBC to take action that people got proper radio coverage of pop music in this country.

My dad, as I said earlier, was blessed with an excellent tenor singing voice and had appeared with dance bands and in stage productions before and during the war. He had been billed as 'The silver voiced Irish tenor,' but Tom unfortunately did not persevere with this career professionally after the war. Instead he took to singing in pubs, especially when he'd had a few, which was most nights. Fishermen in the Bean Hotel in Bean Street would regularly ply him with drinks assured of some decent entertainment once he burst into song. Not normally a man to show that he had a great sense of humour, Tom was always at his happiest when he was getting washed to go out to the pub, which was every night.

Tom was not particularly sporty and did not show much, if any, interest in football or rugby unless a player was a regular in a pub he was using at the time. The only sport that he said he had participated in with any passion was motorcycle and side-car racing in his younger days and he also mentioned Cumberland wrestling. In fact he tried to encourage Brian to take this up and dragged him along to Hull Boys' Club to try it but Brian thought it was crap.

Many people had tales of their dads returning from the pub with a stray dog or cat in tow but they were not exotic enough for Tom who returned once with a pair of Java sparrows. They however were nothing compared to him coming home with Ginny the monkey! This monkey was a grass monkey that he got from some sailor in a pub. The poor monkey had lost half its tail when it had got trapped in the gangplank when being brought ashore and was quite a bad tempered and violent animal. In fact the only person that it liked was Marjorie. This caused much speculation within the family of why this should be with Tom claiming they were kindred spirits.

There's no doubt that Tom was an excellent and skilful engineer, but unfortunately he did not have the skills to be successful in business. Getting paid in money rather than fish would have helped. Originally the business at 241 Anlaby Road and Regent Street consisted of a filling station with pumps on the pavement and a shop, as well as the body and engine repair garage. However, Tom, using his business skills, sold the filling station and shop to a man called 'Piggy' Castleton for £100, much to the annoyance of my mam who considered the filling station as the only profitable part of the business. Anyway, eventually the whole business collapsed and bankruptcy returned Tom to being an employee of others, mainly in the motor trade, except for a brief time as the landlord of the Waverley Hotel in Hull City Centre. He remained working almost up to when he died aged 71 in Harrogate.

Tom always claimed to be an engineer and hated it if he was ever referred to as a mechanic or a fitter as he'd been trained to make tools and parts if needed. In his time he made adaptations to car controls for people with disabilities and, in the early fifties, converted an Austin 7 van into an open topped sports car. However, given the number of house moves the family were to experience, converting the van into a mobile home would have been more appropriate.

So bankruptcy meant moving on. After leaving 241 Anlaby Road the family moved to a house in Staveley Road on the newly built Bilton Grange council estate. A lot of people were moving out from the inner city streets like Bean Street to the new estates in the suburbs of Hull. Hitler had done his best to instigate urban development and rid Hull of its slums by saturation bombing and now the council was starting on a quest to complete the job. The new houses were considered luxurious - compared to the two up, two downs with an outside lavatory – these houses had bathrooms! I don't remember much about Staveley Road as we didn't stay there very long. I remember that there was still some building going on and playing in the mud that was to later become a grass verge. I think I went to the Griffin School while my sister went to Flinton Grove as she was now old enough to start secondary school.

I don't think we were on Bilton Grange longer than six months before our next move to a house on Spring Bank West. This house was situated next door to a butcher's shop that was on the corner of Albert Avenue. The butcher's shop was on the right of our house and in the house on the left, according to my sister, lived a flasher whose hobby was exposing himself from the bedroom window. Our house was a typical old-fashioned, three-bedroomed house with an outside lavatory. Yes, in the housing stakes we had gone backwards and it would not be the last time. Back to the tin bath and the winter nights in the bedrooms where the windows froze on the inside and you could barely move in bed due to the weight of the blankets and coats when it was really cold, and it always seemed that your nose was exposed.

Moving to Spring Bank West also meant changing schools and my sister and I were packed off to Paisley Street School. For me this meant another grim 1870 Education

Act school with iron and wooden desks and slates to write on. My sister liked it there but my only memories were of gloom, spending ages learning how to tie my shoelaces, and wetting myself when I couldn't wait for the 4 o'clock bell. I also had my first and, I think, last experience of performing on the stage as I was picked to play a Christmas cracker in the school's Christmas show. This meant reciting a short poem – 'I am a Christmas cracker' - while standing on the stage with a huge cracker around my neck. I found the experience traumatising as I fretted about forgetting the words, and delivered them in a high pitched staccato without change of expression so that I could rush off as soon as possible. So although my time at Paisley Street was not great I didn't have much time to worry about it as we were soon on our travels again.

This time it was back to a council house, 88 Eighth Avenue on North Hull Estate. This house was in the last block of Eighth Avenue on the corner with Orchard Park Road. This was as near as you could get to living in the countryside, as on the other side of Orchard Park Road was Taylor's farm. The farm stunk a bit because they kept pigs but there were also fields with sheep and cows as well as agricultural crops like wheat and peas. Around the corner from us were some council houses facing a green oval area opposite the farm and just beyond these houses were Barmston Drain and more open fields. I soon made friends in the area and those fields and the drain made the best playground ever. I can still remember some of the people around there. At the other end of our block lived the Patricks. Mrs Patrick was a very big woman and her husband was a very little, partially sighted man who worked at the Blind Institute. They had twin boys Keith and David who were my age and became playmates. Around the corner on the green lived the Sawdens. There were about seven children in total in the Sawden family including Teddy who was my age, and Johnny and Peter who were a year or two older, and these three further added to our little gang of adventurers. Finally, further round the green oval, lived the Newtons and Phillip 'Rusty' Newton was another regular playmate. And play we did: swings were made from old rope on trees; an old tyre would become a swing or a means of transport when we climbed inside and were bowled along; we swam in the drain (sometimes without our costumes so we had to run around the fields naked to dry off); we went bird nesting; chudding - nicking apples and pears from orchards; fishing and getting into mischief - no fence, or anything else combustible, was safe leading up to bonfire night! I loved it.

One day the older lads went off camping to the cliffs near Hornsea. The next day Teddy, Rusty, the Patrick twins and I decided to have a bike ride and visit them. We had a great time messing about by the sea and collecting mussels from the breakwater that we boiled over an open fire and ate with potatoes baked in the embers. The mussels tasted lovely, probably due to their proximity to the sewage outfall but we didn't care. Then we realised it was getting late so we decided to stay overnight. We needed to let our parents know so that they wouldn't be worried but the problem was that none of us had a phone at home. However, the Patrick's next-door neighbour did, so we rang her and asked her to walk around to all of our houses to let our parents know. What a cheek, but she did.

The sleeping arrangements were tight as it was only a two-man tent with about nine of us in it, but again we didn't care. In the morning the older lads threw us out to make breakfast. We needed a bit of water to loosen up the baked beans a bit, couldn't find any, so used seawater. Nobody seemed to notice and everything tasted okay, and would you believe, nobody went down with food poisoning.

Barmston drain was the main attraction as a play area near where we lived as, from the bridge over Orchard Park Road going north towards Dunswell, the drain had been cut through open fields. While people swam near the bridge on Orchard Park Road we generally used a spot we called second (seggy) field where the bank had been eroded, which gave us easy access to the water. The drain itself started in inner city Hull where there were also popular swimming spots, especially near the overflows of warm water from the electricity cooling towers, but where we were, in the countryside, the water was cool and fresh.

Generally the drain water was clear and, apart from the odd floating dead pig, clean. We regularly watched water voles going about their busy business and there was plenty of fish: roach, perch, tiddlers, sticklebacks, eels and some large pike. There were obviously dangers as the drain was quite deep in places and the reeds on the bottom were thought to hold you down if they caught your foot and it wasn't unknown for people to get into difficulties, and occasionally drown. We never saw the dangers though, as the drain was our free source of fun and adventure.

Another playmate of mine at this time was our dog Tanji. Tanji was a black labrador cross whom we'd had for as long as I could remember. Apparently, when we lived in 241 Anlaby Road Tanji was recruited to become a police dog but he didn't like it and trotted home with a piece of blue material between his teeth. In those days dogs didn't have leads – they were just sent out to play, just like the kids and returned home when they were hungry. Tanji was a lovely dog and we roamed the fields together but unfortunately Tanji also took to roaming the fields alone and that was when he was accused of worrying sheep. We argued about this at first but when he returned home with pellets in his nose our suspicions were confirmed and he had to be re-homed.

We didn't get a new dog to replace Tanji but I did get a rabbit of a variety called Flemish Giant. We naturally called the rabbit Thumper but Attila the Bun would have been a more apt name because, as it got older, this bunny was not a friendly giant. At first it was a cuddly, cute little grey bunny but soon it grew into a malicious, bad tempered monster, its size reflecting the 'giant' of its breed. It quickly started to outgrow its hutch and getting it out to clean the hutch became more like a wrestling match as the animal tried to bite and kick as it didn't like being handled. It was more like a boxing kangaroo than a pet rabbit and it had to go. Luckily one of my friends said that he would have it. A few weeks later my mother asked him how he was getting on with the rabbit and if he liked it?

"Yes," he replied, "it was really tasty, we had it on Sunday." On Sunday! On Sunday! That animal was big enough to feed a family for a week!

To replace the rabbit I was allowed to keep a couple of mice that within a few short months multiplied until I lost count at forty-eight. Mother was not too pleased about sharing her kitchen with all these rodents and having the room smell like a pet shop and one day I returned from school to find that my dad had flushed the lot down the toilet.

If you turned left from Eighth Avenue into Orchard Park Road, a short walk would bring you to St Michael's Church, a row of shops and the terminus of the number 17 bus. I briefly tried being in the church choir but my parents were not churchgoers and getting up really early on a Sunday morning was a chore and not as productive as getting up to collect wild mushrooms in the fields, so I gave up the choir. I also tried the Cubs once. That was crap as well – very cliquey and not that welcoming of new members.

The shops were a magnet particularly the chip-shop and a general grocers where they also sold sweets. When you entered the shop there was a row of large boxes, tilted at an angle and with glass lids that contained loose biscuits. Our ploy was to go in as a group and stand with our bums to the boxes and, while one of us bought a penny sweet, the others would lift one of the lids on the boxes and steal the biscuits. Another ploy, legal this time, was to return empty bottles. Most bottles then were recycled so we would get pennies for their return. Usually there would be odd lemonade or beer bottles lying around at home so this was a useful way of getting money for 'goodies'. One day I collected some empty bottles and a couple of them had contained Domestos. I didn't think anything of this at the time, I just took them to the shop and scoffed the bounty they had returned. My favourite sweets at this time were things like kay-lie, a yellow, sugary powder that you ate with a stick of hard liquorice called Spanish or your licked finger, which would stain yellow, McGowan's toffee, peanut brittle, liquorice root, which we chewed until the end looked like a paintbrush, and I was also partial to tiger nuts. I didn't know when I took them but there must have been some residue in the Domestos bottles that must have leaked through the little hole they had in the top. Very shortly my bottle green corduroy shorts were mottled with cream stains as the bleach activated.

Needless to say my mam was not too pleased, as she had to fork out for a new pair of pants! My thrift had not been too thrifty.

On Saturday mornings the children's matinee at the Rex cinema in Endike Lane attracted the urchins of North Hull Estate like a magnet. It was probably very good value for our parents to give us the few pennies entrance fee to get rid of us for a couple of hours. The cinema showed a selection of serials and short films featuring Roy Rogers, Flash Gordon, Our Gang and the like, as well as a number of Looney Tunes cartoons. On our way home we would re-enact some of the scenes we had seen on the screen by running about slapping our bums to simulate horse riding with one hand, while using our other hand as an imaginary gun to shoot each other (usually refusing to die). We were all cowboys; no one wanted to be an Indian.

We only ever went on holiday once. Being in the motor trade dad had no trouble in getting hold of a cheap or borrowed car so usually holidays meant the odd day trip to Hornsea or Withernsea, or a day out to see my father's foster mam, Grandma Pennington. She lived in a small terraced house in Bridlington and I remember that the living room was always dark and smelled of mothballs. There was a table covered with a heavy cloth and a tall dark dresser on the top of which she kept her sweet tin. I would always gaze up at this like a dog at dinnertime until she reached up and offered me a sweet treat.

There were also odd times when we'd go on the ferry to New Holland to visit my mother's brother and his wife and daughters in Cleethorpes but we rarely stayed overnight. This time though, we were going on holiday and were to stay on a houseboat. The houseboat turned out to resemble a small floating caravan on the Leven canal. Yes, the Leven canal, about seven miles from where we lived! Of course I wasn't aware of the closeness of this location at the time and because it was a gloriously hot week it didn't seem to matter especially when dad fell in trying to get out of the small rowing boat that came with the accommodation. We soon realised that Leven was a good location for dad as it meant that he was in easy travelling distance of his favourite pubs.

We had a great holiday even though we were so close to home. However, for my sister the holiday resulted in quite a different experience as she ended up in intensive care in Castle Hill Hospital with TB meningitis. Luckily she made a full recovery but she was in hospital for some time. It was felt that she had picked up the bacteria which caused her illness while swimming in the Leven canal.

The school that I went to - it was now 1954 and I was now aged seven - was 21st Avenue, otherwise known as 'Green Huts' because it was a series of temporary buildings similar to portacabins. Denise went to Fifth Avenue School. I don't remember too much about the teachers at 21st Avenue only that my favourite was

21

an elderly lady. Discipline was kept by use of the ruler but this lady, like all good teachers, never used corporal punishment. Thinking back to my schooldays, it seems that modern-day children, who only have to learn the metric system, have it very easy. We had to contend with pounds, shillings and pence (£.s.d.) with 240 pennies in a pound, 12 pennies in a shilling, and 20 shillings in a pound, further complicated by guineas, three-penny pieces, florins, half-crowns, half pennies and farthings. How would they cope nowadays with a question like, if a dozen eggs cost three pence three farthings, how much would it cost to buy a gross? How would they get by using miles, yards, feet, inches, chains and furlongs? The only time I've come across a use for a furlong is in horse racing, so maybe they were training us up for a gambling addiction.

Every morning, after registration, we had to recite our times tables. True we learned by rote, parrot fashion, but it stayed with you and has always been useful. At junior school I must say that I was not that interested in sport. The only race I ever won was an obstacle race on the school sports day, and football, at that level, seemed to consist of two fat kids in goal with the rest of the teams running around the pitch grouped in one heaving mob chasing the ball!

At the age of fifteen, my sister left school and went to work at Woolworth's in Whitefriargate, first on haberdashery and later as a window dresser. If you have the idea that this was an artistic and creative job you obviously do not remember Woolworth's windows, as the aim was to get as many products on display as possible and any variation from this meant trouble. My two brothers left the family home completely during our stay in North Hull. Malcolm rarely came home for any length of time anyway as when he'd finished his National Service he chose to stay in Cheltenham where he'd met his future wife before moving to London.

Brian, on the other hand, came home and looked for a job after he'd served his time in the Royal Navy. His first job after leaving the Navy was on a tug, the 'Rifleman', and I remember him taking me aboard once when the tug was working in one of the docks. This could be a dangerous job with ropes and wires being pulled taut with always the danger of them snapping. However, I survived this visit and noted that it may be of use as a future career reference. The tug did not stay on dock duty for long before it was required to work out in the North Sea but Brian didn't like this. He said it was his worst sea experience ever and left to become a diver on the docks. Soon he changed his job again and very shortly after he met his first wife Edith and left the family home, with a suitcase on the front of a bike, to set up home with her. Later he became an engineer and eventually owned and ran a car repair garage.

As a child you are very trusting of your parents and accept everything that happens as being normal. But it was during our time in Eighth Avenue that I began to realise that normal wasn't really normal. There were always a lot of arguments and it was often the case that one or the other of my parents left home. Usually this was for only a few days before returning on a Saturday night after the drink had mellowed the ill feeling. Where they went to during these times is anybody's guess but again we just accepted this as normal. In retrospect I think the main problem was my mother working as a barmaid and getting a lot of male attention while my dad was on the other side of the bar drinking a proportion of their joint earnings and seething with jealousy.

At home my mam, like most mothers in those days, had a cupboard in which she stored special food and treats that she saved throughout the year 'for Christmas'. If she left, the cupboard was immediately raided by my dad who used most of the contents to prepare meals when he couldn't be bothered to go to the shops. This kind of lessened the drama of my mam not being home. I don't know who was most to blame for this situation as both of them, shall we say, had their moments of indiscretion. And both of them had a temper, although I never witnessed any acts of violence by them on each other, other than when my mam jumped on my dad's back in the kitchen once. He just shrugged her off and carried doing what he was doing while she went to pack a bag again.

My dad would often give me a clip around the ear if I'd been in trouble and got within clipping range and he did take a slipper to me once but other than that he wasn't too bad. My mother was more formidable both verbally and violently, as she would hit you with anything that was handy if she got the chance. This was the time before political correctness, so parents and teachers could get away with a lot. Even so I think my sister and I were better treated than our half brothers and that's why they chose to stay away as much as possible and leave home as soon as they could.

Anyway, after about three years it was moving time again, this time back to the city centre to the Porter Street flats. Denise had left school and was working, and my parents decided that I should stay at 21st Avenue School to complete the final year before going to secondary school. This meant catching the number 17 bus every day and staying school dinners, although sometimes I'd go to the home of a friend, Barry Jackson, who lived with his grandmother who cooked us chips. The idea was that I would not be disrupted during the time leading up to the 11 Plus Exam. This was in the days of grammar schools and in order to get a scholarship you had to sit a series of exams. These weren't even set during school time as I had to go to a strange school - Fifth Avenue - on a Saturday morning to sit them after filling in a form giving a priority list of schools you wished to attend. This was a waste of time for me as I failed, which wasn't unusual because it was an unfair system, as only about 25% of entries could be successful no matter how well they did in the exam. But I don't remember being bothered, as I wouldn't be with any of my mates anyway and I would be going to a new school no matter what.

Our flat in Porter Street was on the sixth floor, which meant we had good views over the city centre. The flats had been built in an area that had been heavily bombed during the war and next door was an interesting bombed building to play on. This had been the site of the Alhambra Music Hall that later became the Hippodrome cinema. The building was long gone but there were still the stairs to what would have been the balcony and other bits left standing in ruins that made it an exciting adventure playground. The good thing about living in Porter Street was that we were very close to the city centre shops, theatres and cinemas. The Palace Theatre was just around the corner and seats in the upper circle were just a few pennies. Having older brothers and sisters I was very interested in music, rock'n'roll was just taking off, and as well as the early films there were live package tours featuring the latest pop and rock stars that usually took place at the Regal, later the ABC, cinema. I was lucky enough to be one of the few people to see Buddy Holly at the Regal when he came to Hull in 1958 even though I was only ten years old at the time. I also saw package tours with people like Joe Brown, Marty Wilde and Billy Fury who were all popular in that pre-Beatles period.

Above. Class photograph from 21st Avenue Junior School. (Author on the back row, fourth from right).

Left. Author when a student at Hull Trinity House.

Chapter 3. Boulevard to Hessle.

When I reached the age of eleven, I needed to attend secondary school and we found that the nearest was Boulevard High School, which meant a bus trip down Anlaby Road. We were still living in Porter Street when we applied but by the time I started in the September we had moved again to the Waverley Hotel – now known as the Master's Bar - on the corner of South Street and Jameson Street, next door to the White House Hotel, even closer to the city centre. My mam, Marjorie, had worked as a barmaid nearly all her life and my dad, Tom, had spent most of his free time in pubs so they both thought they were well qualified for this job. In fact my mam had worked as a barmaid in the Waverley, which was also a popular haunt for my dad who propped up the bar spending the money my mother earned, so at least now they would both be earning. I'm sure they thought it was a good idea at the time.

The pub consisted of a cellar, where dad spent a lot of time in the mornings cleaning the pipes in search of his quest for the perfect pint, a ground floor bar and an upstairs lounge. Our accommodation started on the second floor accessed by a stairway from the lounge and a private entrance with a steep stairway from a door in South Street. The living quarters consisted of a large kitchen, an even larger lounge with a huge fireplace, three bedrooms on the next floor, and even more rooms on the never used top floor. While I didn't mind living there, it had lots of advantages, the thing about pub life for children is that you hardly see your parents. I'm not sure that they saw each other much as dad always settled himself in the bar while my mam ran the lounge, so it is not a vocation I would recommend for a good family life. Later, when my sister became eighteen she also worked in the lounge where she was to meet her future first husband, a merchant seaman called Jack Collins. He was the brother of the infamous George Collins who pulled her plaits at Bean Street School and the son of Jack and Louise Collins who were drinking associates of Tom from the Bean Hotel. They say, 'It's a small world,' but Hull is even smaller.

Living in a pub was a lonely life for a child although we did have a pet cat. I don't know where we got this cat from, probably a stray that we adopted, or more likely it adopted us as cats do. It was a black cat and was always there on the stairs to meet me when I got home from school. I was very fond of it, more fond of it in fact than my mother who got rid of it one day, so when I got home from school there was no cat on the stairs! I was heartbroken and to this day I've no idea what terrible sin he'd committed, probably crapped in a corner. Anyway to compensate my mother said I could have another dog so we went off to the RSPCA kennels in Clough Road.

What a place. It was as if all the dogs in there were auditioning for the dog version of RADA. Some were barking and frisky as if saying, 'look at me' and 'how cute am I?'

Others just sat with their heads cocked looking sad, and a few others just mournfully howled. We chose a quiet one that just looked at us sorrowfully. The dog looked like a small, brown collie and we called her unimaginatively, Lassie. Lassie proved to be a bargain as within a few weeks it was very apparent that she was pregnant and our one dog became six as she gave birth to five pups. It was then decided, although I was not consulted, that Lassie would also have to go and that we would keep one of the male pups. The pups, except for one, were really cute and were soon snapped up by the pub's customers, Lassie was returned to the RSPCA, and we were left with the ugly pup. This pup was all white with a brown patch over one eye and ear with the other ear also brown and we called him Sparky. As he grew it was clear that Sparky had inherited his mother's looks and soon became a very handsome, collie-like dog - a fine example of the Ugly Duckling syndrome - and I had a new playmate.

While in the pub I also took up fishing after I got a rod for a Christmas or birthday present and some of the pub regulars took me to Broomfleet canal with them on Sundays during the fishing season. I also used to go to East Park on the bus to fish in the boating lake. One day when I went, it was a very cold day and for me it was going to get a lot colder, the fish were not biting although infuriatingly I could see some largish fish lurking in the water but refusing to take my bait. If I could only get a bit closer... if I could just reach out a little more... just one more stretch and a swing of the line...

SPLASH! I was in, and not for the first or indeed the last time, my ability to swim saved the day. I scrambled to the side, fully clothed and dripping wet. And that is how I travelled home on the bus, dripping wet and standing in a pool of water, receiving curious looks from the conductor and the other passengers.

It was also whilst living in the pub that I got drunk for the first time, not on the drinks that were freely accessible but at a New Year's Eve party. We had been invited to the home of one of the pub's regular users, a trawler skipper by the name of Wilf Parkinson who lived in a large house on the outskirts of Hull somewhere. I was only eleven and Wilf looked for something I could drink that was acceptable to my taste and came up with port and lemonade. I loved it. "Just help yourself," he said. So I did... again and again and again - is the room spinning? I don't remember how we got home but I do remember being sick in bed and the red of the port staining my pillow, the awful headache, the inability to speak or eat; my parents were not too chuffed. The hangover put me off drinking port for a long time although in adulthood I now enjoy the odd glass to accompany a cheese board.

Boulevard High School was what was known as a 'secondary modern' as opposed to a 'grammar school'. Schools often determined where you ended up in life and all schools used a streaming system with the top streams of the grammar schools feeding the universities and teacher training colleges. The lower streams of the grammar schools would generally go into office jobs, commerce and technical apprenticeships, as did the top streams of the secondary moderns who had, in theory, been trained for industry, while the lower streams of the secondary moderns became the unskilled workers and labourers.

The school leaving age was, at that time, fifteen, but grammar school pupils generally stayed on to achieve academic certificates. Most children from the secondary moderns left with no qualifications. Post age fifteen education and training in technology, engineering or commerce was provided by colleges of further education through evening classes (night school), day or block release from work, or full time training courses. I know this is a simplified structure and there were many exceptions but this seems to have been the reasoning.

The building used to create Boulevard School had once been used by the grammar school known as Kingston High School that had moved to a greenfield site in Pickering Road. Now it was being used as a boys' school as other old 1870 Education Act schools in the Hessle Road and Anlaby Road areas like Bean Street Boys', Chilton Street and West Dock Avenue, closed. The result was that this was basically a new school in old buildings that were already inadequate. It was also a bit chaotic at first until the teachers sorted the classes out. On the first day we all had to stand in the yard until our names were called out with our class and room numbers; mine was 2C with Mr Braine.

I knew something was wrong almost straight away as this was a second year class and the other lads in the class seemed older and bigger but I was too shy to ask if a mistake had been made. However, Mr Braine must also have suspected this as within a few days he said he wanted to check our dates of birth. He then asked us each in turn to give our full name and date of birth. One or two comedians deliberately got the year wrong, 1947 for 1946, before quickly correcting themselves and getting laughed at by the class, much to Mr Braine's irritation. When my turn came I of course said 1947, which was met with more laughter and jeers but this time Mr Braine told the others to shut up and asked me if I was sure, and I replied, 'Yes'.

Needless to say I was moved straight away to 1C, then after a short period, to 1B, and again after another short period, to 1A. It was obvious that the streaming system was a bit hit and miss. The result of this was that I had managed to make friends in all the classes that I was in so this worked out well for me.

Discipline at Boulevard was maintained by the liberal use of the cane. Some of the teachers were particularly vicious with this form of punishment to the point of sadism. One teacher, Mr 'Daddy' Harpham, who incidentally had taught my sister music at Bean Street, had a particularly old and flexible cane. His method was to make you hold your hand out and he would then tap your knuckles from underneath to get your hand into his preferred position, before swishing the cane down from behind his head and across your palm or fingers. This stung.

On top of this, he usually gave you two, one on each hand, he would then make you say, 'Thank you,' to which he'd reply, 'Liked it did you? Then you shall have another.'

Corporal punishment was the norm in those days as was a clip around the ear. The result was rule by fear and it must be said that you never heard of hyperactive kids although it's a good bet that there were a number of 'punch-drunk' ones by the time they were fifteen.

There were some good teachers at the school who didn't have to resort to violence to keep order, Mr Johnson was one, Mr Allison was another, but generally it was accepted behaviour. Not that we didn't deserve punishment as there was always talking, joking, sometimes fights, and minor mischief and the classes were large so it must have been difficult for the teachers trying to keep order and get us to learn something. However, for the more serious stuff you could find yourself sent to the deputy head, Mr Adams, and if he caned you, you really knew about it. I got sent to him once for a scuffle in the playground, normally a caning, but I got away with a bollocking. Why? Because I'd quickly realised that you could get away with a lot more at Boulevard if you were a member of one of the rugby teams. Rugby was the main sport as we were situated close to the Boulevard, home of Hull FC, the local professional rugby league club.

The rugby played at Boulevard, and indeed at all of the secondary modern schools in Hull in those days, was rugby league (then considered a northern working class sport), whereas the grammar schools played rugby union.

It wasn't easy getting into the rugby teams as competition was fierce and I did not have a track record of being good at sports, so I had to somehow develop my limited skills. Every week we would be bussed to playing fields on the edge of the city to play football or rugby, or in summer, cricket. Boulevard School itself only had a concrete schoolyard that even then, in the days of lax 'health and safety', couldn't be used for these physical games. I chose to play rugby rather than football. And one day, cold, wet and muddy, I was standing on the halfway line supposedly defending, when the biggest, fastest player on the opposing side came hurtling at full pelt towards me.

I looked around and there was no other player close, so it was just me between him and our try-line. My first instinct was to get out of the way but as he side-stepped me and momentarily relaxed thinking he was on his way to the try-line, I stuck my arm in front of his thighs and slipped down to his ankles. It was a textbook tackle and he came crashing down to earth as he cursed me under his breath.

'Well done', shouted my team-mates. I knew then that I could do this and made several more tackles and even scored a try, although the player that I'd tackled got his revenge by jumping on my back as I touched down and nearly sending the ball through my chest. There was no turning back now and I was invited to train with the rugby team and named as a reserve for the following Saturday.

Because I was a little bit tubby, 'puppy fat' as they say, I was put with the forwards as a potential second row. Your size determined your position in those days.

If you were big and fat you were a prop forward; short and stocky – a hooker; medium size and a bit stocky – second row; just big – loose-forward; skinny and short – scrum-half; not quite as skinny and short – off-half. Wingers and centres were generally interchangeable, although the wingers tended to be taller and faster: the full-back had to be a good catcher of the ball and a strong runner.

This was also true for the professional adult game at that time as the tactics depended on the forwards holding the ball and progressing forward in their own half – one pass and charge – until in the opponents' half when the ball could be passed. As this was the tactic from kick off I never saw our full-back pass the ball. Forwards also formed the scrum, and were expected to push the opposing forwards away from the ball, which had to be placed into the centre of the scrum by the scrum-half, so that the hooker would hook it back to the feet of the second-row and then out into play by the scrum-half or loose-forward. Nowadays the scrums in professional rugby league are a parody, as the ball never goes in centrally and the forwards break as quickly as possible without much pushing. In fact the game has changed so much now with the professionals spending most of their days in the gym bodybuilding.

I was watching a match on television recently when my wife came in, watched it for a few minutes and said, "What's happened to all the big fat blokes?"

In the old days of course the players were semi-professionals and held down other jobs when they were not playing or training – all to change with commercialism, sponsorship, cheap air travel and Sky TV coverage making the game a highly commercial financially viable international professional sport.

In keeping with my new found athleticism I asked for a rugby ball for my birthday expecting a fine, leather one that I could 'dubbin' to waterproof it. What I actually got was a plastic oval ball that was pointed at both ends, once more the points were rock hard so that if you happened to kick the pointed end it felt as though you'd kicked a brick. It was lucky I didn't break a toe attempting a torpedo kick for the first time. Anyway I had to wait until Christmas but eventually I got my proper leather ball.

Our rugby training was held after school on Hull FC's ground, the Boulevard. It was a real treat for us to be on the same pitch as our heroes. The forwards trained at one end of the pitch while the backs trained at the other, so for the first session I was sent to train with the other forwards. One of the exercises involved our teacher and coach, standing on the try-line and throwing the ball towards us standing in a group. We were expected to catch the ball and then barge our way through using our power. The result was that the ball was thrown and pounced upon by a heaving malaise of bodies. It reminded me of the tactics of primary school football, except that instead of being in goal all the fat kids were chasing the ball! So I lurked at the back. Suddenly the ball appeared over the heads of the mob in front of me, so I picked it up, ran round the back of the heaving mass and touched down. Try! Then... a bollocking!

'You're not supposed to run and dodge!' yelled the teacher, 'You're supposed to push through!'

We reformed and the game continued. The ball was thrown, the heaving mass scrambled for it, I lurked near the back, the ball fell in my hands, two side-steps and a sprint around the back and I touched down again. Try!

I was immediately banished from the group and told to run up and down the pitch passing the ball with the backs. That's how I came to play centre or wing. In truth I was an okay player, not a star. I learned how to run and pass a bit but my tackling was very good so this made me a good, safe, standby and I played regularly in the back line. I can still remember many of the players' names from those days, even though we were only eleven when we started, including: Greenwood, Moss, Angel, Addey, Mower, Kerwin, Burrows, Hunter, Williams, Simpson, Richardson, Hawker and Pollard.

In keeping with the interest in rugby the main annual school trip was to London in May. Very early on the Saturday morning of the Rugby League Challenge Cup Final we would assemble at the school and board coaches that would take us to Wembley Stadium. It didn't matter which teams were playing as we started saving for this months before the first kick of the competition had taken place, although it was a bonus if our local team was playing. It wasn't just our school that did this: schools, social clubs, pubs and other organisations across the north of England organised trips for the Cup Final which always ensured a full house at Wembley. On these adult trips it was usually just the men who went to the match while the women hit the shops in Oxford Street before meeting up with their other halves later for a meal, perhaps a show, and maybe an overnight stay in a hotel. Our trip though was just for the match and a meal, followed by a seat in 'the Gods' at the London Palladium for the evening show, then a coach ride home in the early hours.

One year I remember fondly that Peter Allison took a couple of us in a taxi to see the sights of London, an act of kindness that I have not forgotten. I can also remember Mr Adams almost exploding with pride shortly after the return from one of these trips when he read a letter that had been published in the 'Daily Express'. It praised the politeness of some of our pupils who had offered their seats on the tube to standing adults. Apparently the writer had asked one of us where we were from and they had told him that we were pupils at Boulevard High School, Hull.

The main curriculum at Boulevard was very firmly industrial based and apart from the usual maths, English, geography, art and German, we had technical drawing and a choice of woodwork or metalwork. The woodwork teacher was fond of mottoes and his workshop was full of posters with slogans such as 'Manners Maketh Man' and the like. Woodwork was always oversubscribed anyway but I decided to do a bit of metal bashing like my dad and chose metalwork. I really enjoyed this, especially using the anvil and lathe. I also enjoyed art as the teacher, Mr Shaw, seemed to recognise that I had some creativity. In general though I don't think the teachers had very high expectations of anyone from the school but this didn't seem to matter. The school system closely reflected the class system only slightly modified by the effects of World War II and the promises made including the 1944 Education Act and improved welfare. The grammar schools were still dominated by the middle classes and middle class values while the secondary moderns were generally working class, particularly in the inner city areas and areas with large council estates. However, there was scope for aspiration and employment was guaranteed.

Hull had been heavily bombed during the war and was being rapidly redeveloped which meant lots of construction jobs. The west of Hull was dominated by the fishing industry, whereas the commercial docks, milling and manufacturing, dominated the east of the city. Wherever you went in Hull you could not escape the influence of the sea. Even in the city centre, where Queen Victoria looked down from her seat above the public lavatories outside the City Hall, there were the bows of trawlers lined up in Prince's Dock with people viewing from Monument Bridge. The salty image was enhanced by the smell from the city centre fishmongers. So from Boulevard, many of the brighter lads with aspirations went into apprenticeships to become electricians, motor mechanics or perhaps into engineering or sheet metal work with one of the companies that serviced the fishing industry. This meant an investment of four or five years on a relatively low wage but with the promise of reaping the benefits of regular, highly paid employment later. Those who wanted a 'quicker fix' could go into one of the semi-skilled or unskilled occupations on offer. These paid more than apprenticeships but were often casual in their nature so there were no guarantees.

Fishing was a good example where everyone started at the bottom as a galley boy and worked their way up. On the fish dock itself many young lads started off as barrow boys before becoming fish porters, salesmen, filleters or bobbers - the men who unloaded the trawlers. One thing everyone had was a work ethic. Unemployment and benefits was not an option, no matter what your school results were, although this does not mean that some of the teachers at Boulevard were not inspirational and encouraged some to aspire to higher achievements. The teachers I remember in this category were the English teachers, Mr Johnson and Mr Allison, the letter writing skills they taught us were very useful later in life, and Mr 'Neddy' Hood.

Boulevard was a school that looked more towards sporting than academic achievements and Mr. Hood was especially enthusiastic about swimming. I still believe that swimming is an essential skill that all children should learn. I could swim before I went to Boulevard and it certainly saved my life on at least one occasion. Every week we'd go to Madeley Street or Albert Avenue baths for a swimming lesson where we gradually collected our various certificates and would occasionally have races. Mr Hood was also into style and picked up that I had a good backstroke style and potential for developing the butterfly, so he invited me to join the swimming team. There were swimmers in the team much faster than me, such as Walster, Williams and Simpson, but Mr Hood was a good coach and encouraged us to join the Hull Olympics Swimming Club in the evenings to receive more coaching from both himself and from the local swimming hero, Jack Hale.

During 1958, my first year at Boulevard, there was more disruption on the home front. Managing a pub was not the dream job that my dad thought it was and we can't have been there even a year before he decided to go back as chief mechanic for the East Riding School of Motoring. This meant that we lost our home as well, so moved to a rented house in Holmes Street off Fountain Road. The house consisted of three bedrooms, two rooms downstairs with a small kitchen and an outside lavatory and coal-house. Hot water came from a gas geyser in the kitchen.

Holmes Street was a cul-de-sac but had once been a through street until a tan-yard was built across it. But the tan-yard was now used as a long distance lorry depot, so lorries trundled up and down all day. At the top of the street was another lorry depot for the Co-operative Society but this closed in the evening leaving the garage doors to act as goalposts and the walls for chalk drawn cricket stumps. On the corner of Fountain Road and Holmes Street was a sweet shop and tobacconist and opposite were some other shops including a general grocer's, a butcher's and a hairdresser's etc. Just beyond Holmes Street towards Beverley Road was a drain and on the corner of the drain footpath was a greengrocer's. Holmes Street consisted mainly of terraced housing although our house number 72, which was on the corner of a terrace, had an on street front door. The back was accessed by a back passage, shared by the houses from two back-to-back terraces. The location meant that I should have changed schools to Fountain Road but my parents agreed that I could stay at Boulevard although this meant a long cycle ride there and back.

Even though I didn't go to the local school I soon made friends in Holmes Street as there were quite a lot of boys and girls around my age, and we'd meet in the street in the evenings and at weekends. Usually this meant playing football or cricket but occasionally we'd get on our bikes and go to Beresford Avenue playing fields, Pearson Park or Beverley Road swimming baths, which closed and became a dance hall during the winter months. We would also occasionally turn a lamppost into a swing using a rope and a tyre. The girls would often join in when they weren't skipping, playing hopscotch or doing handstands. This was quite 'interesting' for us lads, as the clothing then was not as practical as it is now and the girls just tucked the bottom of their dresses into their knickers to give them more freedom.

Another popular game was block, a form of hide and seek, which enabled us to utilise the many back passages of Holmes Street. Again this could get interesting if you found yourself hiding with a girl you liked. I think I had my first proper kiss at this time but that was all we knew then.

However things were about to change again. If my dad had had any business sense he would have taken out shares in 'Mitchell's the Movers', as my mam and dad decided to give the licensed victualler's trade another go by taking the roles of steward and stewardess at the Hessle Golf Club. This involved cooking meals as well as looking after the bar and the clubhouse.

A house came with the job at the golf club, a small but comfortable terraced house, at 8 Barrow Lane in Hessle. The house consisted of three bedrooms, a bathroom, a lounge and a kitchen. It had a small front garden and at the back were an air raid shelter and a corrugated-iron garage that never held a car but formed a play area for me and some rats - until the rat man came. The rent book for the Holmes Street house was then passed to my sister and her boyfriend Jack who were now planning their wedding although they did not move in until after the big event which would now take place at the church in Hessle.

The job at the golf club meant that my parents not only looked after the place and the bar but also had to cook meals so we spent quite a lot of time up there. The course itself was in two parts with the main part to the left of Ferriby Road on the cliff top of the old quarries known as Little Switzerland, and a smaller part on the right of Ferriby Road. It was a good course but eventually had to be relocated to make way for the Humber Bridge. To earn a bit of pocket money I took up caddying, mainly for a solicitor called Precious on a Sunday morning, and because I was around after school I used to pick up some lucrative summer evening caddying as well. I was also allowed to play, using old clubs that some of the regular players had given me.

The professional at the club refaced a couple of woods for me for free and the young apprentice professional, a trawler skipper's son called Graham Fieldsend, used to play the odd round with me and give me some coaching.

There were also other things to do in Hessle. I'd made friends locally as well as some of my mates from Boulevard venturing up Hessle Road to see me. The old quarry known as Little Switzerland was an excellent adventure playground where we could climb the cliffs and trees, build fires and 'dirt track' on our bikes. Flattening halfpennies to make them look like pennies by putting them on the railway lines when a train was due was also an exciting, if dangerous, piece of mischief. There was also the foreshore, the haven where there was still a local shipyard employing lots of people, and woods to roam. Usually I would have Sparky the dog by my side and it was great.

One day, Dave Wise, who lived around the corner, and a couple of friends and me, found an old pram in a ditch. The wheels were all right so we decided to build a bogie. We found - although I don't think it was lost - a large plank on a building site in Ferriby Road just round the corner from Barrow Lane, a few large bent nails and a piece of old rope for steerage and we were up and running. There was a steep hill on Ferriby Road between Barrow Lane and Heads Lane where there was a plateau leading to the golf club: this was a perfect launching point for our first, and as it turned out the last test run. We put the smallest one of us at the front to steer and I jumped on the back after giving the bogie a push start. We started well enough on the flat but when we reached the steep bit we really flew. It was then that we realised we'd have to stop or steer around a bend to avoid crossing the road.

"Steer to the left!" I shouted.

"I am trying," yelled our driver.

"Pull harder!" I exclaimed.

Our driver did as he was told but pulled too hard so the wheels turned under the plank and the bogie stopped dead. This time we really did fly; through the air, then crashed in a writhing heap with the plank - it wasn't a bogie anymore - on top of us. We stumbled to our feet, battered, bruised and bloody. A passing motorist stopped and asked us if we were okay but we feigned nonchalance and said we were fine. Ironically we'd ended up at the entrance to the building site from where we'd stolen the plank so we returned it and slunk off. Our venture had been a failure but it had been fun trying.

I'd been allowed to stay at Boulevard School after our move but very shortly after we were told that because we now lived in Haltemprice and not Hull, I would have to go to the local school, Hessle High School. The school was in two parts, the lower school on Boothferry Road and the upper school for older pupils in Heads Lane. I was sent to the lower school into class 2 Alpha. I didn't like this as there were differences in the curriculum and I was expected to catch up, not so much a problem in some subjects but I was completely out of my depth in French as I'd only learned, and not at all well, German. The teachers were generally very good. I liked our form teacher Mr Pickering and also the games teacher but Mrs Major, who taught French and maths, was a bit of a dragon. The school was also mixed which was a new experience for me as I hadn't shared classes with girls since infant school. Again this should not have been a problem except I had a fear of being humiliated or embarrassed if I gave a wrong answer – a very real concern for an adolescent boy.

To be fair I got on well with the other pupils in the school and soon got to socialise with them. I even had a girlfriend for a short while. She was a girl who lived on Boothferry Road and was also in 2 Alpha. Her name was Jennifer and she was very pretty with long hair done in plaits. We met up one Saturday I remember and she talked a lot about horse riding and horses. The only people I knew who had horses were street traders and rag and bone men, so it didn't mean that much to me. But anyway the relationship did not develop and ended after a school dance when I experienced real humiliation at the hands of a teacher called Mr Wolfe. For some reason the girls in the school liked Mr Wolfe but I've no idea why – another mystery of the female psyche – but one of the things he organised was the school dance. There were rules for the school dance like no jeans being allowed, only 'proper' trousers. Unfortunately the only trousers I owned were my school trousers with a patch on the knee, which I didn't feel would be right especially as I was trying to woo Jennifer, a bank manager's daughter who rode horses.

I've heard the bullshit about not being ashamed of patches and being proud of your mam's sewing but the reality is very different. The answer for me was to take a pair of blue striped jeans that I owned and then press them to make turn-ups on the bottom and a razor sharp crease down the front. I thought they looked just like a pair of trousers. Mr Wolfe did not. It had taken me a while during the dance to summon up the courage to ask Jennifer if she would like to dance. But barely had I set foot on the floor before Mr Wolfe singled me out, took me up on the stage and in front of all assembled, pointed out my flaunting of the sartorial rules and sent me home.

I felt embarrassed, humiliated and extremely upset. I knew I could never respect the school and its petty rules again. I know it wasn't the school's fault but to me the attitude of Wolfe epitomised the institution. The only good lesson I learned from this was that I vowed that should I ever get in the position of some power I would never publicly humiliate anyone. However, until then this was, I think, the event that made me resent authority for the first time. It was also the end of the brief flirtation with Jennifer who, later in life, was to become a Miss England contestant and a model pointing at the prizes on the TV show 'Sale of the Century'. I don't know what happened to her after that but I've no doubt that she did well.

Chapter 4. A Trinity Boy.

Hessle, I think, was the place where I first began to notice that there were discrepancies in the world and that the playing field was not level for everyone. The house opposite ours in Barrow Lane was owned by the Hudson family, well-known trawler owners, and from our front bedroom window you could see over their perimeter wall into the hallway of the house with its grand staircase. It was a mansion. There were lots of other big houses in the area but this was one of the largest and all paid for by the fishermen of Hessle Road braving the freezing wild seas of the Arctic. True, some skippers aspired to the big houses in Kirkella but these were few and far between and even so they had to work their way through the ranks in a cut-throat business to earn their lifestyle.

The golf club was another place that demonstrated the differences in society by the cars in the car park and the houses that the members lived in. I must say however, that I was invited to the house of a member of the club committee by his sons and it was the filthiest I had ever been in, grand from the outside, unkempt on the inside. It was also obvious that there were big differences in affluence and lifestyles of my fellow pupils at Hessle High School but while these things were to formulate my attitudes and political beliefs in the future, my feelings at this time were much more personal.

Added to my dislikes about Hessle High School was that they didn't play rugby; it was all football. The games' teacher did, for my benefit, put in the odd game using the football pitch and some of my schoolmates used to indulge me by a kick around on the rugby pitches on the other side of Boothferry Road, but it wasn't the same. Another peculiarity of Hessle School was that when it was bad weather and the boys couldn't play football or the girls hockey, we had to do old-time dancing in the hall instead. Once more, if you had forgotten your PE kit, you were obliged to do this dancing in your underwear – vest and pants for the boys and vest and knickers, those with a pocket in for the hanky, for the girls. I hope this only applied in the lower school as we were all experiencing or approaching puberty and the embarrassment factor was approaching eleven on a ten-point scale. Many of the girls seemed to forget their kit but I can't remember any of the boys doing this although it may be that I didn't notice, as there were more interesting bodies to look at.

I don't think teachers would get away with this now unless they wanted to be investigated by the police. The types of dances that we did were also a bit suspect. Take your partners for the 'Gay Gordons,' would possibly cause concerns for today's PC police.

My resentment and rebelliousness at the school simmered. But what could I do? Not go, was the easy answer. I recruited a partner in crime, Peter Varley, another recent addition to the school. Peter was a fairly quiet lad, a gentle soul really, but I persuaded him to join me in playing truant. Poor Peter, I really landed him in it. His mother was one of those women who would have cooked a hot dinner (lunch) with a warm pudding and done the same for tea (dinner) whereas my mam always seemed in a rush between work shifts. Peter and his family lived in a house that would not have looked out of place in a Grimm's fairy story, on the way to Swanland, and it was out that way where we built a den in a tree in the middle of a field. We kept this up for a few days pretending to go to school and then meeting up for our outdoor adventures, although to be honest, it soon became boring. Also the time of year meant that it was also cold and damp.

One day Peter didn't turn up. I knew that our cover now was blown but climbed into our tree house and waited. I saw a car draw up at the entrance to the field and thought I could see people in it – like the police with Peter. Had he shown them where I was?

I stayed very still and waited and eventually the car left. Of course in hindsight it could also have been a couple having an illicit liaison but this was not part of my thinking at the time so I was convinced that it was the police. I waited for what seemed like hours before hunger and cold caused me to climb down from my perch, get on my bike and head home. I hid in the garage for a while but eventually I was found – and boy was I in trouble! The police had been involved and people had been looking for me all day. A policeman appeared to tell me off and my mam was fuming, telling me my dad would sort me out when he came home. He didn't though, at least not in a violent, angry way. He just took me aside in the air-raid shelter and talked to me a bit about what was wrong. I think he understood but the reality was that there was more wrong than I understood.

When Peter and I returned to school we were in disgrace, I think Peter more than me because I still didn't care. The headmaster decided what we needed was a beating and caned us with, 'six of the best' as he put it. I'd had the cane many times before and always accepted my punishment but this time it just caused more resentment and I hated the school and the headmaster. We were also required to see an educational social worker to find out what our problems were, something that should have been done before the caning, with the result that Peter decided to settle down and stay at Hessle while I was sent back to the Boulevard. Result!

A number of things had happened on the family front leading up to my school unrest. My sister had married Jack Collins, a merchant seaman, and had moved out of Barrow Lane and back into Holmes Street, despite my dad being a bit awkward about consenting to the marriage because my sister was only eighteen years old. I remember this leading to a big row but he relented in the end. My dad was growing increasingly unhappy with his role at the golf club and eventually decided to go back to the School of Motoring but this time as an instructor. This left my mam in the position of having to run the golf club by herself, which wasn't really practicable. At first it worked because she drafted in a friend to share the workload but I don't think the golf club people were happy with the situation, as they preferred a married couple. As a result our time there was limited and my mother had to find another job as a barmaid, as well as a new home. She also decided that she wanted a new life and the first thing to go would be her husband.

This domestic unrest must have been simmering for some time but it was after my sister's wedding that things seemed to gain pace. It was as if now she had left home, there was nothing between my mam and dad that was worth holding onto. The first I got to know about the break-up was one night when I was woken up in the early hours by someone knocking on the door. I went down to see who it was and it was my dad so thinking he had just lost his keys I let him in. I didn't know my mam had locked him out. Next day she told me off for letting him in and told me not to do it again. I was not too bothered at the time because break-ups had been fairly regular so I was used to them and thought it would all end up with cosy, boozy late night reconciliation; but not this time.

A week or so later I was awoken again, this time by the sounds of a male voice and laughing downstairs. My immediate thought was that my dad had returned. The voice though did not sound like his and when I listened carefully it had a strong foreign accent. I heard the voice get louder as my mam showed him to bed. I cried myself to sleep that night.

The next morning I discovered that the owner of the voice was the Dutch captain of a coaster called the 'Vedette'. A year or so later I was to see the 'Vedette' moored in Humber Dock in the city centre but I never saw the captain again. My mam claimed that she had not 'slept with him' - not the sort of conversation that a thirteen-year-old boy accepts without considerable embarrassment - and it may be significant that she did not bring anyone else home during our time living together, even though that was not going to last for much longer.

My mam and dad were divorced on August 1st 1960 on the grounds, and I've found this hard to believe because he was locked out, of my dad's 'desertion'. I know that dad had slept a few nights in his car when first thrown out but by the time of the divorce he had moved to Castleford to manage the branch of the driving school located there and took lodgings with a mining family in Pontefract.

Castleford had the river Aire running through it, which must have been one of the most polluted rivers ever as it always seemed to be coated in inches of foam like a gigantic bubble bath. Mining was the main industry of that area and Dad's landlord was an old coal miner who sat in front of a coal dust misted television clearing his industrially contaminated lungs by spitting coal dust into the fireplace. Anyway, my dad wasn't there long before he turned the charm on for Margaret, the divorced daughter of his landlady and landlord, and within a short period they had moved to Halifax and set up home there. Margaret had got a job in the Civil Service in an army barracks and my dad had landed the job of transport manager for a large haulage company, Calder Valley Transport. While this was going on, my dad would occasionally appear back in Hessle and take me for a short drive around, nowhere in particular and usually it seemed to be raining, but this didn't happen very often. I did miss him though, even if he wasn't the most supportive or demonstrative of fathers.

I was now back at Boulevard School with no real plans for the future. I knew I didn't fancy the motor trade like my dad. I had always been more fascinated by ships through people I met, like friends at school whose brothers and fathers were at sea or my sister's boyfriends, one who had been on trawlers, and Jack her husband, who had been in the merchant navy along with his brother George.

My brother Brian had also been in the Navy and had gone to the Nautical School. My dad, although not one for great encouragement was always on about wanting me to go to Trinity House Navigation School as it was hard to get into, was linked with the Humber pilotage, and it was, in his terms, 'An honour to go there.'

I was not so sure but there was always the obstacle of the examination. My academic career so far had not been spectacular, I was okay at most subjects but hadn't really excelled at anything, other than mediocrity and playing the fool, so the chances of me passing this examination would not have been a good bet.

Both the Nautical School and Trinity House took boys from the age of thirteen and the examinations took place about the same time. The difference, apart from the uniforms, between the two schools was that Trinity House School at that time was funded privately by Hull Trinity House, whereas the Nautical School (more correctly the High School for Nautical Training) was funded like other schools by the local authority. Later, in 1973, both schools would merge taking the name Hull Trinity House School, but was no longer a private school as it had gained voluntary aided funding status in partnership with the local authority as part of the terms of the merger.

Trinity House also took fee-paying students to cater for those that didn't pass the scholarship. It was easy to tell the difference between the scholarship boys and the paying customers as they wore different uniforms. The scholarship boys wore the traditional uniform of a short black doeskin jacket with a white, 'stick-up' collar, black doeskin waistcoat, and white duck or black doeskin trousers depending on the day of the week. The payers wore a merchant navy officer's style outfit similar to the one worn by the pupils of the Nautical School. All the uniforms were topped by a merchant navy style officer's cap.

I remember that I was not very well on the day of the examination but had to go into school to sit it, along with a few others, in the school library. This was not a good start and I was most surprised when we received a letter saying that I had passed the examination and now the school wanted me to proceed to the second stage of the selection process. This was an interview before a small selection committee made up of members of the Elder Brethren of Trinity House. If this sounds archaic, you should have seen the Elder Brethren!

The interview took place in a boardroom within one of the main Trinity House buildings. The organisation owned a lot of buildings within the city centre bordered by Whitefriargate, Prince's Dock Street, Posterngate and Trinity House Lane. The inside reflected the age of the order and it was a bit like walking into a museum with the walls lined with paintings of antiquated mariners looking stern in their best uniforms. I entered the boardroom to stand in front of a large table seating several, equally stern looking, antiquated mariners in their best frock coat uniforms. The interview, like most bad interviews, was rather intimidating but I answered the questions as best I could although maybe lacking in enthusiasm. Then came the killer question.

'Are you coming here on your own accord?' asked one of the elderly gentlemen.

'No,' I replied, 'My dad wants me to come.'

A moment of loud silence was followed by the cackling laughter of the elder brethren.

'Ha, ha, the only honest one so far,' said one of the inquisitors who I recognised later as Commander Snowden who had served his time under sail.

I was in. A Trinity boy. A cadet of Trinity House Navigation School, the oldest navigation school in the world that had taken its first students in 1787.

But first there was one more test – the eyesight test.

The eyesight test, or to be more specific, the colour blindness test, took place in the Board of Trade offices at the top of the Burton's building on the corner of Whitefriargate. The test was to determine if your eyesight was good enough to be a deck officer (or deck rating) in the merchant navy as being able to determine red (port), green (starboard) and white (mast head and stern) lights was essential for the safe navigation of ships. While it was possible to get away with wearing glasses if you were short or long-sighted, colour blindness was a complete no-no! So to determine this I was shown into a dark room and told where to stand while the examiner projected small beams of different coloured lights onto a large mirror. I was going to be tested again like this on a couple of occasions during my subsequent career but having just passed the school entry examination I had no idea what the significance of the lights was.

"Just tell me the colour of the spots you see," said the examiner.

"Red and two yellows," I said for the first one.

"Red and two whites," said the examiner.

"They look yellow to me," I replied.

"They might look yellow to you but they are white – next!"

"Green, red and two yellows," I said.

"No! They are white!" yelled the examiner, "Next!"

"Yell... er... white," and so it went on.

It was not my fault that his projector was crap. The white lights certainly looked yellow to me but it did not matter as I passed the test and now could start at the school.

Trinity House Navigation School was situated on Prince's Dock Street close to Victoria Square in Hull City centre, where Queen Victoria majestically presided over the public toilets below her with pigeon shit running down her face. Also in Victoria Square were the City Hall, the Dock Offices (now the Maritime Museum) and Ferens Art Gallery. Next to the gallery was a small line of shops that included a fishmonger, newsagents and Maurice Lipman's male fashion shop. Lipman's was on the corner of the building known as Monument Buildings and Monument Bridge. The bridge didn't span anything but used to form the junction between Prince's Dock and Queen's Dock before the latter was filled in to create Queen's Gardens. I don't know of any other city centre that could boast of having a dock. There was always a sense of excitement for me crossing Monument Bridge when Prince's Dock was still in use with the bows of the trawlers clearly visible, coupled with the authentic sea smell from the fishmongers and the seagulls circling overhead. It was much more stimulating than the shopping mall that now dominates the disused dock. I have often felt that the Hull Council missed a trick by not mooring the "Arctic Corsair", Spurn Lightship, one of the old paddle steamers, and an old tug in Prince's Dock to complement the close by Maritime Museum.

Once over Monument Bridge and in front of you was what was once Hull's main shopping street, Whitefriargate, but turn right and you were in Prince's Dock Street with, on the left, Trinity House School accessed by way of a big cream coloured, gated archway with the Trinity House crest on the top. Opposite the archway was Prince's Dock that, at that time, was still being used for commercial purposes as well as a 'fitting out' dock for new and old trawlers. This meant that we had to be careful as the cobble stoned street that was Prince's Dock Street had railway lines for the goods trains that still plied their way and gained their cargoes from the sheds on the dockside.

On entering the schoolyard you were immediately faced with the cream painted Chapel - most Trinity House buildings were painted cream - at the far end, with an impressive flagpole in front of it. While used daily to fly flags this could also be used to hoist your shoes after you'd been dragged around the yard on your bare arse – tradition or just old-fashioned bullying, you decide - if you were ever foolish enough to let on that it was your birthday.

To the left were the main school buildings and at the far end next to chapel on the right, was the bike shed.

The school had two intakes a year, at Easter and summer, with about 30 boys at each. It was quite small and exclusive with a total number of pupils of only about 150.

I started at Easter in 1961. The first term was probationary and only on the successful completion of this did you receive your school uniform. So on the first day we all arrived dressed in a mixture of blazers, sports jackets and suits. We all had to have clean shoes and wear ties, and were termed 'fags', in the public school fashion by the boys who had served their probationary period and were now in uniform. My fellow classmates came from all parts of the city as well as some from other parts of the country who lived in lodgings.

By this time my mother and I had left Hessle and were living in a terraced house in Reynoldson Street off Newland Avenue.

This meant that from the age of five I had lived in nine houses and been to eight different schools, plus one twice! Not bad for eight years. No wonder we referred to mam as Gypsy Rosa Lee! And she wasn't finished.

I don't know how long we were in Reynoldson Street, only a matter of weeks, before she was expressing discontent and a wish to move away from Hull and take up a job she had been offered at Primrose Valley holiday park, which meant living in. Obviously I wasn't part of the plan but to solve the problem I went into lodgings like some of my classmates.

The hardest part of this was saying goodbye to Sparky the dog, who was re-homed with one of mam's friends. I also remember seeing my childhood possessions including my threadbare old teddy bear being assigned to the dustbin. I was left with a few clothes in a suitcase and a heavy Bakelite portable radio.

It was time to grow up...

Above. The class of 1961. The author is seated on the bottom row, second from left.
Below. Cadets on parade. Both pictures by kind permission of Hull Trinity House.

Chapter 5. Lodgings.

I can't say that I had a bad childhood. I was protected until I went to school at five and allowed a great deal of freedom after, so life was mainly fun. The constant moving about didn't seem to bother me and I made friends easily but I could also be happy in my own company.

We didn't do many things as a family, even going to the pictures when I was small, it was usually with my mother to see maybe a Disney offering or a musical that she wanted to see like 'Seven Brides for Seven Brothers'. The only time my dad took me to the pictures was to see Elvis Presley in 'Love Me Tender'. I think he thought it was a western rather than a vehicle for a young man who was to become a rock legend. In the film Elvis sings a few songs before he's shot dead at the end but of course comes into view again as a ghostly figure singing over the closing credits. When my dad saw this he said, "Bloody hell, I thought they'd killed the bugger!" I don't think he was impressed.

As I got older, I'd often go to the cinema on my own with only a couple of concerns. One was when I went to see a film called 'The Innocents' when I was about twelve at the 'Carlton' on Anlaby Road. It was a ghost story and it nearly frightened me to death. It was far more scary than any Hammer Horror film and showed me how suggestion can be much more effective than more direct methods.

Hitchcock had it right.

Another occasion was even more disturbing. This was in the Regent Cinema in Hull City centre but I can't remember the name of the film. It was a matinee performance and there were not many in the cinema so I sat in the middle. After a short while a man came and sat next to me. He had no reason to do this as there was plenty of room but soon he rubbed his leg against mine, so I got up and moved to a different row. He followed after a few minutes, which I found disturbing. My mam and dad had warned me to stay away from strangers and now I had to put their advice into practice. So once again I moved but this time to a seat at the back near where the usherettes sat when they weren't working. This time he got the message and I was able to watch the film although I was uneasy until I got home. Later I heard that one of the usherettes in this cinema was noted for offering men 'favours' on the back row but I must have been too young and wouldn't have known what was happening anyway. So with these experiences I felt reasonably well equipped to face the world on my own.

My lodgings were in a large house in Victoria Avenue on the north-west corner of the junction with Salisbury Street. The landlady gave me breakfast and tea and I stayed school dinners during the day. Most of the other people who stayed there were travelling salesmen who seemed to come and go. The landlady was not married and lived in the house with her elderly mother who slept and lived in the downstairs front room. I was shocked one day to bump into her as she carried the bucket, complete with floating turds, that she used for a toilet to be emptied. I don't know who was more embarrassed, her or me? My room, which was on the first floor was small, with a single bed, some drawers, a chair and of course my radio. There was a large overgrown back garden that had an old, rusting motorbike in it. I found this fascinating but in general the adult world of the lodgings was quite boring so I used to return to Holmes Street where my sister now lived, to meet up with my old mates from when I lived down there. My sister and other members of the family were quite angry and disgusted with my mother for what they perceived as my abandonment for her own selfish purposes, but at the time I found the sudden independence and responsibility initially very exciting, although in hindsight they may have been right. Later in life I was able to joke that my parents ran away from home rather than the other way round. What hadn't been considered was what would happen during the school holidays? My mam could not accommodate me and I hadn't heard much from dad since he had moved with his new girlfriend to Halifax. Anyway I contacted him and he said I could stay with him during the holidays and some weekends. My sister also offered to put me up on other weekends when her husband Jack was away at sea, although he was soon to give up the merchant navy and become a docker like his father.

The school uniform at Trinity House was unique. The normal day uniform consisted of a short black doeskin (bum freezer) jacket with brass link buttons to fasten it and a line of brass breast buttons on each side. The collar of the jacket stuck up and was white, we had to 'Blanco' it, with a brass button on each side. Underneath the jacket was a black waistcoat with brass buttons, matching black trousers, both in doeskin, and black shoes. The shirts were blue and white stripped with a loose collar so they had to be worn with studs although some of us sewed the collar on for convenience, and also it was less draughty as the collars didn't quite fit the shirts, worn with a black tie. On our heads we wore a white covered merchant navy officer's cap with the school crest. The caps came with stiffening wire in them that made them look like helicopter landing pads so we devised ways to bend them to give them, what we thought was, style. For chapel on Wednesdays and for three Sunday church parades each year, we were required to wear white duck trousers with white waistcoats. We were not allowed to wear belts, only braces. The uniform was based on that of an eighteenth century midshipman so that we looked like extras from the film 'Mutiny on the Bounty'. I think some of the teachers thought they had to act like Captain Bligh as well.

The uniform was very expensive, not just because of its 'fancy dress' nature but because it all had to be made to fit us individually. To compensate for this it was subsidised by Trinity House, so that parents only had to pay a one-off payment of £10 to cover the costs of two lots of everything – and a pair of shoes and a tie - and subsequent single items of uniform annually from then on.

Now £10 in 1961 was not an unsubstantial sum of money, about the equivalent of the average man's weekly take home pay, but it was a condition when accepting a position at the school. Unfortunately this point seemed to have been missed by my estranged parents, so that when the uniforms were given out in brown paper parcels, individually in class and signed for, I waited and waited. Slowly the other members of the class got their parcels and I continued to wait until there were no parcels left.

"Sorry, yours hasn't been paid for," said the teacher as he left the room.

Inside I was devastated. This was the humiliation by Mr Wolfe all over again. To be fair my colleagues didn't make a big deal of it and I just explained that there must have been some mix up with the payment. In those days we didn't have telephones in homes never mind mobiles, so getting in touch with my parents in different parts of the country was difficult. I told my sister of the problem and both her and her husband Jack were upset that they couldn't help as they didn't have the money. Jack had given up the sea and was working as a labourer while waiting for his docker's book. Anyway, eventually my dad coughed up and I was given my parcel of clothing, so that I wasn't the odd one out for very long and was soon parading around like Midshipman Easy, the same as the rest of them.

Parading seems the right term because one of the first things we had to learn at the school was marching and parade ground drill, it was like joining the army.

"By the left, quick march!" and all that stuff.

This was done every morning along with an inspection to make sure our shoes were clean, that those in uniform had whitened their collar and that our hats had stiffeners in them. We also had to show that we were wearing braces and to do this we had to turn around, bend over and lift our jackets.

Failure to meet these standards could lead to a punishment of which there were many of varying severity. Lines were one form of punishment which was fairly easy unless given by the English teacher Mr Hibberd as he prided himself on lines that were at least three lines long and more like paragraphs.

This prevented you doing them like lists: I, I, I, shall, shall, shall, not, not, not, and so on down the page. Another form of written punishment was writing out the Rules of the Road at Sea. The Rules were the Highway Code for mariners except that they had been written by over verbose lawyers. They were of varying length from Rule 1 to Rule 32 and over the years we were expected to learn rules 16 to 32 off by heart, or near enough. We could be given any of the rules to write out for punishment but one of the longest and most boring (it was about the lights on fishing vessels), and therefore most popular for this purpose, was Rule 9, which took an age to copy. There was also corporal punishment, not in the form of the cane at this school, oh no, in true keeping with the 'Mutiny on the Bounty' analogy, it was the rope's end across the buttocks. As we didn't have a quarterdeck and railings the teachers had to make do with bending you over a desk while they thrashed you with a length of rope. I've heard that there are people who pay good money for this kind of treatment in adulthood but it certainly seemed an archaic form of punishment for us. But at least it was over quickly, unlike the pointless writing of lines or the Rules of the Road.

There was also a kind of semi-democratic hierarchy at the school where each class was divided into two watches, the port watch and the starboard watch, each with an elected watch officer - I was surprised to come second in the voting for our port watch - who would lead the marching. The class also had an elected class captain. But the main hierarchy consisted of the school prefects, known as officers led by the school captain. The officers were distinguished by stripes of gold braid on the lower sleeves of their uniforms and their job was to keep general order, mainly by being visible but they were also allowed to give out punishments. In fairness they were quite lenient with this responsibility and a good bunch of lads but as always with power there is always some petty despot who oversteps the mark.

My classmates were a good bunch of lads and we all generally got on well together and I think I can still remember some of their names: Baker M, Baker S, Boyd G, Boyd M, Burgess, Byrne, Cannan, Colley, Clifford, Herbert, Harrison, Hawker, Kaye, Markham, Marwood, Nash, Ness, Pendergast, Stocks, Watts, Weldon, Wilkinson and Wood.

Most of them were from Hull and I had been at Boulevard School with Ray Hawker but some came from further afield; Marwood and Stocks came from Goole I think, Nash came from Salisbury, Malcolm Colley from York and Stuart Baker came from Stokesly in North Yorkshire. My main classmates though were Ray Hawker, Dave Harrison and John Wood and it was these three that I met up with for out of school activities like the pictures, youth clubs or, later, dancing at the Locarno.

A good thing about the school was that because it was small all of the lads used to mix no matter their age, so that I also got to know older lads like Steve Gibbs and Stuart Mahoney.

One of the rules of the school was that we were not allowed to go into the main shops like Woolworth's in our uniforms, so at lunchtimes we were, in theory, limited to where we could go. School dinners were held in one of the main Trinity House buildings down Trinity House Lane. To get there we had to march in ranks out of the school, turn left along Prince's Dock Side, left again down Posterngate past the Shipping Office, where jeers from the merchant navy seaman waiting for jobs outside greeted us, then left again at the bottom of Posterngate into Trinity House Lane. If you turned right out of Posterngate you came into King Street and the open air market in front of Holy Trinity Church that was dominated by the delicious smells of Bob Carver's Fish and Chip stall. We weren't allowed to use the market although the temptation was sometimes too much to resist. School dinners were voluntary apart from one day a year when the school had a special dinner when oranges were distributed. Two officers brought the oranges round in a box that was presented to the students' backs who then had to reach behind them to get the oranges. This apparently was to prevent some boys picking the biggest oranges. An unofficial alternative to school dinners, and again you got into trouble if you got caught, was a workmen's café called 'City Diners' in Fish Street. Here they sold a tasty meat pie with chips and gravy and it was cheap. The café was always full but they let us use rooms upstairs so that we couldn't be seen from the street. The room and tables wouldn't have looked out of place on a film set for a Dickensian novel except that the building was probably a lot older than Victorian. After dinner we would sometimes go for a walk around the town docks or visit Victoria Pier to watch the trawlers, merchant ships, ferries and the pilot cutter that was based there. But there was also another place that used to attract us, Prince Street, known as "Fag" or "Smokers' Alley".

Prince Street could be accessed through an archway from King Street where the market was held or from Dagger Lane, which ran off Posterngate. The street looked like an illustration from a Victorian novel in that it was a narrow, cobbled street that curved gently with terraced buildings on one side and the backs of other buildings on the other. Just inside the street near the archway was a small, dark shop that sold cigarettes and tobacco. More importantly though, it sold cigarettes separately so that those of us with a limited budget could feed our new and developing nicotine addiction. It seemed that everyone smoked in those days. The shop also sold Woodbines and Park Drive in packets of five and there was even a cheaper brand called Domino sold in paper packets of four. Usually there would be about a dozen or so Trinity boys smoking their heads off in Smokers' Alley but we had to be careful as the street was regularly raided by some of the teachers or officers, although these seemed to do their fair share of smoking as well.

My first visit to my dad's place in Halifax was tentative, as I had not met his partner - who became his third wife in 1974 - before, so it was a bit of an adventure for us both. She turned out to be a well turned out woman in her early 30s - my dad was about 50 - with a kind of posh accent with a tinge of West Yorkshire and we seemed to hit it off straight away. I liked the West Yorkshire accent in that it was not as flat as the Hull and East Yorkshire accent and they also said 't' instead of the word 'the', like 'going down t'mill', whereas in Hull they don't even bother with the 't', it's just 'going down dock'. Although Margaret had previously been married she did not have children of her own but she did have a younger brother who worked 'down t'pit' and other older siblings including a sister married to a butcher who lived in Halifax. Some years later she told me that I was a bigger surprise than I thought as almost until I arrived on the doorstep my dad had not bothered to mention my existence to her, nor the existence of my sister and two brothers!

At first I would travel to Halifax by train, sharing part of the journey with a number of other Trinity House students who changed trains at York or Leeds. Later on when I had got my full school uniform I would sometimes hitch-hike with a lad called Jones from Keighley as far as Bradford, before continuing our journeys alone. This I suppose was a bit dangerous but by keeping the train fare I had a bit of extra pocket money. It was also quite easy to get a lift when in uniform but one problem was that I arrived in Halifax before the train was due in so had to hang about a bit at the station. It was on the train during my first term at the school that I met an older boy, Dave Mitchell, who was from Huddersfield. Dave was a paying student at the school so wore the merchant navy officer's style uniform. I had seen him around a lot and he had the reputation of being a bit of a 'Jack the Lad', in a Teddy boy sort of way, who really fancied himself with the girls. Anyway one Friday Dave asked me about my lodgings and if I was interested in changing as his room-mate was leaving to go to sea. I said it sounded good to me, so arrangements were made for me to move in with him when we returned after the summer holidays. My new lodgings were in Council Avenue with Mrs Fairweather, a widow who lived in a three bedroomed council house with her twenty-one-year-old son. Dave and I would share the front bedroom.

Halifax was for me a bit boring if I'm honest as I had no friends there and dad and Margaret worked during the day so holiday periods were a bit of a drag. The house itself was in an area known as Ovenden on the way out of Halifax towards Illingworth and Haworth, and all up hill. Our road came off the main road, still going uphill, with a biscuit factory at the top end. The house was part of an old terrace, probably built originally as factory workers' cottages that from the street showed as a continuous stonewall with tiny windows at the top and coal-holes in the pavement. The front doors were on the other side of the house, accessed by way of an arch, where my dad, the only car owner in the row, parked his car.

On the left hand side of the arch was an old laundry or workshop building that was uninhabited and opposite this was a line of four lavatories, each lavatory being shared by two houses. Turning right from the arch was a footpath that led up hill to the eight houses. Ours was the first house and we shared the lavatory with the pleasant old lady next door. At least we had the shortest walk to the loo – I wouldn't have liked to be taken short living in the top one! This made other houses with a lavatory in the backyard and a geyser in the kitchen, appear far more luxurious.

Inside our house was very small, with just one room downstairs with a corner partitioned off as a kitchen. The upstairs had also been only one room but an area had been partitioned off to create a second, small bedroom although you had to pass through it to reach the main room. There was also a cellar for the coal for the downstairs fire. We also had a bit of garden accessed through a gate in another stonewall and beyond that was a graveyard.

For my first summer break there I took my bike from Hull on the train. Hull of course was dead flat and ideal for cycling. Halifax is a different matter as it is all hills, and steep ones at that, all seemingly up hill. The station is in the town centre at the bottom of a valley so it was all up hill to Ovenden. Even with gears I didn't think I would make it as my thighs began to feel like concrete and I was struggling to breathe. I even thought I would be quicker getting off and walking but I persevered. I was though, very careful where I pedalled to after that.

There really wasn't much for me to do in Halifax, as I didn't know anyone there. I tried the local golf club for a while as I still had my golf clubs but I kept losing the balls and I couldn't afford to keep replacing them. Also to get there meant catching the bus or cycling with my golf clubs on my back – all uphill to the course so I was knackered when I got there - although it was okay zooming downhill on the way home. I also played on my own as I didn't know anyone so it was boring. In the end I sold the golf clubs to buy a leather jacket after seeing the film 'Some People' but couldn't afford real leather so had to settle for 'leather look' plastic. At the weekend my dad and Margaret would take me to one of the canals towards Hebden Bridge so that I could do some angling but the fish rarely took my bait. There was only one person about my age who lived further up in our terrace, an attractive young lady with auburn hair. We exchanged glances once or twice but I was too shy to approach her. I used to see her walking by and given that there was only one way in or out of the terrace and that everyone needing the lavatory had to pass our house this was quite regularly. But what could I say to her when she seductively walked by clutching a toilet roll and holding her lavatory key? How could I break the ice? "Been for a shit have you?" didn't seem romantically appropriate, so that was that.

In September 1961 I was welcomed into the home of Mrs Fairweather but because my room mate, Dave Mitchell, was considerably older than me - I think he was just about eighteen - our social lives didn't compute, so I had to find new friends. Luckily one of my classmates, John Wood, whose father was a fish merchant, lived on the Gypsyville estate and he introduced me to the local youth club held at Francis Askew School and some of his friends so I took to knocking about with them for a while. One of the lads I remember from this time was Dave Preston who had already left school and was an apprentice engineer with a firm that serviced trawlers called Shiphams. We didn't do much, just roamed the streets or played billiards in the youth club in our leather (plastic) jackets and with our hair combed and greased – Brylcream wasn't strong enough so we used Vaseline - in a Tony Curtis, teddy boy style. Sometimes I would also go out with some of the lads from school. Wrestling or roller-skating at Madeley Street baths, which was closed for swimming in the winter, were a good laugh and cheap but the main thing was the youth club. After a while at the youth club, a young lady by the name of Sylvia began to attract my attention. So with Sylvia in mind I looked forward to the youth club Christmas dance with the hope that I would use the opportunity to get to know her better.

On my way home from school I had to walk through the city centre to the bus station to catch the bus for Gypsyville. Doing so inevitably meant looking in shop windows and one night something in C & A's window caught my eye. It was a blue and brown checked suit in the new high-buttoned Italian style and it was very cheap. I mean really cheap. Every night I looked at that suit and wanted it thinking I would cut a real dash at the youth club dance if I could buy it. The trouble was that I hadn't any money but I used my charm to convince my dad it would be my perfect Christmas present and he surprisingly agreed. There was a bit of a delay in getting the money and it arrived only just in time for the youth club dance. And as my sister had to come with me to buy it I was pushing it fine and it was actually after school on the day of the dance that we went to C & A to buy it. Of course I had to try on several before we found the right size trousers and jacket (allowing for growth) and then I had to catch the bus to Gypsyville, looking forward to dashing in, getting washed and changed, and then making a grand entrance at the dance.

I arrived at my lodgings at about 6.30 p.m. The doors were locked. No Mrs Fairweather. No anybody. No spare key. I could have got changed in the outside toilet that was not used but I would still of had to go in my school shirt and clunky shoes, which would have spoiled the image. So I sat and waited for someone to come in thinking that Dave, Mrs Fairweather or her son would appear shortly. I waited and waited. Eventually, about 9.00p.m. Mrs Fairweather turned up.

It wasn't a disaster. It wasn't a major catastrophe. But for me it was traumatic. I'd planned my night and spent a lot of time persuading my dad to pay for the suit and it had all been a waste of time. Mrs Fairweather said that she must have only missed me by about five minutes, but five minutes was five minutes that led to over two hours waiting in a toilet. To console me she offered me some money to go and buy some chips. In Hull chips can cure everything from major disappointments to broken hearts; but not for me that night. It was too late to get changed, too late for the dance, and too late for Sylvia.

Anyway, soon it would be Christmas.

I went back to Halifax for Christmas to spend it with my dad and Margaret. During the autumn (probably after the main season at Primrose Valley had finished) my mam had appeared in Halifax and asked my dad if he wished to go back with her. He said no! The marriage was well and truly over and he was happy as he was. My mam then went off again, after asking for her radio back, and during the winter moved to Blackpool to work at the Winter Gardens. So Christmas passed but I'd been invited to stay for the New Year with Dave Wise and his family in Hessle, so I took them up on it. The Wises were a really nice family with just Dave, his older sister and his mam and dad. I stayed there a couple of days over the festivities before returning to my lodgings. I had a little bit of money left over from Christmas so took myself off to the January sales. It was then that I saw them - the perfect accessory for my C & A suit – a pair of winkle-picker shoes. They were in the window of Northern Clothing in Hull and priced at less than ten shillings. A bargain! True they were white with black patent leather toecaps so I could have looked a bit like a spiv but a bottle of black leather dye would soon cure that. Sure enough they looked okay after I'd dyed them. Well, they looked okay until it rained and then they turned a purple-blue colour but with a bit of black shoe polish who would notice? All I wanted now was somewhere to go.

Back at the lodgings my room-mate Dave Mitchell was busy applying for an apprenticeship in the merchant navy and eventually got an offer with a company called Hogarths, also called the 'Baron Line' as most of their ships were called after barons. I'd heard my brother-in law and his brother George talking about the company after George had completed a voyage with them. Hogarths ran tramp ships, slow cargo ships that tramped around the world on very long voyages, and had a pretty bad reputation. They were known as "Hungry Hogarths" because of the poor quality of food and a lack of stores that they carried in order to save money.

There was even a song that sailors used to sing about Hogarths in which the chorus went:

Heave away you hungry bastards, heave away,

Heave away you hungry bastards, heave away,

PSNC are very fine,

But 'til you ship the Baron Line,

Heave away you hungry bastards, heave away.

I pointed this out to Dave but he dismissed it with a contemptuous, "What is he this George? An EDH! I will be an officer and we will have different food to the crew."

Little did he know. He also didn't find it funny when he said that he was joining the "Baron Minto" and I said "Baron Hardup" might be more apt. I thought I would let him find out for himself what it was like and didn't come down to earth with too big a crash and, I hoped he didn't get too hungry.

Anyway with Dave gone there was just me left with Mrs Fairweather and her lovesick son who spent every evening sitting on the sofa with his girlfriend while they saved up to get married. Also because it was mid-term it would be a long time before Mrs Fairweather found a replacement. Then I got a better offer. I used to spend odd weekends at my sister's house and one day my brother-in-law Jack asked me if I would like to lodge with them rather than at Mrs Fairweather's as they had a spare room. Of course I said yes and shortly after, it may have been half term or Easter, I moved in. This was a brave step for Jack as he was only about twenty-three and here he was taking on a fourteen-year-old boy, although Jack was very mature and sensible for his age, as was my sister. Of course there were rules, like I had to have my homework done before I could go out and had to be in by 10 o'clock unless it was something special like the pictures or a dance. I still went to Halifax some weekends and during the school holidays so didn't impose too much on my sister and brother-in-law's private lives and the added income of my lodgings' money may have also helped in those early years of their marriage.

My mother had moved to Blackpool to work at the Winter Gardens and she invited me to stay for a few days during the summer holidays and said that I could take a friend with me, so I asked John Wood from my class at school along. We travelled by train from Hull to Blackpool and had a pretty good time as I remember although we didn't see much of my mother as she was working all the time so we were able to continue our hobbies of under age drinking and smoking. The only other holiday I had while with my dad in Halifax was a week in a cottage in Wensleydale with Margaret, her mother, and Margaret's pet goldfish! Yes, we took her goldfish on holiday in a big sweet jar. We all loaded into my dad's Riley car, a lovely car with a running board and a swept down back, and trundled off. I really enjoyed that holiday as I got into the geography and geology of the area with its mountains, caves and waterfalls. The cottage itself was on its own in the middle of a field full of delves and small hills.

One night we got back and a big storm started. Thunder, lightening and torrential rain; and then the lights went out. We sat downstairs with lighted candles talking for a while and then we noticed the carpet moving, and then floating as the cottage began to flood. We decided to vacate the ground floor and took to the stairs as the water began to rise so that we were marooned in the bedrooms for the night. Next morning, the rain had stopped and while the flood water was no longer in the cottage the place was soaked and the field with the delves was now a field full of lakes. I'm sure for the goldfish it was the perfect holiday but for us it meant dragging the carpets out to dry. However, it wasn't long before the farmer, who owned the cottage, and his wife appeared to see if we were all right and told us to leave everything to them to sort out, so we did.

Moving back to Holmes Street meant that I could link up again with some old mates but many were now leaving school. In those days people left secondary school at the end of the term when they reached the age of fifteen and then went straight to work. I had already been knocking about with school-leavers in Gypsyville and now this applied to my Holmes Street mates. I'd also met up with a mate from Boulevard, Colin Williams, who was a galley boy on trawlers with a wad of cash. My pocket money didn't compete with the lowest paid apprentice so as I turned fifteen myself, I started to look at them with some envy. I know my dad did his best but if I complained he would come out with the same old, "You should think yourself lucky, I was out working at fourteen."

However, even with my limited cash, sometimes supplemented by hitch-hiking instead of buying a train ticket, I still managed to get out a bit. Two of the lads at school, Dave Harrison and Ray Hawker, had somehow discovered a couple of pubs that were not too choosy about who they served. One was 'The Manchester Arms' in the old town and the other, which we used the most because it was close to the Locarno Ballroom (also known locally as Mecca and had opened in 1961), was known as 'Tony's', and was near the corner where the road that buses used to leave the bus station met Ferensway.

Here we plucked up the courage to walk to the bar and, using a gruff voice, ask for 'a pint of mixed'. I don't know why we chose to ask for 'mixed' but we did and were never asked our age. Fortified with a pint down us we would then venture forth to a cheap, no-alcohol, Monday night session at the Locarno designed for young teenagers. Here we'd try our hands at bopping and a dance called the 'Twist' while we tried, and mostly failed, to pull a girl.

Another of our haunts around this time was the 'Coffee House' in Prospect Street, a fancy café really that attracted students and those of a bohemian ilk. We would sit in there in the evening nursing our drinks of hot orange and thinking that we looked cool when we probably looked just like what we were – daft schoolboys.

Left. Prince Street, Hull, otherwise known as Fag or Smokers' Alley. Below. A school assembly. The author is sitting with arms folded, the second in on the second row of boys.

Chapter 6. Out with a bang!

Trinity House was very different to Boulevard or Hessle High School in terms of discipline, uniform and the curriculum. The teachers were also different in that they were a mixture of those from an academic background, that liked to show this by wearing black academic gowns, and those from a nautical background.

The curriculum consisted of maths, including arithmetic, geometry, algebra and trigonometry, English, history (of sorts), navigation, seamanship (including boat work), signals, physics, and PE. But oddly, given that it was expected that one day we would be making our way around the world, no geography. There were also no facilities for arts and crafts although I do remember doing some rudimentary woodwork - making a box - in the seamanship room. The teachers were what you would expect, a bunch of eccentrics trying to keep order and create an environment for learning amongst students representing a cross section of society and hand-picked by a bunch of geriatric old salts.

Our form teacher at first was Mr Hibberd who looked like a teacher you would find on the pages of the 'Beano' teaching the 'Bash Street Kids' or 'Dennis the Menace', complete with a sports jacket with patches on the sleeves and a toothbrush moustache. Mr Hibberd generally kept order by his demeanour (kind of military) and the threat of lines, which he managed to extend to nearly a paragraph, for punishment.

He also used verbal rebukes. "Take that asinine grin off your face, boy!" was one that I was on the receiving end of regularly. "Stop lounging like a lizard, boy!" was another of his regular remarks along with, "Sit up boy, you look like a rat peering out of a hedge!"

I never witnessed him ever using corporal punishment, which testifies to how good a teacher he was, a fact that was not appreciated at the time. Because I was prone to 'playing the fool' at any opportunity, I have been able to retrospectively evaluate my schoolteachers' ability in class control based on the extreme provocation that I must have put them through and Mr Hibberd certainly passed this test.

On one occasion we had been asked to prepare a talk to be given to the rest of the class. We could choose any subject we liked and I racked my brain for something that I could talk about with some authority. In the end I chose speleology.

That may seem an odd choice but that summer I'd been on holiday for a week with my dad, Margaret and Margaret's mother in a cottage near Ingleborough. There, I'd become interested in the caves, mountains and geology of the area and had gathered some leaflets and booklets on how the caves were formed in the limestone.

I duly prepared notes, diagrams and cut up the leaflets to make handouts. One day during a lesson Mr Hibberd must have run out of things to say so he said we would be starting to give our talks. And with a name like Addey, it was inevitable that I would be called first.

"Let's start with you Addey," said Mr Hibberd.

"I would rather not sir," I replied.

"Why boy!" retorted Mr Hibberd, obviously irritated.

"Because I need to use the blackboard to draw some diagrams so it would be better if I gave my talk in a lesson after a break," I said.

I could see that Mr Hibberd was very sceptical and considered this to be another one of my stalling ploys to avoid work – I excelled in the art of procrastination. But he had to give me the benefit of the doubt and arranged for me to give my talk at the beginning of the lesson that followed the morning break a couple of days later.

When the time came, I duly arrived early and prepared the diagrams on the blackboard. When the class came in I could see that Mr Hibberd was quite impressed with my efforts on the board, although he did quietly correct a spelling mistake. After the register I began my talk by going through the diagrams and sending around the handouts, then, at the end, answering questions. The talk lasted most of the lesson and it showed me what I could do if I put my mind to it and applied myself. I also think that it showed Mr Hibberd what I was capable of if motivated and I know that he gave me one of the top marks for this exercise.

Maths on the other hand was taught by Mr 'Pop' Darley, a stocky little man who wore an ill-fitting, grubby, navy pinstriped three-piece suit in the pocket of which he kept a thin length of rope for thrashing you with if you stepped too much out of line. His main teaching style consisted of issuing us with dog-eared textbooks with a minimum of blackboard tuition and even less explanation. Most of it was easy enough but some questions remained, certainly for me, unanswered.

For example: what kind of person invented logarithms? Who the hell went to the trouble of making all those calculations and writing them down? What did the poor compositors and printers think when asked to meticulously recreate these columns of numbers? What happened to the proof-readers? Did they ever recover? In the days before the calculator when only the slide rule ruled I could see the point of these tables, as I could the navigation tables produced by Norie and Burton... but what kind of mind? Pop Darley's first line of punishment was to send you to stand in the corner of the room but if you then moved or did something else, the little length of rope would appear and he would give you a couple of whacks across the buttocks. Whatever turned him on I suppose. He could also be rather short-tempered at times.

On one occasion he asked my unfortunate classmate Burgess, who was prone to stammer, a question:

"Be quick with the answer, Burgess," said the impatient Darley.

"Ah, ah, ah, tha, tha," Burgess began.

"Come on boy, we haven't all day!" spluttered Pop.

"Tha, tha, tha, tha, tha," continued Burgess.

"Spit it out boy! Spit it out!" Darley pressed.

The class was now getting a bit fed up with this insensitive bullying when John Cannan piped up with, " He doesn't stammer when he sings sir."

Pop Darley contemplated this for a few seconds and then yelled, "Then sing it boy, sing it!"

Mr Darley also took us for history. You would think that this subject would be approached with enthusiasm and some imagination given the history of Trinity House itself and the wealth of historical information on the development of the British Empire and Britain's use of its maritime dominance to exploit the trade routes of the world. We are an 'island nation' for Pete's sake. But not Pop! His idea of history was reading Joshua Slocum's 'Sailing Alone Around the World' to us, before getting more adventurous with passages from a book about the sinking of the 'Lusitania', interesting if you consider the aftermath and the unnecessary loss of life, but not the way Pop Darley did it. I'm sure he would have his rope end out now if he could read this but he should have stuck to his logarithms.

Mr Spinks and Mr Bole taught physics. Mr Spinks was one of the teachers who always wore a gown and, like Mr Bole, was a very good teacher. I never saw either of them resort to corporal punishment, in fact Mr Bole kept order completely by a 'look'. Just one look and you knew you were on the verge of going too far. We were all pretty frightened of him but looking back I don't know why because he always seemed amiable, in a serious way, and in control. Some of us though who used to go to Madeley Street Baths in the winter to watch the wrestling were convinced that he moonlighted as a wrestler called 'The Mask' as he had the same build and used the same eye glare that Mr Bole used in class. The billing for 'The Mask' was that if he was ever beaten, he would be unmasked. But of course this never happened as he usually resorted to foul means to make sure that he won, getting the crowd excited and booing in the process to ensure a good value show.

Mr Bole did turn out to have a talent that nobody knew about though, when he accompanied himself on guitar while singing a song that he'd written for the soundtrack for a film of the school's traditional 'Noah Play' that was put on in the streets of Hull one weekend. He also sang the narrative throughout the soundtrack in, if I remember right, a calypso style. I hope he didn't use a West Indian accent!

Mr Spinks also had a bent for music and composed one of the school songs sung to the tune of the cowboy song 'Streets of Laredo'.

One of the lines was, 'Wrap me up in my bum-freezer jacket', but I can't remember the rest. School songs were often sung at school assembly which occurred every morning except Wednesdays when we had chapel, presided over by the head teacher, Mr Eddon. He was quite elderly when I was there and always wore a suit covered by an academic gown. He was a bit 'bumbling' with very thick eyebrows and often looked as if he was about to fall asleep when he wasn't actually addressing his congregation. What used to always wake him up was when we used to sing one of the school songs that started, 'Rejoice with me my mother dear, I'm now a Trinity Boy', and change some of the words. The original words were, 'It's an English ship and English crew, so give three cheers for your boy in blue', which we changed to, 'It's an English ship, and Chinese crew'. Not particularly politically correct but it always made a startled Mr Eddon glare around the room from beneath his bushy eyebrows. Of course Catholics and Jews, there didn't seem to be any Muslims then, were excused the religious part of the assemblies and I always envied them for this.

The practical seamanship tutor at the school, Mr Jack Haylett, also took PE. His main domains were the gym, his seamanship room, which resembled a kind of workshop or rope loft, and Victoria Dock, which was used for boat work. Jack always wore a smart, grey three-piece suit except in the gym when sport attire meant that he took his jacket off and substituted his polished black shoes for a pair of white plimsolls. Some said that he'd been a PTI in the Navy, while others said that he'd been an AB in the merchant navy. I don't know which was true, he may have been both, but what was for sure was that he taught practical seamanship brilliantly. In his loft we learned all of the major knots and hitches, along with some fancy knot work. We also learned how to splice ropes and wires, where to use the different knots and splices, how to rig stages, blocks and tackles, boatswain's chairs and everything you needed to be a competent seaman. I certainly left the school with a range of practical skills that made my transition from schoolboy to sailor very easy.

Mr Clark, known as 'Nobby', was our signal instructor, developing our skills in recognising the International Code flags, and transmitting and receiving semaphore and the Morse code. He was a short, stocky man with a gruff voice and fingers that had been kippered dark yellow due to his fondness for Capstan Full Strength cigarettes. Nobby also instructed at the Nautical College and always wore a uniform that I believe was that of a Royal Navy petty officer although it also could have been a merchant navy officer's rig.

Nobby was very down to earth and while he was a hard taskmaster his lessons were also a lot of fun as the messages he asked us to transmit, which the rest of the class was supposed to receive, were often ribald and risqué. We all liked Nobby.

Navigation was taught by Mr Lancaster, an ex Lieutenant Commander in the Royal Navy. He was a big man who normally dressed in a blazer and slacks and travelled in from Hornsea every day with Mr Hibberd. Mr Lancaster was a good teacher and also had a very good sense of humour, which was a good job because our paths crossed regularly due to my tendency to play the fool rather than concentrate on my learning. His line of punishment, on the rare occasions he used it, was to write one of the Rules of the Road but often he would forget that he'd given you the punishment so you just kept it for the next time. I saw him lose his temper only twice. One was when we were in Jack Haylett's seamanship loft for some reason when the unfortunate Burgess did or said something. I don't know what, but Mr Lancaster went ballistic, grabbing one of Jack's display pieces off the wall - an example of a wire splice in a short length of wire rope - then laying Burgess over one of the tables and thrashing him several times with it. Burgess screamed with pain. I was transfixed thinking, fuck this for a game of sailors, keep your mouth shut Bob or you'll be next. When he'd finished beating Burgess, the wild-eyed Mr Lancaster looked around the room, saw me and said, "You, you... I just know you are going to do something so get out now before you do!"

"But where shall I go sir?" I replied.

"Anywhere. Just get out of my sight and don't come back!"

So I went for a walk around town before my next lesson. I hadn't done anything wrong, I just looked, at least in Mr Lancaster's eyes, that I might.

This wouldn't be the only time that we had problems. One day Mr Lancaster asked who hadn't done their homework. I put my hand up along with several others. After giving all the others a reprimand he just looked at me and said, "I'm not interested in you, you're just a waste of time."

On another occasion he said, "Addey, you are nothing but a bum, a deadbeat, and a coffee bar cowboy, and you will end up selling French letters on street corners."

It was good advice that I wish I'd taken, as that's how Richard Branson started out! I got my own back on Mr Lancaster though when he was reading out the class positions in navigation following the end of term examinations. I'll never forget his expression when he read out my score and I'd come third.

One of the funniest things that happened to me at Trinity House also involved Mr Lancaster. We had been to boat work with Jack Haylett where we had to launch a lifeboat into Victoria Dock, row it around a bit, and then bring it back alongside and hoist it in the davits on the dock side. When we came alongside the majority of those on board climbed a steel ladder set into the dockside to prepare the davits and tackles. The trick was to time your step from the boat to the ladder, and this time I missed and my bottom half plunged in soaking my trousers and part of my jacket. This meant that I had to go home for a change of clothing while my uniform was cleaned and dried. As I only had the one uniform at the time it also meant returning to school in my civvy gear, the blue checked Italian style C & A suit, accompanied with my winkle-picker shoes that by now turned up at the ends. Next morning, because I was not in uniform, I wasn't allowed to stand in the ranks with my school colleagues so I had to stand at the side with the teachers. There I was with my drainpipe trousers and my winkle-pickers with the curled-up toes, when Mr Lancaster spotted me. He sidled up alongside of me, looked me up and down, and said, "Now then Robin, where's Little John?"

My final run-in with Mr Lancaster, and what probably led to my downfall at the school, was an incident involving my mates Ray Hawker and Dave Harrison. Ray and Dave sat at a desk just behind me and I could hear that they were up to something. Dave had managed to get some fireworks, which he was taking to pieces and he and Ray were pouring the gunpowder into an empty inkwell; all desks had a hole and cavity for inkpots in those days. There was no teacher present at the time so we were expected to do some preparation or revision. I pretended to be doing some work - that should have got their suspicions up for a start - before turning with a lighted match and dropping it into the inkwell.

Baroof! A minor explosion erupted that sent a flash and a cloud of black smoke up to the ceiling. Mr Lancaster had been watching from outside and with an agility that defied his size and age he leaped through the window, bounced across several desks, grabbed Ray and Dave by the scruffs of their necks and marched them towards the door.

Ray raised his arm and shouted, "Get off!" to which Mr Lancaster replied, "Want a fight do you? Let's go to the gym and sort this out!"

It was a bit ridiculous for a six-foot, sixteen stone, man against a fifteen-year-old, five foot six lad. Anyway it didn't come to violence as he marched them to the headmaster's office instead. Obviously he had not seen my involvement. Shortly after our class was dismissed, I went to the headmaster's office myself and stood outside with Dave and Ray. Mr Lancaster was still inside giving the details to Mr Eddon. After a while Mr Lancaster appeared and asked what I was up to. I told him that as I had lit the match and fired the gunpowder, I didn't think that my mates should take all of the rap.

"Right," said Mr Lancaster, " you can join these two."

Inside the office we were asked to explain ourselves after Mr Lancaster had given his perception of the events. It really was a fair cop, we had no excuses and the black soot mark on the ceiling of the classroom would remain as testament to our guilt.

At last Mr Eddon said, "I think, Mr Lancaster, we should now consider an appropriate punishment." We waited in anticipation. "I think writing the Rules of the Road from 16 to 32 would be fitting, given the severity of the offence." Our hearts sank, 16 to 32, that was a lot of writing.

"I don't think so," said Mr Lancaster, "I think all of the rules from 1 to 32 is a fairer punishment."

Not in our eyes it wasn't and our hearts sank further as we waited for Mr Eddon's reply.

"Very well," said Mr Eddon as Mr Lancaster smirked. "All the rules from 1 to 32 it shall be, but Addey because of your honesty, I will let you off this time with a warning."

It wasn't good news for Ray and Dave, or even Mr Lancaster but it was a great outcome from me, or so I thought. There was a moral there somewhere but for me this was the beginning of the end.

I returned to Halifax at the end of the autumn term in 1962, to spend Christmas with my dad. A couple of days before Christmas whilst my dad and Margaret were out at work, a letter arrived. I knew immediately where it was from, Trinity House. I held it for a while and then put it with the other letters for when my dad came home at lunchtime. I picked it up again, and then again, until finally my curiosity got the better of me and I got the kettle and steamed it open.

The contents were a shock. I knew that I'd been in a bit of trouble but I didn't expect this. The letter from Mr Eddon questioned my commitment to the school and said that my behaviour left much to be desired. It went on to invite my dad to make an appointment in the New Year to discuss my future or, alternatively, "We would have no objection if you withdrew your son from the school."

Shit! What should I do? Elvis Presley was number one with 'Return to Sender' at the time, which seemed like good advice. The fire was also tempting but in the end I put it back with the rest of the mail.

When my dad came home he read the mail and I waited for the outburst. It didn't come even though he sussed immediately that I had steamed the letter open. He just said, "You know what this means? You've got the sack. But you knew that already."

Well, not quite I hadn't. I was still expected to return to the school if I was prepared to knuckle down. I could do the work with no problems, I just needed to apply myself more for the next year or two. The problem was that I'd had enough of school and not having enough money and the thought of another year or so in that position was not an attractive one. In addition, the wage of merchant navy apprentice officers was notoriously low, even lower than shore-based trade apprentices, so this again wasn't attractive. And I'd also learned that it was possible to work one's way up from being a rating to being an officer while getting paid more in the process.

Over Christmas, while in the doghouse, I got a bit of a grilling in between the "You should consider yourself lucky, I was out earning a living at your age," routine.

Did I want to work in a garage? No. Did I want to work in a mill? - Halifax was big on carpets. No.

Do you want to go 'down t'pit' like Margaret's brother? No, but it would be better than the mill as it paid more on the coalface.

I didn't say much but in my head I was concocting another plan and contemplating another possibility. I still found going to sea the most attractive option because of the tales that I'd heard, the prospect of decent money and because if I was going to live out of a suitcase I may as well do it professionally.

I knew that I was too young to join the merchant navy as I was only fifteen and you had to be sixteen. You also had to go to sea training school, which would be as bad as returning to school. But I also knew that you could sail as a galley boy on the deep-sea trawlers out of Hull at fifteen. Some of my old mates from Boulevard School had done it and one of the older lads from Trinity House, Steve Gibbs, had gone to sea on the trawlers. I was also aware that this was one of the most dangerous jobs in the world, that many trawlers got lost and hundreds of fishermen got killed and injured. One of my schoolmates from Boulevard had been lost at sea when, as a galley boy, he fell over the side emptying the gash (waste bucket). And one of my classmates at Trinity House lost his skipper father when a mine that he caught in his trawl went off on the deck of his ship.

Most of the lads from Boulevard and Trinity House who had chosen this path though had started their sea careers in the summer. What kind of an idiot would contemplate doing their first trip on an Arctic trawler in the middle of one of the worst winters for years? – Me!

During my final term at Trinity House, a trawler owner, Tom Boyd, had presented the school with a new lectern. So I had a contact name, as Tom Boyd was the head of Lord Line as well as his own Boyd Line and his office was in the famous Lord Line building on St Andrew's Dock. I had been to the Fish Dock a few times but this was the only company that I knew, as the building dominated the eastern end of the dock. I'd no idea how to get a job on the trawlers. So, unknown to my dad, I used my letter writing skills and wrote a job application for a post as galley boy and addressed it to: Mr Tom Boyd, Lord Line, St Andrew's Dock, Hull, and put it in the post.

Immediately after Christmas I told my dad that I wanted to go back to Hull for the New Year and he agreed.

On my arrival in Hull I left my case at my sister's house and that afternoon went down to the Fish Dock and the Lord Line office. The dock area was very quiet as most of the work and ship recruiting went on in the morning. I'd no idea where to go so I went into the main entrance of the Lord Line offices and started to climb the stairs only to be surprised by Tom Boyd himself coming down. He asked me what I wanted and I said I was looking for a job on the trawlers. He told me that I was in the wrong place and took me down to the ship's husband's office where the crews signed on. I said that I'd sent them a letter and Tom Boyd asked if it was the one that he'd picked up from the ship's husband's desk and was holding in his hand. I said it was and he told me that I needed to come back the following morning as that was when they would know if there were any jobs going. I thanked him and off I went.

The next morning I was there bright and early, but there was a little bloke, who I found out was the ship's runner and did all the running around for the ship's husband, blocking the office door. Nothing seemed to be doing so I went off for a walk about. As I crossed the swing bridge, I met Steve Gibbs and he asked me why I was there and said that he'd show me the ropes such as where to go for jobs with other companies. But first we visited Stanton's Coffee shop for a hot, sweet, coffee and a delicious bread cake, hot and dripping with butter, just what you needed on a cold winter's morning.

After Stanton's, we were walking back across the bridge when we heard the runner from Lord Line who was on the opposite footpath shouting, "Anybody know a galley boy called Addey?"

"That's you, Bob," said Steve.

We yelled to the runner and he took me back to the office. It seemed that my letter to Tom Boyd, and my encounter with him had paid off. The ship's husband said I could choose between three ships, two old ones and one that was nearly brand new.

I chose the new one, the 'Lord Jellicoe', which was due to sail the next day. Before that however, there was a lot to do.

First of all, because I was under age, I needed parental permission and a consent form needed signing. This was impossible for me as my mam had now moved again and was somewhere in London and my dad knew nothing about what I was doing. I told the ship's husband that I lived with my sister and asked if it would be all right for her to sign the form. He said this would be fine, so I went and told my sister what I was doing and told her that my dad had said it was okay. He hadn't of course but my sister signed the form and I returned to the dock and signed on the ship. I had to go now as I'd seen in the Hull Daily Mail that fishermen who didn't sail after they had signed on were taken to court and fined!

Next, I had to get ready to sail. I didn't have any working gear so my school shirts had to do along with some old jeans. Jack, my brother-in-law who my sister said was so excited it was if he was the one that was going to sea, gave me lots of advice as he had also been a galley boy on the trawlers. Soon the clock ticked by and it was time for my first trip to sea.

My dad duly arrived back in Hull early in January to be informed by my sister what I'd done. He then went to the school to see Mr Eddon who said to him, "Your son hasn't been back to the school since the beginning of the new term Mr Addey, where is he?"

My dad just stared at him and said, "He's gone to sea."

PART TWO – TRAWLERS.
Chapter 7. A Pan of Shackles.

On January 4th 1963 I joined the 'Lord Jellicoe' as a galley boy, official title 'Assistant Cook', on the princely wage of seventy-three shillings a week. That was three pounds thirteen shillings in old money or three pounds sixty-five pence today. This was for working over twelve hours a day over a seven-day week with no overtime. It was just the basic wage plus tips (backhanders) from the crew if they liked you and they had made a good trip as everyone else got paid their wages plus a percentage of what the catch sold for (settlings) after their expenses. I'd been given some advice by Jack, who'd also left school at fifteen to become a trawler galley boy, on how to maximise the backhanders, like make sure you looked clean - the fishermen liked that, don't be cheeky - the fisherman didn't like that. Make sure that the mess-rooms are kept clean and everything is ready for the men coming in off the deck. They may not have washed for days, they may be covered in blood, scales and fish guts but they liked their food served in a clean environment. It was good advice and I did my best to follow it.

The 'Lord Jellicoe' (H228) was a sidewinder trawler, which meant that she fished for fresh fish with the trawl over the side rather than the newer, larger stern trawlers that froze the fish on board and dragged the trawl over the stern using a ramp for hauling. She had been built at Beverley, by Cook, Welton and Gemmill, where she was launched in 1961 before being fitted out in Prince's Dock, Hull, and being registered for service in the summer of 1962. At 163.6 feet in length, and with a breadth of 30 feet and a gross tonnage of 594 tons, she was slightly smaller than the average Hull deep-sea trawler.

I think a note of clarification is necessary here in regards to the term tonnage in relation to the size of a ship. A ton in this context is not referring to weight but to volume in terms of cubic capacity in that the measurement used is 100 cubic feet. The gross tonnage of a ship is the internal volume of the ship including all enclosed spaces - holds, engine room, accommodation etc. If the tonnage calculated to include the areas for the engines, steerage, crew accommodation and navigation is deducted from the gross tonnage we are left with the net tonnage.

The crew of the 'Lord Jellicoe' consisted of: Skipper, mate, boatswain, third hand, nine spare-hands and a deck-hand learner; a chief engineer, second engineer (the 'Lord Jellicoe' also had an extra engineer for this trip), two motormen, a cook and cook's assistant (galley boy) and a radio operator.

A classmate, Ray Hawker, who would himself leave Trinity House to start work on the trawlers later in the year, had come down to see me off,

It was a dark, gloomy, cold morning when we first looked across St Andrew's Dock towards the trawler, now with lights burning and engines humming, as it waited for the crew to arrive. We were sailing late that morning and the first thing I needed to do was to go to the fishermen's stores and buy myself a mattress. Neither these, nor any bedding, were provided but I'd brought a blanket from home with a pillowcase, so all I wanted now was a 'donkey's breakfast' mattress, the cost of which would be taken out of my already meagre wages. Ray and I then went on board to find my cabin. 'Lord Jellicoe' was a new ship, only a few trips old, and all of the accommodation was aft. On older ships the spare-hands (deck-hands) slept in the fo'c'sle but on the more modern trawlers everyone slept aft. I shared a small cabin with the deckie learner. It was a tiny room, just big enough for two bunks, one above the other and a small seat locker. There was no natural light. As it turned out I had the top bunk and this was where I placed my donkey's breakfast mattress. We then had a walk about to see where things were.

What got me first was the smell. The mixture of old fish, fish liver oil and fuel oil smells was overbearing and, for me, nauseous. I felt sick already and we hadn't even left the dock. I was already apprehensive, although I couldn't show this in front of Ray, and wondering, with a mixture of fear and excitement if I'd made the right decision.

Soon the rest of the crew were climbing on board and Ray took his leave to watch the ship sail and then tell my mates what I'd done when he went back to school. Soon the tone of the engine changed. The ropes were cast and we were heading for the bull nose and the lock head. There was no turning back now and I was experiencing a buzz that I was to experience nearly every time I was on a ship heading for the open sea.

One of the last people to jump on board, and a little the worse for wear, was the cook, Gordon, who found me, introduced himself, and took me out on deck. Holding himself steady by gripping my shoulders and breathing rum fumes in my face, to add to the other nauseous smells that I was experiencing, he pointed at some stacks of sacks and bags and told me to put them away in the vegetable locker aft.

He then said, "When you've done that I want you to make a big pan of shackles for tea."

I looked at him blankly.

"Do you know what a pan of shackles is?" he asked. I shook my head. "It's a big pan of stew so do your best, I'm going below for a drink. Oh, and another thing it's blowing out there so if you start to feel sick, turn in, and fuck them, they'll get no tea!" And with that he was gone.

Bewildered, I started to move the sacks starting with the potatoes. By now we were out in the river Humber and heading for Spurn. The deckie learner then joined me. He introduced himself as Dave Wooldridge. Dave was a really nice bloke who took a lot of ribbing because his brother and father were both skippers and indeed Dave eventually became a skipper himself while still in his early twenties. He obviously realised that it was my first trip, and offered to help, so between us we fairly quickly cleared and stored the vegetables. We then went into the galley and Dave asked what I had to do next and I told him about the pan of shackles and again he said he'd help. We found the largest pan we could, which looked like an enormous soup tureen and part filled it with water and put it on the stove. I then got a load of vegetables: onions, carrots, potatoes and swede, and peeled and chopped them up, then threw the lot in the water. But there was something missing? Meat! We didn't know what to put in, so we found a likely piece of meat - to this day I've no idea what it was – and chopped it up and threw that in as well along with some salt and pepper and some powdered soup that we found in a tin. That was it. We stood back and admired our work, which was now simmering nicely, so we put a lid on it and left it.

We were now in the open sea and heading for Norway and the Norwegian fishing grounds off the north coast. We were heading into a strong wind that would soon become a gale, but was now just causing the ship to pitch and roll. I was having trouble in keeping my feet even though the movement was mild compared to what was to come and the pitching, rolling, oil, stale fish, and now cooking smells, really started to take its toll. I felt dizzy, nauseous and as green as the sea and I knew it would only be a matter of time before I was throwing up.

Seasickness is an awful feeling. I felt like I was dying. The motions of the ship felt like I was experiencing every ride at Hull Fair at the same time. Up, down, side-to-side, round and up, and, down with a mighty splash and crash. Everything in the whole world seemed to be moving in different directions and, as I tried to keep my balance, the deck seemed to fall away of its own volition causing me to stumble. So I spent the rest of the afternoon in my bunk. All I wanted to do was sleep but the motions made even that impossible as I slid around my bunk. Early in the evening the door of the cabin burst open and a number of the spare-hands entered.

"Did you make this pan of shackles?" one of the men said, waving a pint mug filled with the stew. "Best pan of shackles we've ever had, do you want some?" They all laughed. I looked at the mugs with the fat glistening and floating on the top of whatever was underneath, wished for an early death and rolled over.

Next morning the cook called me very early, about 5.30, to prepare the mess-room for breakfast. This was the start that for me would be about a 15-hour day with maybe an hour or two break in the afternoon, a good introduction to the world of work for a fifteen-year-old boy. The weather had not improved and my condition was made worse by the cooking and other smells circulating as the ship had been battened down since we passed the Spurn Lightship. On top of this was the continuous throb of the engines. The cook kept on at me, continuously telling me what to do, urging me to get a move on, and, "Don't let it get to you," all apparently for my own good.

After breakfast I was told to scrub the mess-room deck. All I wanted to do was sleep and I wasn't fussed where, but if I slacked and for a moment rested my head against one of the seats, the cook was immediately on my case and shouting through the hatch to wake me up. And so it went on throughout the day as we prepared the vegetables for dinner and tea. I seemed to be peeling potatoes all afternoon, when not washing up and making sure the mess-room and the little cabin that the skipper, mate, boatswain, radio operator and engineers used, were kept clean.

The day's work was interrupted when the skipper opened the bond locker to distribute cigarettes, tobacco and other goodies that were duty free. I was told to take a pillowcase up to the bond locker where the skipper filled it with cigarettes and some other stuff and said he would pay for it. It was better than Christmas, or at least it would have been if I hadn't felt so ill.

During the course of this second day one of the spare-hands came into the galley and was chatting to the cook when he turned to me and said, "So you're the one are you? I was in the office when Tom Boyd came in and told the ship's husband to give the lad from Trinity House who wrote the letter a job, as he was the type we wanted in the fishing industry." By the tone of the spare-hand's voice and the way he looked at me I don't think he was too impressed with what could become the future of the fishing industry.

The next day went pretty much like the first although now I was getting a bit more used to it but still feeling seasick. We were nearing the Norwegian coast when the cook sent me up to the bridge with a mug of tea for the skipper, Alf Fletcher. Alf was looking out of the clear view window when I staggered onto the bridge still with most of the tea in the mug.

"Come over here Snacker and have a look at this," he said. Snacker was a term usually relating to a deckie learner but often used for any young starter. I made my way across and looked through the spinning glass of the clear view and the ship was entirely covered in ice from the rigging to the deck and every splash of spray was adding to it. It was a wonderful and exciting sight for my naïve eyes but I also knew the dangers. Ice had taken many trawlers by making them top heavy. This was a modern trawler built to withstand all the hazards of the Arctic but nevertheless the deck-hands were out on deck with axes and steam hoses to clear what they could. I watched for a while but not wanting to get in the skipper's way went back down below.

Later we got a message that the skipper had decided to seek shelter by steaming through the fjords and that we'd be stopping briefly in Tromso for some engine part that the chief engineer had requested. We were also told that if we wanted we could send letters home, which some of us did. No doubt many of the letters from the crew were about how much they loved and missed their families at home, some may just simply have been apologies for their behaviour when they were last at home, mine was just a big moan. I wrote to my sister along the lines that I wouldn't be returning home as the seasickness would do for me before then, and that if I did get back I would never set foot on another ship. I also said that the cook was a slave driver and if I'd realised then that there was a thing called child abuse I'd have thrown that in as well. Seventy three shillings a week, twelve plus hours a day, seven days a week – did they still send kids up chimneys? I then finished off the letter by saying that I couldn't write any more as I was about to be sick again.

I awoke the next morning to a new sensation. No rocking. No rolling. No pitching. The engines were throbbing rhythmically but now all was calm. I looked out of the galley porthole and got my first glimpse of a foreign country. If I thought the iced up ship was spectacular, it was nothing compared to the Norwegian Fjords. As it was the middle of winter there was not much daylight in these parts but still the views were fantastic. The mountains, large and snow covered, came down directly into the sea, and waterfalls, some of them frozen solid, cascaded down their sides. Pastel coloured houses could be seen outlined against the snow in the dim lights that illuminated the tiny villages and hamlets we passed in the darkness. Tromso was also a delight, more densely populated but still with the pastel coloured buildings and a bridge that spanned the fiord, with people carrying skis crossing it. To me it appeared to be a magical place and I wished that we were staying there and that this was the end of our voyage. But not so, we only stopped at Tromso for a very short time before carrying on through the fiords to Honnigsvag for the engine part.

Fishermen like all seamen try to take advantage of anytime ashore that they can get, so in Honnigsvag some of us decided to venture ashore. It must have been about twenty-five degrees below freezing but what the heck. There wasn't much open and little to do but we wandered up the hill away from the quayside and found a café where we were talking to some local young people when we heard the ship's whistle blowing to let us know that we were about to sail again. So it was a quick 'goodbye' to our new acquaintances and then we were slipping and sliding down the hill on the snow and ice as we dashed back to the ship and on with the voyage.

It was only a few miles from Honnigsvag to the North Cape and the open sea; we were now about 300 miles inside the Arctic Circle.

Once we left the sanctuary of the fiords we were once again at the mercy of the elements. The bad weather was relentless and fishing was difficult. For several days the skipper was restricted to one or two hauls a day around the 'midday twilight zone' as this was the closest to daylight that we would get. The rest of the time we just dodged at a slow speed into the wind, rolling and pitching about. At least when the trawl was down it seemed to settle the ship and the movement eased. One afternoon, we may have been dodging or steaming to try new grounds, the ship almost turned over. I was in the mess-room listening to the spare-hand's banter as they enjoyed a mug of tea and a smoke, when suddenly the ship rolled to starboard. It was if we were surfing sideways down a massive wave. I held on to the mess-room table and looked down through the portholes at what looked like a wall of water coming towards us. We hit it beam on with a big bang.

"That's it," someone said, "We're going over!"

There was a moment's silence but no panic. We just clung on to the tables with white knuckles. The sea seemed to swallow the ship and we could only see water through the portholes. Then slowly we started to come up and we were back to the, what was now normal, rolling and pitching.

"That was a close one," one of the lads said, but then it was back to the jokes and banter.

The crew generally were a jovial bunch most of the time and were a mixture of young and old, although I may have mistook some for being older than they were because they didn't have their teeth in and hadn't shaved since we left Hull. I didn't have a lot of time to spend with them as I was busy at mealtimes but liked listening to their chat when I could. I know there was one old spare-hand who the others were wary of because he always sailed with the skipper and always wore his oilskins on watch on the bridge so he was ready for any emergency and the others thought this odd.

In their spare time the crew usually slept, played cards, or read. Their reading material consisted mainly of comics, magazines and paperbacks, including westerns - Zane Grey was very popular, thrillers of the Mickey Spillane variety, and books with explicit sexual activity, known as 'c**t yarns'.

It was with interest that I read in a newspaper some years later that a Hull trawler owner had objected to a request from the Seafarers' Education Service, a charity supported by the ship owners, that wanted to put libraries aboard the large freezer trawlers, which were away for up to three months. His reason was that reading books could lead to 'subversive ideas' amongst the crew. Talk about Victorian educational values, no place for enlightenment here.

On the few days when it wasn't blowing a gale there was a kind of freezing mist and fog and it was on those days of poor visibility that we caught glimpses of the Norwegian Fisheries Protection vessel that was monitoring our position relative to the exclusion zones. I'm sure that our skipper pushed it as finely as he could while playing this cat and mouse game but the finest protection for the Norwegian fish was the appalling weather. We were not catching enough and there was talk of a Jonah aboard. Were those sidelong glances directed at me?

"You must be a Jonah," one of the men said. Of course he was joking... I think.

By now I had got into the routine and was learning how the cook liked things organised. Mealtimes were hectic, not just in preparing the food but in serving it in a clean mess-room, with clean cutlery and plates. All meals were served in two half-hour sittings so that the turn around had to be very quick as the men had no time to waste if they wanted to get their meal, a drink and a smoke in that short period.

We had three main meals each day; breakfast, dinner (lunch) and tea (dinner) that were timed were possible to correlate with the watch changes, and then cold food was left out for those hungry during the night. Dinner and tea consisted usually of something like soup, main course and sweet. Main courses could be: roast meat, suet duff, stews, meat pies, pork chops - the biggest I had ever seen - served with vegetables, mashed potatoes or chips. A dessert could be a: sponge pudding, duff, roly-poly and things like that except on Sundays when it would be tinned fruit served with evaporated milk. In addition to this, once we got to the fishing grounds there was always fried fish that was served at breakfast and tea. And what wasn't eaten would be left out for sandwiches during the night (there is nothing like a cold fish sandwich) along with tins of jam and big pieces of cheese.

The bread, after the first few days when we'd run out of white sliced, was baked on board by the cook. All the food was high in calories and carbs as was needed for men doing a hard physical job in the freezing temperatures at sea inside the Arctic Circle. You can also see why it is said that the cook was the most important person on a ship next to the captain as a good cook and baker could make a lot of difference to the quality of life of the hard-working sailor.

No matter how good the cook though, the skill was keeping the food on the plate or bowl as the ship tossed about. The tables were webbed with wooden battens to keep the plates and serving tins in place, and the table cloths dampened with water to help stop things sliding about. But it was still necessary at times to hold the plate or bowl in your hand and move it constantly, sometimes at very acute angles, to stop the food flying off in all directions. Similarly in the galley, which in bad weather was a dangerous place, the stove had large metal battens to hold the pans in place and the floor was covered in tied down woven coconut matting, again sometimes wet, to stop us sliding around. Even so there were times when the weather was so bad that it was too dangerous to cook and the crew had to make do with a cold meal.

I was also now coping with or had got over the seasickness. Gordon had been right about this too as the key was to keep yourself occupied and not think about it and his driving me on with no quarter given played its part in this. Then something else started to concern me. While peeling potatoes and vegetables I must have nicked my finger, but thought nothing of it, and carried on handling the dirty peelings and water. Soon I was starting to feel a tingling sensation in the tip of my middle finger on my right hand but again I didn't think anything of it. A couple of days later and the end of the finger was red, swollen and throbbing. I pointed this out to Gordon and a couple of the lads and was given the advice, "Cob it."

By this they meant stick it up my arse. I didn't take this advice. Instead, when it got even more painful, I went to see the skipper.

The skipper diagnosed that the finger had gone septic and he tried bringing it to a head with a hot poultice. After a couple of days doing this he then thought the best thing to do was to lance it, so he took a scalpel to my finger to get the puss out. Unfortunately he didn't get all the puss out, so the finger swelled up again and once again the scalpel came into use. Again it failed and I was now coming out in boils on my face. At the time we were about to give up on the fishing and head home so the skipper decided that the best thing to do was put into Harstad in Norway on our way home where I could get hospital treatment. So it was back into the fiords and on arrival in Harstad I was taken up to the hospital, where my finger was anaesthetised - a luxury I hadn't had for the lancing by the skipper - and a surgeon cut a cross into my finger end. I still have the scar today without flesh under it, so that it's always sensitive in cold temperatures.

Once that was done and bandaged up he started work on my face. I can still remember seeing the yellow puss squirt out over his gloved hands as he squeezed the boils. All done, bandaged and plastered, I thought that was it, but no. There was just one more thing, a nurse would give me an injection of antibiotics in my buttocks so I had to drop my trousers and bend over the operating table.

I remember my mother saying, 'Always wear clean pants in case you get run over and taken to hospital.' Well, we'd been away nearly three weeks!

I looked at the nurse who smiled at me as she entered the room with a syringe in her hand. She was about eighteen years old, blond, blue-eyed and a true Nordic beauty. Smitten, smarting with pain and scarlet with embarrassment, I left the hospital and returned to the ship.

Back on board with my bandaged hand that the surgeon had told me not to get wet, I was restricted in what I could do. The deckie learner, Dave, had to take over most of my wet galley duties and I just did what I could for the three or four days it took to get back to the Humber. We were quite shocked as we made our way to the Killingholme anchorage to await the tide, because we passed a number of ice flows drifting out to sea as parts of the upper Humber had frozen over during one of the worst winters ever.

At Killingholme I experienced a new illness for the first time, the 'Channels', the feeling of restlessness and excitement that you feel when you are about to return home.

The next shock was when we put alongside the Insurance Buildings just outside St Andrew's Dock so that the ship could be towed stern first into the dock. Here, one of the shore staff told us that the Lord Line had been sold and the 'Lord Jellicoe' would be based out of Grimsby and that Boyd Line would now become a separate company still operating out of the Lord Line offices.

It was accepted that members of the crew not needed to tie the vessel up in the dock could leap ashore at the Insurance Buildings and that is what the cook and I did and this, for me, was the end of the voyage. It was January 27th; we had been away twenty-five days for a very poor return.

Early next morning I went down the dock for a fry. All members of the crew were entitled to a fry if they could be bothered to go to the fish market once the trawler had landed its catch. The mate was quite gloomy as he handed me my parcel, as the trip had not been at all successful. In fact it made me feel guilty when accepting the fish to the point that I nearly gave it him back and told him to sell it with the rest of the catch. Anyway I took half my fry to the Collins's, Jack's mam and dad, who lived down Bean Street, and the rest I took home. Guess what was for tea that night?

Later that morning, about ten, I returned to the dock and the company office where the men were getting the money for their share of the catch (settling) and hung about there for any backhanders that would come my way. I didn't do bad even though some of the men were probably settling in debt, but I felt that the money I received was really in sympathy as I'd not be able to return to sea until my scars had healed up, which would take a few weeks, and then I'd have to find a new ship. I had of course, now that I'd conquered the seasickness, decided that I'd be returning to the sea.

Above. Lord Jellicoe.
Left. Arctic Adventurer.
Below. Tom Addey (my dad), and me holding my newly born niece,Paula Collins.
Bottom. Arctic Crusader. All trawler pictures by kind permission of the Hull Bullnose Heritage Group.

Chapter 8. Three Day Millionaire.

It only took a couple of weeks for my hand and face scars to heal up but getting back to sea was not as easy as I thought it would be, so I was 'out of ship' almost as soon as I started. I was also not entitled to any sick benefits or unemployment pay as I did not have enough in National Insurance stamps, so I had to make do with what I had and some money my dad had left for me to buy some working gear after his visit to the school. While I still had to sign on to get credits for National Insurance I was sent for careers advice where various suggestions were made like eat humble pie and go back to Trinity House, try an apprenticeship in engineering or whatever I fancied. It was like that in those days as there were plenty of opportunities if you were capable, but I rejected them all. One reason was that I didn't have what I felt was a regular home and the apprentice wages would not cover my lodgings. The sea seemed a good answer to this as I would be away most of the time and it was possible to earn good money at a young age. In fact it was possible to become a trawler skipper at a very young age if you had the right approach and a lot of luck. Nearly all trawler skippers started at the bottom and worked their way up: galley boy, deckie learner, spare-hand, third hand, boatswain, mate and skipper. Similarly you could also work yourself up "through the fo'c'sle" to be a captain in the merchant navy if you put the effort in, so it seemed the best for all concerned that the sea would form the basis of my career. I also wanted some fun.

As it happened my sister was pregnant at the time with her first child, which meant that their small house would become a bit more cramped, particularly if more children came along, but still they were happy for me to stay. After some discussion Jack came up with a solution in regard to the board and lodging money as my dad couldn't be expected to pay this any more as if I was not at school, I should be earning money. The answer was simple, I would send a payment to my sister while I was at sea and I wouldn't pay anything while I was home. This seemed more than fair to me although it was more of a gamble for him as I was already out of a ship!

1963 was a horrendous winter and February was as brutal as January. When I was fit and ready to go back, my routine every morning was to go down to the fish dock and hang around the Boyd Line offices and near to the other trawler owners' offices to see if there were any vacancies for a galley boy. It was freezing cold and meant crunching through ice and frozen snow to get there and it was even colder on the dock. If I could afford it I would warm up with mug of hot sweet coffee and a hot bread cake, oozing with melted butter in Stanton's Coffee Shop.

I didn't know many people at first but Steve Gibbs came home from one of his trips and by hanging about with him I got to know some of his mates like Terry Rowan and Dave Calvert. This in turn eventually led to a whole network of young fishermen, mainly deckie learners, who I'd meet up with on the dockside or maybe at a café or pub although I was still under-age and 'bar shy'. We were not confined however to the fish dock and Hessle Road as we would also roam a bit venturing into the city centre where one of our haunts was a café in Market Place and then to the top floor of Hammonds department store opposite Paragon Station. Here there was a record department, where we used to chat to the girls who worked there and on the nearby sweet counter and in a self-service restaurant called 'Pick a Dish'. I still managed the occasional visit to the Locarno and the pictures but money was a bit tight and it wasn't until the beginning of March before I was called into the Boyd Line Office and offered the job of galley boy on the 'Arctic Adventurer'.

The 'Arctic Adventurer' (H381) was a much older ship than the 'Lord Jellicoe'. Built in Beverley in 1936, originally as the 'St Loman', she was an oil burning steam ship of 565 gross tons, 172 feet long and 29 feet wide. In this ship the deck crew slept forward under the fo'c'sle in a cramped space with three-high bunks. The rest of the crew slept aft and my bunk was in the cabin, the officers' saloon, which took the round shape of the stern of the trawler. The cabin (saloon) had a large, half-round, built-in table with a built-in seat locker for seating. The whole cabin (saloon) was lined with panelled, polished wood, but some of the panels above the seat locker were sliding doors hiding cupboards. Some of the cupboards were for our personal storage but others served as bunks. My bunk was across the stern so that I had to slide around the table, kneel on the seat locker, and open the pair of sliding doors and climb into the narrow bunk with my head and feet thwart ships.

This ship certainly wasn't as comfortable as the 'Lord Jellicoe', particularly when it was rolling. It was like trying to sleep on a see-saw with the addition of the vibration of the propeller and the rumble of the steering gear, and let's not mention the noise from the liver house when we were fishing. When she rolled in bad weather it was as if one minute I was about to stand on my head, followed by a period when I seemed to be standing on my feet. A slight exaggeration perhaps but I remember that even if I laid on my front and hooked my feet under the mattress it didn't seem to help much.

Whereas the 'Lord Jellicoe' had been closed in on the port side of the after accommodation and only fished from the starboard side, the older trawlers like the 'Arctic Adventurer' had been built to fish both sides. So the after accommodation had open decks on either side, hence the need for the deck-hands' accommodation to be forward under the whaleback.

The 'Arctic Adventurer' didn't have a bathroom or showers so washing was done by using a bucket of hot water from the engine room or boiled on the galley stove. At the stern of the 'Arctic Adventurer' was the liver house where the fish livers were boiled in big vats to extract the oil. This was extra money for the crew but the radio operator also usually did the job so that he got a share of this cash. The after accommodation of the ship was accessed by a watertight, steel door that led to a short alleyway. On the left were the mess-room and the galley.

Next to the galley door was the entrance to the engine room. Across the alleyway from the galley and almost in front of the engine room door was a hatchway rimmed by the bulkhead on one side and by a steel plate about eighteen inches high on two other sides, leaving the remaining side clear for the steep ladder leading down to the lower deck.

Down here was the pantry, where the cook would prepare his bread, an area where I used to peel the vegetables, the cabins used by the engineers, mate and boatswain, and the saloon where they ate and we slept.

The cook on the 'Arctic Adventurer' was called Bill, a small, wiry Irishman, with thinning dark hair and hairy hands and arms, who scurried about a lot. I don't know why the hairy hands and arms are so memorable but maybe they were his only redeeming feature. To be fair he turned out to be a very good cook - his secret ingredient was 'on yons' – I think he was Northern Irish - and an excellent bread maker, even if he was a bit pedantic and always worrying about running out of food. This was an issue on the older ships that didn't have fridges and relied on ice or a ventilated locker on deck to keep the food fresh. The bread making was also important in that Bill would make batches of hot cakes, as good as Stantons, in the afternoon when we were at the fishing grounds. They would look and smell delicious and tasted as good as they looked. Bill would look outside and when he saw the men coming aft between hauls would say, "Quick, get these in the mess-room (a tray of hotcakes) and then they won't eat so much at tea." It was a ploy that worked – he really was a master baker.

Bill was obsessed with potatoes, well he was Irish, and the first thing that he inspected as far as I was concerned was how thinly I peeled them. Not a morsel of potato could be wasted, so my knife had to be sharp and the peelings razor thin. This also applied to one of his culinary specialities, hot pot, where he expected the potatoes for the topping to be sliced in such a way that you could see your knife blade through them, rather than the quarter-inch thick scallops that the cook on the 'Lord Jellicoe' had wanted. The slices were as thin as crisps and this is what they were like on the top of the hot pot when it came out of the oven, and very popular it was too. Such was his pedantry Bill even showed me how to cut bread. It was all in the wrist action, apparently something that he obviously knew quite a lot about. Bill was also very good at producing suet puddings and duffs, some of which were sweet but also there was the inevitable 'on yon duff' to 'fill them up' during the main course. Sometimes the men would ask how many chops or other items they could have and the answer was usually one per man perhaps, or as Bill would say, "Warn pore mon pore harps."

When we did find ourselves running short of food Bill would do a fish dinner. This would consist of fish soup followed by halibut cooked in a milky white, 'on yon' sauce. You would think that the fishermen would have had enough of fish seeing as it was always there, fried in batter for breakfast and tea, but in fact they loved the halibut and looked forward to it. They also used to make their own sauce using vinegar and mustard powder called 'Hessle Road' but I never cared for it myself preferring the old standby, tomato ketchup.

Fish and chips were fried in beef fat and one of the worst smells for me was when the cook rendered down big tins of the fat to fill the vast rectangular pans used for deep-frying. This really stank when it was done but not after when used for frying, but nevertheless it didn't help my feeling of nausea when battling the seasickness again on my return to sea, not helped by my thwart ship bunk.

The galley on the 'Arctic Adventurer' was simply a small room with a temperamental oil-burning stove on one side and a work surface and sink on the other. Hot water for the sink came by way of a steam pipe that by opening a valve projected a jet of steam into the sink filled by a cold-water tap. This made a bit of a racket but was very effective. The stove was topped by an arrangement of heavy metal battens to keep the pans in place and the floor was covered with the usual coir matting tied down at the corners.

The routine for me was much the same as the 'Lord Jellicoe' as far as the meal times were concerned. At other times my main concern was maximising the backhanders from the crew by making sure that everything was clean in the mess-rooms and the table battens were scrubbed white. In addition, I would also make sure that the big teapot in the mess-room was full and accompanied by clean mugs for when the men came in off deck between hauls. The fishermen, if there was any spare time between hauls, were expected to keep the alleyways and the lavatory, situated outside on the after end of the accommodation, clean but I started to do this when we had a slack period in the afternoons. I also used to clean and scrub out the fo'c'sle, taking care to be quiet and not disturb the sleeping watch.

It was a long day but worth it in the end as my bond was paid for by the skipper and I used to do very well on settling day, often walking off the dock with over £20 in my pocket when the average wage for a working man was about £10 – not bad for a fifteen year old. In addition, I used to get some backhanders when we went back to sea from the skipper and the mate, and I remember a boatswain who, usually pissed, would give me all the money he had on him when the ship sailed on condition that I'd give him his taxi money when we got back if he needed it.

I was quids in and experiencing what it was like to be one Hull's 'three day millionaires'. The term used to describe the fishermen who were away for three weeks and then having only three days - actually five tides - to spend their money.

Most fishermen were easily recognisable, not because of their money and western ocean roll when walking down the street but because of their clothes and, in some cases, their look. The look was to cultivate an image that borrowed from James Dean, Robert Mitchum and Marlon Brando but without the film star looks or lifestyle. This meant kind of half closing your eyes so that you looked half-pissed all the time, a half sneer (Billy Fury style), pout the lips slightly and on no account smile while trying to look cool and hard. It was also required to talk in a gruff voice with a strong Hull accent punctuated with rhyming slang, for example, "Nar then china," for, "Hello my friend." All this was topped off with heavily Brylcremed hair pulled down in a Teddy boy quiff. Obviously it was hard to keep up this pretence for any length of time due to the joking and banter that went on, particularly at sea, but a few did have a good try.

Fashion wise the fisherman was easily spotted with his pale grey or powder blue suit, with bell-bottom trousers with a Spanish waistband and back pleated, usually double breasted, jacket. The style was certainly pre-war and stuck in the 1930s, so the young ones developed their own styles with single-breasted jackets, still with the pleats but more often just one, with a yolk on the back, fancy cuffs and pockets, and drainpipe trousers with the Spanish waistband. Shoe styles varied but white moccasins were popular, as were white socks. The only time that I've seen people dressed like this has been in films of the nineteen twenties, or the suits, usually black, worn by Mississippi gamblers. These suits had to be made to measure as they were not high fashion and nobody would be seen dead dressed like that anywhere except in Hull, but there were many tailors that catered for the sartorial needs of the young fishermen. This in turn led to some competition between the more adventurous into who could devise the most outlandish suit by colour and embellishments. I had to have one.

My C & A suit that I'd had since I was fourteen still fitted me but made me stand out, not in a good way, when I was out and about with my deckie learner mates. So after my first trip on the 'Arctic Adventurer' it was down to Jackson the Tailor in Whitefriargate to be measured for my first deckie learner suit. The suit would be ready for when I returned from my next voyage. I chose a powder blue material with a fine check in it. It had thirteen-inch bottoms on the trousers and a four-inch Spanish waistband. The jacket had a shawl collar with a single link button for fastening, and delta-shaped, top pockets, one on either side. It had turned-up cuffs with buttons on them. The back of the jacket was yoke backed with a single pleat and a half belt. We went through the book as far as detail was concerned, even to selecting the colour of the jacket lining. I already had the greasy quiff and the winkle-picker shoes so this suit, I thought, would complete my image. I was brought down to earth though a few trips later when one of the spare-hands on the ship I was on said to me, " I saw you on Hessle Road while we were home Snacker... and you looked like a fucking spider!"

The skipper of the 'Arctic Adventurer' for three of the four trips I did was Phil Garner or 'Fascinating Phil' as he was known, due to his habit of pushing his hair into shape using the reflection in the bridge windows. For one trip we had a skipper called Albert Thompson who the crew were wary off because he was supposed to be a hard taskmaster and wasn't noted for his sense of humour. True he was a bit miserable but he was always all right with me but Phil Garner was more approachable even though I was, at that time, in awe of the skipper or 'Old Man' whose word was law.

During my time at home between voyages it was a case of grabbing what entertainment was going at night. The 'Locarno' and 'Majestic' were always good and there were also other venues cashing in on the beat boom that had been kick-started by the Beatles, meaning that there were new groups appearing almost every day. In fact the Beatles appeared at the Majestic, as did rockers like Joe Brown. There were also pubs that didn't seem to be too bothered about checking the age of potential under age drinkers. These included the Norfolk Arms, the Neptune, where the girls from Smith and Nephews used to spend their dinner times, King Edward and some of the many pubs that were to be found along Hessle Road. In the evenings there were also pubs like Halfway House on Spring Bank West, the George on the corner of Walton Street, and Blue Heaven in east Hull, that often offered live music and other entertainment.

My daytime activities after settling, which for me as a galley boy took longer than anyone else as I hung about for all the crew to get paid waiting for my back handers, consisted of a trip into town to the shops and maybe to a bar if I was with some other lads. This usually ended up with a visit to Hammonds' record shop and chicken and chips in 'Pick a Dish'. I remember doing this with a spare-hand called Sammy Gee who came from Stratford upon Avon and spoke with quite a posh, probably public school, accent and was a great bloke.

On another occasion I was there with a mate, Terry Rowan who was a couple of years older than me, when Terry said, " Have you seen Barbara today?" Barbara was a girl who worked on the sweets' counter, next to the record department and was a very pretty blond girl, so I said that I had seen her.

"She's all done up today, didn't you notice?" he asked.

I replied I had noticed and she looked really nice. "Well it's for you, you daft bugger, get over there and ask her out!"

I've never been very good at reading the signs and I still didn't believe Terry's assessment but I plucked up courage, sidled across and after a little small talk I asked her if she would like to go out with me that night; and she agreed.

Should it be the Dorchester or The Carlton? No, not for high class dining out as we didn't do that then, they were just the names of a couple of cinemas in Hull at that time although the venue for our first date would more likely have been the ABC Regal or Cecil. Like most dates in Hull then we met at the preferred rendezvous of promise and sometimes heartbreak, the newspaper kiosk in the bus station. The date went well although I can't remember the film we saw and by the time I'd taken her home I didn't have much time before it was time to sail again in the early hours of the next morning.

Sailing day meant arriving on the fish dock two hours before we were due to sail and started with a trip to the fishermen's stores. This was where the fishermen bought their gear, mattresses and other subsidised goods. As a galley boy I didn't have much to buy unless someone else wanted something like a shirt, if a pal saw you off it was usual to buy them a nylon shirt, or an order for nappies. The nappies sold in the stores were of very good quality and cheap so I was often asked to buy them for people, including my sister who would shortly give birth. At the stores you could also order flowers, gifts and cards that they would send on your behalf while you were away. These included lovey-dovey, 'remember me' type cards for wives and girlfriends. I'd heard about these, so while at the stores buying some nappies and T-shirts to work in, I decided to send some cards to Barbara. This was seen by one of the spare-hands who asked me who the cards were for as we walked back to the ship and I told him that I had been seeing a girl called Barbara who worked in Hammonds. Of course I got a little bit of ribbing by the lads but it soon passed and I forgot about the incident. Then one evening I was quietly clearing the table in the cabin where the skipper, Phil Garner, was chatting after his tea to the mate and chief engineer. The skipper then turned the conversation to me, asking me where I lived and what had I done during our two days at home. He then asked me if I had a girlfriend so I told him, "Yes."

"What does she do?" he asked.

"She works on the goody counter in Hammonds," I replied.

"What! They don't call her Barbara do they!" he exclaimed.

For a moment I was flummoxed, "Ya, yes," I stammered, "Do you know her?"

"Do I know her? Do I know her! She's my niece! You had better not have been up to no good with her or else there'll be trouble."

I could have died. I didn't know what to say. My face was bright red with embarrassment. The others said nothing, just watched me, waiting for my response.

"We've only been to the pictures," was my feeble reply. Then they all looked at each other and started laughing.

"I was just winding you up Snacker, your face was a picture, I don't know the girl," said the skipper as he slid off the seat locker and headed back to the bridge.

I went out with Barbara for a couple of trips but I felt that I was missing out on the 'wild side of life' shared by the other young fishermen, who spent more time hanging around the pubs I mentioned earlier. It wasn't anything to do with Barbara as she was everything a young man would want in a girlfriend. I was just too immature to appreciate her and most of the other girls I met while I was in my early teens. Sometimes this was because I wanted to go further quicker than what the girl did, even though I wasn't sure how far this was, or what to do when I got there! Quite a common trait for an adolescent, testosterone high, young teenage male, but eventually I would learn the lesson – it was a long lesson – that patience generally paid off.

This was the beginning of the swinging sixties with changes in music, fashion and sexual mores. When our black and white world of the 1950s turned into Technicolor. Girls started to wear their skirts shorter and the pill revolutionised contraception. This would be the era of free love and we all wanted some. Unfortunately however, most of it passed me by.

Back on the 'Arctic Adventurer' everything was going fine. I was getting on with the job and picking up a lot of money on settling days. I got on well with the fishermen and would share in their jokes without being cheeky and in return I got the best of their advice. A good example of this concerned tattoos. Jack, my brother-in-law had already warned me about tattoos but as most of my mates had them it was still tempting to get one myself, particularly as I'd accompanied some of them to a seedy, unhygienic little shop in Midland Street while they had badly drawn dolphins and swallows inked on to their hands and arms.

Others had things like anchors or sailing ships with 'Homeward Bound' written underneath. 'Mam' was popular, as was a heart with a girl's name in it. Girls' names were risky however, as you never knew how long a relationship would last although one solution was to have a whole list of popular girls' names tattooed up your arm so that you could just underline in biro the one that you were with at the time. Perhaps not. Anyway, during one of my first trips to sea an old spare-hand advised me not to get a tattoo, as I would regret it later. And if I didn't believe him, I should look at the arms of some of the older fishermen and try to work out what the big smudges of blue ink once represented. He had a point. I dread to think what some of the people we see nowadays with tattoos, male and female, will look like when they reach a pensionable age. It was also the fashion amongst young fishermen, many years before it became high fashion, to have your ear pierced for an earring and again I took the advice not to have this done.

Whilst on one of my returns home during my time on the 'Arctic Adventurer' I was told that my old schoolmate, Steve Gibbs, had collapsed on the deck of the 'Cape Spartell' and was in Castle Hill Hospital with TB. So after the settling business was over, I went up to the hospital to see him. By coincidence, one of the girls from Hammonds' record counter, Irene Shearsmith, was also in there so I took the opportunity to see her as well. In fact Steve and Irene started seeing each other when they were finally released; a hospital romance! Steve asked me to bring some things for him the next time I visited, which I did, and then started saying that he hated it in the hospital and wanted to sign himself out and would I help him. We plotted an escape as though he was imprisoned in Colditz - clothes, time of escape, taxi waiting, etc. Unfortunately Steve's mother got wind of the great escape and scuppered the whole plan, so I left Steve in hospital with Irene and returned to sea.

The main hazards of being a galley boy seemed to be cuts, scalds and burns, but during one time ashore while standing outside the offices I overheard a conversation between two other galley boys which alerted me to other possible hazards. The two lads were quizzing each other about how they had been subjected to 'initiation rites'. They both seemed to be trying to out brag each other in regard to the extent of these rites that they had been subjected to, which ranged from having their genitals covered with mustard and tomato ketchup to extreme sexual assault. The receiver of the latter appeared particularly proud of the act to which he had been subjected. I listened with interest and with some horror, pleased that luckily I hadn't been subjected to anything like they had. There had been an old spare-hand on my first trip who asked me if I'd be his 'special friend' but even with my inexperience and naivety I realised that he was after more than a cosy chat. So I made sure that I was never alone when he was around, which fortunately was easy to do in the cramped accommodation of a trawler. It seemed I'd also had a lucky escape from any of the 'initiation rites', no doubt the perpetrators of these acts would have described them as just a bit of fun or harmless banter. I would agree with them that harmless banter and practical jokes could alleviate the tensions on board ship and helped to develop good camaraderie. As soon as the attention becomes unwelcome though, then someone becomes a victim and the 'high jinks' can turn into bullying or worse, featuring any combination of verbal, physical, sexual and psychological abuse that can have far ranging consequences. If we add to this that the victim could be a vulnerable, under-age teenager just out of school then you can add child abuse to that list. I know that initiation ceremonies or rites also take place in other occupations and within sports and social groups but it still does not make them right.

I did four trips in the 'Arctic Adventurer' starting in early March towards the end of winter, and through the spring. We still had some bad weather in freezing conditions but the days got longer and it was possible to get outside a bit more, essential in fact if I wanted to use the lavatory, empty the gash bins and scrub the tablecloths and mats.

Here I got my first glimpse of the Northern Lights; to see the spectacle of a full trawl breaking the surface, and observing the thousands of seabirds that scavenged around a working trawler. Some of the birds looked to me like penguins but a spare-hand soon pointed out that we didn't get penguins in the Arctic and that these penguin 'lookalikes' were guillemots. Interested, I asked another deck-hand the names of the other birds, which I now know were black backed gulls, herring gulls and fulmars, soaring about above our heads.

He looked for a while, shrugged his shoulders and said, "Fucking shite hawks" and walked off.

Top. Sidewinder trawlers await the tide in St Andrew's Dock, Hull.

Right. St Andrew's Dock.

Below. St Andrew's Dock wet side.

Chapter 9. Going Overboard.

My aim was to stop being a galley boy and become a deck-hand as soon as I reached the age of sixteen. However, I was really disappointed when I overheard a couple of the fishermen talking about me and saying that the skipper, Phil Garner, thought I was "too frail" to be a good deckie learner. Too frail! I couldn't believe it. I knew I was thin and had yet to grow a few more inches, so I resolved to prove him wrong.

About this time my sister had her baby while I was away and Jack, her husband, sent me a telegram saying simply, "It's a girl!" This got me a ribbing from some of the crew who made out that I was a dad. When I got home my dad came through with Margaret to see his new granddaughter and I have a photograph of me holding the baby with my dad and Margaret looking on. My dad was not that tall, about five feet eight, and I was certainly a couple of inches smaller than him then (I ended up several inches taller) and thin, so maybe, despite the greased Tony Curtis and sneer, the skipper was right and I did look frail.

My last trip on the 'Arctic Adventurer' was a bit fraught. The problems started in the stores when one of the spare-hands saw me buying some tea towels.

"What are you buying those for, to take home?" he said.

"No," I told him. "Bill the cook was complaining that he always had to buy them and I should pay my share."

"You shouldn't have to do that, he should be doing that!" he said. And when he got on board he told the cook how he felt and Bill wasn't too pleased.

The next thing that happened was during some bad weather when the ship was bouncing around a bit. It was the beginning of teatime and I was taking the food from the galley down to the cabin via the steep ladder. Meal times were always hectic and Bill was one of those cooks that scurried about, rushing here and there, trying to do everything at once. I left the galley with a tureen full of soup and was heading for the hatch and ladder when the ship took a lurch. My feet went from underneath me and I fell backwards and head first down the hatchway. By luck the back of one of my knees landed on the edge of the steel coving that shielded two sides of the hatchway, and I managed to grab hold of the other coving with my free hand. Hanging there, suspended over the drop to the deck below and still holding on to the boiling soup I shouted for help. I don't know how long I was shouting but the chief engineer, I think his name was Ray Knight, heard me down in the engine room and rushed up to haul me to my feet. At this point Bill appeared out of the galley, a couple of feet away, and shouted, "Is the soup all right? You haven't dropped the fucking soup have you?"

The chief immediately started pointing out that Bill should get his priorities right and that it was lucky I was not seriously injured. This again didn't go down well with Bill, but at least the soup was all right; I hadn't spilled a drop.

It was now time to part company with Bill and the 'Arctic Adventurer', so I signed off on June 6th and immediately signed on the 'Arctic Crusader', again as galley boy, to sail on June 10th. During my last trip on the "Arctic Adventurer" I had my sixteenth birthday and so was old enough to become a deckie learner. But the "too frail" comment was still ringing in my ears and I felt I needed a little longer and a bit more sea experience before taking this next step.

The 'Arctic Crusader' (H74) was slightly younger than the 'Arctic Adventurer', having been built at Selby in 1949, originally as the 'Boynton Wyke', and was 676 gross tons, 178 feet long and 30.6 feet wide. The layout was not a lot different from the "Arctic Adventurer". The deck-hands slept forward in a two bunk high fo'c'sle and my berth was down below near the cabin aft, only this time my bunk went fore and aft which was better for sleeping. Now however, it was mid-summer, the weather was much better and it was almost daylight all the time with just a little 'twilight' to signify the middle of the night.

The skipper of the 'Arctic Crusader' was called Terry Thresh and I was pleased to see that a couple of the spare-hands from the 'Arctic Adventurer', Dick Taylor and Carl Skow, had also changed ships. The cook originated from Ceylon, now known as Sri Lanka, and, I believe, was known as Sid although my memory, sadly, may have failed me here. I was initially a bit wary of Sid as I had overheard some galley boys saying they didn't like him and that he was a "right bastard." This though was not my experience. The first couple of days I agree he was a bit taciturn and watched my every move but he obviously liked my way of working and we started working well together. In fact we got on like a house on fire. He involved me in all aspects of the cooking and bread making as if I was his apprentice and he also liked the way I kept the mess-rooms and accommodation clean. My tablecloths and table battens were always scrubbed white and the mess-room floor was swept several times and scrubbed once every day. This went down well with everyone apart from the time when I thought it was a good idea to tow the tablecloths, rather than scrubbing and rinsing them in a bucket.

We used to attach the galley coir mat to a rope and throw it over the side and tow it while the sea cleaned it. I thought it might be a good idea to do the same with the tablecloths rather than hand-rinsing them after I'd scrubbed them on the afterdeck. I duly tied them on the end of a heaving-line, tossed them over the side, and secured the rope on a cleat. We seemed to be steaming along nicely so I left them streaming astern and went off to do another job. After a while I was aware that the engines had stopped and I could hear voices outside so went to investigate. The skipper, chief engineer and some other crew members were hanging over the stern looking at something, so I joined them to see what it was. The Arctic waters were fairly clear and to my horror I could to see my tablecloths and rope hanging off the propeller. The skipper was not pleased and showed it. I, to put it bluntly, was shitting myself as I envisaged being thrown over and told to dive down and clear it. But fortunately for me, the chief engineer and skipper used the engines to eventually free the propeller. What a relief! That was the last time I towed anything while the vessel was fishing.

One afternoon I decided to scrub the fo'c'sle. I knew I had to be quiet as there was a watch below and with the men working eighteen hours on deck with only six hours off they would not want to be disturbed. I started scrubbing at the forward end and was stacking the sea boots under the seat lockers as I progressed aft. All was routine until I grabbed a stray sea boot sticking out from under a seat locker and felt something in it. I felt the toe and then moved to the heel. There's a foot in this, I thought. My hand then moved down the boot. Fuck me, there's a leg in this! Had someone collapsed? What should I do? I grabbed the leg with both hands expecting the resistance of a body, only to fall backwards with the leg in my hands. It was a prosthetic leg with thigh straps. I was still shaken by the experience even when I found out it belonged to an old spare-hand called Harry Abrahams. You would never have noticed as he got about the ship and did his job without any apparent difficulty. Even with two good legs it was sometimes difficult to keep your footing so he immediately got my respect.

The cook kept up his encouragement throughout the voyage saying that if I stayed with him he'd teach me the ropes and then I could go for my cook's certificate, six weeks at the Nautical College, and then become a cook myself at the age of eighteen. I did think about this but I still favoured going on deck, which meant changing to being a deckie learner before again doing a six-week course at the Nautical College and becoming a spare-hand at eighteen.

I'd already used my little spare time on the 'Arctic Adventurer' and 'Arctic Crusader' to pick up tips from the deck-hands about working on deck. I'd also spent some time down in the engine rooms where the firemen showed me how to change the burners and do other jobs, in case I fancied that as my next step. Each time though, I returned to the deck, as I preferred to be outside and to see which way we were going.

In fact, as spring turned to summer I spent most of my spare time on deck. I wasn't allowed to be around while hauling for obvious reasons but I could help the deckie learner fill the needle basket between hauls, so I got to know the technique and how many needles to fill of nylon and single and double twine. I'd even spent some time down the fish-room helping to store the fish and chop the ice but I liked being on deck gutting the best. The spare-hands had loaned me some gear, like boots and an oilskin frock, and I already had gutting knives that I used for preparing vegetables.

They soon showed me the technique: pick the fish up by the gills, slip the knife between the breastbone just below the head, cut down to the arsehole of the fish, being careful not to cut the bag that held the intestines, lift out the intestines and slide the knife back up to cut them free. Then use your fingers to flick the liver into the basket for boiling later, use your thumb to flick the heart out, toss the guts on the deck, make sure the inside of the fish is clean and throw it in the washer. With practice it was possible to process six to ten cod or haddock a minute in this way if you got into a rhythm. Obviously it would take some time before I reached anything like those speeds but for the moment I was only a galley boy and enjoying being with the men and learning from them during the hour or two I did in the evenings.

During one of these early sessions I'd been quite happy in the corner of one of the pounds gutting smallish cod and haddock when I was suddenly aware of some different types of fish that up until then I'd avoided. I hadn't noticed but a couple of the spare-hands had been quietly kicking these fish in my direction until I could avoid them no more.

What could be different? I thought, as I bent to pick up what to me looked like a cross between a cod and an eel.

Strangely, I couldn't find the gills but picked it up anyway only for it to slide out of my hands. I picked it up again and the same thing happened. The next one went over my shoulder. In desperation I was juggling with another, still trying to get a grip. Up and over it went. I was now aware of some amusement around me but I wasn't going to be beaten.

I tried another type of fish. I knew it was a catfish and I'd been told that they bite, so avoiding its mouth I searched in vain for the gills, which resulted in a second juggling act.

By now the others in the pounds were nearly finished and between stifling laughs were saying, "Come on Snacker, hurry up and stop messing about!"

Then the bridge window dropped and the skipper shouted, " Which of you lousy bastards has left that snacker with all those tusks and cats?" Everybody was laughing now. I think I'd experienced an initiation ceremony of sorts.

The trick with 'cats and tusks' was to use your finger and thumb in their eye sockets to get a grip and then go through the normal gutting process. People are sometimes shocked when I tell them that we didn't kill or stun the fish before we gutted them and that the fish were alive and wriggling while we disembowelled them. But I bet they didn't complain when they were tucking into their haddock, chips and mushy peas on a Saturday night.

Soon I'd learned to recognise all of the main food fish that we saved and landed. The only ones that we didn't gut were red fish (bergylts) that were put in baskets before being sent down the fish-room to be stored separately. Catfish, which indeed could bite, were also kept in baskets to be sent down after the main food fish including cod, haddock, skate, plaice, coley, turbot and halibut etc., had been washed and packed. There were two types of cats: tiger cats that we gutted and saved, and black cats (schmoos) that were thrown back overboard.

The voyage on the 'Arctic Crusader', as far as I was concerned, had gone well. I liked working with the cook and I got on well with the crew and, because I knew I'd done a good job, I expected good backhanders when we landed. I'd also decided that because I got on so well with the cook I would return as galley boy and he was delighted with this. So that was the plan as the 'Arctic Crusader' swung hard of starboard and approached the quayside at the entrance to St Andrew's Dock prior to backing through the lock pits and being towed to her discharging berth on the wet side of the dock. As the port side of the ship nudged the quay known as Insurance Buildings the cook threw his bag ashore and then leapt for the quayside and the waiting taxi driver.

I then, following the cook, climbed on the ship's rail, threw my bag ashore and leapt towards the shore. The fall was a bit blurred and I don't remember the splash but I was conscious that I was under the water and it was dark. My instinct was to swim and above me I could just make out an area of light. I was wearing my trusted C & A suit, which after long service had now become my going away suit, and although it weighed heavily, I still managed to reach the surface.

"Swim for'd!" someone yelled. "Swim aft!" shouted another. "No swim for'd!" was the cry again.

Shocked and silent, I swam around in circles as directed, before a heaving-line appeared, which I wrapped around my arm. I was then hauled back on board and flopped on the deck like a giant cod. The skipper had run down from the bridge and I was taken under the whaleback where, with shaking hands, the skipper stripped my clothes off (that was the end of the C & A suit) and asked me if I was all right. I said yes but that my arm hurt so he decided I should be sent to the hospital for a check up. Some clean dry clothes were found from somewhere and one of the spare-hands, Dick Taylor, took me in a taxi to Hull Royal Infirmary, which at that time was in Prospect Street. After an X-ray, it was discovered that I had broken my wrist. I must have hit the ship's side or the quayside during my fall.

The accident happened around about 10 o'clock at night but it was the early hours of the morning before we left the infirmary and Dick Taylor dropped me off at home. My sister had been expecting me earlier and was already worried when Dick knocked loudly on the front door. She opened it to find a strange man telling her that he was sorry but there'd been an accident. My sister immediately thought the worst and that I'd been killed, until seconds later I appeared with my arm in plaster and it was explained what had happened.

Despite my accident, I was back down the fish dock later that morning to ensure that I didn't miss out on my backhanders, especially now that I could count on the sympathy factor from the very visible plaster cast.

Everyone said how lucky I was to be alive and that it was a good job I was a strong swimmer although that would have not been much use if I'd been crushed by the ship against the quay. Someone said that the skipper of the trawler ahead of the 'Arctic Crusader', which was about to go astern through the lock pits saw me fall and rang his ship on ahead to catch the stern of the 'Arctic Crusader' and hold it off until I was saved. I don't know if this was the case but if so he has my thanks. I knew I'd been very lucky; maybe there was something in the old wife's tale about the protection of being born with a caul after all.

The accident happened on June 30th and so the summer month of July was spent with my arm in plaster but that didn't stop me enjoying the summer and the social life that went with it, even though it meant learning to bop with one hand during trips to the Majestic and Locarno. I liked bopping although I wasn't that good at it. One of the attractions was that the girls at the time wore shortish skirts that flared out when you spun them giving you a glimpse of their stocking tops or sometimes their knickers, although most of the girls developed a style where they kept one arm holding their dresses or skirts down while they swirled about. The girls also wore their hair in the back-combed bouffant style that had so much lacquer on it was like a crash helmet. We didn't get up and ask girls to dance if they were sitting down, instead it was always the 'split'. This meant that two of us lads would approach two girls who were already dancing, usually around their handbags, and ask them, sometimes using sign language, if they wanted to 'split' (dance). This was when the girls would use their sign language or other pre-arranged means of communication to look at each other and decide yes or no. This took seconds but both girls had to agree: if one showed any doubt, it was over and they would shake their heads and carry on. Snubbed, we would walk away licking our wounds or, if we'd had a bit of Dutch courage, respond with a quip like, "You'll never get another chance like this." Or, "What do you expect for half a crown," which was the admittance fee, "Paul Newman?"

The bars in the Locarno were 'members only' and the Majestic didn't serve alcohol at all, so if we wanted a drink we had to use the local pubs or smuggle in a half a bottle of rum or other spirit to drink in the toilets, often getting drunk in the process. Sometimes this led to a bit of trouble with people being thrown out, but to be fair most of this was caused by the bouncers in these places who wanted to justify their jobs.

There always seemed to be plenty of things going on while I was home and it was easy to join in with the other young fishermen who were home at the time. I wouldn't call them all good friends but we shared a few good times. Some of them were a bit wilder than others, but mostly they just wanted a good time before going back to sea.

Trouble did happen in some of the bars, often for the most trivial reasons such as "You knocked my drink over!" (Answer: "I'll buy you another," or fight) Someone buying a round, but not getting a drink himself, (considered some type of slight as though they would have an advantage by being the more sober). And " You've been looking at my bird/wife." (Answer: "she should be so lucky" ending usually in a fight, as you couldn't win on this one).

One evening I was in a packed-out Half Way House on Spring Bank enjoying a few drinks and listening to a live band. Then a fisherman, who seemed much the worse for wear, insisted on getting up on the small stage saying that he wanted to sing a song. "Which song?" said one of the band.

"Mule Train," replied the fisherman, "give me an E"

A guitarist in the band plucked a note.

"I said give me an E!" slurred the fisherman.

"That was a fucking E!" said the guitarist as he plucked the string again.

"Oh, right", said the would-be pop idol,"just a minute."

He then went into short discussion with some people at a table in front of the stage who passed him a metal drinks tray. The band began to play rhythm.

"Ma...u al tra....EEEN!" screamed the band's new singer followed by a mighty metallic smash as he crashed the tray against his head to simulate the sound of a cracking whip.

"Clipperty, clipperty, clipperty, clipperty, clipperty, clopping a-longong AH!"

"Ma...u al tra...EEEN!" Smash! The tray came down again.

Clipperty, clipperty, clipperty, clipperty, clipperty, clopping a-longong AH!"And so it went on.

It was obvious that these were the only words that the man knew and to save him from brain damage the band quickly ended the song.

The man sat down again but after a short while he decided he deserved another claim to fame and asked the band if he could get up and sing again.

"What do you want to sing this time?" asked the band leader,"and no trays."

"Ole, I Am A Bandit," replied our would-be singer loudly.

But before the band leader could reply a voice from the floor said, "You're a bandit alright... a fucking arse bandit!"

Then all hell let loose as a fight started between the want-to-be singer and his heckler and which soon involved most of the customers in the bar as the band unplugged and ran for cover.

Most of the time no one knew why a fight broke out like the one I witnessed which, once again, started in the Half Way House on Spring Bank and continued down Walton Street. This began as a scuffle between a couple, then a few more until everyone was at it with everyone else but even so the only things bruised at the end of the night were a few egos. While there were one or two fishermen who didn't think they'd had a good time unless they'd had a fight or been "filled in", these were in the minority, the rest just wanted to do as much as they could in their two days at home: get paid, get laid, get pissed, and usually have a row with their missus or girlfriend; not necessarily in that order. Remember that these guys were up to their knees in blood and guts in freezing conditions, while shore workers were going out and doing these things every weekend: the fishermen had earned their right to a good time during their brief time ashore.

It was after a session at the Majestic when I first arrived home drunk. We'd already been in the pub before we got there and then there were a couple of bottles of rum to be passed around in the toilets. I must have had too much and staggered home to find my sister and brother-in-law still up and watching TV, when normally they'd have been in bed. There is nothing so funny, apparently, than watching a drunk trying to act sober. I saw them and realised that I had to act sober, as I'd only just turned sixteen and didn't think they would be too pleased.

"Hi," said my sister, "had a good time?"

"Yush," I slurred, "I yam off to tut toilet and bed."

Then, taking extra slow long steps and trying not to sway, I staggered through the living room and kitchen to the outside toilet before doing the return journey in an equally ridiculous manner. My sister and brother-in-law watched in amazement while trying to stifle their laughter. The next day they asked me if I had a hangover and that it served me right if I did.

This was 1963, the year when, according to Phillip Larkin in his poem Annus Mirabilis, sexual intercourse began. The first stanza reads:

"Sexual intercourse began

In nineteen sixty-three,

(which was rather late for me)

Between the end of the Chatterley ban,

And the Beatles first L.P."

I could have added another line – "But it never did for me". However, this didn't stop me trying, and failing.

As it was summer there were also Saturday night dances at Withernsea Pavilion Ballroom. In those days, before the Beeching axe, there were regular trains from Hull to Withernsea, so a few of us decided to give it a try. When we got off the train in Withernsea, we decided to have a drink in the Spread Eagle before we went to the dance. I went to several of these dances at Withernsea Pavilion and never set foot in the place, as I never got beyond the Spread Eagle. One night though was, for me, a bit different.

I was with Steve Gibbs, who was now out of hospital and available for work, and a few others in the Spread Eagle when we met some girls from Hull who also had set out for the dance but had found the Spread Eagle was more interesting. After several drinks we decided to take a walk around the town and ended up on the beach under the building that looked like a castle but used to be the entrance to the long demolished old pier. Somehow we had managed to pair off with the girls and I had ended up with one called Maggie who was a little older than me. Soon everyone was lying in the sand in a line under the sea wall, heavy petting.

Maggie and I were on the end and, after a while, I looked at my colleagues and all I could see was a line of bodies engaged in rhythmic passion that reminded me of the pistons on a diesel engine; but one wasn't firing! I quickly became more amorous with Maggie and the positive response meant that the engine was soon firing on all cylinders. This wasn't exactly the first time for me, there had been a bit of fumbling in earlier experiments with girls, but this was the first time the earth really moved. Whether it moved for Maggie is a different matter.

During my time ashore with my broken wrist the 'Arctic Crusader' had returned and then gone again. I'd met up with Sid the cook and he'd asked if I would be returning on the next voyage when I should be free of the plaster. I told him that I was considering looking for a deckie learner's job. Sid said he thought that would be the case but if I changed my mind there would be a job with him, he then wished me luck and that was the last I saw of him. I was going to be a deckie learner...

Above. "Arctic Buccaneer".
(Courtesy of Hull Bullnose
Heritage Group)

Right. The Deckie Learner.

Below. "Stella Altair".
(Courtesy of Hull Bullnose
Heritage Group)

Chapter 10. Snacker.

In early August, as soon as my plaster came off, I went straight down the fish dock to look for a job as a deckie learner and within a week I'd landed a berth on the 'Arctic Buccaneer' sailing on August 8th 1963.

The 'Arctic Buccaneer' (H516) built in Aberdeen in 1948, was 613 gross tons, 180 feet in length and 30 feet wide. She was very similar in build to the 'Arctic Crusader' with a two bunk high fo'c'sle, which was where I'd sleep for the time I was on the ship.

My first call was to the stores where I not only needed a new mattress, my old one had never been retrieved from the 'Arctic Crusader', but also a full set of heavy working gear. I was lucky that it was summer and I wouldn't need the heavy 'fear-nought' or mole skin trousers favoured by fishermen in the winter months. But I did need an oilskin frock, sou'wester, guernsey, fish-room smock, muffler, sea boots, gloves (rubber for hauling and cotton for gutting), and two gutting knives, one large and one small. This obviously would take a considerable slice of my earnings from the trip, which were as yet unknown. My wages had gone up to over £5 per week and I would now be on poundage, a share of the catch, so there was no more relying on backhanders to supplement my wages.

The sea boots I bought were the cheapest that they had in the stores. This was a mistake. What I found was that the rubber that they were made from was thin and sloppy. This meant that they tended to fall down at the back, which could be very draughty when the wind was blowing and very wet when we shipped a sea that splashed up the back of my frock when working on deck; even in summer the Arctic Ocean is pretty cold! The next trip I invested in a pair of heavier, black thigh boots that offered much more protection and my cheap ones became 'clumpers' for general deck work.

While heading for the fishing grounds (running off) I was on day work helping to get the nets and fishing gear ready and preparing the fish-room. Once we started fishing it was eighteen hours on and six off (midnight to breakfast) and then running home it was back on days again, stowing the gear and cleaning the ship. When a trawler returned to Hull the crew would clean the ship from top to bottom. The deck would be scrubbed white with holy stones and the brass work would be polished until it gleamed. The brass work did not just consist of the ship's bell and a few portholes. On the older ships it was also the large engine room vents, so this was a big job and to prevent the damage done by salt water, the brass work, including these vents, were lightly smeared with grease for protection. This was my first job as deckie learner, to grease the brass work. Unfortunately the word lightly didn't register so I liberally smeared everything to a depth best used by a channel swimmer. Three weeks later I learned my lesson well when I had to remove the grease to polish the vents on our way up the Humber.

In charge of the 'Arctic Buccaneer' was a well-known and respected skipper named George Kent. The mate was called Ron Dodsley. I didn't think I'd know anyone on board when I joined but I was pleased to find that the galley boy was a lad I knew from Boulevard called Teddy Sanders. The cook's name was also Ted, Ted Brady. Brady was not in the same class of cooks that I'd been used to and the standard greeting from the spare-hands was, "Now then Brady, what's that you are spoiling for tea?" We used to joke that we needed to put out a shipping warning when Teddy was emptying the gash bucket after Brady had served his baked dumplings. The rest of the crew were the usual mix of young and old and were all good for a laugh. A young spare-hand from Fleetwood called John Gibson showed me the ropes and running off everything went well, although it was all a new experience for me and before long we were at the fishing grounds.

All ships depend on teamwork for maximum efficiency and a deep-sea trawler is no different, especially shooting and hauling the trawl, processes that are significantly dangerous. Once the trawl had been shot and the warps had reached the required depth calculated by the skipper, the warps were dragged together and secured in a snatch-block close to the stern of the trawler. The first job on being given the order to haul was to release the warps from this block, a process called 'knocking out'. This involved one of the hands leaning out over the side and knocking a pin out of the snatch-block, which would release the warps. The trick was to do this without losing a limb or having your head sliced off. The massive winches forward of the bridge would then noisily kick into gear and begin winding the warps on to their drums. Eventually the doors (otter boards, that kept the net open wide) would appear and be hauled up to the gallows (the large steel horse-shoe shaped contraptions situated fore and aft on the sides of a sidewinder trawler) where they were secured by a shackle and a chain and then detached from the warps. The ship would also have been turned to starboard so that the net, when it appeared, would be broadside on to the waiting deck.

The warp winding was then continued until the dan leno bobbins (which looked like large, steel half globes with a swivel called a butterfly attached) appeared. At this point the net would break the water, sometimes in spectacular fashion.

Attached to one end of the butterfly was the footrope that held the string of large steel bobbins designed to run along the seabed and keep the net weighted down. These were then lifted over the rail by the winch and dropped onto the deck in a trough. The trick here was to not get your foot crushed. Next, the head-line, containing the string of floats known as bogs, would be hoisted aboard and dropped on the deck. The trick here was to not have your head caved in. Now it was time to haul the net using strops and a block attached to the bridge housing. My job during this process was to stand amidships holding a wire with a hook on it called the gilson. The gilson wire was rove through a block on the foremast and hoisted or lowered by turns on the drums on the end of the winches forward of the bridge, on which the warps were being hauled. As the trawl broke surface I would grab a length of rope called the poke line and haul it in until a wire with a spliced eye on it appeared, into which I hooked the gilson. The trick here was not to get washed overboard. The gilson wire was then heaved tight which in turn tightened a wire loop around the trawl and dragged the cod end forward before being hoisted aboard.

The mate or boatswain then reached under the cod end to release the cod line and the catch would tumble onto the deck. The mate then tied the cod line and the cod end dropped over the side and, if there was more than one bag of fish, the process was repeated.

The mate, Ron, was, shall we say, a stocky man who had to run or charge past me to get from whatever he was doing to attend to the cod end and it didn't seem to matter where I stood as he always managed to knock into me saying, "Gerout the fucking way!"

It wasn't long before I suspected this was deliberate but maybe, like the cook on my first trip, this was for my own good, and to be fair the cook had been right in that the only cure for seasickness is to keep your mind occupied. So this could have been Ron's attempt at training rather than the bullying that I initially suspected.

Once the trawl had been shot again we then had to clear the catch. The mate and a couple of others went down the fish-room to stow the fish while the rest gutted the catch on deck.

As deckie learner I was expected to spend some time down the fish-room chopping ice. This was a backbreaking job particularly when you reached old ice. The fresh stuff was okay, like snow that fell down when you hit it with your shovel before throwing it up on to the area known as the stage where the fish was sorted. The hands then used the ice in the storage pounds.

Sometimes you came to ice that was difficult to crack and seemed to have formed into a solid, frozen wall. This called for a large ice axe but you knew you were in trouble when you swung the axe and came up standing with a shudder that vibrated down to your sea boot socks. But you still had to keep going.

I confess that I had difficulty in keeping up with the men sorting the fish. Speed was the king and the nagging pain in my wrist didn't help me. I was now aware that I'd come back to sea far too early and would have benefited from some physiotherapy.

Luckily I was only required down the fish-room in the mornings, so spent the rest of the day gutting. I quite liked gutting on the open deck, well it was summer. My wrist still ached but I couldn't do anything about that. I soon was given a nickname to replace the universal 'Snacker' when one of the older hands started calling me 'Wand'. When I asked why he called me this he replied that it was because I was very thin and swayed about in the wind; and the name stuck. Gutting could be boring but there was always, except when we were all really tired, some chat, banter and singing. It was even better if the skipper let Sparks play pop music through the outside speakers. However, the skipper only allowed this if we'd had a good haul. If he was disappointed the bridge window would slam and that would be it, silence.

Once all the fish had been sent down below to the fish-room and the decks hosed down, sending the guts and throwbacks through the scuppers for a feast for the scrounging seabirds, my next job was to attend to my net needle baskets. After every haul when there had been a tear or some damage to the nets I had to make sure that I'd enough needles filled for the next emergency. This meant that I was often one of the last ones in the mess deck for any short break we had between hauls.

The needle baskets were kept near the engine room 'fiddly top', so that I got the benefit of a warm draught of air from the stoke-hold below. It also got me constant complaints from the firemen whose standard greeting for me was, "You been dropping fucking twine down my fiddly top?"

This did happen but it was much more fun to drop a piece of twine down the 'fiddly' with a shackle pin on the end, rattle it against a pipe, and watch the fireman and engineer drop their comics and start turning the valves and looking at the gauges. The needles were made of a piece of flat wood about six inches long and just over an inch wide and the twine was wrapped tightly around a spike in the centre of the needle; some single, some double, and the same for the smoother, stronger, nylon cord used on the cod ends.

Filling needles was quite easy but a bit boring and the coarse twine made my fingers sore until I got used to it.

The main types of fish that we caught were cod, haddock, coley, skate, plaice, turbot, halibut, cats (wolf fish), dogfish and reds (soldiers, squadies or bergylts). What some people don't realise is how big some of these fish can be particularly the cod we caught off the Norwegian coast. Some of the cod seemed almost as big as I was. Halibut could also be massive and worth a lot of money on the market, so particular care was taken when gutting this fish and storing it down in the fish-room. The aim was to gut about ten fish a minute. Most of the fish, once gutted, was flung into the washer, a galvanised rectangular tank raised off the deck above the fish-room, where the fish swilled around before being washed down a chute onto the fish-room stage.

The rougher fish; reds, cats etc. were thrown into baskets and then sent down to the fish-room last for bulk storage. The reds were the only fish that we didn't gut for some reason, although they said that the spines on their backs were poisonous if they penetrated the skin.

Sometimes we also caught sharks, that the fishermen called orekettles. These were not little dogfish but real sharks known more properly as Greenland sharks, very large and formidable beasts that had massive livers if you could be bothered to hack through the three inch thick skin. When we caught an orekettle it usually meant that there was not a lot of fish in the cod ends. Whether this was because the shark frightened them away or it had eaten them on the way to the surface was hard to tell.

Obviously we didn't keep the sharks but instead we hoisted them over the side using the forward derrick and cut their tails off so they went straight to the bottom of the sea. Only the tails were kept as the White Fish Authority paid a bounty on them at that time. Sad really, as now we know that these harmless beasts can live to be over four hundred years old.

Catfish (wolf fish) also had a formidable reputation as biters with their mouths full of sharp teeth. It was said that their bite could penetrate the toughest sea boot and that they had a reflex action that made them bite even after they had been gutted.

One day we had cleared the pounds and someone said, "Send the cats down the fish-room Snacker." There was only one basket full of catfish so I picked it up and carried it to the fish-room hatch.

"Cats coming!" I shouted as I tipped the basket down the hatch and on to the chute.

"Arrrrr! You little bastard! I'll fucking kill yer!" screamed Dodsley as he tried to get at me up the washer chute, slipping and sliding and knocking the odd catfish off his neck.

"You're supposed to let them know before you throw them down Snacker," said one of the spare-hands.

Needless to say I took a little longer than usual to tend to my needle basket that haul and waited until I thought Dodsley would have calmed down before returning to the mess-room for a mug of tea. When I finally did, Dodsley was in there.

"You do anything like that again Snacker and you're in fucking big trouble," was all he said.

As this first trip wore on we started to get into some heavy fishing and fatigue started to creep in. One day when we hauled, the skipper as it happened was having a nap leaving the mate in charge, one of the spare-hands called Charlie was late getting on deck.

"Where have you been Charlie? Can't get out of your pit?" asked Dodsley.

"Sorry Ron, didn't hear the call," Charlie replied.

"What's the matter, not enough sleep? Everyone else gets up! Different rule for you is it or are you just a lazy bastard?" Dodsley sneered as he continued to harangue Charlie, who was a good, conscientious spare-hand who didn't deserve this treatment.

"I said I was sorry and it won't happen again," said Charlie.

"Fucking right it won't happen again, you need to get your fucking act together and spend less time in your berth," carried on Dodsley, deliberately goading Charlie for several minutes.

"For fuck's sake Ron, give it a rest," said Charlie.

"You going to fucking shut me up?" replied Dodsley.

Charlie had had enough. I don't know who threw the first punch but a scuffle started. I was stunned, as I'd never seen grown men argue in this way, never mind fight. They were wearing their oilskins, which obviously hindered them physically, but it also reminded me of two knights fighting in armour, like the bad black knight (Dodsley) versus the good, white knight, Ivanhoe figure, Charlie (although to be accurate Charlie was also a bit dark and grizzled). However there was no chivalry here. I was willing Charlie to be the triumphant victor but this was real life and in real life the good guys don't always win.

"Let's stop fighting like girls Charlie and take our frocks off," said Dodsley.

Charlie momentarily stopped when he heard this but as he did Dodsley head-butted him. A gash opened above Charlie's left eye and the blood streamed down his face and onto his yellow oilskin frock. That was the end of the fight.

"Go and clean yourself up Charlie," said Dodsley. But Charlie refused. He still had his pride and carried on working on deck until we'd shot the trawl and Dodsley had left the deck. Later, in the mess-room some of the men said that if the skipper had seen the way Dodsley had behaved he'd have given him the sack. I hoped someone would tell the skipper but to my knowledge no one did.

I was struggling a bit on this first voyage with my wrist. The repetitiveness of the gutting made it painful but I persevered. Then I started to get a painful rash, more like running sores, on my wrists and arms. This was so uncomfortable that I had to try to sleep with my hands on my chest like a pair of paws. As the sores got worse, I was advised to go and see the skipper to see if he had anything I could put on them to ease the discomfort. The skipper, George Kent, looked at my wrists and arms and said it was 'haddock rash', caused by some irritant found in the guts of the haddock.

That was his diagnosis and unfortunately his cure for the problem was even more worrying.

"I'll give you some zinc ointment Snacker but the best cure, and you'll think that I'm joking, although I assure you I'm not, is to piss on them," he said.

With that I left the bridge to contemplate the 'treatment'. After a few days the rash began to clear up, I don't know whether it was the ointment or the piss. I only know that no one asked me to pass the cheese in the mess-room.

When we first started fishing on this first trip we were a few days catching very little fish and just a few duffs, a type of worthless sponge found on the seabed, which meant naps between hauls unless you were on watch.

We were working eighteen hours on and six off although in reality it was only five hours and a half off. In addition we had only half-hour breaks for our meals so these naps were welcome. After a few days though the skipper found what he was looking for and the fish started coming on board with every haul. This seemed to be the pattern with George Kent, a few days searching and then bang on it. Normally we towed the trawl for three hours but when we were working lucrative grounds the tow could be as quick as an hour and a half. At these times we never managed to clear the pounds between hauls. Fish piled on fish as we hauled and gutted for our entire eighteen hours on deck. Any few minutes for a smoke or a mug of tea were cherished. For days we'd be like this and you knew when the fatigue was setting in when the chat in the pounds dried up and we all sank into our thoughts of our loved ones and how we'd spend our money when we got home. That kept us going. We wanted fish of course because they paid our wages but it was soul destroying to get up after a watch below and see that the fish in the pounds had not gone down and you would be spending the next eighteen hours mostly on your feet. The job was already dangerous enough but when you added on the severe tiredness, the stakes were even higher.

Only the skipper could decide when we'd enough stored in the fish-room to make a good landing. He also had to time the run home to make sure we landed on the day that the market price for fish was high to maximise the earnings of the ship. The skipper and the mate didn't get a wage but got a percentage of the ship's profits after all expenses had been paid, so it was vital to them that the voyage made money. The rest of us were on poundage, so we got a percentage of what the catch was sold for on top of our basic wages. So it was all a bit of a gamble.

After a week or so of heavy fishing, the fish took off again and the decks started to clear. One night I came off deck for my watch below at midnight. I was absolutely knackered as were my other watch mates so we just crashed out in our berths to get as much sleep as possible. Then, about three in the morning, I could hear voices.

"Come on lads, all hands on deck, we're clewing up and going home." My heart sank. I was glad we were going home but the thought of dragging myself out of my bunk and back on deck for several more hours was daunting.

My curtain moved but then I heard a voice say, "No, the skipper said to leave the snacker, we won't need him."

Result! I couldn't believe my luck. I waited until the fo'c'sle went quiet and then got myself properly ready for sleep and snuggled down under my blankets. I slept until teatime. And I also slept that night as well.

The next day it was back to work stowing gear and cleaning the ship ready for it to be 'filthied' up, good and proper by the bobbers and the other shore trades that traipsed over the ship when she was in dock. Trawlers entered the dock spotless with all the brass polished and the decks scrubbed white. But you would never know it the day after the fish had been landed.

On arrival at the fish dock there was no jumping ashore (or like my last voyage, jumping in the river) for me, as I was now a deck-hand so had to stay on board until we'd tied up on the wet market side of the dock. Then it was a taxi home.

Early next morning I was down the dock again to get my fry. I took that home and then went back down the dock to settle. To my surprise I was not given the sack following my couple of run-ins with the mate, so I signed on again and then collected my settlings. There was no hanging around for backhanders now as I was on poundage, a proper fisherman. But I was quite disappointed to see that my settlings were less than what I'd been getting in backhanders as a galley boy. Previously the skipper had paid my bond, now that expense was mine, alongside the costs of the oilskins, sea boots and other gear that I'd bought on credit from the stores when we sailed. Anyway, I was still a three-day millionaire, even if a somewhat down at heel one.

The next voyage was uneventful and I was now into the routine of being a deckie learner and knew what was expected of me. It was about this time that the Hull trawler owners decided that it was a good idea to carry two deckie learners. This of course was not an act of philanthropy to ensure that more young people were trained, but one that saved them money by carrying one less spare-hand. The practice didn't go down too well with some of the fishermen who felt that the trawlers were already undermanned. The owners countered this by saying that there would be a junior and senior deckie learner based on age and experience. The irony of this was that the trawler owners were fiercely against the fishermen ever having a collective voice by forming or joining a trade union, whilst contrarily the owners themselves had their own association that enabled them to impose changes to the conditions of employment of their (casual) workforce whenever they liked. However, as far as I was concerned, this decision didn't make much difference to me except that during my next three days at home I met up with my old mate Steve Gibbs, who told me that he'd signed on as the senior deckie learner on the 'Arctic Buccaneer'. And as I still hadn't got the sack, it looked like I'd be having two old school pals as shipmates.

While I was at home I decided that now I was a proper fisherman I needed a new deckie learner suit, to wear against the pale blue one that I never had off my back. This time I went for a more serviceable dark brown, retaining the shawl collar and link button but without the decorative cuffs and pleats. I still kept some fancy pockets and a half belt at the back, but reduced the waistband to two inches as a four-inch one, that seemed to go from my waist almost to my chin, would concertina up and had proved not that comfortable. As it was autumn and getting colder I also invested in an overcoat from Waistell's on Hessle Road. This was light-grey coloured tweed - Donegal - with a half belt at the back. I'd seen a few lads with these and it seemed part of the deckie learner uniform.

Back at sea, Steve's first question was, "Why do they call you Wand?"

"Because I'm thin and sway about in the breeze," I replied. The addition of Steve to the crew at the expense of a spare-hand didn't change my role at all. I carried on working the poke line when hauling, working a watch down the fish-room and the rest of the time gutting. Steve worked the fore door with a spare-hand at hauling and spent most of the rest of his time down the fish-room chopping ice. During the trip Steve started saying that he was getting fed up of fishing and fancied big boats - the merchant navy. There was always a lot of crossover in Hull with merchant seamen and fishermen in that many merchant seamen had started on the trawlers rather than go to a sea training school. They also used many of the same pubs in the city centre when home on leave. The conditions were supposed to be a lot better in the merchant navy and there was always the prospect of a voyage to somewhere warm and exotic. He sold the idea to me.

When we docked after this trip, we both signed off and headed for the Pool - British Shipping Federation - in Posterngate. Here we were told that they needed confirmation of our sea time on trawlers, a reference from our school (Trinity House) and that some of our school time, because it was a nautical school, would count towards sea time, so that we could start as ordinary seamen rather than deck-boys.

This sounded good to us and we went straight away back to our old school, Trinity House, which was only around the corner. Our luck was in and the headmaster, Mr Eddon, called us into his office without any waiting. He asked us what we were doing and what we wanted, so we told him. He suggested that maybe a reference was not really appropriate given the circumstances in which we had left the school but he would give us a letter saying we had attended the school. We said that this would be fine and thanked him.

He then turned to me and said, "While you were at the school Addey it was noted that you demonstrated a great deal of ability and I would like to suggest that should you wish to progress in the merchant navy we can offer you a correspondence course to assist you in going for your officer certificates."

I thanked him and said I'd think about it - and I'll never forget Steve's face when he didn't ask him.

Back at the Shipping Federation our fishing records and letters for the school were checked and Steve was told he could sail as an ordinary seaman because of his age and the time he'd spent as a deckie learner. Unfortunately I was younger and didn't have enough sea time on deck to qualify. Bollocks!

So leaving Steve to sign on a tramp steamer and head for tropical climes, I went back down the fish dock looking for another deckie learner berth and wishing I'd stayed on the 'Arctic Buccaneer'.

I'd signed off the 'Buccaneer' on October 15th and after a couple of days I was doing the rounds of the trawler offices but with no luck. Generally if you hadn't been offered a job by about eleven in the morning it was time to give up. One morning I'd just done that when someone suggested going to Stanton's for a coffee. I was just enjoying sitting in the café and drinking a hot coffee with a bacon sandwich when another fisherman came in and said that Charleson-Smith's were looking for a deckie learner. I didn't hesitate and went straight to the Charleson-Smith's office and presented myself as a deckie learner.

"Just what we need," they said, "The Stella Altair's sailing on tomorrow morning's tide…"

Above. The entrance to St Andrews Dock where the author fell in.

Below. Deckie learners at leisure in the King Edward pub The author is seated far right, Steve Gibbs seated third from right. (by kind permission of Lisa Maree Gibbs)

Chapter 11. Stella Altair – The Last Sidewinder.

The 'Stella Altair' (H279) had been built at Selby that year, 1963, so was brand new. I think she had only done her maiden voyage. She was 677 tons and 180.2 feet long by 32.11 wide. This would turn out to be the last purpose built sidewinder out of Hull. The accommodation was quite luxurious compared to the old Arctic boats I'd been on and reminded me of the 'Lord Jellicoe' with everyone sleeping aft with decent bathrooms and a mess deck. To be honest I'd got used to sleeping in the fo'c'sle even in bad weather, although the feeling of weightlessness when the bows took a dip and left you momentarily suspended in mid-air for a second could be disconcerting. So the thought of good aft accommodation with winter pending was very attractive.

We sailed on October 19th heading for Bear Island under the command of skipper George Atherton and mate Jim Wilson. There was a slight delay in leaving the dock as we were a man short but as we edged towards the lock pit someone shouted, "McGee's on the bull nose skipper!" McGee was a young spare-hand, only about eighteen-years-old and married with a small child. As the skipper nudged the bow up close to the bull nose McGee jumped on board and so now with a full crew we entered the Humber and headed for the open sea.

Bear Island turned out to be bare of fish so the skipper headed further north to Spitzbergen (Svalbard) about as far north as you can get in the Arctic Ocean, about 800 miles inside the Arctic Circle. Here we were approaching the ice cap to which Spitzbergen, an island, was attached. In the past it had been a whaling and seal catching station but I think the only living things on Spitzbergen at that time were copper and gypsum miners, the people who manned a Norwegian weather station and polar bears.

The weather up there was unpredictable and very cold as winter had already set in. At first we didn't catch much fish here either although orekettles seemed more prolific. The skipper, in search of a bigger and better catch, decided to tow up to a glacier which had the effect of us coming fast (a foul trawl caused by catching rocks on the seabed) a lot and tearing great holes in the trawl. Rather than patch the trawl the skipper kept telling us to lace it - roughly sew it up - until the trawl was beyond repair and we had to bring out the spare. This, in turn, was holed and laced until it had to be repaired properly.

The crew were not too happy about where we were fishing and moaned, "What the fuck are we doing up here? He's an Iceland man and knows fuck all about fishing here, just because they've given him a new ship he thinks he's got something to prove."

The skipper though makes the decisions and the quality of the fish was good so he persevered. This was a new ship with new gadgets, one of which was a loudspeaker system placed in strategic places for the skipper to bark orders into. The speakers also had a concealed microphone so that the crew could answer back when necessary, like when knocking out at the start of the haul.

One night we'd just come into the mess-room for our tea after gutting in the pounds and were sitting down for our meal, when the telegraph rang for us to get back on deck and start hauling. As we scrambled out through the stern accommodation door we had to pass under a loud speaker and McGee was just doing this when he said, "Fucking hell, we can't even get our tea in peace. He's always hauling at tea time."

McGee didn't know that the loudspeaker was on and relayed everything that we said to the bridge, or that the reason for the haul was that the trawl had come fast on some obstruction on the seabed. After a while the trawl was freed but when it was hauled aboard we saw that it was ripped from end to end and as we'd already used our spare trawl, it had to be mended. Even the skipper came down on the deck to supervise and do some net mending and I was working flat out to keep the men supplied with full net mending needles. During this work the skipper managed to sidle alongside McGee and said, "By the way McGee, I don't make a habit of hauling at meal times... but you won't have to worry about that next trip."

Such is the reality of casual employment...

It was a relief to get home from that trip but I signed on again as it was a good ship. My two days at home passed by very quickly with the usual round of taxis here, taxis there. It was like living your life like one of the Keystone Cops, dashing about to get as much living in as possible in a very short period of time. I still hadn't been very successful in the 'lady stakes'. While there were girls who hung around the bars and dance halls frequented by fishermen, many were just looking for a few drinks and a good time, things that fishermen and seamen in general were happy to provide. The girls were certainly hot due to the amount of clothing they wore and the mottled evidence of their 'corned beef legs' showing where they'd been sitting too close to an open fire. On the sexual side, some of these girls did and some of them didn't. And those that did, didn't for me.

It was also winter which made it even more difficult, as if you found a girl and took her home you were rarely invited in. Instead it was the porch or back passage (not a euphemism) for a quick kiss and, if you were lucky, a grope, although the temperature was often a dampener on amour. Knee tremblers were particularly risky in case of frostbite or grazing if you missed. First of all though you had to negotiate the layers of resistance in the apparel of the Hull young ladies at that time. Overcoat, cardigan, blouse, vest, bra – they had more skins than an onion. Down below was not much better: dress, underskirt, suspenders (sometimes over knickers as an added hazard), knickers with elasticised legs (wrist trappers 'keep the heat in and the dirt out!'), and foundation garments, particularly one dastardly thing called a roll on. Negotiate that lot and then you may hear the heart dropping words, "I'm not like that." I found a lot like that. There was also the passion killing, "Careful! I'll drop me chips!" if you got that far.

Another heartbreaking fact was that it was a lot to ask a girl to stay faithful while you spent most of the time at sea. Several times I returned home to find that 'my girlfriend' - or at least who I thought was my girlfriend - had now a new, usually older (I was still young and most of my girlfriends were older) and earning more, boyfriend. The girls were too kind to say, "Come back when your balls drop and you start shaving," but they would have been partly right. This was a hazard of a seafarer's life.

It was no surprise that McGee was not on the next voyage which was again to Bear Island and the White Sea. We also had a new senior deckie learner, a small, wiry ex-miner, aged in his late twenties from a coal-mining village in the West Riding. His West Yorkshire accent contrasted considerably with the flatter Hull accent especially as he had a high-pitched voice and a speech impediment caused by a cleft pallet. There was also much speculation amongst the crew about what he had packaged in the trouser department, given the mountainous bulge that he paraded like a massive codpiece. Turned out he wore very baggy long johns under tight jeans. He was okay although a bit annoying with his squeaky voice but he seemed to enjoy it down the fish-room which suited me as I preferred to be on deck; maybe he was used to shovelling coal. On deck, however, there must have been some problem as I suddenly found myself throwing chains around on the fore-door, which was normally the station of the senior deckie learner, rather than standing mid-ships and pulling on the poke line prior to hooking on the gilson.

The winter was now setting in with a vengeance. It was bitterly cold to the point that our oilskins were starting to freeze as we stood in the pounds gutting the fish, and if we didn't clear them quickly, the fish were also freezing before we got to gut them. A further discomfort was the sea spray that froze before it hit you in the face. It was like being showered with ice pellets from a gun.

When the fish's guts and blood failed to keep our hands warm we would take to buffing. Buffing meant swinging your arms and slapping your hands on your shoulders to get the circulation going. One day when a couple of us stopped to do this the skipper sent a bottle of rum down to give us a dram. The next day the same thing happened. After that we would buff as if we were bats trying to take off but it didn't work all of the time.

The skipper though was good enough, but only if we got a decent haul, to get the sparks to play Radio Luxembourg through the loud speakers on the front of the bridge while we were on deck gutting. We always looked forward to this as it helped to pass the time in pretty grim conditions and this is how I know where I was on the day (it was early evening for us) when President Kennedy was shot on November 22nd 1963. It wasn't so much about getting the tragic news on the radio but that Radio Luxembourg as a matter of respect cancelled the normal scheduling and played mournful music continuously instead. We knew that the tragedy was very sad but after a couple of hours of this music we were begging the sparks to turn it off.

The accommodation on the 'Stella Altair' was warm and comfortable but during fishing we didn't have a lot of time to appreciate it and on deck there was no escape from the winter conditions. It was a relief when the skipper gave the order to clew up for home, rang the telegraph full ahead, and turned in. Unfortunately it was starting to blow a gale and we were heading straight into it. We hadn't caught much in the last haul but it took us ages to clear the fish as we spent most of the time clinging on and trying to keep our feet. Calls were made to ease the ship down but the skipper had said he wanted to meet a particular market and no time should be wasted. Having cleared the fish and battened down the fish-room, we started to clear the deck of the rest of the gear. One job was to remove the pound boards and stow them under the whaleback and again this was made difficult by the appalling conditions. Working from the well of the main deck I unshipped a stanchion just when the ship dipped and she took a tremendous sea that picked me up and threw me, still clutching the stanchion, into the well deck scuppers. I was on my back clinging on for dear life and awash until the ship rose and I could feel the pull of the seawater as it flowed through the scuppers. Some of the others rushed to help and the mate said he'd had enough and dashed up to the bridge. He opened a window and said he was easing the ship down but we had to clew up quickly. It was much easier at a slower speed and we managed to store the gear, in a fashion, under the whaleback. Then it was full ahead for home.

Days of the week didn't seem to matter on the trawlers; Saturdays and Sundays were the same as all the other days except that on a Sunday there was tinned fruit for tea. I remember this because when I was galley boy the cook let me eat any fruit that was left over – a real treat at the time. But for the rest of the days of the week the only one that mattered was which market would be the best to land the catch. Friday was always the prime target, but it also depended on the owners who could over-rule the skipper if they felt the need. One thing was for sure and that was that any fish landed on the dock described as 'fresh' certainly wasn't – it could be anything from a few days to over two weeks old.

At sea the fishermen talked about anything, their wives, girlfriends, what they'd done at home, things in the news in Hull, music, previous trips and skippers. When they were home the conversation was often about fishing, something like this when fishermen met in a pub:

"Na then, china."

"Na then, you all right?"

"Yer, well you know, fair to moderate, getting stronger later."

"Saw you steaming past at Bear Island, what happened."

"Skipper got pissed off, if you remember you were here, we were there, a Scrob was on our quarter, the 'Leonis' was hauling, you came around our arse end." (At this point the glasses (ships) are being moved around the table, tracking your drink was like trying to follow "the lady" on a street spiv's "find the lady" trick). "We turned to starboard and picked up the scrob's gear. By the time we got clear the fish had gone so we steamed east. I'll tell you china, the bastard steamed so far east that we were fishing alongside Chinese junks!"

"Where's me fucking beer gone?"

"Don't get obstrockuless (obstreperous) pal! Don't get obstrockuless!"

"Is that mine?"

"No, that's the Norwegian gunboat."

"Who wants another?"

It was obvious that the fishing industry was changing in that the 'Stella Altair' was the last sidewinder to be built to order by Hull trawler owners. The new trawlers were much larger and built to fish from the stern. The fish was not just gutted and stored in ice but frozen on board into big slabs which meant that the ships could stay at sea for months, usually three months, before returning with their catch. Three months working in a floating factory was not a very attractive proposition for me especially as this time would be spent entirely at sea. The merchant navy seemed much more exciting and inviting.

During my last voyage on the 'Stella Altair' I'd been thinking that there must be an easier way of making a living and trying the merchant navy again seemed very attractive. I liked the idea of working in warmer climates and seeing different parts of the world while getting paid for it so after settling and signing off the 'Stella Altair', it was back down the shipping office to see if I was acceptable. Within a couple of days I had a medical with the merchant navy doctor, Dr Massey who also happened to be my GP. I had a colour blindness test (again) and was issued with my seaman's discharge book (a blue book that looked like an old passport), my British seaman's ID card (a red book that acted as a passport in an emergency), and my National Union of Seamen's membership card (it was compulsory to be a member of the union to sail in the British merchant navy). My time as a deckie learner and some of my school time at Trinity House was calculated towards my sea time and I was given the rating of junior ordinary seaman.

That was the end of my time on the trawlers but not the end of my association with fishermen as often when I was home I would meet up with old fishing mates for nights out, and big boat lads and fishermen used many of the same pubs anyway. I will never forget the fishermen who, despite all their brusqueness, were caring, supportive and the most generous people you could ever meet. They were also some of the most hard-working who earned every penny they received and deserved much more. Everyone enjoying their fish and chips on their way home from the pub on a Saturday would appreciate them much more if they realised the atrocious conditions that these men had to endure in order to bring home this staple of the British diet.

I was lucky that after a year on the trawlers and surviving blood poisoning, falling overboard, breaking my wrist, and nearly getting washed overboard in the Arctic, that I still had all my fingers and limbs in tact and indeed I was still alive.

When I left the deep-sea trawlers there were still about 200 of them sailing out of Hull, the largest fishing port in the world. However within the next fifteen years or so that would change. Iceland had long been complaining that its only source of income in terms of a natural resource was fish and therefore resented the fact that most of Iceland's fish was caught by foreign vessels. At first, in 1958, Iceland imposed a 12-mile limit which, while opposed by the British Government, was verified by the United Nations International Conference of the Law of the Sea in 1961. Nevertheless the imposition of this limit had led to the first Cod War and the foreign trawlers being harassed by the Icelandic gunboats. After 1961 things quietened down but in 1972 Iceland started to impose a 50-mile limit and the second Cod War began with this time the Icelanders cutting the warps of offending trawlers. Things continued to get worse and in 1975 other countries started taking their cases to the Law of the Sea Conference and some of these like Chile and Peru were asking for a 200-mile limit. Shortly after this Iceland also declared a 200-mile limit and the Third Cod War started.

Britain at first sent Royal Navy frigates to protect the British trawlers from the Icelandic gunboats but these could not really cope with the ramming techniques used by the Icelanders. The answer was to supplement these with deep-sea tugs, most of which ironically, were provided by United Towing of Hull which was part of the Boston Deep Sea Fishing Company. So in effect the government was paying this trawler owner to protect its own vessels. Iceland really could not have taken on Britain's naval might but it had one good trick up its sleeve. It was host to the Keflavik American Nato base, which was strategically crucial in the Cold War then in operation with the Soviet Union, and there was no way that the Americans would let a dispute over fishing rights put that base in jeopardy. The British Government still pushed to retain fishing rights until the Law of the Sea Conference ruled in Iceland's favour for a 200-mile limit along with Peru and Chile. The limits were agreed along the lines of the 1961 Conference that had offered protection of resources related to the continental shelf belonging to the named member countries of the United Nations making the claim. Britain then suggested to the Law of the Sea Conference in 1976 that if this applied to the named countries, then a precedent had been set that should apply to all and the Conference agreed. Win some, lose some. What price a few tens of thousands of jobs in Britain's fishing ports when you have just assured the largest portion of North Sea oil!

The Government's answer to the loss of the deep-sea grounds was to say that the owners could build smaller trawlers to fish the North Sea. But Edward Heath, as part of his Common Market moves, had signed the Common Fisheries Policy which gave all European countries equal access to the fishing grounds and also implemented quotas of what fish could be caught. Some trawler owners did commission some smaller trawlers but many never cast a net as the North Sea became a Klondike for oil and natural gas and the smaller trawlers made excellent support ships in these new lucrative businesses.

Long before this happened the St Andrew's Dock had closed and the fish landings moved to Albert Dock but very quickly the fishing contracted leaving only a small fish market to deal with Icelandic imports and the tiny number of local fishing craft that remained. About 8,000 jobs were lost in Hull, not just the fishermen but the people who worked in fish processing and all the other associated businesses that were supported by the trawlers: engineering firms, painters, dry dock workers, shipwrights, rigging companies, equipment suppliers, chandlers and so on. The worst hit were the fishermen themselves in that while the trawler owners got some compensation, the fishermen got nothing as their employment was considered casual and it would be over thirty years before any form of recompense for losing their living was agreed.

Today, the once bustling St Andrew's Dock and the south side of Hessle Road is filled with retail parks and as yet undeveloped wasteland, while the council debates what will happen to the still standing, but derelict, Lord Line building and the remains of the lock gates and bull nose.

But cheer up – time for a song I think!

PAY ME MY MONEY DOWN

(Traditional, arrangement and additional words by Bob Addey. Feel free to add your own verses.) You may have heard of the three-chord trick, well this one only uses two, 1st and 5th in any key you wish.

Well, I thought I heard the captain say,

Pay me my money down.

Tomorrow is my sailing day,

Pay me my money down.

Chorus:

Oh pay me, pay me,

Pay me my money down,

If I don't sail, I'll go to jail,

Pay me my money down.

Sailed next morning on the tide,

Pay me my money down,

And down the Humber we did glide,

Pay me my money down.

Chorus

Well if I'd been a rich man's son,

Pay me my money down.

I'd sit by the river and watch it run,

Pay me my money down.

Chorus:

North half west from Spurn light,

Pay me my money down,

Batten down for a stormy night

Pay me my money down.

Chorus

We're heading for the Iceland grounds,

Pay me my money down,

We'll shoot the trawl and fill the pounds

Pay me my money down.

Chorus

Through freezing spray, ice and snow,

Pay me my money down,

We'll stow the gutted fish below

Pay me my money down.

Chorus

Clew up lads our fish-room's full,

Pay me my money down.

Heading home to the port of Hull,

Pay me my money down.

Chorus

After twenty days and nights at sea,

Pay me my money down.

I'll get me settlings and pissed I'll be

Pay me my money down.

Chorus

Them Broadway girls with their back combed hair,

Pay me my money down.

They'll rob you blind and skin you bare,

Pay me my money down.

Chorus

One to another you will hear them say,

Pay me my money down.

Here comes Jack with his three weeks' pay

Pay me my money down.

Chorus

Spend our money in three days ashore,

Pay me my money down.

Pack our bags and to sea once more,

Pay me my money down.

Chorus

Well, I thought I heard the captain say,

Pay me my money down.

Tomorrow is my sailing day,

Pay me my money down.

Chorus

Pay me, pay me,

Pay me my money down,

If I don't sail, I'll go to jail,

Pay me my money down.

Top. "Silvio".

Middle. "Rollo"

Bottom. "Palermo". All belonging to Ellerman's Wilson Line.

PART THREE – GOOD LIFE MERCHANT NAVY, SUNDAY DINNER EVERY DAY.

Chapter 12. Junior Ordinary Seaman.

In the cold December of 1963 I was dreaming of working in shorts on a pristine ship heading for exotic, tropical locations, maidens beckoning from the beach with garlands round their necks and playing ukuleles and all that stuff. Instead, on December 21st I signed on my first merchant navy vessel, the ss 'Silvio'. Built at Leith in 1947 (1797.72 gross tons) the 'Silvio' was one of Ellerman Wilson Line's ten-day boats, ships that, before the days of ferries, ran on regular trips to designated European ports, in this case, Oslo. Yes, for my first trip I was heading back to Norway, in winter. I suppose I was the merchant navy's equivalent of a 'Christmas Cracker' so beggars could not be choosers. I just remember spending my first Christmas away from home in a snowy, and freezing cold, Oslo.

The merchant navy was a different life to that of on the trawlers so I had a lot to learn about the job and my, very low in the hierarchy, position. All ships have a hierarchy that reflects, in a way, the class system. However, I soon saw that it was a much stronger hierarchy in the merchant navy. On the trawlers the officers, skipper, mate, engineers etc., ate in their own mess-room called the cabin and had their own cabins to sleep in but did not wear uniforms, and everyone but the skipper was called by their first names. In the merchant navy on the other hand, the officers ate in the saloon, wore uniforms on duty and expected to be called "Sir" or by their title 'Chief', 'Second' or 'Third.'

To be honest it stuck in my craw to call anyone 'Sir', and I never did. This was not to be disrespectful as I did respect some of them, but because I felt that they were no better than anyone else on the ship as we were all there to do a job. I also felt that because I'd been to Trinity House there was no mystique about what they did and I was perfectly capable of achieving their positions if I wanted to. At the moment though I was quite happy to be just a silly sailor and earn as much as I could. If I'd wanted their job I would have suffered as a very low paid apprentice for four years, instead I was earning better cash while still getting the sea time in. The class structure was further emphasised by the location of cabins, the further up the hierarchy, the higher your cabin above sea level. Our cabins were down below, aft, next to the steering gear.

One of the first things that I noticed was the sleeping arrangements. This was a shared cabin with another sailor but there was no need now to take my own bedding like on the trawlers as mattresses, sheets, blankets, pillows and pillow cases along with a Wilson Line bedspread were all provided and changed regularly. However, in keeping with the class differences, the crew's bedding was blue and the officers' white. When I asked why this was I was given the excuse that the crew generally had dirty jobs while the officers didn't. I thought this was bollocks as I had never seen a clean engineer coming off watch.

The food was also different. I'd been with some excellent cooks on the trawlers who managed to do wonders with what little they had at their disposal but the food on this ship was something else. The problem was that this was my first experience of the catering in the merchant navy and it led me to false expectations on other ships that I would join later. The reason for this was that the ten-day boats carried a small number of passengers and there was only one galley, so what the passengers and officers could have in the dining salon we could also have by collecting our food directly from the galley. As a result my first breakfast was a revelation: cereals, porridge, fruit juice, and a full English breakfast.

The 'Silvio' had a regular crew as was usual on ten-day boats as they were ideal for married seamen in that they got to see their wives and children regularly, so the positions on these ships were coveted. Most of the rest of the crew were pretty nondescript, although one of the greasers, Charlie Bilocca, was a bit of a character. Charlie was originally from Malta but had married a Hull girl called Lillian. Later, Lil was to get a lot of publicity campaigning for greater trawler safety. It was hard to imagine Charlie and Lil together as Charlie was rather small and Lil was, shall we say, formidable. The main thing about Charlie was that he was constantly complaining that a breakfast hadn't been saved for him when he got up in the morning - he must have been on the twelve to four watch.

"Where's my breck-a-fust! They throw away my breck-a-fust! Every day the same – they throw away my breck-a-fust!" He was right, everyday was the same, which led me to think that the cooks were doing it deliberately to hear Charlie's constant whine.

The main jobs for the deck crew when sailing was battening down the four canvas covered hatches - two before the bridge and two on the afterdeck, securing the eight derricks and stowing the mooring ropes and wires for the sea crossing. Then it was watch keeping, an officer and three seamen per watch working four hours on, fours hours off, made up of steering, lookout, and standby. In port we just worked days on general maintenance. It was cold and wet on lookout but generally warm and cosy on the wheel, while the standby just waited in the mess-room until needed.

This was my first trip in the merchant navy so I had a lot to learn about how things were different to on the trawlers. Certainly the accommodation was more comfortable and the food seemed better but the relationships between the officers and the crew were a bit more formal and I wasn't sure who was who at first but I soon found out. One of the crew asked me if I would go and ask the chief steward if he had finished with the washing machine, as he needed to do some washing. This is even better, I thought, they even have washing machines in the merchant navy. The chief steward, when I found him, said that he had finished with it and I needed to ask the second engineer. The second engineer said I should ask the cook, and then the cook sent me to the second mate who directed me to the boatswain, and it was then that I realised that I'd been had.

I only did one trip on the 'Silvio' as I was looking for more adventure. I'd had enough of Norway in the winter so on January 6th 1964 I signed off hoping to find something more exciting.

It took me ten days to find my next ship when I signed on another Wilson Line vessel, the ss 'Palermo', which was even older than the 'Silvio' as she'd been built in 1938 and had managed to survive the Second World War. However, the ship was slightly larger than the 'Silvio' at 2,838 gross tons. Wilson Line ships generally had a green painted hull with a red funnel. She had two hatches on the fore deck and two hatches on the afterdeck with a smaller hatch between the centre castle and the mid-ships accommodation. In total the ship had ten derricks, with a heavy lift derrick, serving hatch two on the foredeck.

The 'Palermo' however was heading for somewhere a little warmer than Norway in January, the Mediterranean, after first 'going round the land'. This meant visiting a couple of other ports before starting off on our main voyage. To be honest the ship was crap but at that stage of my merchant navy career I didn't have much to compare it to. The deck crew's accommodation was aft but I can' t remember whether there were three or four sharing a cabin, but whatever the arrangements it was cramped and not that comfortable. Also aft were our mess-room and a bathroom. The deck crew consisted of about four or five efficient deck-hands, (EDH) or able seamen (AB), a senior ordinary seaman (SOS), a deck-boy, boatswain and a chippy (carpenter). The deck officers included the captain, chief officer, second mate and third mate. There were four engineers, along with three greasers and a donkey man.

The ship also carried a chief steward, a second steward, two stewards, two cooks and a couple of cabin boys. The chief steward was the one who looked after the bonded stores, so if we wanted anything we went to him. The chief steward also dished out the subs on our wages if we wanted any money to go ashore. The unusual thing about this chief steward was that he brought his old motorbike with him, which was kept on deck lashed under an old tarpaulin. If we got to a suitable port he would ask the dockers, or us, to lift it ashore on a derrick.

Our first port of call was Antwerp in Belgium. I really liked Antwerp with its mixture of new and old architecture including a spectacular cathedral and clean streets. In those days if you were in a Catholic country and wanted to find the good time district you usually had to look no further than the area around a cathedral. It was like a beacon for sailors and other travellers. What I found was that the bars and the people in general were very friendly and every time I went back to Antwerp I found the same atmosphere. Antwerp also introduced me to the delights of crispy fried chips with a big blob of mayonnaise on top – I still like salad cream with my fish and chips!

The next stop was London and the West India Docks, where half the Hull crew felt they'd already had enough and asked to be paid off and were replaced by seamen off the London Pool. Two of my cabin mates were the deck-boy called Dennis from York, and the SOS who I think was called Gerry and came from Worksop. They were both older than me, which made me the youngest deck-hand. The new crew members included two from Birmingham, Royston Benyon and Julian Flint, and a fellow from London who I think was called Roger.

 All of these were characters. Royston was an always-smiling joker with a broad Brummie accent. Julian sounded more middle class but fancied himself as one of the missing Beatles with his hairstyle and guitar, whereas the immaculately dressed Roger thought of himself as a kind of womanising James Bond figure but was constantly getting into scrapes and not coming out of them very well.

The East End of London in those days was very rough and the West India Dock Road was well known for muggings – 'getting rolled' as seamen called it. It was particularly dangerous at night especially if you showed signs that you'd had a drink. Rumour had it that if the local police saw someone staggering along on their own they would arrest them and keep them overnight in a cell at the Police station for their own protection. Needless to say we didn't venture ashore alone at night but we did frequent a couple of local pubs including the 'Blue Posts' and a notorious one called 'The Railway Tavern', better known as 'Charlie Brown's'. This pub was full of dockers by day but at night it was the haunt of sailors, a few locals, good time girls – full-time and part-time girls of the night - and gangsters. The 'girls' were only really interested in anyone with money, which counted me and most of my shipmates out, as we didn't have any. Most of the gangsters were local Del Boys or Flash Harrys usually flogging something that had been nicked from the docks. You knew when a real crook came in because the noise level in the pub momentary hushed before a bit of backslapping occurred. You could tell the difference by the cut of their suits and the camel-coloured Crombie, draped over their shoulders. We generally kept away from them but still had a few good nights out in there until we'd finished loading for our main voyage. One thing that I noticed was that the draught beer in London was not very good and that the dockers' favourite was a 'light and bitter'. This was a half pint of bitter in a pint glass topped up with a bottle of light ale which made the drink more expensive but at least palatable and a bit more lively than the flat, mud-coloured slop that was described as draught bitter. A good tip; always look at what the locals drink.

After a few days loading we left the lock pits of the West India Dock and nosed out into the Thames and headed for the open sea. One of the attractions of a seafarer's life for me was the buzz of excitement and anticipation as the ship pushed its way slowly through the black, oily waters of the dock and out into an open seaway. Even letting go of the tugs was exciting, never mind the captain ringing the engines full ahead after dropping the pilot. No matter what the vessel or where we were going I never lost the buzz.

Watch-keeping on this ship was four hours on with eight hours off. There were three of us on each watch as the ship didn't have an automatic pilot so had to be hand-steered all of the time from the little wooden wheelhouse on the bridge. Lookouts were generally on the monkey island, on top of the wheelhouse from where we had to shout down a pipe if we saw a light. In busy waterways lookouts were sent to the forecastle where lights and ships were reported by using a bell – one clang for starboard, two for port and three for straight ahead. Lookouts were generally only needed at night or during poor visibility so during the day, when not actually on the wheel, we were expected to work with the boatswain on general maintenance. We were also expected to work some overtime when we were not on watch. The maintenance could be anything from chipping and painting, to overhauling the blocks, tackles and running gear on the derricks and any other jobs that needed doing. The deck-boy also had to act 'Peggy' which meant he had to look after the bathroom and mess-room, make tea at break times, and wash the dishes as well as fetch our food from the galley at meal times.

The first port of call for the 'Palermo' was Gibraltar for bunkers (fuel and water). The weather had got warmer as we progressed south and it was a nice sunny day when we tied up to the quay with the backdrop of the magnificent 'Rock'. It would only take a few hours to load bunkers so the captain issued the order that no shore leave was allowed. Of course Roger, Julian, Royston and a couple of others were not having this and promptly bounded down the gangway heading for the town with the captain and chief officer dancing up and down like pair of performing monkeys shouting for them to come back. They did come back, a few hours later, with several drinks down them and clearly in high spirits.

Disobeying a lawful command is a serious offence at sea so it was no surprise that the next day after we left Gibraltar the fun-loving few were called to the captain's cabin for their punishment. The captain of course is judge and jury on board a ship and has the power to inflict punishments. Much to the chagrin of one or two captains that I sailed with, flogging, apart from at Trinity House School, had been outlawed decades ago so the only punishments available were financial – the captain could inflict fines.

In this case the lads had to forfeit half a day's pay and were logged a full day's pay. The forfeit was for the hours that they were not available for work and the 'loggings' were fines that were held until the end of the voyage when the captain could decide whether to cancel them or to have the deductions made from the crew member's pay. Another form of punishment was through the seaman's discharge book, when the captain would stamp the boxes for ability and general conduct at the end of the voyage. Usually this would be very good (VG) but he could also use the word satisfactory (which wasn't very good) or worse 'decline to report' (DR), which could mean going before a shore disciplinary panel with the possibility of suspension or complete dismissal from the service.

We sailed from Gibraltar in the evening and because we were entering the Mediterranean and a potentially busy seaway the watch lookout was posted on the forecastle head. I was on the eight to twelve watch so ended up there for the last hour. It was a lovely clear night with a flat, calm sea and on top of that there didn't seem to be much other shipping around so I contented myself by singing and thinking about how I'd spend my wages when I got home to counteract the boredom. Then something in the sea on the port side caught my eye. It was long and narrow and looked like a torpedo clearly outlined by phosphorescence. Within seconds, several others had joined the first outline. I looked to the starboard and a similar formation was outlined. The torpedoes paused for a few seconds as though waiting to attack and then homed in on the bow of the ship at full speed leaving a phosphorescent trail. The pod of dolphins then swam, jumped and danced in the ship's bow wave. It was magnificent, it was spectacular, it was a private show just for me. I leaned out over the bow to get a better look. I watched amazed for several minutes before I was brought back to earth by the third mate calling to tell me to leave the forecastle and resume lookout on the monkey island on the bridge top. I was disappointed and I'm still not sure whether I was brought back amidships because the seaway was quiet or they didn't like the idea of having to turn the ship around to look for a man overboard should I have leaned out too far.

Our next port was Valletta, the capital of Malta, which at that time was still used as a major naval base. We were looking forward to this as we hoped to get a good run ashore, however our moorings somewhat limited our access to the delights of the town. Instead of mooring alongside a quay, the ship was required to drop its anchors and swing round, stern to quay and then use mooring ropes to secure her in position. This meant that we were always fifty or so yards from ashore. Cargo was worked using the derricks into barges and the only way for us to get ashore was by using the local water taxis. These gondola type, oar driven boats, were known as dghaisas and of course we had to pay for this service. Once on shore we could make our way to Strait Street known as the 'Gut', a narrow street lined with bars that normally served the needs of the naval fleet. As it happened the fleet must have been out as the 'Gut' was very quiet but that didn't stop Roger causing a fracas with some Royal Air Force men, but it was more of a bar room scuffle than a bar room brawl and nobody was hurt.

Getting back to the ship after a night out meant using a karrozzin, a horse drawn taxi rather than one with a motor, so we would come back pretending to be on a stagecoach in the Wild West. Inevitably there was one occasion when a few of us got back to the quay to find that there wasn't a dghaisa in sight as they'd finished for the night.

"What shall we do?" someone asked, not fancying a night sleeping rough on the quayside.

"I have an idea," another replied - I'm not sure whether it was Roger, Julian or Royston - who then strode purposefully towards a small building just off the quayside. It turned out that this was a local police station. Inside was a lonely, indifferent, policeman; no one else was in attendance. Our leader told the policeman of our plight. The policeman merely shrugged his shoulders. Our leader asked him what we could do? The policeman shrugged his shoulders again.

"Right, we'll stay here for the night," said our leader.

"You can't do that," said the policeman who had finally found his voice.

"Yes we can, you've got some empty cells."

"No, it is not allowed."

"Who said so? There is only you here!"

"It is against the rules."

"Sod the rules," said our spokesman as he started to walk towards the cells with us following closely behind.

"Stop! You'll get me in trouble," shouted the policeman.

"Well, get us a boat back to the ship then."

"I can't."

"Have you got a boat? The police must have a boat."

"Yes, but I'm not allowed to leave the station."

"Right, we'll stay here then."

"No stay!"

"What do you want to row us back to the ship?"

"You have tea? Sugar?"

"We'll get you some tea and sugar, you get the boat."

We all then left the police station while our newly bribed policeman went and got the rowing boat. When we arrived back at the ship we provided him with a couple of big tins of tea and sugar and off he went back to his lonely desk in the police station but at least now with plenty of refreshment and quiet, still empty, cells.

While we were in Malta the weather started to turn. It was still warmer than Britain in February but a strong wind sprung up, which meant no dghaisas and no means of getting ashore. We could see the lights of the shore beckoning us as we looked out from the afterdeck with our cans of beer and mugs of tea. How we wished we could get ashore. The wind and the heavy swell was making the ship surge, even though we were in a harbour. The anchor cables were holding firm at the forward end but the stern ropes would slacken as the ship moved astern and then tighten as she surged forward. Sometimes the ropes dipped under the water only to be pulled up bar tight quivering with tension and spraying water into the night.

There was some debate about using the ropes for getting ashore with the majority agreeing that it was too dangerous but Royston wouldn't have it. After a couple more beers he said he was going for it.

"Don't be daft," we all said, but Royston was so daft that he couldn't help himself. With his trademark grin on his face he watched the rhythm of the ropes so that he could pick the time when there would be the least rise and fall, and then he was over the rail. He dropped onto the rope and then, hanging by his hands, started towards the shore. Hand over hand he slowly made his way towards the quayside. He had picked his time well and the surging was kind to him. Then, when he was about twenty feet from the shore and still bone dry, the ship surged backwards.

For moment Royston disappeared under the water. We all watched in silence. The ship began its forward surge and up rose Royston, dripping wet through and clinging on for dear life. The rope almost pinged as it became tight and stretched giving Royston a massive shaking as it vibrated and we expected him to be thrown off. But then, instead of proceeding the few feet to the shore, he carefully turned around and started, hand over hand again, to come back to the ship.

"No, it can't be done," he said with a grin.

From Malta we sailed on, into the Mediterranean to the island of Cyprus. Our first port was Limassol and here we didn't even dock, as all the cargo was worked into boats while we rode at anchor which was a bit boring. Next we went to Famagusta where we did dock but it was a time when troubles were brewing between the Greek and Turkish Cypriots. Hostile exchanges had started to take place in December 1963 and the British Army was trying to keep the peace. This meant that there were restrictions attached to going ashore at night and there were soldiers with guns on rooftops overlooking the main streets and the main dock areas. The restrictions meant that there was not much for us to do in the evenings. The daytime was taken up with painting the ship's sides, using one of the punts that were available in the harbour.

Bored one night a couple of us decided to explore the harbour in one of the punts. It was a nice, warm, clear moonlit night as we paddled slowly around, exploring the extremities of the harbour but even this became boring after a while, so we paddled back.

It was a bit of a shock to find ourselves looking down the barrels of guns as we clambered ashore after mooring our little craft. It was even more of a shock to be informed by the soldiers that we were lucky not to have been shot, as if they'd not heard our laughing, English voices, we could have been taken for terrorists! Anyway, that was the only excitement in Cyprus.

From Cyprus we sailed to Israel to visit Jaffa and Haifa. Here we could spend more time ashore and the Chief Steward was able to get the dockers to put his motorbike ashore for the first time to allow him to disappear into the hills. We were content to just wander about ashore and drink fresh orange juice from the street stalls where the vendor squeezed the juice from the oranges as you waited. Israel was, and still is, a place of political tension but no one got into trouble there except for the deck-boy, Denis from York, who had a very narrow escape and had to run back to the ship for safety when some locals took offence to his swastika belt buckle. He didn't wear the belt again.

While in Haifa I developed toothache and was sent to a local dentist. I think it must have been a very cheap one as it seemed that I entered it from an open doorway on the corner of an alleyway in a shopping street. It was more like the local barbers rather than the dental surgeries I had used at home. I didn't even have time to assess the hygiene of the place if there was any, before I was in the chair and injected with a needle that I thought would penetrate my jaw. Then the guilty molar was yanked out and I was sent on my way, nursing a sore mouth with a bloodied handkerchief. The dentist must have got paid more for extractions than fillings as no attempt was made to save the tooth. I heard later that some sailors used a visit to the dentist as a way of getting a run ashore but that seemed pretty drastic to me if they'd had the experience that I'd had. On the other hand, it may have explained the number of toothless shipmates I would encounter on my travels.

After we had discharged the cargo in Israel it was time to load for home. The intention had been to load fresh oranges but the port health people put a stop to this as they didn't think the ship hygienic enough. The cause was not helped by a dock worker falling through one of the rusted deck plates next to number three hatch, so we were only allowed to load concentrated orange juice in large cans along with other canned produce. This meant that we had an unlimited supply of orange juice but we were all fed up of drinking it after about a week.

Once loaded we started our passage home calling again at Malta and at Messina in Sicily for bunkers. We weren't allowed ashore in Messina but we did have a 'bum-boat' on board which gave us the chance to spend some of our money on rubbish although a few of the crew did buy guitars which were cheap and of quite good quality. Italy was part of the Common Market, one of the six countries linked together for economic purposes that the UK was trying to join, so I was very concerned to see women with small children begging for food on the quayside. I had never seen anything like this before and it was unheard of in the northern European countries; why would we want to join this? I know that things did get better and the European Union has been very effective in fighting poverty and creating opportunity but at that time it was, to me, a shock.

One of the rituals of the merchant navy was the Sunday inspection. This was when the captain and an entourage of the chief officer, chief steward and the chief engineer, in full uniforms and regalia, inspected the accommodation to see if it was clean and tidy. 'Spying' we called it, giving the captain a chance to nose about amongst the crew's possessions – some captains even opened lockers! To me it was another example of the class-based nature of the crew structure of the merchant navy. The officers didn't actually use a white glove to check for dust but they did use their fingers. Normally the inspection went without comment but one Sunday on the 'Palermo' the captain took issue with a bit of dirt left in a scupper in the alleyway leading to our accommodation.

"This is not good enough, who's responsible?" the captain asked.

But before anyone could own up, Roger was out of his cabin like a shot.

"How dare you? How dare you come down here inspecting this slum of an accommodation? You should be ashamed of yourself. You should be ashamed of calling yourself the captain of a decrepit old ship like this. Would you like us to inspect your accommodation? Would you like to live down here? Look at it! You should be praising us for trying to keep it as clean as it is, never mind strutting around in your gold braid and looking at a bit of dust in a scupper. Get out!"

And the captain and his entourage did just that. We expected another logging for Roger for insubordination but it never happened; maybe the captain saw his point.

We ended our voyage back in West India Dock, London and signed off on March 31st 1964. We'd docked the day before so got a night out before paying off. Most of us stayed local but Roger, because he was from London went off to his local area, returning late the next morning, looking the worst for wear and with his suit trousers stapled together down each outside seam. Apparently the police had done this for him when releasing him after a night in the cells. There's always one...

Chapter 13. Slow Boat to China.

After paying off the 'Palermo' it was home by train to Hull but less than ten days later I was back, with a few other Hull seamen, in London at the Prescott Street (also known as Dock Street) Pool office. We'd been sent there as we'd been recruited to join a Shell tanker, the 'Hindsia', at Saltend in the Humber but the ship had changed orders and had been sent to the Isle of Grain in Kent instead, so we'd been sent to London to join her and the Prescott Street Pool office was to arrange our transport to the ship.

We'd set off from Paragon Station in Hull early in the morning and had gone straight to the London Pool office where we were kept hanging around until early in the afternoon. Worse followed however, when we were informed that the 'Hindsia' would not be docking in the Isle of Grain after all, and that we would have to travel up to Grangemouth in Scotland. We were pretty fed up by this time and we were not looking forward to another, even longer, train journey that day. In fact a couple of the Hull men wanted to give up and go home and planned to get off the Scotland bound train at York as we assumed we would be travelling on the east coast railway line from King's Cross. Unfortunately the Pool shipping officers must have suspected this plan and sent us up on the west-coast line by way of Euston Station. This was an overnight train but we did not have sleeping berths so had to make do. It also meant having to sit in a cold waiting room for a few hours in the early hours of the morning waiting for our connection to Grangemouth. And, on finally arriving in Scotland, cold and hungry, guess what? No ship! It wasn't due for another two days!

This meant that we needed somewhere to stay and we were told to go to the Seamen's Mission where the shipping company would pay for our accommodation. The Seamen's Mission in Grangemouth was hardly used by the seafarers it was intended for and the bloke that ran it had a nice little side line in renting out the bedrooms to travelling salesmen. He was quite shocked and put out when we arrived saying that we were seamen wanting accommodation for at least two nights. Eventually he got rid of his lodgers and we moved in but the next day a couple of the lads said they'd had enough and went back to Hull, but the rest of us stayed.

We signed on the 'Hindsia' on March 11th 1964. She was a typical tanker with a centre castle containing the bridge and deck officers' accommodation with the crew's accommodation, saloon and mess-room and engine room aft. Built in 1955 at 12,212 gross tons (19,246 tons deadweight) she was the biggest ship I'd been on to date but was, never the less, small by comparison to many other tankers. The articles that we signed were a 'foreign going running agreement', which meant that the vessel was operating in European waters and we could give our notice and leave the ship anytime it docked in a UK port. The thing about tankers is that when they dock it is usually at the end of a long jetty serving a refinery, miles from anywhere. Also, because the discharging and loading of the cargo is done by using high pressure pumps, turn rounds are very quick, so shore leave can be a problem.

During my time on the 'Hindsia' we visited Rotterdam, Copenhagen, Isle of Grain and a few other places but I only remember spending some time ashore in Copenhagen and visiting the Tivoli Gardens. I was not too pleased about this although the accommodation with single berth cabins, recreation room and serviced mess-room was much better than I had ever had before.

Shell then decided to send the ship 'foreign going', which meant signing new articles. However I didn't fancy the tanker life so when I signed off the running agreement in Ellesmere Port on May 2nd, I said I didn't want to do the deep-sea trip. In their wisdom the shipping master doing the transfer of articles had already assumed I'd be signing on and had made the entry in my discharge book, so I ended up with two records of the 'Hindsia' in my book, one reading the usual VG, and one reading Engagement Cancelled. This is not counted as a 'bad discharge' but it didn't look very good, especially next to the record from my next trip.

My next ship was another tanker, this time one of Cory's coastal vessels, the "Pass of Glenclunie", which I signed on at Saltend on May 5th 1964. The 'Pass of Glenclunie' had been built in 1963 so she was a fairly new ship of 1,416 gross tons (1,880 deadweight), and had been designed to carry mainly chemicals. This meant very quick turn rounds so I only had time to sign on, go home and get my gear, and then get back on board in time to sail that afternoon.

The ship seemed comfortable enough and the captain, called Morrison, seemed okay. The mate was a small Scottish chap and the second mate an ex-trawler skipper from Hull. The rest of the crew seemed all right but I was disturbed to find that when I was in the mess-room having my first meal on that evening of May 5th that they seemed to be speaking in a foreign language. I asked one of the crew a question and he responded in English before gabbling to his mates again.

"What's that you are speaking?" I asked.

"Gaelic," was the reply.

"Where do you come from?" I asked, as this was something new to me.

"We come from Barra and he comes from Stornaway."

"Is that how you talk all the time?"

"Yes, mostly because we all come from the Hebrides."

"Well I would prefer it if you spoke English while I'm around if you don't mind. It's not very nice listening to you lot when I can't join in the conversation. You might even be talking about me!"

To be fair they could see my point and I never had to ask them again, in fact they turned out to be a good bunch of lads.

During one conversation in the mess-room, I overheard a couple of them talking about the 'Moonman'.

"Who is this Moonman?" I asked.

"Morrison the captain," one of them replied.

"Why do you call him the Moonman?" was my next question.

" He comes from Skye," was the answer.

It was pretty hectic on the 'Pass of Glenclunie' with the quick loading and discharging. This needed constant vigilance and while we were in port there always had to be at least two on deck, one of the mates and one of us, to be ready to open and close valves as the tanks filled or emptied. Once discharged we then had to make sure that the tanks were clean and gas free, before we could load our next cargo. All this meant that we didn't get much chance of getting ashore although there was a lot of overtime so we were getting paid well. We did manage to get ashore in Grangemouth a couple of times but there was nothing there so we used to go to Falkirk instead, which had a bit more lively nightlife. I also tried Canvey Island once but this was before it became a holiday resort and again there was nothing there. I asked at the local shop if there was anywhere to go and the shopkeeper suggested Southend but there was no transport to take us there.

Some of the chemicals we carried were quite dangerous so we had to be very careful that we didn't have any spillages, as these could be costly. One night I was on watch with the second mate in Dunkirk loading acetone, which smells like nail varnish remover, and we thought we had got the timings down to a fine art for opening and shutting the valves. We'd been warned that on no account should we spill any acetone as the fire brigade would have to be called out because of the fire risk and the ship would be fined heavily for polluting the harbour. It was a nice night and between tank changeovers we decided to have a mug of tea in the ship's office. While having our break we started 'swinging the lamp' with some fishing stories as it turned out that he knew some of the people I'd sailed with. Every now and again we popped our heads out to see what was happening with the tanks and then carried on with our yarns. Then suddenly the second mate looked out and shouted, "Fucking hell!" and dashed for the door. I followed him to see a fountain of acetone shooting up from one of the tanks. We slipped and slid our way to the valves and turned them frantically to stop the flow and start the next tank. We didn't have time to survey the damage as we dashed about trying to stop the flow of the chemical as it raced towards the scuppers. We did our best to mop up the spillage and run a hosepipe over it before the shore watchman appeared and looked suspiciously at us and asked if any acetone had gone in the harbour.

"Nooo," we said shaking our heads furiously.

The next day we could see the damage that had been done. Rather than stripping nail varnish, the gleaming steel showed clearly how the rivers of acetone had stripped the paint from the deck. While the second mate took the main rap neither of us was very popular with the captain. Despite this I quite liked being on the 'Pass of Genclunie' because it was a bit different. I also got on with the mate who liked me to assist him in working down in the pump rooms between ports, all extra overtime. Unfortunately, or fortunately, depending on how you look at it given future events, my time on the ship was limited.

Arriving back at Saltend, I asked if I could pop ashore for a couple of hours. I was given permission but was told to be back by sailing time, about three in the afternoon. Off I went as I had couple of things to sort out during the few hours I would have at home. All went well until I jumped in a taxi to take me back to the ship. I'd allowed myself an hour to get back to the ship, plenty of time as it was only about twenty minutes to Saltend. What I hadn't allowed for was the local high tide. I was on the west side of Hull and Saltend is on the east, which meant crossing the river Hull using one of the two bridges close to Hull city centre, North Bridge and Drypool Bridge. Both of these bridges opened, if needed, at high tide to allow the passage of small ships, tugs and barges. It was because of one of these closures that I found myself sitting in a taxi watching the clock as five minutes turned into ten, then into twenty, then thirty, then – oh shit! Once over the bridge the taxi driver did his best to make time to Saltend. I paid him and then legged it down the seemingly endless jetty just in time to see the stern of the 'Pass of Glenclunie' heading down river.

There was nothing I could do except return to Hull. I contacted the Seamen's Union the next day and, after some enquiries, they found that my discharge book and personal belongings had been put ashore in Billingham and sure enough, the day after, my discharge book arrived. The entry for the 'Pass of Glenclunie' showed I had left on June 9th and written in large handwriting across the spaces for conduct and ability were the words 'Voyage Not Completed' - a bad discharge! Not as bad as a DR (Decline to Report) but almost. This implied that I had jumped ship!

I'd only got five recorded discharges and one was an 'Engagement Cancelled' and another a 'Voyage Not Completed' (VNC) - so my discharge book didn't look too good. My next port of call was the Pool office where I was informed that I would have to go before a disciplinary committee - things were not looking good. I was also told to report back to the office the very next morning. Chatting to some of the lads outside the office I was concerned to hear that because shipping was a bit slack I should expect a suspension of at least six weeks. Six weeks! I started to think that I might have to go back fishing.

I arrived early the next day, June 12th 1964, and reported to the Pool office. The officer in charge of the office that morning was called Claude Locke who told me to wait in the office as 'they' (the committee), were not ready for me yet. I'd spoken to Claude the day before about missing the ship because of the bridges being up so he knew why I was there. While I was waiting I noticed Claude thoughtfully watching me while sucking his pencil, he then called me across.

"How would you like to go to China?" he asked. I said that I would go anywhere rather than be given a 'walk around'.

"Leave it to me," he said. After a few more minutes, which seemed like hours, the telephone rang and Claude answered it and entered into a short conversation before he turned to me and said that they were now ready for me upstairs.

The disciplinary committee turned out to be three or four people, one of whom was a union official. I wasn't too sure about the others but the main man was in full uniform with more gold braid than I'd seen since watching the gathering of the Elder Brethren at Trinity House. His jacket must have weighed a ton! After I was given the opportunity to say why I'd missed the 'Pass of Glenclunie', 'Gold Braid' launched into what could only be described as a bollocking. He said that I should have been back on board at least two hours before the ship sailed (she was only alongside for a few hours) and that he had never seen such a disgraceful discharge book belonging to someone who had been in the merchant navy less than six months. Next, he said that I should have been ashamed of myself and not to let anything like it happen again or I would be in serious trouble. He then told me to go downstairs and see Mr Locke as he had a ship for me.

Phew! I'd got off lightly, and in hindsight I was also very lucky as the young man who had taken my place on the 'Pass of Glenclunie' was killed a few weeks later when he was gassed in the pump-room. Apparently, like me, he had become the mate's favourite for helping him in this work.

Feeling suitably chastised, but also that I'd got away with it, I descended the stairs. It was then that I started to think what was the catch. Claude was waiting for me when

I returned to the office and I thanked him for his support although I was still a little suspicious.

"Go straight to the Board of Trade shipping office where the 'Brighton' is signing on," ordered Claude, so off I went.

In the shipping office I approached the desk and said to one of the shipping masters that I'd been sent to sign on the 'Brighton'. There were a couple of other seamen in there signing on and we were joined by an old jovial Geordie chap who turned out to be the captain who said, "Hope you realise you are signing on the original slow boat to China," and he wasn't joking.

The m.s. 'Brighton' was a tramp ship of 8,572 gross tons (5,309 net), built in South Shields in 1960 for Chapman and Willan of Newcastle, with a top speed of 11 knots (but why push it). Although the ship wasn't very old, the design and layout was very dated, she may as well have been built in 1940. She had three hatches on the fore deck, two hatches on the afterdeck and a hatch amidships between the bridge housing and the amidships accommodation, each hatch having two derricks (twelve in total). The crew's accommodation was aft and accessed by way of a steep companionway that led to a fair sized mess-room, three double cabins on the port side and two single cabins - doubles really - and a small recreation room on the starboard side. The cabins contained double bunks, a seat locker, lockers and a wooden chest of drawers with a bit that pulled out to make a writing desk. There was no air-conditioning apart from wind chutes stuck out the portholes of the cabins.

The crew came mainly from Hull and my cabin mate, a senior ordinary seaman, was an old friend of mine from when I lived on North Hull Estate called Johnny Sawden and we took the middle cabin on the port side. Next to us were two EDHs or ABs whose names I can't remember, but one was about thirty with ginger hair and the other was in his mid twenties and a little overweight. In the other cabin on the port side was a tall seaman called Jack who had been in the army and had an electric guitar, but thankfully no amplifier, and sharing this cabin was a small, older AB called Tommy Marshall. Tommy was all right most of the time but could become a bit obnoxious when he'd had a drink. In the two single cabins were an EDH called Albert Sparks (known as Sparky) and a DHU (Deck Hand Uncertificated) called Mally McRitchie. The boatswain was a big chap from Nottingham and there was also a middle aged, easygoing, carpenter. Of the officers, the third and second mates were okay, as was the captain who was a typical tramp ship man who only wore his uniform when going in or out of port, most of the rest of the time, in the tropics, he wore old khaki shorts and a vest. The chief officer however was something else.

This bloke had just come out of British India and it was his first experience of a British crew, and it showed.

The ship was still discharging when we joined it in King George Dock and the plan was for us to leave Hull light to load grain in France and take it to Dairen (later known as Dalian) in China. This meant that we had a few days before we sailed during which the mate (chief officer) started barking orders which soon got the crew's back up. One wheeze was to say that we had to go to the dole office to sign off so the first afternoon we all disappeared ashore. The next day we again started to slink off when the mate challenged us, "Where do you think you lot are going?"

"The dole office," was the reply.

"You went yesterday," said the mate.

"Yes, and we're going again today!" was not the answer he expected.

After a few days we eventually sailed to load grain at Rouen which meant getting the holds cleaned and rigging the shifting boards. There was no urgency to do this as we didn't have a berth in Rouen so we had to lie up for a few days up river from the main port. There was nothing much where we berthed, just a small village with a bar and a wine shop but it was summer and it was quite pleasant. Then we moved down river to Rouen to start loading the grain. It was already very hot and the talk amongst the crew was that we would be away for many months so someone suggested that we should all shave our heads as it would have grown by the time we got back. Thinking this was a good idea we duly shaved each other's heads. Bear in mind that this was the sixties when the hairstyles for men were getting longer and shaved, shiny, baldness was not a fashion statement, even given the efforts and popularity of Yul Brynner. It then dawned on us that the person who had made the suggestion was Tommy who was already bald, didn't look any different and, anyway, always wore a trilby hat! Duped or not, we decided to make the best of it and every night before going ashore we would re-shave our heads and put Brylcreem on it to make our domes even more shiny.

We'd found a friendly bar in Rouen where we spent our evenings and the first time we went ashore with our newly shaved heads we were surprised that cars were honking, buses nearly crashing and people were staring at us as we walked over a bridge to where the bar was located. The bar owner was shocked when we walked in before falling about laughing, so we asked her what all the fuss about. She then explained that in France they shaved the heads of prisoners so people would have been shocked to see what they thought were half a dozen convicts walking down the street!

The thing about bulk cargoes is that they can be loaded almost as quickly as fluid cargoes on tankers, so after enjoying a week or so in France in the summer, loading part of our cargo in Rouen and the rest in Le Havre, it was soon time for us to sail on the voyage proper.

The normal routine after leaving the final port on a long voyage was to clear the decks of all the dunnage and rubbish left by the dockworkers before stripping, oiling and stowing the running gear of the derricks, a dirty and at times, dangerous job that involved a fair bit of climbing to reach the topmost blocks.

Clearing the decks someone had the idea of building a canoe out of some of the dunnage and an old hatch tarpaulin we found, so these were kept while the other rubbish was thrown over the side. After that it was back to the normal routines of watch-keeping and carrying out general maintenance, usually sugi mugiing (washing paintwork), and painting, which could be anywhere on the ship from the deck to the topmast. Because we didn't carry a deck-boy the senior ordinary seaman, my old friend Johnny, had to share the duty of being 'Peggy', keeping the mess-room and accommodation clean, collecting the food from the galley and washing up. As Johnny really resented doing this I ended up doing more than my share. I wasn't too endeared to this role either but there were advantages as you could take your time to finish before joining the others on deck. Our work rate reflected the pace of the ship, leisurely, and it got slower mainly due to the attitude of the chief officer – a perfect example of a bad manager. I mentioned earlier that the chief officer (mate) had appeared officious and had recently left the British India Shipping Company where he'd worked with Indian crews and had been used to shouting out orders and the recipients jumping. Unfortunately this method didn't work with our crew and the more he barked and shouted the less work he got out of us, to the point that we would drift along just going through the motions. We still got most of the jobs done but in our time not his, and there wasn't a thing he could do about it. I learned a good lesson then that would serve me well later in my working life.

Our spare time was made up of reading, chatting and a bit of keep fit when we changed the recreation room into a makeshift gym later in the voyage. The first thing though was to build the canoe. Using the salvaged dunnage and some tools borrowed from the chippy, the wooden frame of the canoe took shape before being covered with the old hatch canvas. To waterproof the boat we painted the canvas hull with boot topping and topside paint. The canoe looked okay but was a bit heavy and we had no idea of its stability in water or even when we would be able to launch it. Anyway it gave us some interest in the evenings as we slowly steamed through the Mediterranean towards the Suez Canal.

On arrival at the canal we were subjected to the usual onslaught of bum-boats and other traders trying to sell their various wares. One guy was a barber who, although Egyptian, had developed the skill of mimicking English accents that caught his ear so that he could shout, "Want a haircut?" and you'd think he was down your street in

Hull, Glasgow, Liverpool, Newcastle or wherever. Another thing for sale by the Egyptian wide-boys was pornography of dubious literary merit disguised by the cover of a Reader's Digest. I must confess that the sight of a pile of these magazines in a doctor's or a dentist's waiting room has raised my pulse rates only to have them crash down again when opening the magazine and finding "Laughter is the best medicine" - I'm sure the moral arbitrators at the Reader's Digest are right.

The Suez Canal itself is an exciting experience in a boring way, if you get my drift, because on either side there is nothing but sand. Yet on the other hand, you are passing through this magnificent man-made ditch that links the Mediterranean with the Red Sea, thus saving the thousands of miles that the old sailing ships would have had to travel to sail around Africa to reach the ports of Asia and the Orient. The canal isn't wide enough for ships to pass so you move in convoy and even then we had to stop in a cut to allow a northbound convoy to pass. This is also spectacular as the ships seem to be actually passing whilst moving through the sand as, because of the banks of the cut, you cannot see any water. There is a scene in the film 'Lawrence of Arabia' that exploits this illusion.

The stop in the cut gave us our first chance of launching the canoe. Some of us had decided to cool off with a swim anyway and the companionway and a pilot ladder were lowered so that we could get back on board after jumping in from the ship's side. Using ropes, the canoe was lowered carefully into the water and to our surprise it floated. Even with three people in it, it still floated, a little unstable perhaps but we soon got the hang of it as we paddled around. It wasn't far to the nearest shore so a couple of us swam there to explore but found only sand and an angry scorpion, we were in the middle of the desert after all. On the opposite bank we noticed what looked like a couple of military men with guns but they paid us little attention and moved on their way. We also felt it was time to get on our way and swam back to the ship. On board we were informed that sharks from the Red Sea were sometimes found in the canal along with poisonous sea snakes – thanks for that!

Soon we were on our way again and left the Suez Canal to pass through a hot, but tranquil, Red Sea before stopping at Aden for bunkers. There was no shore leave here but we didn't expect any as the port was considered dangerous for foreign sailors. We did see some sea snakes however but didn't test them to see if they were poisonous or not. After Aden there would be no stopping until we got to Dairen (Dalian) in northern China, although we did see signs of life and land as we passed through the Malacca Straits where we also had our excitement heightened by being asked to keep a good look out for pirates, although I don't think any self respecting pirate would have wanted to be seen onboard a crap Chapman's tramp ship. Our next bit of excitement was showing a large Union Jack as we passed Taiwan, then still known as Formosa, in case they mistook us for a disguised Chinese warship and opened fire – some disguise.

Our passage so far had been pretty uneventful as we spent our days carrying out routine maintenance, oiling the rigging and using boatswain's chairs heaved up and down on a winch to white lead the shrouds, plus the usual cleaning and painting. During this period it was decided that some of the winches needed new covers so the boatswain asked if any of us could sew canvas. This got the usual non-enthusiastic reaction but somehow Tommy found himself the only volunteer. This meant he spent hours and hours and days and days on his own with a palm and needle in his hands developing sore fingers, while the rest of us did our best to waste time on deck. The mate still occasionally barked orders and we responded by working even slower. Eventually it was time to drag the derrick rigging and runners out of the winch houses ready for when we docked in Dairen (Dalian).

What we noticed when getting the derrick gear out of the winch houses and hold hatchways was the number of mice that had made their home on the ship after arriving on board with the grain. They were even more noticeable when we lifted the hatch boards as thousands of them scampered for safety. I've no idea what happened to the mice, as they seemed to disappear with the cargo that was shovelled by the Chinese dockers into canvas slings and lifted ashore. They left the hatches spotless. Not a grain was wasted except for some that had escaped into the bilges and had been spoiled by damp making it ferment and stink.

One morning I came up on deck after clearing the mess-room to find the boatswain and a couple of others looking over the side. "Just in time," said the boatswain. "We need you to go over the side and free a scupper, it's only a bit of grain so it won't take much shifting."

Naively I thought that seemed easy enough as I climbed over the rails with a metal rod into a boatswain's chair that was then lowered to the offending scupper. I reached over and poked the rod in. Nothing happened.

"You need more leverage," said the boatswain. "Swing under it and use both hands to really free it."

I obligingly swung under the scupper and rammed the rod in.

"Aaaahhh! You bastard!" was all I could shout, as the stinking bilge water and swollen grain gushed all over me like a Niagara Falls of putrid porridge. The boatswain and the others thought it was hilarious and could barely pull me up for laughing, although they kept well clear when I landed, dripping and stinking, back on the deck before the boatswain sent me aft for a shower.

Our time in Dairen (Dalian) was quite interesting. This was Communist China, guards were placed on the gangway and a curfew operated for foreign sailors that meant we had to be back on board by a certain time. Not that there was a lot to do in Dairen (Dalian) then, although there was a club with a restaurant and a shop that we could use. To get there meant walking through the streets, which gave us an opportunity to see how the local Chinese lived, but there was no social interaction. No one spoke to us, in fact it was as if we were invisible as the people went about their business and completely ignored us. Even the children, and there seemed lots of them, noisily playing cards, Mar Jung, and other games on the pavement, barely gave us a glance. It was strange but we didn't know the consequences that the locals would have had to face for fraternising with foreigners.

The main form of transport was the bicycle; there was very little motorised transport. Hull at that time was a big cycling city and I'd been to Rotterdam also known for its cyclists, but I had never seen as many people on bikes as I saw in Dairen (Dalian). At the club and in the shop the people were friendly enough but we were buying things like ornaments expertly carved in wood or ivory, intricately carved camphor wood chests, and bicycles – big green heavy 'sit-up and beg' jobs that looked as if they'd last for ever.

The food on the 'Brighton' to be fair wasn't very good. Our two West African cooks did their best with the meagre supplies but it was an uphill task for them. These cooks were a pair of really nice guys who kept their 'checks' and T-shirts immaculately clean along with their galley, although this may have been because they didn't have much food to cook. When we complimented them on their cleanliness they told us that with their colour they had to be spotless and efficient, as they'd experienced racism in the past, but thankfully they did not experience any on this trip. Mind you they always managed to get fresh fish for themselves (we were saved from this treat) as every morning they'd collect any misdirected flying fish that had landed on the deck, a regular occurrence in the open ocean.

Anyway, ashore and faced with a tempting restaurant and bored of the bar, we thought we'd try a meal so we ordered chicken and chips (very adventurous) and vodka to drink (I don't know why). The shock came when the waiter brought a full spring chicken on a platter surrounded by chips and vegetables. We thought this was to share but it turned out we had one each, along with a small bottle of vodka each. And it cost us 'next to nowt' as we say in Hull. It was a good night, even though we all ended up a little drunk.

On returning to the ship we thought it was time for a bit of music. A few of us, including one of the stewards and a cabin boy had been messing about with a kind of skiffle group. I'd borrowed a guitar from one of the apprentices, a nice lad from Newcastle, and the others played tin cans and scraped metal mosquito nets. One of my sister's old boyfriends had taught me three chords, C, F and G7, when I was about eleven and he was angling to get in my sister's good books (and failing) and the apprentice had taught me a few other chords like A, D, E and G – so I could use the three chord trick of guitar strumming in at least two keys. The result was that our little skiffle group created a right racket but we nevertheless trundled on deck and bashed out a bit of Lonnie Donegan and Buddy Holly. The dockers in Dairen (Dalian) worked all night so they were working when we started but soon stopped to watch and listen and clap. To them it must have sounded okay and a rare chance to hear western 'music', but to our crew mates it was an awful row and they begged us to shut up. Their wish was soon granted when we were ordered off the deck and not to disturb the workers again.

At first we were the only foreign ship in the port but then a Norwegian and another British ship joined us. Up until this point we'd adhered to the curfew imposed upon us by the Chinese authorities but now there were other dimensions to our social lives this soon went to pot. The problem was that there was a lot of to-ing and fro-ing between the ships, with people returning late and sometimes not at all, until the Chinese authorities had no idea where any one was or was supposed to be. This led to some altercations between crew members and the unfortunate Chinese soldiers guarding the gangways and checking we were aboard our correct ships at the right time. One high-octane argument led to a wooden hatch wedge being thrown from the ship at a guard on the shore. Now there really was trouble. The guilty party never came forward but the main suspect was Tommy, which seemed about right given that he was one of the last on board that night and had 'had a few'. Nevertheless, the Chinese authorities decided we all deserved a bollocking so we were summoned to the captain's cabin later the next morning. We were met by a desk full of Chinese 'gold braid' with the most bedecked example sitting in the middle from where he addressed us in, quite good, broken English by listing all the rules we'd broken and how this would not be tolerated. I remember one of his sentences quite clearly, "Danish ship come – no trouble. German ship come – no trouble. Swedish ship come – no trouble. English ship come… PLENTY TROUBLE!"

It about summed us up really…

Chapter 14. Fiji and Home.

We left China completely light with the hatches swept clean and barely a grain of wheat left. Even the mice had gone. Nowadays China is the largest exporting nation on Earth but not then, so without a cargo we headed for Japan for bunkers while the company sorted out our next cargo. The Chinese charter had been for six months which, apparently, wasn't enough, given the speed of our ship, to make two trips so whatever the shipping company could come up with would be a bonus for them.

In the end they decided we should proceed to Fiji to load sugar, a cargo that could be easily sold on our way back to Europe. First though, we needed to take on bunkers in Japan.

We were all looking forward to a brief stay in Japan but, as usual with bunkering, there was no shore leave. The port was Moji, now part of the port of Kita-Kyushu on the island of Kyushu. Instead of shore leave the captain allowed us to have a bum-boat, except it wasn't an actual boat but a kind of large market stall on one of the hatches selling mainly Japanese electrical goods. These were top of the range technically and relatively cheap, although haggling was always expected when buying from a bum-boat. A middle-aged woman assisted by her teenage daughters ran the bum-boat. While we were interested in the electrical goods, Sony radios with short wave bands were much coveted by merchant seamen, the girls also caught our attention which led to, not a little, flirting, although the matriarch in charge ensured that was as far as anything would get.

As a marketing ploy the all female bum-boat worked a treat and they did quite a lot of trade. I know I bought a little reel to reel tape recorder, which wasn't very good but I used it to record our little skiffle group with the result that this convinced me that I would never make the grade as a singer or a guitarist so the machine was worth it from that point on, saving the human race from the aural violence of my attempts to create music.

Many of us looking for gifts to take home also bought these little fluffy electronic dogs that walked, yapped and begged. While these were bought as gifts for children at home they also gave us a bit of amusement - and some annoyance – when we took them for 'yapping walks' on the afterdeck in the evenings.

So we left Japan without stepping foot ashore and headed in a southerly direction for Fiji. This entailed crossing the equator. On passenger ships they make a big deal of this with a 'crossing the line ceremony', and make Neptune rising from the sea part of the passenger entertainment. They also organised one on a cadet training ship I was on later where they initiated the first trippers. I'd also heard that a 'crossing the line ceremony' was used as an initiation ceremony for first trippers on some merchant navy vessels, that gave the crew the excuse to paint the genitals of the unfortunate victim with fish oil, white lead, red lead and anything else they could clap their hands on. On this ship, thankfully, nothing like that happened and crossing the line was just another day. It may have been because none of us aboard were first trippers and it was assumed that we had crossed the equator before, or, like most other things on the ship that involved some effort, the crew simply couldn't be arsed.

Anyway, unscathed we arrived in the Fijian capital of Suva, which gave us the chance to have a run ashore. There were bars and a seamen's mission where we could play snooker and have a drink. One of the first things that we noticed was that the policemen in Suva were about seven feet tall and wore what resembled a normal UK policeman's tall helmet and a tunic on the top and a white jagged edged skirt on the bottom. I think their shear size kept us quiet.

At least we were having a little bit of a change while we prepared the ship to load sugar. In fact we didn't load sugar in Suva but we did take on board about 200 'crew boys' – Fijian men to load the sugar as we travelled round the islands. The crew boys slept under makeshift tents on the hatches and had a portable kitchen on deck, they even had their own toilet, a kind of wooden shed with a plank with a hole in it for sitting on, suspended over the stern of the ship by lashings. The Fijians were big men and very friendly and easy-going so we soon got to like them. However, because they tended to wear what looked like skirts and often held hands with their mates when walking down the quayside or jetty to a shower, they did get a few raised eyebrows – although I don't think anyone dared make a comment questioning their sexuality.

On the first evening after we left Suva we noticed that the crew boys would sit in a circle on a hatch top while a couple of them played guitars and sang local songs. In addition they had buckets of a muddy brown liquid, it resembled the water of the river Humber, which, using half a coconut shell as a cup, was passed around the circle. Each time the cup was filled from the bucket and passed to one of the crew boys who then clapped his hands and said, "Bula bula," before accepting the cup, drinking the contents in one, and throwing the dregs over his shoulder before saying, "Bula bula," again and passing the cup back to be filled and passed to the next man. This looked interesting to us as we assumed this drink had some intoxicating properties. It turned out to be a drink called 'kava' made from the fermented root of a tropical plant with mildly narcotic properties. The root came in a powdered form and was squeezed through a kind of cheesecloth bag to produce the muddy looking drink which, to be honest, didn't look very appetising.

The next night the crew boys were again on the hatch. The music played, the men swayed, only this time they were joined by several white faces swaying with the music and saying "Bula bula," in Yorkshire accents – we were not going to miss out on this! In the event it was a bit of a disappointment as the kava tasted of, well, muddy water tinged with a hint of aniseed, so we soon lost interest.

Loading the sugar in Fiji was quite different to the way that we'd loaded the grain. The grain came down chutes that were directed to where needed in the hold. The sugar though was loaded in a more labour intensive way. The sugar was lifted on board in sacks using the derricks as most of the places that we visited consisted of little more than a wooden jetty in a lagoon so cranes where out of the question. On top of the open hatch the crew boys laid a metal grid, it looked a bit like a spring bedstead. The sacks were landed on this contraption and then cut open and the crew boys trampled the sugar through the grid with their feet.

The knives they used to cut the bags were made from six-inch nails that one of the crew boys made by hammering the end of a nail flat using a hammer and one of the bits on the forecastle head as an anvil. When flat, the blade was sharpened to an almost razor like edge.

With the grain we'd noticed dust while we were loading it, which was like itching powder and the unwanted passengers were mice. But with the sugar, we suffered a nauseating, sickly sweet, smell and our unwanted passengers this time were spiders, big brown ones. We also soon found out that one or two of our 'macho' sailors were frightened of creepy crawlies. We were able to exploit this by capturing a large cricket one night and putting it in one of their cabins, so that he was up all night searching for it. Sometimes he could hear it and sometimes he couldn't, but he always knew it was there and dare not go to sleep until it was caught.

Being in the tropics it was very hot and the clear blue water of some of the lagoons looked very tempting for a swim but the crew boys warned us if it was dangerous and also told us to keep out if the area was known for sharks. However, we became a little sceptical of their judgement when we were tied to a jetty in a lagoon and decided to swim ashore to cool off. Washed up on the beach we noticed some fish heads with razor like teeth, barracuda! If they were in the water what else lurked in there? We walked back to the ship along the jetty.

While travelling around the islands our main job was carrying out maintenance by painting the ship's side. This meant rigging stages and using rope ladders to access them. I had no problem in helping to rig the stages as Jack Haylett's Trinity House practical seamanship training had left me in good stead for all this type of work, although he didn't teach us how to paint! We had no intentions of rushing the job to ensure that we kept up our ploy of annoying the mate as much as possible but the poor boatswain found it a bit frustrating at times.

One particularly hot day we were painting on stages over the bow and were wasting time, waiting for the boatswain to call us for smoko (tea break). We were sitting on the stages smoking and dangling our feet over the water when suddenly a shoal of small fish leapt out of the water over our feet, followed by a larger fish snapping at them. This happened several times before it went quiet. It was so hot and the water was really tempting but the idea of snapping fish put some of us off. But not Sparky, who, when the boatswain called us, dived off the stage, swam around for a couple of minutes, and then shinned up the guide ropes to the stage and climbed the ladder.

We all went aft to get our tea from the mess-room and then went up on deck to see what was going on as we'd seen some of the stewards hanging about on the afterdeck and wondered what they were up to. When we saw what they were doing Sparky's face drained white. Shark fishing! They had several lines out with baited meat hooks suspended from makeshift floats made of biscuit tins. Leisurely and gracefully swimming around the hooks were some very big sharks indeed. Obviously they were discerning about their diet as they were completely ignoring the lumps of meat on the end of the hooks. I knew the food on the 'Brighton' was pretty bad but even the sharks were turning their noses up at this free lunch. We quickly berated the stewards for putting us at risk. Didn't they realise we were working over the side and one slip and we were in – obviously not. But they did reel in the lines when we pointed this out.

When we had some free time we would mess about with the canoe or wander ashore although there was little to do except explore the palm tree lined beaches as we were never near any towns. I loved it. It was like going back to nature. This was why I'd joined the merchant navy. I remember one day when several of us decided to take a walk along the beach. The sand was nearly black, obviously from volcano eruptions in the past, but the beach looked orangey-yellow with the millions of fiddler crabs that basked in the sun and then dived into their holes as we walked along. Except that Sparky felt that they had a personal vendetta against him and was insisting that we stamp the ground in front of him to make sure it was clear of crabs. Walking along with the clear blue sea on one side and the palms on the other we passed local women fishing in the shallows with nets, smiling, laughing and giving us a wave, but they were busy working so we didn't bother them. After a while we moved to the edge of the palm trees and noticed that many were heavy with coconuts, so we decided that we'd harvest a few. At first we tried throwing sticks up to knock the nuts down but this didn't work, so Johnny Sawden was elected to climb the trees and throw some nuts down to us. It was when he was halfway up that we first noticed the cobwebs. Massive cobwebs suspended between the trees, and in the middle of the cobwebs were the biggest spiders we had ever seen. They were about the size of a man's hand with a big yellow body. Sparky took one look at them and was gone, soon to be seen jumping up and down on a log on the beach pleading with us to run. Instead we knocked the webs and spiders down and urged Johnny to carry on climbing while we did a little dance in case the spiders returned for revenge. Eventually we collected our booty and returned to the ship where we found how difficult it was to open the nuts. Well difficult for us but not for the crew boys who made short work of opening them with a machete.

One Saturday morning we were given the job of painting the funnel using stages and boatswain's chairs. By about 10 o'clock in the morning we had little done except preparing the stages and chairs because, as usual, we were taking our time. Just as we were about to haul ourselves up the funnel we were distracted by some shouting from the crew boys who were pointing to some turbulence in the water of the lagoon. We stopped work immediately as this looked more interesting than a Chapman's funnel. Out in the lagoon we soon saw a shark fin circling something in the water. It was a turtle. The shark would circle; the turtle would swim for its life. The shark would attack; the turtle would withdraw in its shell. When the shark backed off the turtle would begin swimming again - I'm sure it was doing over-arm - while the shark circled before attacking again. It was very exciting but not as exciting as what was to follow.

The crew boys asked to borrow our canoe and of course we agreed and three of them jumped in it and, using our makeshift best quality dunnage paddles, made their way as fast as they could to the commotion in the water. Once there they began to beat the shark with the paddles. The canoe wasn't that stable at the best of times and this made it rock to the point that it looked like it would turn over. At one point the shark seemed to turn its attention to the canoe and came up under it, lifting the bow before it crashed down back into the water. After a few more scares the shark gave up and the crew boys turned their attention to the turtle. How kind and brave of them to risk their lives for a turtle we thought, we had never seen anything like it. The crew boys in the canoe then started to direct the turtle towards the beach where, in the meantime, several other crew boys had left the ship and were gathered waiting. Once the turtle got within reach it was grabbed and brought aboard the vessel where some photographs were taken. It was a big turtle. Then they cut its head off with a machete and gave the turtle to their cook for their evening meal. We were shocked, but that was life on these islands and this was part of their culture. Later they gave us the turtle shell complete with scars from the shark's teeth. That was our excitement over for the day and realising he would get little more work out of us, the boatswain, on the instructions of the mate, abandoned the planned painting of the funnel.

The next day was Sunday and as we had nothing to do, a few of us decided to take the canoe out ourselves and go exploring. The sea was calm so we decided to paddle across the lagoon to a beach that we could see on the other side. We landed on the beach and started to walk along the edge where it was green and lined with the usual palms but seemingly deserted. Then, through the trees we noticed a village. A proper native village of small huts with thatched roofs. Then out of the trees a smiling man approached us. He didn't look Fijian but more Asian, perhaps from the Indian sub-continent. In broken English he told us his name and invited us into his hut in the village, which he shared with his wife and children. The hut had mud floors and probably mud walls as well but they were wallpapered with newspapers and magazines. It must have been like living in a collage. There was no furniture except for some wooden boxes and what I assume was a bed that also doubled up as the seating. He told us that he worked on a sugar plantation, as did the rest of the villagers, and to us it was obvious that they were paid very poorly. Even so he offered us a drink and produced some water flavoured with sugar which, to be polite, we accepted. It was obvious that this family had very little to share but they were friendly and we were humbled by their kindness and hospitality and it was with smiles and handshakes that we left them. Unfortunately we had not brought any money with us on this expedition or anything else but we said on our way back to the canoe that we would return if we could with some tea, coffee and anything else we could find. We were glad that we hadn't promised these items as we never got the chance to return as we sailed early the next day for our next loading point.

On the way back we were surprised that the water was a little choppier. Then someone said that the sharks liked it a bit choppy. We then all remembered the encounter between the shark and turtle the day before. Did someone see a shark fin? We returned as if we were turbo charged. We paddled so hard the bow raised and we left a wake. I don't remember using the canoe again.

Our final port of call before dropping off the crew boys was Lautoka. At least there was a town here even though it resembled something out of the Wild West with its raised sidewalks. What we discovered here was that there were shops that sold electrical goods and the Japanese radios, with a bit of haggling, were cheaper than in Japan. Radios were important in the merchant navy as they were our only connection with the world as well as home news and, occasionally given the strength of the reception, entertainment. The most desired was a Pye Cambridge but these were quite big and expensive and used valves rather than transistors in a wooden cabinet but the short wave range and the tone of the radio made it probably worth it. The next best thing was a Sony transistor or some other Japanese brand. Normal FM, medium and long waves were generally useless unless close to shore, so short wave bands on the radio were essential. I purchased a nice tabletop Sharp radio as I could not afford a Sony, but nevertheless it sounded good and it had good short wave bands. A few others also bought radios and other equipment.

What we noticed in the town was that Indians owned the shops and businesses, obviously a different caste from those that worked the plantations, which were, in turn, owned by Europeans. This indicated that the amiable free and easy Fijians owned nothing. Someone said that this was because it was not part of their culture to exploit others and preferred to work when they or nature dictated. We just felt that it would only be a matter of time before the indigenous islanders woke up to what was happening and do something about it. It took them about another twenty years but this is precisely what happened.

While in Lautoka the boatswain tried to get us to finish the ship's side in our final couple of days in Fiji but we just cruised along as usual. Most of the hull had by now been painted grey despite our efforts to work as slow as possible so the last part of the process was to cut-in and paint the red boot-topping that showed above the water using the ship's jolly boat (a small rowing boat that some ships carried). Tommy had decided to make himself 'Captain' of the jolly boat as he could scull, so every day he sculled to the work section and then every evening he sculled back for the boat to be lifted out of the water.

It was one evening when, for Tommy, the worst happened. Remember the location of the crew boys' toilet? Tommy was sculling along, happily going around the stern when he looked up to the crew boys' toilet and realised there was no turning back, as the blue sky through the toilet hole suffered a sudden total eclipse, followed by what appeared to be two thirds of a pawnbroker's sign and a shower of shit! We heard the screams from the mess-room.

At least in Lautoka we had somewhere to go in the evening and we made sure that we had a good time on the last night to use our money up. It was like a big party around the bar that we had chosen to use. There was music, drinks - a lot of rum, local girls and a general good time. I don't remember that much of it to be honest as I fell asleep under a palm tree after drinking too much but I know I had a good time as did the rest of the crew.

Leaving Fiji was a bit sad as we'd had some good times there but our consolation was that we were heading in the right direction across the Pacific for home, although we were not sure which port yet as our cargo had to be sold on passage. Our next stop would be the Panama Canal.

In Fiji we'd lost the third mate who had been hospitalised with some tropical virus and we wouldn't see him again until Panama. The third mate was a pleasant young man who had only recently completed his time and he was always complaining about the food in the saloon and that he thought the cooks prepared special meals for the crew. He stopped me a few times when I was carrying the mess tins aft and asked what was in them before saying, "We didn't get anything like that."

The food on all ships is important as it is one of the only regular things to look forward to and I'm sure our cooks did their best from the meagre Chapman rations. Nevertheless, the minimum, and on the 'Brighton' it was the minimum, you could expect in the merchant navy was a breakfast of cereals and a full English; lunch would be a three course roast dinner (good life merchant navy, Sunday dinner every day); and the evening meal, again three courses, would consist of a starter, a main course and a dessert. In addition food would be left out overnight should anyone need a snack or a sandwich. On most ships if you ate it all you would end up like a barrel but this was not a problem on the 'Brighton', in fact the food was so good on some ships that it was much better than some hotels I've stayed in since. The food on board was usually issued from the galley on trays and in mess tins and kept warm in a hot press, not that welcome a piece of equipment in the tropics without air-conditioning. Most mess-rooms had a sink for washing up and a geyser for boiling water for tea and coffee. Standard issue on long trips to the tropics were lime juice to prevent scurvy and also salt tablets to combat the effects of the tropical heat.

Another absentee, well at least from the decks, was the chief officer who had managed to fall down a companionway and damage his knee so that he was confined to the bridge and his cabin for the journey home. This was a bit of a relief for us but I think he'd realised that his attitude was counter productive before then and had given up on trying to get more work out of us. It was too late though, as the unfinished paintwork on the ship's hull made the ship look like a patchwork blanket, not a good look after a long voyage.

After leaving Fiji and stowing the derrick running gear and clearing the decks of rubbish we started our leisurely 6,000-mile journey across the Pacific. Our final wild nights in Lautoka meant that a number of the crew started playing 'bingo', not the pastime favoured by old ladies but a more practical version by observing their privates' department where it was 'eyes down and look in for a full house.' This was one game that you didn't want to win and, in this case, most of the players lost but there was one crew member that had to take his unlucky member along to show the chief steward who was in charge of the medical chest. The chief steward duly recognised the symptoms and issued the appropriate antibiotics but this wasn't the end of the adventure for the unfortunate seaman. Immediately the mess-room banter started with comments like 'unclean' and insisting that he used his own knife and fork although everyone knew that there was no chance of him passing on his disease in this way. The next thing was that they said he should be taken away from our accommodation altogether and housed in the hospital and arrangements were made for this to happen. We all knew that this seaman was very superstitious so the rest of the crew played on this by spinning a tale that on a previous voyage there had been an explosion in the engine room and one of the greasers had been so badly injured that he died in the hospital and from that point had been haunting his place of death.

As it happened the hospital had been badly painted and there were some places where paint which had been flaking had been painted over. These were pointed out to the unfortunate new occupant as bits of the skin of the dead greaser that had stuck to the bulkhead and been painted over. All nonsense of course but the bloke fell for it.

That night, after he left our company, we could see him sitting on the hospital bed looking around him with a great deal of apprehension but eventually he fell asleep with the lights on. Not for long though as each watch keeper on his way to and from the bridge would scratch on the mosquito gauze covering the portholes. This immediately woke him up with a start so that he would jump off the bed and look around the room. This happened for a couple of hours before he was back down aft begging to be allowed to return to his cabin. Of course he was allowed back as the whole thing had been a, somewhat cruel, joke.

The passage across the Pacific was going to be a long one so to pass the time some of us who'd bought radios in Fiji decided to make carrying cases for them. The easiest way to do this was to sew canvas around the boxes which we did by borrowing palm and needles and using some of the canvas that had been left over from Tommy's prolonged tailoring exercise making winch covers. Our stitching was neat and some of us also introduced fancy piping and knot work to make our cases look even better. Mine was so strongly made I used it as a DIY tool bag for years after I had given up on the radio. Of course Tommy and the boatswain were not too pleased, as when asked previously, not one of us professed that we could sew but now the accommodation resembled a bespoke canvas tailor's workshop.

It took us almost four weeks to reach Panama where the third mate rejoined us. We saw him waving from the pilot boat and of course we waved back before pelting him with some old vegetables that the cabin boy had been told to save for the mules in the Panama Canal. The machines known as mules in the lock pits of the canal are of course large, heavy, traction engines designed to move the mooring ropes of the vessels moving through the locks and the cabin boy was not the first to fall for this jape.

The Panama Canal itself is a wonderful thing. Cutting through mountains and jungle it is more spectacular and interesting than the Suez Canal, which just cuts through sand. Here the landscape was green and there was the chance to get a glimpse of the wildlife like alligators and monkeys, although the really wild nightlife was in Panama City itself apparently. Unfortunately we didn't have the chance for any shore leave at either end of the canal and we resumed our journey home via Curacao, with again no shore leave, for bunkers.

What we did pick up in Panama was our mail from home. These were the days before satellites, computers and mobile phones so our only contact with the outside world was through the radio and our only contact with our families and loved ones at home was through letters, which obviously meant delays of many weeks in getting news from home. At the time I didn't have a girlfriend but I did get the odd letter from my family. However Johnny, my cabin mate, did have a girlfriend but struggled to compose letters to her so I would help him out which allowed me a bit of creativity in the word department. This worked well but it was a bit embarrassing when we got home and Johnny introduced me to her as, "the bloke who wrote you the letters."

We had now learned that our first port of call in the UK would be Avonmouth, near Bristol, and that we would have to take the vessel around the land before being discharged. Going around the land was bad enough on any outward voyage but worse when returning home after months at sea. Home was so near and yet so far, with the added temptation of spending your hard-earned money before being paid off, so that you had less to spend while on official leave.

In Avonmouth for our first Saturday night ashore in England for many months a few of us decided to visit a village on the river Avon called Pill, which we learned had lots of pubs. To get there we had to catch a ferry, more like a big ship's lifeboat, to cross the river to the village. The boat was full of young people dressed in their best gear for a night out with many of the girls wearing white as they gingerly boarded the ferry by the flimsy gangway. In Pill the booze flowed as people moved from one pub to another and by about 9 o'clock the local lads were balancing chairs on their chins after consuming vast quantities of the local scrumpy. The whole night was a good-natured laugh and after the 10.30 closing time, as it was in those days, the crowds made their way back to the ferry. It was now low tide however, so the passengers had to negotiate a muddy narrow path on the steep bank on the other side. Inevitably, because many were already unsteady because of the drink, some slipped and fell in the mud and those girls' white suits? Well let's hope that their mothers used a good detergent.

The deal was that we discharged half our cargo in Avonmouth and half in Liverpool before taking the ship around to the dry dock in South Shields. What I remember most about taking the hatch covers off to begin discharging in Avonmouth was the nauseating smell of the sugar. It nearly made us retch, as it seemed to stick in our throats. The good thing was that we didn't have much else to do except let the dockers get on with it. Our next stop was Liverpool and some of us took the opportunity to visit the Cavern. Mally was impressed with the dingy club and went back on other nights but most of us thought it was crap and once was enough. Instead we found another backstreet club where you could drink after time called the Green - or was it Blue? - Parrot. This, if anything, made the Cavern look like the Ritz and got over the licensing laws by serving 'food', like a restaurant or hotel. What this meant was a waitress sidled up to us - I'm sure she had a fag in her mouth - and said, "What do you want, sausage and chips or egg and chips?" Eventually she returned with some greasy plates of food and told us not to eat it all, as we had to look like we were eating if we wanted to carry on drinking the bottled beer that the club sold at extortionate prices. The club was filled with what looked like a range of alcoholics, petty criminals, pretend or maybe real, local gangsters, and some, not very attractive, ladies of the night. We decided not to overstay our welcome.

Finally we left Liverpool and had one night in South Shields before paying off. There was some kind of argument on that last night involving the boatswain and a couple of the others. I don't know what this was about and it seemed stupid as we'd all got along together during our long voyage and the boatswain was always, in my opinion, a gentleman, a gentle giant if you like. But this final hiccup, it wasn't a major incident, was probably caused by Tommy who always seemed to be the centre of any trouble when he'd had a drink.

So on November 22nd 1964, nearly six months after leaving Hull and having sailed over 27,000 miles on an around the world voyage, we left South Shields by train and headed home to Hull.

Chapter 15. Senior Ordinary Seaman.

Home on leave in Hull made a nice break but unfortunately my wages as a junior ordinary seaman on the mv 'Brighton' were not that much, given that we'd been away over five months. I hadn't considered what you could actually spend at sea particularly when having to spend the final couple of weeks going around the land before we paid off. The married men may have stayed on board but the footloose and fancy-free needed to make up for all the Saturday nights missed while at sea so every night was a Saturday night for a silly sailor home from the sea. My Saturday nights had started when we first docked in Avonmouth and had continued in Liverpool until we had finally discharged our cargo of sugar there and taken the ship to our final port of Soth Shields for dry dock. So, after less than ten days' leave, I headed back to Posterngate looking for another ship.

The first stop I made though was not at the Pool office but at the Board of Trade offices next door, to have one of the shipping officers check to see if I qualified for the rating of senior ordinary seaman (SOS). For this I needed to show that I'd done nine months' service, under articles, on deck. This was easily calculated, so armed with my new rating I headed to the Pool office. Senior ordinary seaman was still pretty low in the pecking order but it meant that I received a bit more pay, which was worth having.

My first ship as an SOS was another one of Wilson's ten-day boats, the s.s. 'Rollo'. This wouldn't have been my first choice had I been given one but it was a job. The 'Rollo', built in 1954, was a bit younger than my previous ten-day boat the s.s. 'Silvio', and at 2,499 GT was also larger and carried more passengers on a regular trip to Gothenburg, Sweden. We sailed on December 4th 1964. The best thing about the 'Rollo' was the food, as we could just go to the galley and have the same meals as the passengers. To this day I can still remember my first breakfast when I was offered bacon, sausages, black pudding, kidneys, eggs to order, flap jacks, potato fritters, beans, tomatoes, kippers, smoked haddock, and kedgeree. I've only come across such a choice since in four star hotels in Scotland. In fact there was so much choice I didn't know what to have. Unfortunately that was about the only highlight of this voyage.

Having been at sea for nearly two years and now a senior ordinary seaman I was a little bit cocky and perhaps over confident. The thing with the ten-day boats was that they attracted crews who stayed on them for years because they offered the chance of being at sea but getting regular time at home, so they naturally attracted married men. All ships depended on the crew working as a team and this lot had it down to a fine art with everyone knowing precisely what job they should be doing as we battened down the hatches and secured the derricks and running gear for our passage across the North Sea. I say everybody but nobody had briefed me so I got told off immediately for working on a starboard derrick when this was 'Tom's job' and I should have been on the port fall guy apparently. The next thing I had to contend with was the seating arrangements in the mess-room for our first meal after we left Hull. I got my food from the galley, found a seat in the mess-room and sat down. It all went quiet for a minute and then someone said:

"You can't sit there."

"Why not?"

"That's Old Con's seat."

"Who the fuck's Old Con?"

"Old Con's been on the ship since she was built and has sat in that seat for ten years."

"Well it's about time that he sat somewhere else then!" was my final and not well-received, reply.

My only words with Old Con was when he burst into the mess-room after coming in off the deck and blowing his nose on the tea towel, which I pointed out was a filthy habit. He never said a word back because he realised there was no excuse, nor did he complain if I managed to get to the mess-room before him and sit in his seat, he just sat somewhere else and glowered.

To be fair I didn't like the 'Rollo' and I don't think the 'Rollo' liked me as I also had a couple of bust ups with the mate who, apparently, "didn't like my attitude" and asked me which school I had been to and "didn't they teach you respect?" He didn't know what to say when I told him Trinity House, probably because he went there himself, so it was with mutual relief when I left the ship after one voyage on December 14th.

Ashore again, my social life revolved around which fishermen or merchant navy lads were home at the time. I also had a mate who lived down my street but as he was an apprentice motor mechanic he could only afford to go out at weekends. Everybody in those days wore suits to go out, as most dance halls and clubs would not allow you in if you were not wearing a tie, and jeans were banned. My taste in suits had become modified while in the merchant navy and I had moved away from the flamboyant styles favoured by the young fishermen, towards the more modern styles that were coming into vogue. I didn't tend to have regular girlfriends in those early years as I didn't think it fair as I never knew how long I'd be at sea for, but I did go on regular dates with some of the girls who hung around the pubs and dance halls that we frequented. The main dance halls were the Locarno, Majestic and, in winter, Beverley

Road baths. The pubs could be anywhere where there was something going on, like live music or simply because they had a good jukebox. One such pub, not too far from the city centre, was the Norfolk Arms in Norfolk Street, which was a regular haunt for young fishermen and merchant seamen during the week when there wasn't much else going on. Mostly, people were out for a good time but the over indulgence in alcohol of some meant that the threat of violence was also not too far away from the laughing and joking.

I was in the Norfolk Arms one night chatting to a couple of lads that I knew. The pub was quite busy for a mid-week but everyone seemed to be minding their own business in their little groups. The time came when I needed to relieve myself and headed for the gents and opened the door. I didn't see the first punch but I certainly felt it along with the next and my head hitting the brick wall. I felt myself falling and then hearing a woman screaming, "Not him you idiot, you've got the wrong one, he's only a young kid!" I heard another voice saying, "Sorry," and then there were more voices as my mates picked me up. It was no consolation that it was a case of mistaken identity that led to the cowardly attack but I couldn't report it as I didn't want to get the landlord into trouble as I was under age and I shouldn't have been in the pub in the first place. My assailant was gone but I was a bit of a mess and my mates took me to the Infirmary for a check up. Thankfully, no bones were broken but my face had taken a bit of a battering.

Being out of a ship meant going to the Pool office every morning - and every afternoon if you were desperate - and asking if anything was available, then hanging about yarning with the other out of work seamen in case anything came in while you waited. There was a lot of luck involved. Sometimes we'd leave the Pool and spend some time in the 'Before Eleven Club', otherwise known as the Kardomah Café in Whitefriargate, but after eleven it would be one of the local pubs, if we could afford it, close to the Pool like the Monument, a small pub in Whitefriargate, or the Bonny Boat, Kingston or Malt Shovel, all near the market.

Running out of money, and with two black eyes and Christmas looming, I was getting desperate when finally I signed on the mv 'Baltic Merchant' on December 22nd 1964. The "Baltic Merchant" was owned by a company called the United Baltic Corporation, which ran a fleet of ships on short trips serving the countries of the Baltic, not exactly ten-day boats as they didn't have the regularity needed for passenger travel, but close. Some of the ships ran regularly out of Hull but there was always the possibility in this company of a change of destination and this would prove to be the case in this instance.

The ships themselves were usually of a more modern design than the traditional short sea traders, with electric winches and strange steering arrangements like, in the case of the 'Baltic Merchant', press button steering. On others you may have found a wheel like an aircraft joystick rather than a conventional wooden ship's wheel. These mechanisms where more sensitive than the traditional wheel and took some getting used to but were easier physically, although they lacked the lounging support of the larger wooden wheel. Most of the company's ships were built in Germany; the 'Baltic Merchant' for example had been built in Rensburg in 1954. She was 1,689 gross tons and had ten derricks, six on the foredeck and four aft. She also had steel hatch covers that ran on tracks. This was the first time that I'd come across these as up until then all the cargo ships that I'd sailed on used beams, hatch boards, tarpaulins, battens and wedges; so the steel hatches on small wheels that we closed with a winch were a bit of a novelty.

Our destination was Leningrad, now called St Petersburg, in what was then the Soviet Union, so we knew that we were heading for some cold weather. I signed on, on December 22nd, joined the ship the next day and we sailed from Alexandra Dock, Hull on Christmas Eve afternoon. It was a cold, grey afternoon and as we edged our way through the lock pits, the quayside was lined with dockers making their way home, one of them was my brother-in-law Jack.

"Merry Christmas!" they shouted with some irony as we left the lock pit and headed out into the Humber towards Spurn Point. Was I bothered? Not really, as the thought of being home for Christmas and New Year with no money was not tempting, and I knew I was heading for somewhere different and felt the buzz.

Christmas day found us in freezing fog tied up in the Kiel Canal. Because of the fog we had to keep watch on the forecastle head so that we could ring the bell if we saw anything moving. But nothing seemed to be moving that day, not even the fog, and it was freezing cold. The temperature was nowhere near as low as it would be when we were further up the Baltic but the damp of the fog seemed to make the cold penetrate our clothing to our bones. Captain Littlejohn, who later became a Humber pilot, had decided that it would be best to postpone any Christmas celebrations until New Year's Day when we'd be in Leningrad. This seemed a good idea given that we were all watch keeping but the cook still put on a bit of a Christmas dinner and we had a few beers to wind down.

After our passage through the Kiel Canal we began our voyage through the Baltic towards Leningrad. Soon, ice flows began to appear and eventually we reached sheet ice that made it difficult for the ship to progress so for the rest of our journey we had to follow an icebreaker. The ice was well over a metre thick and we could actually see the sea freezing between the icebreaker and us. If we fell too far behind we would get stuck and the icebreaker would have to return to break us out. Steering in these conditions was easy as it was like being on tramlines as we followed the track of the icebreaker, although the ice did strip the paint from the ship's side leaving just gleaming steel. Sometimes, ahead of us, we could see 'ice roads' with lorries and cars crossing on the ice. The traffic would stop when the icebreaker approached and, like on a level crossing on water, waited until our little convoy had passed. A few minutes later the sea would freeze over and be strong enough to carry the traffic again.

The temperatures were obviously very cold, well below −25° centigrade, and to prevent condensation on the bridge windows freezing it was necessary to keep the bridge doors open, this made being on the wheel (buttons) very cold indeed so that we had to make relieving more frequent. In fact if we were doing any jobs while in Leningrad that didn't involve a lot of movement our time on deck was limited to twenty-minute sessions to prevent frostbite. Frostbite, like sunstroke, deemed a self-inflicted injury in the merchant navy, was pretty nasty but I only saw one crew member get it. He had to have his sea boots cut off after going on deck without proper woollen socks on, with the result that his toes turned black. Luckily he recovered.

We were not sure what to expect when we arrived in Leningrad especially when armed guards were placed on the gangway. Eventually a woman came down to the ship and told us that we could go where we liked within the boundaries of the city but were not allowed to travel anywhere else without a permit, and that we needed to be back on board each night by midnight. In fact there was not much chance of us wandering about given that the temperatures were so low and that there was little daylight at that time of the year. In saying that though the cold in Leningrad, because it was dry cold, didn't feel as cold as that of the freezing fog at Kiel, which made it a bit deceiving and consequently made the risk of getting frostbite greater. Anyway, the woman said that she would arrange for a coach to take us ashore that evening and show us what was available to do in Leningrad. I had heard tales of being taken ashore in blacked out buses in communist countries but this had not been the case in China and it wasn't here either. The bus came and we were given a guided tour of where things were in the city, before we ended up at a place called the International Club. The International Club seemed to be the only place open to us where we could have a drink and experience some entertainment.

The drinks were very cheap so we soon got into the routine of going there in the evenings even though it meant walking through the icy cold night, the coach, much to our annoyance, had been a one-off and after that we were on our own. What we did notice though was that the streets were swept clear of snow every night so that the city kept moving; a stark contrast to management of heavy snowfalls in our country.

Our nights at the International Club were very pleasant. It wasn't in fact that International as we were the only foreign ship going to Leningrad - the only ones daft enough, we said - at that time of the year, so we had the place much to ourselves apart from a few locals. It amused us to see the Russian women lumbering in, wrapped in their fur coats looking like polar bears, only to be surprised when they had taken off their several layers of outdoor clothing - we knew where the idea for Russian dolls came from - to reveal these slim attractive young ladies. Unfortunately there weren't enough of them to go round.

We soon realised that there was an active black market operating in the Club, with British currency and British-made female clothing and lingerie very much in demand. We made a note of this for future reference and it was noticeable that on future visits to the Club we left the ship looking like a cross between Humpty-Dumpty and the Michelin man, as we padded out our normal clothing with our contraband. The Russians must have thought we fed our seamen very well. We went ashore looking like Oliver Hardy and came back like Stan Laurel. We also learned to get a small sub in roubles so we could show where our money came from and then take more money ashore in the form of pound notes that we could sell on the black market.

The boatswain of the "Baltic Merchant" was a big Latvian man, another gentle giant, who had found himself a refugee in the UK after the war. The boatswain, who we called Ed, had a Russian girlfriend who he'd take to the International Club. We asked him what she did for a living and he told us that she was a crane driver on the docks. We knew there was more equality in Russia than in the UK but we couldn't help joking that we were off ashore to see if we could pick up a little curvy, blue eyed, blond bricklayer or hod carrier. In fact we didn't pick up anything much at all but the drinks were cheap and quite good especially the dark beer, more like a porter, and the vodka.

One night there was a dance at the International Club and the manager came down to the bar to tell us about it and that we should go upstairs to the ballroom. But there was no bar in the ballroom and we were well stuck into the vodka and beer. The manager made several trips up and down the stairs to try to persuade us to move upstairs but we stayed put. However, about 9.30, he finally gave up and persuaded the orchestra (I'm not kidding) to come and play in the bar, which was as big as the ballroom anyway, with the hope that we would join in the dancing. He didn't have to worry about that, as the vodka had kicked in by then and as soon as the music started we were dancing and flinging ourselves around the room like demented dervishes, much to the shock of the ladies who'd followed the orchestra down and others using the bar. Watching this performance was the boatswain and his girlfriend.

"Why they do this?" she said.

"Why they do what? replied the boatswain.

"Dance like, like, lunatics and mad men."

"Oh that. Well you see it is very hard to get a crew to come on this Leningrad run in the winter. Now all of these men are qualified seamen but they are also criminals and as soon as we return to Britain they are locked up by the police until it is time for us to sail again. So the only time they are free is when they are over here in Russia."

"Ah, now I see, now I understand."

On leaving Leningrad on our first trip we learned that we would not be returning to Hull and that for the foreseeable future the ship would be sailing out of Surrey Docks, London. This meant that a number of the Hull lads paid off over the next couple of voyages and were replaced by seamen from the London Pool until there were hardly any of us left, but I didn't mind as the replacements were all good lads. I chose to stay on the 'Baltic Merchant' as my dad and stepmother, Margaret, had recently moved to London, my mother had been living there for about eighteen months, and I also had a brother who lived in south London and worked at Abbey Road studios as a recording engineer. My mother, at that time was working in the bar of the Empire Ballroom, Leicester Square, and was living with the caretaker of a posh block of flats in Marylebone. My dad had moved to London because of Margaret's job in the Civil Service, where she was working in the offices of MI5 paying out spies by sending money to obscure PO boxes. Apparently the whole family had been vetted before she was appointed to this job, it must have looked really good that I was working on a vessel going regularly to the Soviet Union. Anyway having these family connections meant that if I had any free time at the weekends I had people I could visit, so it was no sacrifice sailing out of London for a few months.

Surrey Docks are situated on the south bank of the Thames and our local pub was called 'The Warriors', where you would find us most nights of the week and where we got to be pretty well known as locals. The landlord employed a couple of young Irish live-in barmaids called Bridie and Mary. I took Mary out a couple of times to the pictures and up the West End once. While in the West End we decided to go dancing so I took her to the Empire Ballroom, Leicester Square. We entered the ballroom and as usual I went straight up to the bar. The barmaid looked very surprised and I knew that she knew that I was under-age, I was still only seventeen, when I ordered our drinks. Luckily she didn't embarrass me and we entered into some good-natured banter.

"Do you know that lady?" asked Mary.

"Yes, she's my mother," I replied.

The brief flirtation with Mary was what it was – brief – because on returning from my next voyage to Leningrad she'd had her fancy, and maybe other parts of her anatomy, tickled by a camel Crombie coat wearing, loud mouthed, travelling salesman. He had offered her a flash car, fancy restaurants and other treats that I, on my ordinary seaman's pay, couldn't. Another lesson in life learned the hard way. My one consolation was that Mary was not the brightest star in the sky as one rainy night when returning to the Warriors in a taxi she said, "Oh look, it has stopped raining!" as the car passed through the Rotherhithe tunnel!

I didn't know that people could get drunk on water but I experienced it on this ship. One of the motormen, an elderly Scotsman who we obviously called Jock, we noticed got drunk very easily and this was indicated by him breaking out in song. Well, one song, "You are my sunshine" which he sang with a lisp. One afternoon a couple of us exploited this by filling an empty Russian vodka bottle with tap water. Amongst our number was an EDH from Hull called Mick Temple who also entertained us from time to time with a number of ribald songs and sea shanties. We sat in the mess-room with glasses of this water and, when Jock appeared for a cup of tea before he was due to go on watch, we started laughing loudly, and slurring our speech. Jock watched us for a couple of minutes.

"What's that you're drinking?" he asked.

"Thish Jock hic, is very, very, very strong vodka, hic, the strongest in Russia! Do you want a dram?"

"Yes, please."

We gave him a glass full and carried on laughing and talking louder. Then we gave him another dram and Jock joined in our banter. One more dram of water – vodka - and Mick burst into song, some old Japanese folk song that went something like;

"Me no likee British sailor, me like Yankee one much more,

Me no likee British sailor, Yankee sailor pays ten dollar more!"

"Give us a song Jock!" we shouted.

"You are my shunshine, my only shunshine."

We then reminded him that he was due down the engine room for his watch and he staggered off. About ten minutes later the second engineer burst into the mess-room saying, "What have you done to my motorman? He's flopping about down there as drunk as a skunk!"

We laughed and said that he'd only been drinking water and gave the engineer a taste of the 'vodka'. He couldn't believe it and started to laugh, although he also said that we were a bunch of trouble causing bastards.

All was going well on the 'Baltic Merchant' and I was looking forward to the spring and the summer when the ice would have melted and I'd be able to explore Leningrad more closely as we could see that it was a beautiful city. However, things were not going to work out quite how I expected...

After about four trips Captain Foss, a completely different personality, replaced Captain Littlejohn. While Captain Littlejohn was rather quiet and dour, Captain Foss was much more vocal and flamboyant and had the habit of coming on to the bridge in a silk dressing gown voicing his outlandish opinions and knowing that it was unlikely that they would be challenged. Sometimes it was like Noel Coward or a ham actor from a 1930s amateur dramatic society play was on the bridge. Along with Captain Foss we also picked up a new second mate who was arrogant, really full of himself, and officious. Our happy little ship was changing.

During the previous months we'd grown together as a team and developed routines that made working in the extreme weather conditions bearable. One of these was if you were the next wheelman and the ship was sailing, instead of going straight to the bridge from the stern or forecastle where you'd been involved in letting go, you would go to the mess-room for a hot drink before relieving the previous wheelman. It was not much of a concession but it meant that you got a bit of a warm before having to stand on the bridge for an hour with the doors and windows open. This was my fifth trip to Russia on the 'Baltic Merchant' and although it was now the beginning of April, it was still very cold and although the ice was breaking into flows on the open sea we still needed an icebreaker in case we got stuck. I was on the forecastle with the second mate when we let go and pulled clear of the quayside, so I expected the others with me to stow the mooring ropes and wires away while I prepared to take the next wheel by having a warm in the mess-room.

"Is it okay for me to step down?" I asked the second mate.

"Why?" he replied.

"Because I'm due to take over on the wheel and the next wheel-man always stands down to get a warm before taking over."

"Well you can stay here until I say so."

"What do you mean? You expect me to go straight from the freezing deck to the cold bridge?"

"Yes."

I gave this due consideration of about half a second before responding, "Well you can fuck off because I'm going!"

I hate injustice and unfairness and I felt that in this case I was being treated unfairly by an officious prat who wanted to show his authority. Sadly Captain Foss didn't see it that way and promptly logged me a day's pay for 'insubordination and refusing to obey a lawful command'. I still felt it was worth it though.

Captain Foss obviously was not impressed with my act of rebellion and watched me like a hawk while I was steering the ship following the icebreaker. The problem now was that as the ice was melting there were fairly wide patches of open sea-water rather like lakes within the pack ice. This meant keeping a close watch on the icebreaker's course, as if you misjudged it the ship could become stuck or, at best, collide with the ice with a bang and a crunch, not quite Titanic stuff but you get the picture. Following the ice breaker into one of these lakes I noticed that it had veered towards a more starboard course before beginning to break a passage through the pack ice, so I started to turn to starboard to line up for the newly cut pathway.

"Where do you think you're going?" said Captain Foss.

"Following the icebreaker," I replied.

"No you are not. The icebreaker is over there. Go to port."

"But the icebreaker made the passage over there," I said, pointing to where I believed the icebreaker had entered the pack ice.

"Do as you are told and go to port. Port more. Midships. Steady!"

Bang! Crunch!

The captain stopped the engines and then went astern to free us from the ice.

"I said that the icebreaker had made the passage over there Captain," I said.

The captain rang the telegraph to go slow ahead again and said, "Port easy. Midships."

We didn't get as far as "steady" before we hit the ice with another sickening crunch. Again we backed off but this time, away on our starboard side we could see the icebreaker returning and it was with reluctance that Captain Foss said, " All right have it your way go to starboard."

We found our track and continued on our passage through the ice and to be fair captain Foss didn't interfere again.

Inevitably I was asked to leave the ship when we docked in London. I had expected this and wasn't that bothered other than I'd spent the best part of three months working in unbelievably cold temperatures and now when things were getting better,

I had to leave. My pay off was delayed while the Nation Union of Seamen representative argued with the captain over my logging and whether I deserved a bad discharge or not. In the event the logging stood but my discharge book showed "Very Good" "Very Good" – can't win them all.

Back in Hull I realised that I was only a couple of months away from my eighteenth birthday when I'd be eligible to sit my Efficient Deck Hand Certificate. There were a couple of ways to do this. One was to attend a two-week course at a merchant navy training school in London, and the other was to just take the examination, which you could do in Hull and some other ports. Why waste time at college? I thought. But I still needed to prepare myself so I invested some of my earnings from the 'Baltic Merchant' and bought a copy of the bible for deck-hands, 'The Boatswain's Manual' by William A. McLeod. Jack Haylett, the seamanship teacher at Trinity House had given me a very firm basis in the practicalities of seafaring but the Boatswain's Manual, which would make up my main reading matter on my next voyage, would I hoped, help fill in any missing details. Armed with this I went looking for my next ship.

This turned out to be the m.v. 'Tremorvah', one of Haines' general freighters chartered to Manchester Liners. The 'Tremorvah' had been built in 1954, weighed 5,605.44 G.R.T. and had five hatches, ten hatch derricks and two heavy lift derricks. Most Manchester Liners were built to navigate the Manchester Ship Canal but the 'Tremorvah' wasn't, so there was some discussion about whether we'd have to lower the topmasts or even remove the funnel for the passage up this waterway. As it happened our air draught was just low enough to pass under the bridges.

I signed on the 'Tremorvah' on April 23rd 1965 and we duly left Hull and went round the land to negotiate the Manchester Ship Canal and load in Manchester prior to our trip to the southern states of the USA.

The crew were mainly from Hull and I shared a cabin with another SOS, while the ship also carried a JOS, a couple of deck-boys and five ABs. The boatswain was a cocky little guy from Australia. One of the ABs left the ship in Manchester to be replaced by a young EDH from Cheadle Hulme, who we nicknamed Parkin because his mother had packed him up, with what must have been a trunk full of the local ginger cake of the same name. Every mealtime and 'smoko' he seemed to bring out a slab of this stuff, until one night we persuaded him to bring out all that he had left and the deck-boys, who always seemed hungry, made short work of it.

The ABs were a pretty boozy lot and the ones I can remember were Bob Taylor from Hull and his mate Harry Cooper who lived in Leeds. Harry would be found dead in his flat in Leeds a year or so later surrounded by empty whisky bottles. Two others from Hull were Jimmy Fernley and Ken (the Animal) Johnson. Johnson, a big heavy bloke, who was noted for bellowing "they call me the Animal," when drunk, and indeed Animal Johnson was the name that he was known by in Hull. He was also noted as being a bit of a bully but to be fair I didn't notice this behaviour on this trip. However, you could tell when the booze was taking hold on Animal as he would burst into song, well, a high-pitched yowl in an American accent.

"I never knooow...ed God made hooorn...ky tonk aye...en.. gels!" was the only song he knew. A few years later Animal came to a sticky end when his body was found floating in Auckland harbour. Most people, and the coroner, believed that he had fallen in returning to his ship drunk. Local rumour however, preferred suggestions of an end that was far more suspicious.

Our first port of call was Wilmington in North Carolina, and our first stop was an industrial clothing shop. In those days British jeans were really crap and American jeans like Levis, Wrangler and Lee were almost impossible to get hold of in the UK and very expensive. In the USA jeans were still considered work wear and very cheap, so we found a little store and stocked up. My preferred options were Levis for going out and Wranglers for work wear although the usual thing was to wear them for going out for a while and then wear them for work when they could be patched up for years. Nowadays these patched up rags would be considered cool fashion and command ridiculous prices – I've seen some in the shops that were worse than the ones I've thrown away! We also bought denim jackets to match our new jeans and we referred to the whole outfit as a denim tuxedo. My nickname on the ship was Donovan because I had curly hair and wore a denim cap similar to the folk singer of that name who was popular at that time. The denim tuxedo completed the image.

From Wilmington we visited Charleston in South Carolina, Savannah in Georgia and Jacksonville and Miami in Florida, before revisiting Jacksonville and Charleston again on our way back up the coast to Newport News to load for home.

The drinking age in the States was twenty-one, so as there was little chance of us getting in the bars our evening entertainment was a few beers on board the ship or a visit to a coffee bar or diner. This was a time when British beat groups were really taking off in the USA and we were forever asked if we were part of a group while we were out. In retrospect we could have exploited this if we'd tried. Everywhere we went people were friendly and welcoming, although we did cause a bit of stir in Miami when half a dozen of us in our new denim tuxedos decided to go ashore together and were stopped by a gun-wielding cop in a car who thought we were a new neighbourhood gang out looking for trouble. Luckily he soon realised his mistake and after chatting to us for a while wished us well and let us go on our way.

One of the good things about visiting the USA coast was that we came under their regulations in regard to fresh food entering the country, so that all the contents of our storerooms and fridges were condemned and replaced by fresh American produce. This meant that we were living on steaks and salads although the American bread was pretty rubbish, almost like eating cotton wool, a bit like the slimming bread Nimble.

The radio stations in the US were also very good. There were hundreds of stations so we could always find music we liked because, as I said earlier, a lot of it was British. In fact we were listening one day to a DJ raving about a new group that were near the top of the US charts called 'The Hullabaloos' who, according to the DJ, "Came all the way from Hull, England!"

Well, we'd never heard of them and we didn't find out until we returned home that they were a well known local group who played the dance halls and pubs in Hull called Ricky Knight and the Crusaders, who had been signed up for a record deal and had to change their name.

What we noticed about the USA in contrast to the UK was that everything appeared to be spread out. In some of the places like Savannah and Charleston there was evidence of older, what we would term Victorian style, properties but these tended to be in the run down and less salubrious districts close to the docks. Beyond this, apart from the central zones of the towns and cities, the buildings were laid out in blocks with wide roads like our modern out of town developments. There certainly didn't seem to be anything resembling the rows of terraced streets with tiny houses and outside toilets that we were used to in Hull.

When we left Miami and headed back north to Jacksonville a strange thing happened. We were all on deck on a lovely sunny afternoon without a breath of wind and with a flat, calm sea when we heard a roaring in the sky that got louder and louder. Looking up we noticed three bright lights in a perfect triangle in the sky on our port side that seemed to come straight out of the sky and then hover, very, very high in the sky, for several minutes before disappearing back into the heavens. The noise faded and then within seconds started to return and the three orbs again appeared, this time in the sky on our starboard. Again the lights and the noise faded to return seconds later directly above our heads. Whatever had shone those lights and made the noise had not directly travelled across the sky within sight of normal vision, and the speed that they were moving must have been tremendous to cover so much air space in so little time. We were stunned, shocked and searched for an explanation. We were very close to Cape Kennedy (Canaveral) and we wondered if the Americans were testing a new aircraft of some sort? Were they drones? Although to be fair we hadn't heard of drones then. Or were they – and I hate to say it, UFOs? We were actually in the vicinity of the Bermuda Triangle - could that have anything to do with it? You decide.

In Jacksonville we got a request from a car factory that challenged us to a football match. This was immediately taken up by the second mate who set himself up as our player-manager and coach. He must have been planning this as he was the only one on board who had brought football boots so he was a bit like the kid who owned the football always being the team captain, even though he was the worst player. I'm not much of a soccer player myself but I put myself down for the team as it looked like a bit of a laugh and a chance to socialise with some of the locals. Unfortunately the day before the match I was attempting to stop a runaway derrick when I suffered rope burns to my hands and across my stomach that needed treatment ashore, but it didn't stop me working on light duties. The burns were also superficial so I knew they wouldn't take long to heal. The next day I looked at the second mate's team list and noticed that I wasn't playing, so I went to see him.

"Why have you left me out of the team?" I asked.

"Because you're injured," he replied.

" Yes, but I can still play."

"No you can't, you're injured."

"Only my hand and stomach. Not my fucking feet!"

"I don't care, as far as I'm concerned you're injured and that's that. You can come and support us if you like?

Disgruntled I had to accept this and decided that I would go along to support the team and that would give me a chance to meet some of the American supporters.

A coach had been laid on for us that evening and we duly arrived at the soccer ground. No one on our team, apart from the second mate, had football boots nor did they have any proper kit just white T-shirts, or shirts and shorts of various colours. We piled out of the coach and joined in with the lads while they had a kick around as a warm up before the arrival of the opposing team who were getting changed in a pavilion. Then they came out. You would have thought they were a national side coming out of the tunnel at Wembley Stadium. Their kit, including boots, socks, shorts and shirts was pristine, all matching and co-ordinated, as was, as we soon found out, their playing tactics. They ran rings around our bunch of scruffs and no amount of our clogging and dirty play could suppress their playing superiority. By half time I was glad I wasn't playing and anyway had made contact with some of the opposing supporters of about my age and was enjoying socialising with them. Although we ended up losing, the evening had been a great success socially as we were treated to the usual American friendliness and hospitality.

Our final port in the USA was Newport News before we sailed for home, where we paid off on June 23rd in Manchester. I'd had my eighteenth birthday when in the USA so my plans were to take my bit of leave and then take my Efficient Deck Hand Certificate.

I'd been reading my Boatswain's Manual while away on the 'Tremorvah' and the other seamen had given me some coaching and advice. In fact I had a lot of advice, most of it contradictory, on what to expect and how to approach the examiner, who was noted for being strict and not having much of a sense of humour. Some said the examiner was a stickler for making sure that the ends of the strands on the wire rope used for the splicing demonstration were whipped with twine at all times (in practice you rarely bothered or used insulation tape). Some said he liked to see you in working gear so that you looked the part and were prepared to get dirty while doing any practical exercises. Others said he liked you to look smart as though you were going for an interview and so on. I decided that I would wear a blazer that I could take off and a pair of trousers that were reasonably smart but I wasn't bothered about if they got stained, and a shirt and tie.

The requirements for the EDH Certificate were that you had to have had twelve months' service at sea under articles, that you'd reached the age of eighteen and you had a steering certificate issued by the captain of the ship on which you'd served. I knew that I met all of these criteria and after visiting the Shipping Federation was given a day and a time to sit the examination, which was purely oral and practical. The examinations were held in the Board of Trade offices, where nearly all maritime examinations took place, on the top floor of the Burton's building on the corner of Whitefriargate in Hull.

I arrived early and eventually I was called in and asked by the examining officer a number of questions, mainly about lifeboats, swinging the lead, and boxing the compass. We then moved on to more practical work, like demonstrating some knots and hitches and answering questions on when and where they were best used. This was followed by having to reeve some guy falls and doing an eye splice in a rope. We then came to the wire splice, when the examiner said that he was leaving me while I did it and would be back shortly when he would want to see an example of a locking splice. I duly got to work remembering the advice on the whippings which, inevitably, slipped off and I was busy putting them on again, splice completed, when the examiner came back in. I felt sure he had noticed and thought, Oh shit!

After some questions about where the splice would be used - on derrick runners and other wires that may revolve - and where it would be safe to use a three, two, one splice, he asked a couple of more general questions and then, to my surprise, said that I had passed. Certificate number 63917, issued on June 30th 1965.

I was now an EDH.

Above. The "Tremorvah".

Above. Crew of the "Baltic Merchant", Jock, the singing motorman, extreme left, Ed, the boatswain, extreme right.

Below. A Soviet (Russian) icebreaker comes to our rescue while on passage to Leningrad (St Petersburg).

Chapter 16. Efficient Deck Hand.

I was now looking for my first ship as an EDH. Using my usual criteria of looking seriously for a job when I was down to my last fiver, it was with disappointment that I found that there were not that many jobs available to choose from. After a few days of being offered nothing I was in the Pool office when Claude Locke, the shipping officer, said that all he had was a Shell tanker. I said I didn't fancy it but was overheard by a few other seamen who were in there who had already agreed to sail on the tanker. I knew one of them, Mick Temple, who had been with me for the first couple of voyages on the 'Baltic Merchant' who said, "Come on Bob. Sign on with us and we'll have a laugh."

"I don't like Shell and I don't like oil tankers," I replied," You are always miles from anywhere, you don't get time in port and you never know when you will get back."

Claude Locke then came back with, "This one is a new ship on a regular run between Tranmere and Bonny in Nigeria and back. Regular as clockwork. Four weeks max. Do one trip and then shipping may have picked up here."

"There you are," said Mick.

"I'm still not sure," I said. "It's still a tanker and I've just met a new girlfriend and don't want to be away too long."

"But you heard him, four weeks max," said Mick.

"That's right," said Claude.

By now the others, who I soon found out were Mick Parkinson and Charlie Hoodless, started to join in saying, "Come with us and we'll all have a laugh, its only four weeks."

Finally I gave in and the next morning we all met at Paragon Station with our rail warrants for Liverpool. On our arrival there we went to the Pool office, where we were bungled into a taxi that took us through the Mersey tunnel to Birkenhead where we signed on, and then on to the ship berthed at Tranmere as it was due to sail as soon as we got on board.

As we approached Tranmere I looked at the various tankers berthed on their jetties looking for one that looked like the new tanker Claude had promised. Eventually the taxi pulled up alongside a large rusting old tanker that I faintly recognised. On the stern I could see in bold newish white letters the name 'Verconella' but underneath I could also see the outline of the original name of the ship, the 'San Gerado'. I did recognise the ship as I'd seen it under its original name in Rotterdam while on the

'Hindsia' and thought it a rust bucket then; so much for Claude's 'new ship'. But what about the rest of his promise? As soon as we got on board we were told to change into our working gear as we were sailing straight away, I asked where to and was told Bonny. So far so good but what I didn't know was this was the last we would see of Tranmere – we were on our way to Bonny but would not be coming back for a very long time.

On sailing we learned that the ship had had a full crew change in Tranmere that included the five EDHs from Hull, including me, George Gower from South Wales, Ted Sheringham from Wigan, a DHU (Deck Hand Uncertificated) from the Wirral, an ordinary seaman from North Wales, and an old AB called Ernie from Carlisle who we annoyed by calling him Geordie because of his accent. Amongst the stewards were Jimmy Cain from Liverpool, a lad from Doncaster named Bill, and our mess-steward called Alan. However, the crew list would change as the voyage progressed.

The st 'Verconella' was a typical tanker with a centre castle which housed the bridge and officers' accommodation, and at the stern was the engine room, galley, saloon and crew accommodation. The ship had at one time carried a foreign crew and there were signs that bunks had been removed from the cabins leaving us with a single cabin each with cabins to spare, so we had a choice. Storm doors from the main deck accessed the crew's accommodation, with the deck crew on the port side and the engine crew and catering staff on the starboard side. The two sets of cabins were linked by a recreation room at the forward end of the accommodation. The deck above our accommodation housed the engineering officers' cabins, officers' saloon, our mess-room and the galley. The deck officers' accommodation was in the centre castle where they also had a recreation room which housed the ship's library provided by a wonderful organisation called the Seafarers' Education Service, which also provided us with films that were shown once a week in our recreation room. Just aft of the centre castle was a small swimming pool, which was useful for cooling off in the scorching tropics.

The ship was six hundred and sixty feet long and weighed 31,465 GT, large by the standards of the day but tiny compared to modern super tankers. Our cargo, although we obviously sailed light from Tranmere, was crude oil. The ship, as mentioned earlier, had been built as the 'San Gerado' in 1958 at Birkenhead but had had her name changed to the 'Verconella' when the Eagle Oil Company had been taken over by Shell in 1964. For obvious reasons smoking was restricted on the ship to our accommodation and decks aft of the funnel which meant that you felt obliged to smoke as many cigarettes as possible during breaks, like three in a half hour smoko!

The voyage down to Bonny near Port Harcourt was uneventful. There was no shore leave in Bonny because we didn't moor up to a jetty and the oil was pumped aboard from floating pipelines while we remained at anchor in the Bonny river. However, our presence did attract lots of local interest as people in dugout canoes surrounded us. It was obvious that these people were living in poverty in what was an oil rich and potentially wealthy country. This raised some questions from amongst us and it was no surprise that some years later the area would be ravaged by civil war. At the moment though things there were peaceful although we had been told to keep vigilant watches due to the possibility of pirates and other people with criminal intentions getting aboard. For the most part the only people we saw were the ones in the canoes begging for anything they could get or selling local wares like fruit and wood carvings and the like, some were even selling their sisters. There was a little trade in the local wares done through buckets on ropes but no one got on board. Sometimes some of the crew would toss items to the young lads on the canoes who would dive in for them, although we noticed that they were in and out of the water so quickly that they barely got wet. This got us speculating about what was in the water to make them so skittish.

At this point we still expected to return to Tranmere from Bonny but before we left we learned there had been a change of orders and we were to take our cargo to La Plata near Buenos Aires. So from the tropical Nigeria we crossed the Atlantic to a cold and damp Argentina in winter.

Winter or not we decided to brave the damp and cold to sample the delights of La Plata. Tankers always tie up miles from anywhere but this didn't deter us either, after all we had been over a month at sea without setting foot on dry land. Our first thoughts were that La Plata was closed as everything seemed shut down but eventually we came to a bar cum restaurant cum - er, decide for yourself. In true sailor fashion it was a case of the first bar would do but this one, although we seemed to be the only customers, served not only cheap drinks but also food and what is Argentina famed for? Steaks! So we ordered steak and chips to be washed down with whatever we were drinking. Soon we were each presented with a platter with an enormous slab of meat on it. What a disappointment as we all agreed that it was the toughest steak we had ever attempted to eat. It was a good job that none of us had false teeth. We decided that the Argentines must export all the best quality meat and keep the rubbish for domestic consumption and then settled down to some serious drinking.

Apart from the barman there were no other customers in the bar at first but soon we noticed a dark haired lady of indeterminate age propping up the bar and looking our way. I wouldn't say that she was ugly because it was hard to tell through the thick layer of make up that she wore offset by the bright red lipstick that exaggerated her mouth, but it's a good bet that she was. After a while, with a sway that was more pronounced than a first trip fisherman's Hessle Road version of a Western Ocean roll, she walked over and plonked herself down at the end of our table. To be fair none of us was much interested at first but chatted to her politely. Before long she started to talk 'business' and again we didn't show much interest as it was early in the evening and the price was too high. As the night progressed though, the beer goggles began to make our surroundings and company more acceptable and in addition, the price kept getting lower. It was also apparent that we seemed to be in a one-whore town. As the alcohol waved its magic wand our female companion, who probably looked like an average middle-aged Latin woman with too much make-up on, transformed into a vision of youthful beauty to rival Sophia Loren. On top of that the price had now come down to only a pound which, I felt, was close to a bargain, so I accepted the deal. I'd had no previous experience of the 'ladies of the night' so this was to be enlightening for me, a part of my continuing education so to speak, or so I thought. It was certainly that all right.

She took me to a room across the courtyard behind the bar. This was where she plied her trade; this was her workshop. It contained only a bed covered by a grubby blanket; a bedside table with a jug and a wash bowl, and above the bed was shining a dim red light. Now it was time to get down to business but it was obvious that there would not be any finesse about the deed, no foreplay, no small talk, no caressing, just straight down to the deed, which for my part I now didn't fancy and was finding it difficult, to shall we say, meet expectations.

Back in the bar Mick Temple noticed that I'd gone missing. "Anybody seen Bob?" he asked. He was answered by Taffy, the ordinary seaman who said, "I know where he is, I saw him going into a room with that woman, I can show you."

A few minutes later I was lying on the bed on top of the woman and just about to try and take up a position when she let out a piercing yell, shouting, "Get out, get out!"

I wondered what I'd done. Had I got the wrong hole? But then I looked over my shoulder to see several faces along the end of the bed. The bastards had stolen in to watch. She shooed them out of the door and we again began to align positions. Suddenly she again let out another yell, threw me off like a dog with a rat and started screaming at my drunken colleagues who had crept back in. This completely did for me; there was no way I could rise to the occasion now. A true Yorkshireman would have asked for his money back but instead, riddled with guilt and some shame, I ventured back to the bar, not so much to drown my sorrows but more to try and forget what had just happened. The rest of the lads thought it was a huge joke of course and after a while one or two of them went on to sample the delights of our female friend and I think George Gower negotiated to stay with her for the rest of the night.

After our one night ashore adventure in La Plata we sailed across the river Plate to Montevideo in Uruguay for bunkers, before heading back to Bonny again to load another cargo of crude oil.

While loading at Bonny we were subjected to the usual requests for trade from the people in the canoes milling around the stern of the ship. Only this time George Gower managed to smuggle one of the girls to his cabin. I've no idea how he managed this due to the supposedly vigilant lookouts that were posted around the ship whose only task was to prevent unwanted boarders. George's mistake was that he accomplished this act shortly before we were due to sail, so the ship was held up as he refused to open his cabin door. We'd warned him first to try to avoid him getting into trouble but he was obviously too busy to listen to us. Then the boatswain tried. The apprentices and the mate appeared only to receive muffled, impolite requests to go away from inside the cabin.

Finally the captain himself, a small wiry man, appeared and started jumping up and down while hammering on the door shouting, "Open up Gower, I order you, open up and get that woman off the ship! I am the captain! Open the door!"

After a few minutes of this the door was flung open and the half-naked girl made a dash for it. Like greased lightening she legged it out of the accommodation door and slid down a rope into a waiting canoe.

We left Bonny straight away. The ship used an automatic pilot for steering while in the open sea but close to the coast, or during pilot assisted passages, the ship was hand steered, so it was that after leaving Bonny I took my turn at the wheel. The captain was on the bridge still complaining about George Gower to the second mate.

"A disgrace, the man's a disgrace!" he kept saying. "How could he do that with that woman? Did you see her? It doesn't bear thinking about. How could he? How could any man go with a woman like that?"

It was time to change course so he kept quiet for a while before continuing.

"Did you see her? That girl that Gower had in his cabin; I don't know what to think although she wasn't too bad looking."

Another course change and a lapse of silence led to the captain saying to the second mate, "You know what? That young girl that Gower was with was quite pretty." It was obvious to all of us on the bridge who had been listening to this contradictory monologue that the girl had made quite an impression on our captain, but not enough to stop him logging George a day's pay the next morning.

Anyway we were now heading in the right direction that we all hoped would lead back to Tranmere but we hoped wrong, our orders were to take our cargo to

Hamburg before taking the ship to dry dock in Greece. We all felt the disappointment but this was the life on a tanker, never knowing when you would get a change of orders and never knowing when you would return home. The boatswain, a kindly, elderly Scotsman, was one of the few, apart from the officers, company men on board the ship who told us that one of the advantages of signing a company contract was that they relieved you and flew you home after twelve months away. Twelve months was considered good! Things were not looking good at all.

Passing through the Bay of Biscay one of our crew, an AB from Hull called Eric, slipped on the deck and fell onto one of the numerous pipes that criss-crossed it, badly hurting his back. His injury was so bad that he was confined to the ship's hospital because he could not move. The captain made the decision to have him put ashore and the nearest place in the UK that we would pass was Penzance. Of course there were a few people who thought that he was feigning his injury in order to get off the ship but I don't think that this was the case. So it was that on a beautiful late summer's day we dodged closely off the beach at Penzance while our crew mate was lowered on a stretcher into the waiting lifeboat. I looked longingly at the beach and the people on it and it did cross my mind that the shore looked close enough to swim to with perhaps a few belongings in a plastic bag to aid buoyancy. But with the sudden ringing of a bell down in the engine room and the corresponding roar of the engines and the swirling of the water around the screw, I realised I was too late for a great escape this time but it had got me thinking of other ways that could get me off this ship.

A year earlier, on board the 'Brighton', I'd shared a cabin with a boyhood friend of mine, Johnny Sawden. In the cabin was a chest of drawers that had a pull out shelf that made a writing desk, quite a common piece of furniture on ships and in fact there was one in each cabin on the 'Verconella'. One day on the "Brighton" I'd been for a shower and was combing my hair in the mirror above the chest of drawers when my towel slipped and I pressed forward with my body to catch it. Unfortunately for me the writing desk shelf must have been sticking out a little and the force of my body pushed it in, trapping my foreskin. If you've ever done this with a trouser zip you will understand the pain. I let out a mighty yell asking Johnny to free me. Johnny of course couldn't do anything for laughing but eventually, after a bit too long if you ask me, he came and freed me. Johnny then said, "You've only got one ball, Rusty (a mutual friend from childhood) was like that but he had an operation."

I had thought that there was something not quite right in the 'tween decks' but had been too embarrassed to broach the subject. Was it natural? After all I'd had numerous medicals and it had never been mentioned, and I certainly seemed to be functioning all right physically and I didn't have a high-pitched voice. I could vaguely remember that one time my dad had had a bath with me, something very out of the ordinary, and then my mum had taken me to the doctor and him saying something like, "With time, these things sometimes correct themselves." With this reassurance my parents must have thought, that's that then, and thought no more about it. So now it seemed was the time for me to try and sort it out.

In Hamburg I asked to see a doctor. The doctor spoke very good English and gave me an examination stating that it looked like I had an undescended testicle. He went on to say that this could sometimes be cured with a simple operation and that he would recommend that I be sent home to the UK. Result! He asked me when the ship was due to sail and I said, that night.

"Where's your next port of call?" he asked.

"Greece," I replied.

"That's not too far, I'll recommend that you're sent home from there," said the doctor.

I should have asked him to send me home from Hamburg but because we were already a man down, I could see his point that Greece wasn't too far. Mistake! In the meantime, happy with what I'd heard, I asked the taxi driver to drop me off at the bar where some of my mates were having drink. It was time to celebrate.

Life on a tanker was much different to that on a dry cargo vessel. In those days when a freighter docked to load or unload, the chances were that you'd be tied up for several days, watches would be stood down, a night watchman appointed and the rest of the crew would be on day work with evenings and sometimes weekends, or parts of the weekend free. On tankers loading and discharging could be accomplished in hours and rarely lasted more than a day - on the 'Verconella' it was usually about twelve hours - with the consequence that watches would not be broken and the crew would be expected to work through. You could of course go ashore once your watch was complete but you were expected to be back on board for your next stint. So, for example, if you were on the eight to twelve watch you could go ashore after mid-day but you would be expected to be back on board for eight o'clock at night. Bear in mind that you were expected to adhere to this rule even though you may have not set foot on shore for weeks. In our case, we'd not set foot on shore since our night in La Plata, which must have been over five weeks previously. It was tempting therefore, to miss a watch and stay ashore as long as possible even though this meant risking a fine, or forfeiting half a day or a day's pay (lost completely) or being logged a day's pay (cancelled at a later date at the captain's discretion) – and some of us felt that sometimes it was worth it!

So it was that I joined the others in the bar in Hamburg, had a few beers and then a few more and got back to the ship in time to sail but had missed my early evening watch. Next morning, along with several others we received our forfeits and loggings and went back to work as we made our way to dry dock in a place called Scaramanga near Athens in Greece. On our way to Greece we had to make the tanks gas free and clean them by lowering hoses with rotating heads that sprayed hot water on the tank sides. When the tanks were considered gas free and the hoses had finished their work we would go down and check and clear any build ups of oil residue in the bottom by using hand shovels and buckets. This was a dirty and unpleasant job but one that we would have to do several times while on the 'Verconella'. One thing we noticed was that if we started singing the boatswain would tell us to come back up thinking that there was still gas down there and it was effecting our heads. We would just want to get the job over with, so in the end worked mainly in silence.

Scaramanga is situated in a large bay near to Athens and consisted mainly of a large shipyard owned by the Greek shipping tycoon Niarcos. Outside the gates of the shipyard was a line of bars looking for clientele from the ships and the shipyard workers. A little further around the bay were more bars and restaurants that were close to the beaches used by holidaymakers. In those days international holidays were not as popular as they are now so these beaches never seemed that busy with most tourists sticking to the sights of Athens and other developing ancient Greek attractions. Our stay in Greece would be about three weeks and the main attraction turned out to be the Daphne wine festive – pay your entrance fee and drink as much as you like! What an invitation!

I didn't expect to be sampling any of these attractions because the good doctor had given me a letter for the captain instructing him to send me home. So, soon after we docked, I went to see the captain and asked him when I would be sent home.

"What do you mean?" he said.

"I gave you a letter from the doctor in Hamburg saying I should be flown home," I said.

"I'm not sending you home, you're not ill," he said.

"But the doctor said I should have medical attention as soon as possible," I insisted.

"You were not that ill that you couldn't go to a bar and get drunk!"

He was getting angry now.

"You can't be ill in the morning and drunk in the afternoon! Get out! That's the end of it!"

What right had he to say that? What was his medical knowledge? I may not have had a deadly disease, I may not have been incapacitated, but I certainly needed medical attention to offset the psychological impact of my predicament. The captain may have been angry but not as angry as I was. I was seething. The little bastard and there was nothing I could do about it. I was stuck on this crap ship that I should have only been on for a month. I hated him. I hated Shell. How I regretted not insisting that the doctor send me home from Hamburg. Eventually the resentment and stress took its toll and I flipped. The mate, a guy called Thompson, made a comment that I took exception to, although in hindsight he was correct to do so, and I just flipped and burst into his cabin to remonstrate with him. I was pretty drunk on wine from the Daphne wine festival and he soon bungled me out of his cabin and I was dragged away by Mick Temple who took me back to my cabin where we were joined by Mick Parkinson. Of course they showed a great deal of sympathy and empathy.

"What the fuck do you think you're doing? Why are you acting like a c**t? You're lucky the mate didn't flatten you because I would have done!"

I was wrong to take out my frustrations and angst on Mr Thompson, it wasn't his fault and the man hadn't done anything previously to warrant my behaviour. On the contrary, when I'd been on watch with him he'd often chatted to me. He also used the ship's library and had noticed that I also borrowed books and he would discuss these with me. He was a good man.

The next morning I was duly called to the captain's cabin for whatever punishment he would feel appropriate. In the back of my mind I had the feeling that he would send me home after all as I was too much trouble. Although this would mean a bad discharge, at least I'd be able to get my medical problem sorted out. However again I'd got this wrong. Instead Mr Thompson said I should be treated with leniency because I obviously had problems and issues otherwise I wouldn't have acted out of character and that he didn't want any action taken other than we put the matter behind us, and he would accept a simple apology. I told you he was a good man.

After this incident I resolved to accept my fate and complete the voyage but first we had the rest of our stay in Greece. We were in the shipyard in Greece for about three weeks I think, certainly for two weekends as the shipyard went to the trouble of providing us with coach trips to see some of the sights of Ancient Greece including the spectacular Corinth Canal. While most of us appreciated this kind gesture as it provided us with something different to 'the first bar syndrome' it wasn't to everyone's taste. I asked one of the greasers, Paddy, if he was coming with us on the second Sunday and he said, "No. I see enough bombed buildings at home without looking at theirs!" It was good to see culture appreciated.

I also managed a trip to Athens on the bus to visit the Acropolis. My watch mate, Ted Sheringham, came with me but gave up halfway up the hill and camped out in a café until I got back. One of the bars on the beach, a little further from the ship, also seemed to adopt us and would treat us to a different local dish each night we visited. This made a change from the food on the ship as we tucked into fresh octopus, squid and other local fish cooked in a variety of very tasty ways.

Inevitably our last call of the night when returning to the ship was to the first bar outside the gates and this was to be our downfall.

One night we all ended up in this bar for our final few drinks of the evening. The bar was quite full. Inside were some seamen from a Swedish ship; we were sitting outside, as were some seamen from a West African ship. To this day I don't know what happened, only that there were some words exchanged in the toilet between some of our crew and the West Africans that led to a brawl that would not have looked out of place in a Hollywood western. What started as a skirmish spread through the bar and eventually involved everyone using the outside seating. Tables were overturned and chairs became weapons. One of the African seamen was knocked flying through one of the large plate glass windows that fronted the bar and landed at the feet of a giant Swedish seaman sitting inside the bar who looked down, picked him up and threw him through another window. The West Africans decided enough was enough and legged it out of the bar with us in pursuit. They ran through the gates of the shipyard and back to their ship. This was the sensible thing to do. We watched them run off and then went back to the bar to finish our beer. What did we expect? We sat down and then realised that some of us were bleeding. I had a small cut above my eye and a cut wrist that the bar owner very kindly bandaged up for me, but his kindness only went so far. The police scrambled out of about five or six cars about twenty minutes later and we were promptly arrested and taken to a police station where we were threatened with the cells overnight. Instead they released us in the early hours and we returned to the ship thinking that was that. But it wasn't! Two days later, the captain was visited by the police with the ship's agent saying that we would all be in court unless we paid damages to the bar owner. We said this wasn't fair as we hadn't caused the trouble, what about the seamen on the other ship? Unfortunately for us the other ship had already sailed leaving us as the only people who could be liable. We felt aggrieved and debated going to court and fighting the case but decided that we would probably lose, so agreed to pay the damages thinking that it wouldn't be a lot. We were then presented with the bill. We were each (about six of us) to pay twenty-seven pounds, seven shillings and six pence to cover the costs of two plate glass windows, seven chairs, five tables and replace broken glasses! We thought we were paying damages not paying for a complete refurbishment! This was over two weeks' wages. The captain, who had taken umbrage about a comment made by the agent, then said that he was about to be relieved but if he was staying he would have helped us fight the case but, in the circumstances, he was grateful (not that grateful incidentally to send me home) that we'd decided to settle the issue amicably.

The captain left the ship just before we sailed from Greece. The new captain was called R.S. Walker, a big man who would stomp along the catwalk from the bridge to the saloon with his legs splayed below his enormous belly like a modern day Henry VIII. He also let it be known that he'd worked his way up "through the forecastle," so knew all the tricks. Later in the voyage he'd sometimes have special meals sent up to him in his cabin and the steward showed us the platter that contained a mound of fried rice surrounded by steaks. No wonder the bloke looked like a heart attack waiting to happen.

We knew we wouldn't be going home from Greece without a cargo and we were not surprised when our orders were to proceed through the Suez Canal to load crude oil in the Persian Gulf. Later we were informed that we'd be taking the oil to Geelong in Australia and that this could be our regular run for the next few months.

I hadn't had a haircut since we'd left England and my hair was now shoulder length. Some of the lads said that it would be really hot in the Red Sea and Persian Gulf and that I'd suffer greatly with the heat if I didn't have it cut. Somewhere at the beginning or the end of the canal we were boarded by the usual Egyptian tradesmen plying their wares and one was the barber who could impersonate any British accent when shouting his call, "Want 'aircut?" So I employed his services and had it all cut off and consequently suffered greatly with the heat, as I no longer had my hair to shade and insulate me from the hot desert sun. We also had a bum-boat on board in Suez so I bought myself a little Japanese radio for some entertainment in my cabin, well more like to pass some time trying to find a short wave station where English was spoken and didn't fade out at crucial points. I already had a radio at home but because I'd been told I'd only be away about four weeks, I'd chosen to travel light.

The ship left Suez and we entered the calm, blue Red Sea. The outside temperature was hot but the 'Verconella' had air-conditioning, which meant that for the most part the accommodation was cool and it was possible to sleep with bedclothes on. Except that the air-conditioning was prone to break down so that there were times when you woke up during the night fighting with sodden sheets, gasping for air and searching for a wind chute to hang out the porthole.

The working set up on this ship was that we were split into three watches. On the open sea when the ship was steered by the automatic pilot - iron mike - there were two on a watch with one on lookout, usually the wing of the bridge or monkey island on top of the bridge, and one on standby (sitting about drinking tea and reading mostly) in the accommodation. During times when the ship was hand-steered, near coasts and in pilotage areas, there would be three on a watch. If you were not required on watch you became a day worker and when on watch you may also have been called on to do three or four hours overtime. For example, eight to twelve watch keepers would also work one to four or five as overtime, twelve to four would work nine until twelve in the morning etc. This was a way of making up your wages to something really worth having, although overtime in different ships was varied and often at the whim of the captain and chief officer.

I was on the twelve to four, graveyard watch, when I was called about fifteen minutes before midnight for my watch by the DHU from the Wirral, I think his name was Steve. I was a bit miffed as even though I'd only had about three hours sleep I liked to be called half an hour before my watch so that I could get a wash, have a coffee and wake up before going up to the bridge to relieve the lookout but I didn't think any more about it, did my watch with Ted Sheringham and turned in just after four in the morning. At that time we were well on our way and had almost completed our transit through the Red Sea.

The next morning I was called just after eight for breakfast and to do some overtime and I was also asked if I'd seen the DHU Steve. I said no but suggested they tried the mess-steward's cabin as he would often talk to him. At half past eight the boatswain came and asked me when I'd last seen Steve as he had not turned up for his watch and no one could find him. I said that he had called me at quarter to twelve and, as far as I knew, he went back to his cabin. We then went to his cabin and noted that his bed had not been slept in and that he'd been in the process of writing a letter home. The pad and pen were still on his writing desk, as were the ashes of a cigarette that had been left burning in his ashtray. The last words of the letter said something like, "I'm not feeling too good and just going up on deck for some fresh air."

All hands were then called to search the ship for him but there was no sign. The captain then ordered the ship to be turned around on her course and lookouts were posted as we sailed back through the Red Sea. We sailed back for eight hours, about the time from when he was reported missing to the last sighting of him, which was by me at a quarter to midnight. The search, in daylight and perfect sea conditions, proved fruitless; there was no sign of him. The consensus was that he had gone up on deck and fallen overboard although the captain pointed out that the ship's rails were designed so that you couldn't accidentally fall overboard. But in saying that there were gaps in the ship's rails to allow for mooring ropes, so if he had stumbled he could have slipped through there. Whatever happened he was lost at sea and even though the Red Sea is warm, the chances of him surviving had been slim. He may have been sucked into the blades of the propeller; sharks may have got him, or even both. The atmosphere on the ship became very sombre as we again turned around and continued on our journey.

Above. Mules in the locks on the Panama Canal.

Below. The Shell tanker "Verconella".

Chapter 17. A Tankerman's Life.

The Persian Gulf was even hotter than the Red Sea and the Suez Canal and this was when we really valued the air-conditioning, when it was working. Our first port of call was Bahrain but it didn't matter which port we went to in the Persian Gulf as they all looked basically the same; a long jetty sticking out into the sea from the desert. There was no shore leave as there was nowhere to go, unless you needed to visit a doctor or a dentist when you'd be taken by taxi to the nearest town. I went to the doctor to see if I could swing an early passage home based on my Hamburg experience but the Arabian doctor didn't see the urgency. I also mentioned that I was suffering from constipation and he suggested more roughage and vegetables but also said beer was also supposed to be good for relieving the condition. I was quite surprised about receiving this advice from a Muslim and it immediately raised my interest but he pre-empted me by saying, "No, I will not give you a prescription for it."

Our beer on the ship was rationed to six cans on a Wednesday and six cans on a Saturday but we would save our Wednesday ration so that we could have a decent drink at the weekend. This was usually a piss-up in a cabin that led to a sing-song. We had a couple of singers on board, Mick Temple who I'd sailed with before had a repertoire of bawdy sea shanties, and a steward from Liverpool called Jimmy Cain, who also had a good line in bawdy songs once he'd had enough to drink. We all generally had a good laugh during these drinking sessions although one of Jimmy's songs was, for me, upsetting although I didn't let it show.

The song went:

My name is Sammy Hall, Sammy Hall,

My name is Sammy Hall. Sammy Hall,

My name is Sammy Hall and I've only got one…

You can guess the rest!

It took over three weeks to run from the Persian Gulf to Geelong where we got a night in port but only because the pilots refused to navigate the ship in the dark. We arrived there on October 28th 1965, I know this because we were issued with Australian seaman's identification cards as we'd be making regular visits to the country. Even the night in port was not much to look forward to as we didn't break watches and although Geelong was, for Australia, a fairly large industrial city of 100,000 people, there still didn't seem much to do. There were bars that we could

189

visit if we got the chance but, at that time, the pubs in Australia closed at six in the evening leading to an event called the 'six o'clock swill'. This meant that people leaving work would dive into the bars on their way home and drink as much as they could before the pub closed. I say pub but these bars had only one function and that was to serve beer through what looked like small petrol pumps, a kind of small hose with a gun on the end that pumped cold lager into glasses called schooners. Most of the bars had rooms with walls covered with green tiles, which made you think you were actually drinking in a Victorian toilet, and you almost expected to see urinals in the corner.

Life on the tanker was also very boring. There were no satellite communication systems then nor were there things like mobile telephones and wi-fi. News of what was happening in the world or back home came by means of our short wave radios and the fading in and out signals of the BBC World Service and the Voice of America, which always seemed to be on the air. Occasionally we'd get our hands on an out of date International Daily Mirror that we'd read from front to back and from back to front. Nowadays papers are flown all over the world and the latest you get them is the next day but then there were not the air services that we have today, so the Daily Mirror and some other national newspapers would staple together the whole week of its copies into one package and send it out for international sale.

Personal communications were generally confined to the medium of the letter. In emergencies it was possible to contact relatives by telegram, which could be used to wish loved ones happy birthday or for correspondence of a more urgent matter such as bereavements or the birth of children. The radio telephone (RT) was rarely used other than when the captain needed to contact the shipping company. So generally we contented ourselves with letters. Writing them in our spare time and looking forward to receiving them at the next port, when the letters from loved ones would be devoured and re-read time and again during the voyage, even though often they contained nothing much more than the details of the mundane daily rituals that we were all missing. Sometimes though they could be very frustrating especially if they involved anything resembling a discussion. If we received a letter in the Persian Gulf we could not send a reply until we docked in Geelong over three weeks later then, if we were lucky, we'd receive a reply to that letter over three weeks later when back in the Persian Gulf, and so on. You can imagine what anguish this could cause especially if you received the letter that all seamen dreaded: the Dear John.

This happened to me on this ship as a girl I'd been taking out before sailing on the 'Verconella' took umbrage when I made a comment in a letter about her going out. I fully understood her point of view and I accepted that I'd been completely unreasonable in my expectations but having it spelled out in a letter that we were finished was still hard to take. I had first met this girl in the summer of 1963, when I was with a friend who knew her, as she crossed Whitefriargate and returned to her job in accounts at 'Burtons the Tailors'. I remember I was attracted to her because she was so pretty, but I didn't have the courage to ask her out then. However, at the time I also felt that she was attracted to me as she gave me a 'look', although this could have been simply because she was squinting because the sun was in her eyes. The next time I met her was while I was on leave from the 'Tremorvah', prior to signing on the 'Verconella'. It was at an open night at Hull College, where I was with a friend who did his part-time day release there, and she was also visiting a friend who studied there. She looked even more beautiful than I remembered walking down the street with her long hair, parted in the middle, catching the evening sun. This time though I didn't hesitate in asking her out and we spent as much time as we could together during my leave. I really felt she was the 'one' and expected a long-term relationship. I still continued to write to her after receiving the "Dear John," and every time we received our mail I looked desperately for her handwriting on the envelope, but sadly, I was always disappointed.

However, it must have been much worse for married men. Charlie, a bloke in his thirties who was one of the guys that had persuaded me to join the 'Verconella' because it was supposed to be a short trip, was a case in point. Charlie's wife had been several months pregnant when we'd left the UK and he'd expected to be back for the birth, but on our way to or from Geelong he received the message that his child had been born and it hit him hard. Charlie wanted to be home with his wife and family so he hatched a plan to get sent home. Unfortunately this turned out to be wrong in so many ways; his plan was to get paid off insane.

We must have been on our way back from Geelong and approaching the Persian Gulf again when he started his campaign by going on lookout dressed in a duffle-coat. This may have been sensible in the Baltic in winter but not in the Persian Gulf with temperatures somewhere between 30° and 40° degrees centigrade. He kept this up for a short while and then collapsed on the wing of the bridge. The captain was called and Charlie was hauled to his feet. Captain Walker was a wily old salt and was immediately suspicious of Charlie's behaviour so he said that Charlie, who was still acting groggy, should go back to his cabin for a rest and helped the staggering Charlie towards the bridge ladder. As they approached the ladder the captain gave Charlie a push and Charlie responded by catching himself on the handrail. This was part of Captain Walker's process of medical examination as if Charlie was really on the verge of collapse he would not have been able to save himself and would have crashed down the stairs to the deck below. It wasn't quite 'ducking stool justice', but close.

Charlie then swung things back his way by grasping the captain's arm and staring at our accommodation door while saying, "Don't send me back there! Don't send me there! They will throw me over the side like they did the lad from Birkenhead!" The captain, though he was still suspicious, knew he had to act on this accusation, so instead of sending Charlie to his cabin he ordered that he should be taken to the ship's hospital and kept there under observation on a liquid only diet. I read later in a ship's medical book for captains, that if in doubt about anyone claiming an illness, just put them in the hospital on a liquid diet and if they are still there three days later then they are genuinely ill.

The captain then started to call each of us in turn to his cabin where we were questioned about Charlie's allegation. Charlie then changed his story and claimed only a couple of the crew were involved. The whole scenario was ridiculous, we all knew it and the captain knew it. However, he still had to complete an investigation that led to the conclusion that there was no evidence of foul play and no further action was needed. After a couple of days of starvation in the hospital, Charlie returned to the accommodation but, as you can guess, he wasn't very popular. His next ploy was to claim, by sign language, that he had lost his voice. While he was not forgiven for his ridiculous accusations this latest antic caused us great amusement as we threw ourselves into an all day and all night game of charades.

"What am I? A teapot!" and "What am I? A tram!", were quite tame efforts in our attempts to mime our daily activities. However Charlie soon found his voice when he called me for my watch one night. I looked up from my bunk to watch his elaborate mime which attempted to inform me that it was time for me to get up and relieve him and then I said, "What the fuck is that? That's not a call!" Then rolled over as though I was going back to sleep.

"Half past eleven, tea's made," said Charlie. The game was over.

Our main source of oil was the Persian Gulf where we visited, at different times, Bahrain, Mena Al Ahmadi, Kargh Island, Kuwait, Abu Dhabi, and Abadan. There was no excitement or shore leave to look forward to on our visits there so any distractions were always worth it. One of these was being caught in a sandstorm. I've been in many storms at sea but this one was unique. We couldn't see a thing as the high winds whipped up the sands of the desert and blew it in our path, landing on the decks like gritty snow. We had a pilot on board as we were heading for port and, as it happened, I was on the wheel when the pilot, after lifting his head up from one of the radars said, "Starboard easy."

Immediately Captain Walker, who was on the bridge and looking at another radar, then said, "No, port easy!"

There then followed a short argument between the pilot and the captain which ended when the captain said, "I'm the captain, I'm in charge and I'm saying go to port!" He then turned to me and said again, "Port easy."

I turned the wheel and the ship turned to port. "Steady as she goes," said the captain.

There was a short silence and then a crunch and a grinding noise as the ship came to a stop on what was obviously a sandbank. "I told you the channel was to starboard," said the pilot.

Trying to get the ship off the bank by going astern didn't work but it wasn't long before one of the tugs standing by to assist us to our berth appeared out of the sand and with its help we re-floated quite easily. Needless to say Captain Walker kept his mouth shut from that point on as the pilot guided us safely to our moorings.

The only other excitement that I remember from the Persian Gulf was when I was asked a couple of times to change the feature films that were provided by the Seafarers' Education Service. This meant collecting the metal cases containing the reels of film, and wheeling them a mile or so down the jetty in the boiling hot sun to a depot where they could be exchanged for other boxes containing films. The number of films in a box depended on the number of reels for each film, usually three reels but could be more for 'epics', so normally with two boxes we would expect four or five films. We all looked forward to watching films so selecting boxes that contained films that reflected all tastes, or as near as possible, was important. The films were quite up to date but the favourites amongst the crew were the usual war films, adventure stories and westerns, but the boxes would often contain a mixture of genres. Generally my choices went down well but I remember that a very modern film called 'The Knack' got mixed reviews with some loving it and some hating it. I also got a bit of criticism for borrowing 'Lawrence of Arabia' especially when the air-conditioning broke down while it was being screened with outside temperatures of about 40° centigrade.

While we'd been told that the our regular run would be from the Persian Gulf to Geelong there were variations to this as changes of orders happened quite regularly, often with rumours that we were going home which were without foundation. There was also a rumour that we were to take a load of oil up the Mekong river in Vietnam. We were briefed that if this was so our time on deck would be limited so as not to be targets for snipers, and that we'd get double pay while in the war zone, but thankfully this change of orders didn't happen.

One change of orders that did happen though meant that on one trip we loaded up in the Persian Gulf and discharged half our oil in Bombay (Mumbai), India, before moving up the coast to unload the other half in Karachi, Pakistan. This happened just after the two countries had been at war but I'm sure it wasn't to maintain good international relations that Shell chose to provide both sides. Again we were required to work watches so there was little time to visit these ports but we worked time off between us so that a few managed to experience the delights of Mumbai and some of us got a run ashore in Karachi. Being in a Muslim country Karachi was dry except for bars in hotels, where the prices for beer were quite high, but it made a change to be able to stretch our legs and walk around the city. Karachi was bustling with street vendors peddling their wares. The roads were also quite busy with vehicles of various kinds, mainly animal driven. Most of the vehicles looked like they needed repairs with many on their last legs particularly those pulled by donkeys and horses; to own a bicycle here was considered a sign of wealth. They were supposed to drive on the left but they also seemed to sometimes drive on the right but mostly drove up the middle of the road. What struck me and what stayed with me was the extreme poverty of many of the people, clearly visible by the number of beggars on the streets and whole families homeless and living with their meagre belongings at the roadside. It was quite shocking.

After this change of routine it was back to the Gulf to load a full cargo for Geelong. After leaving Geelong we headed back towards the Gulf but again we were given a change of orders and told to proceed to Indonesia instead.

Indonesia and the Malacca Straits were areas noted for piracy so again we were given warnings and told to be more vigilant than usual, especially while at anchor and awaiting orders. Eventually we were told to go to Palau Sambu, a small island in Indonesia close to Singapore, to load wax - a kind of very thick crude oil that had to be kept warm to keep it fluid - for Sydney. We arrived in Pulau Sambu on December 24th 1965, Christmas Eve. Of course we felt that we had to take any opportunity for a run ashore that we could, so a few of us decided to venture forth and see what we could find. Not a lot as it turned out but eventually we found what resembled a kind of bar in a clearing in the jungle and sat ourselves down to enjoy a few cold beers in the equatorial heat. We each in turn bought a round of drinks using British currency, which the barmen took with no problems but gave us change in local currency. The problem for us was that when we tried to buy a round with this local currency the barmen wouldn't take it, he only wanted pounds sterling! We started to argue and ask what we were expected to do with this local currency. After much shoulder shrugging and other negative hand gestures the barmen, who may have also realised that they were outnumbered by a visibly irate bunch of foreign sailors, said that we could exchange the money for brandy. This seemed a good deal for us so we handed over all our change and waited for the brandy. There couldn't have been a lot of money so we only expected a bottle of brandy at best but were amazed when the barmen appeared with two packs of six bottles tied together with string. We couldn't believe our luck as we ambled back to the ship.

We got some idea of what the wax was like to work with when, as we were disconnecting the loading pipes from the ship's flanges, we had a spillage. The wax immediately solidified into a mass of thick black jelly on the deck that we had to slice up and shovel over the side after we sailed that night. It was Christmas Eve so we decided to continue our little drinking session and began eyeing up the brandy. Eventually we cracked open a bottle. It was foul. Someone put a match to some in an ashtray and it ignited immediately with a flash and a blue flame. We concluded that it was wood alcohol and that we'd been done. No wonder they had given us a dozen bottles. Then the second cook suggested using the brandy to make a punch and went off and returned with a massive metal pan into which we poured all the 'brandy', followed by several cans of Coke. He then took this off to the handling room, which was really a big walk-in fridge, where he added fruit juice and any bit of fruit he could find, and left it there until Christmas night when it was dragged out for us to try. We eyed it with some suspicion before one of us dared to try it. It was delicious and we all had a very Merry Christmas.

Chapter 18. Homeward Bound.

After leaving Pulau Sambu we sailed through the islands of Indonesia and then picked up a pilot off Thursday Island. The pilot guided us through the Great Barrier Reef off the east coast of Australia and down to Sydney. We were then told that they didn't want us in Sydney until early January so we had to steam dead slow for the most part of the passage. Of course we had all been looking forward to arriving in Sydney with the promise of a run ashore in a proper city as we'd now been away for six months but, once again, our luck wasn't in. This was because the Australian authorities insisted that once wax had been discharged the tanks on the ship had to be cleaned and the dirty water pumped ashore for processing, rather than doing the job at sea and pumping the waste into the sea as we'd done previously. This meant that the mate needed a team to attend to this work as it meant dropping large pipes with rotating heads spraying hot water down the tanks, ten feet at a time, every twenty minutes until the bottom of each individual tank was reached. Even then there would be some sludge left at the bottom of the tank that had to be removed by hand using buckets and small shovels. Access to the bottom of the tanks was through a manhole and a long climb down a steel ladder on the side of the tank. Obviously volunteers for this work would not be forthcoming given the delights of Sydney, so Captain Walker came up with a simple solution, not to give a sub to those that the mate and boatswain wanted for the tank cleaning gang. No money, no shore, simple. Unfortunately I was one of the chosen few. As we couldn't start cleaning until we'd finished emptying the tanks of oil I did manage to get ashore on the first Sunday but with no money there wasn't much to do except go for a walk. I walked all the way to the Sydney Harbour Bridge where there was what looked like a closed theme park. I thought about crossing the bridge but during this walk I don't think I saw a soul, so didn't think it was worth it so turned back. Sydney seemed shut on a Sunday.

Once the cleaning started we seemed to be working around the clock doing a very dirty, hot job, not just because of the hot water but that it was also summer in Australia. While we didn't have the benefits of going ashore our colleagues looked after us by bringing back cheap bottles of Penfold's wine to keep us going during the several days it took to complete the task. Towards the end of the cleaning, when it looked like we'd be ready to sail within twenty-four hours, Captain Walker told the chief steward that we could have a small sub for the hard work we'd put in. I didn't like proving Captain Walker right but once I set foot off that ship I had no intention of returning until my money had run out or it was sailing time, and putting the gear back could wait until then.

From Sydney it was back up to Indonesia to Balikpapan and then on to Miri in Sarawak to load for home. Yes home. So it was with some excitement that we slipped the loading buoy at Miri and headed for the Suez Canal. However, our hearts fell when we were told that we'd had the dreaded change of orders and that we were to discharge our cargo in La Spetzia, Italy. While this was at least back in Europe, it was not home and there was no chance that we'd be returning to the UK from there light, so we knew we'd be returning again through the Suez Canal.

La Spezia is in northern Italy not far from the Riviera and as I remember it is situated in a bay where the mountains, green and spectacular, seem to come down to the sea. Again this was a place where we didn't tie up and the pipes were floated out to us for the oil to be pumped ashore. The only means to get ashore was by boat and a small ferry, like a floating minibus, that moved around the few ships at anchor at fairly regular times. We were told that the last trip back from shore would be at ten o'clock so not to miss it. Of course half a dozen of us missed it as there was no way we would be clock watching when we were having a good time drinking cheap beer and wine in what was a very friendly port on a Saturday night. The first boat the next day wasn't due until about 9 o'clock in the morning although we had no intentions of even catching that as we were enjoying being on dry land so much. When it dawned on us that the night was cold and that we had nowhere to sleep we booked into a small hotel for the night. Then on a cold, damp January morning, got up with our hangovers to look for somewhere for breakfast. We walked through La Spezia, which still seemed to be asleep, until, right on the edge of the town where the houses started to give way to forest and the foothills of the mountains, we found a café bar. The bar, even at that time of the morning, was surprisingly busy with, mostly men, drinking strong coffee and small glasses of brandy. It was obvious that the local pastime on a Sunday morning was hunting as more men came into the bar with shotguns under their arms clutching an assortment of dead and bloody animals in their hands. Pheasants, rabbits, even a large fox were amongst their proudly held trophies.

After an hour or two in the warmth of the bar we returned to the town centre and I decided to get the boat back to the ship to do my twelve to four watch, although I expected a logging for missing the one during the night. My mates, the two Micks from Hull and a steward from Doncaster, decided that they'd stay ashore for a bit longer. As it turned out, it was a lot longer as they decided not to return at all, and sat on a bench on the quayside and watched as the 'Verconella' let go and proceeded out to sea.

The two Micks were just fed up and had had enough while the steward from Doncaster just couldn't see the point of continuing the voyage after Captain Walker had just fined him a month's pay for smoking on deck. The steward had actually been smoking inside the accommodation dropping his ash into a gash bin but had had a foot resting on the ledge of an open doorway when Captain Walker had appeared to gorge himself in the saloon. He fined him immediately. Everybody thought this was harsh but that was Captain Walker's method of maintaining, on his terms, a happy ship.

The loss of these crew members meant that of the original five from Hull there was only Charlie and me left, but replacements were flown out as needed. There were also other replacements as the officers were replaced after their contracted time was up after six months. The captain had already been replaced and thankfully would be replaced again before we went home. We also had a new chief officer, a little, wiry Geordie guy with bandy legs who offered the image of Stan Laurel to Captain Walker's Oliver Hardy, except that there was no hilarity with this 'comedy' duo. Bramley spent most of his time dashing about the deck on his bandy legs barking orders as well as watching us like a hawk. He was always trying to catch us not working, which happened a couple of times to me, for example when we were painting the outside bulkheads of the after accommodation. I was using a roller to paint and the others were slowly cutting in behind me and chatting. If I got too far ahead I'd stop for a rest, chat or smoke - if we were aft of the funnel - and that would be the point when Bramley would come hurtling around the corner. One day, when we were painting near to the funnel he came up to me and said: "This morning between 9.25 and 9.45 you were missing from the deck. Where were you?"

I'd no idea what he was talking about but replied, "I don't know; maybe I went for a shit."

He thought for minute and then said, "Well don't make a habit of it!"

I had to laugh and so did my colleagues as he scampered off.

On several occasions we heard Bramley instructing the boatswain with comments like, "Separate them boatswain they are laughing, they can't be laughing and working at the same time!" and "Separate them boatswain they are singing, they can't be singing and working at the same time!"

Another example of Bramley's lack of communication skills happened when we were loading or discharging and I was on watch working with the pump man, turning valves on and off as needed. The pump man was a middle-aged man with many years of experience, so he really knew the ropes. We were working on the tanks on the afterdeck nearest the centre castle as Bramley charged past shouting, "You two go and look over the port side!" before disappearing into the centre castle. The pump man and I looked at each other, shrugged our shoulders and went to the port side and looked over.

"What are we looking for?" I asked the pump man and he just shrugged his shoulders again. We then heard a lot more shouting and looking forward we could see Bramley hanging over the side and waving his arms like a demented monkey shouting, " Not like that! I meant look forward and wait for my signal! Shut the valves quick!"

I didn't like Bramley much and it must have showed as one day after we'd had a disagreement about something he turned to me and just said, "I don't know what's wrong with you, you've got a king-sized chip on your shoulder and it's weighing you down."

He was right of course. In fact it wasn't so much a chip but a whole bag full swimming in vinegar. I didn't like the uncertainty of tanker life, I resented the fact that I'd not been sent home when I had a medical condition, I'd been dumped by my girlfriend and couldn't do anything about it, I felt that my parents' divorce had contributed to my rebelliousness at school and since, I thought the symbolic class differences on board ships were petty, and I looked at the officers and thought, who do you think you are? I could do your job!

This latter feeling was reinforced when a young man who had been a couple of years ahead of me at Trinity House, Neil Brocklesby, replaced the third mate. I felt hard done by at the time and this probably was the basis for my lifelong support of the underdog and anything that supports equality.

After Italy it was back through the Suez Canal to the Persian Gulf and a Geelong run again. One of the replacement crew members was a chap called Ted Sheridan from Sheffield, which caused some confusion because my watch mate was called Ted Sheringham but he came from Wigan. Ted Sheridan was a middle-aged ex-Royal Navy man who arrived on board with a reel-to-reel tape recorder and a library of music tapes, which immediately made his cabin the party cabin. At some stage Ted managed to dislocate his shoulder and was in tremendous pain so he took himself along to see the chief steward and Captain Walker for some pain relief and to request medical treatment at the next port. The injury also made it difficult for Ted to work as one arm was completely useless. Captain Walker ordered him to take his shirt off so that he could have a look at it. One shoulder was perfectly straight but on the other side you could see that the arm socket was about two inches below the line of the shoulder.

"Looks all right to me, nothing wrong with it," said Captain Walker, and that was that. The chief steward gave Ted some painkillers and Ted was expected to continue working although the boatswain made sure he was only doing light duties. At the next port Ted insisted he be sent to hospital and his shoulder was reset. This again showed what type of man Captain Walker was.

Then, in Geelong, Captain Walker was relieved by Captain Annette. We had suffered Walker for six months but it seemed a lot longer. Captain Annette immediately made his mark by stating that everything and everyone was starting with a clean sheet and that included loggings – all wiped out – and the atmosphere on the ship changed overnight.

Captain Annette was good in other ways too. After our final visit to Geelong, instead of proceeding to the Persian Gulf we were ordered to return to Indonesia again and anchor off Jacarta to await instructions for loading at Miri or Balikpapam. It was obvious that we'd be waiting for a few days and Captain Annette wasn't happy with this so he called Shell to ask if we could anchor off Singapore instead, but the answer was no. The next day Captain Annette had a word with the chief engineer and guess what? We'd developed an engine fault and needed to go to Singapore for a spare part. What a coincidence. The captain also let it be known that he'd grant shore leave but that we must all be back on board by the time specified, as we'd only be allowed to anchor for a limited period. I was on the wheel as we steamed towards Singapore when the chief steward appeared on the bridge with a crew list and said to the captain, "If there is shore leave how much sub are the crew allowed?"

"What do you mean how much sub are they allowed?" replied Captain Annette.

"Well Captain Walker used to stipulate how much each individual could have," said the chief steward.

"What nonsense. These are grown men, it's their money, they have earned it, they can spend it how they like. They can have as much as they have in the ship as far as I'm concerned, give them what they want," said Captain Annette.

When we anchored in Singapore we could only get to the shore by using one of the little ferries that worked among the ships in the anchorage and we were told to be back by midnight, plenty of time to explore the delights of Singapore. Singapore in those days was like a massive, bustling bazaar of small traders and bars. It seemed you could buy almost anything there at knock-down prices and we enjoyed walking through the maze of tiny streets looking at the items for sale. I remember buying some Joan Baez and Bob Dylan albums, taking in the delicious smells of cooking from some of the stalls selling food, and stopping for a cold beer in a bar when we felt like it. In one of the bars I was attracted by some pretty giggling girls at the bar who were looking in our direction, when I was told by Ted, "You'll get more than a surprise if you end up with one of those girls Bob; they're all men, known as lady boys," so that ended any carnal desires that I may have had. Eventually it was time for us to make our way back to the ferry quay to be taken back to the ship. By then we were getting a bit hungry so we stopped by a stall selling what looked like big fried prawns, which were absolutely delicious. We then caught the ferry back to the ship. Nobody was late; Captain Annette had treated us fairly so we made sure we didn't let him down.

We sailed on time from Singapore and returned to our previous anchorage until we received orders to proceed to Miri to load for Rotterdam. Rotterdam! Rotterdam was considered within home trade limits, so we'd have to be paid off there. We couldn't believe it and thought it was some bad joke particularly as there had been talk of a seamen's strike looming. The seamen's strike was due to start on May 23rd but would it be called off before then? We were certainly excited, if not a little sceptical, as once again we entered the Suez Canal north bound. We had to stop in the canal to allow the south bound convey to pass and, as I was on watch, I was observing the passing ships while talking to the third mate Neil Brocklesby, the second mate and the second mate's wife (this was another perk of officers in that they could bring their wives occasionally). One of the ships passing was the liner 'Oriana' looking like a magnificently lit floating block of flats. As she passed the second mate's wife, with much cooing said, "Oh isn't it a beautiful ship?"

"Yes," we all agreed, and then the silence was broken by the sound of our straining mooring lines as the backwash from the 'beautiful ship' tried to part the 'Verconella' from her moorings making us fly along the decks to attend the damage fore and aft.

May 23rd came and went and the seamen in home ports were now on official strike to try and get an improved pay offer and a reduction in the working week, rather than the increase to fifty six hours a week that had been proposed. We thought we must get a change of orders now but still we headed towards Europe. Every day, every hour, we expected to hear the worst but we still kept ploughing on. Through the Mediterranean, through the Straits of Gibraltar and the Bay of Biscay, at any time we expected to hear that we were going somewhere else. We had wished our lives away many times on this voyage but my, how the time dragged now. Even losing money to George Gower, an Everton supporter, when Sheffield Wednesday were beaten 3-2 in the Cup Final didn't douse our flames of excitement on the possibility of getting home. We were still on edge when we entered the English Channel and even kept our fingers crossed as we lowered the pilot ladder for the Rotterdam pilot.

The lines went ashore and that was it, the voyage was over. We paid off on June 2nd 1966 and had been away almost eleven months but it seemed a lot longer. We were taken from the ship to Amsterdam airport where a KLM plane flew us to Heathrow. We had not been given any rail warrants and were told to pick these up from the Shell Centre in the centre of London if we wanted them. My intention was to stay in London at my mother's flat for a couple of days anyway. My dad no longer lived in London and had moved back to Halifax so I would visit him there later. I had close on a year's wages in my pocket and wanted to buy some clothes while in London by visiting Oxford Street and of course Carnaby Street. I remember cord jackets and hipster trousers were the fashion at that time so I made some attempt to keep up with trends.

What concerned me most about being back on dry land was the traffic. I was actually frightened at first to cross the roads, as I'd not been used to any (or very little in the short time I had the opportunity to get ashore) never mind heavy traffic.

Soon I was ready to head back up to Hull and was crossing one of the main thoroughfares in London when I bumped into Ted Sheriden who had booked into a hotel in London. He was also heading for the Shell Centre for his warrant but suggested a coffee in a café first. While in there we saw another crew member of the 'Verconella' walking past and called to him. This was quite a coincidence, the three of us meeting by chance in the centre of London so we decided to go and get our warrants before the day became a full shipboard reunion. Then, for me, it was back to Hull.

Britain was in the throes of the World Cup that summer which generated a great deal of excitement especially when we went on to win it and have reminded people about it ever since. World Cup Willy was not the priority for me though as I had other things on my mind at that time. The first thing I did was visit the girl who'd ditched me while I was at sea as I'd missed her very much and wanted to continue where we'd left off. Dressed in my new hipsters and cord jacket, equipped with a deep suntan and a bunch of flowers, how could she resist me? Quite easily, as a matter of fact, as her excuse was that she couldn't go out with me now as people would talk about her and think that she was only after my money, so come back when I was skint. So I took her advice and did as I was told.

The seamen's strike was in full swing now with hundreds of ships clogging the docks, officially though, I was not on strike as I'd accumulated a lot of leave during my eleven months on the 'Verconella' which was a good job as some of the seamen started to suffer financial hardship as the strike dragged on. A few of the Hull men who'd started their sea careers on the trawlers went back for a few trips to get some money while some other deck-hands who had not had the experience of trawling signed on as deckie learners although they were comparatively old for this role. I didn't have to worry about this as I enjoyed my leave spending the money I'd earned on the long voyage, and I was never short of helpers in the spending department as a lot of my mates were among the strikers. So it seemed like an endless cycle of pubs, dance halls and carry out parties if someone offered a venue. There were also a few seedy clubs like the Speak Easy on Spring Bank that were open until the early hours. The clubs were not allowed to sell booze but plenty was smuggled in. I also spent a couple of enjoyable days at the Beverley races although I've never been much of a gambler, but the all-day licensing on a beautiful summer day was a much bigger attraction.

I had not forgotten the next most important thing that I had to do on returning to Hull; go and see my doctor in regards to the concerns in my tween decks. Dr Massey, who was also the Hull merchant navy doctor as well as my GP, referred me to a specialist surgeon at Hull Royal Infirmary who told me that I needed an operation if there was any hope of saving my testicle and said that he'd fit me in as soon as possible. The 'soon as possible' though seemed to be dragging on so I returned to Dr Massey and told him that there could be a problem as I was a seaman and I could be away when needed for the operation.

"No problem," he said. "When it's time for you to go back I'll give you a note for the Pool saying home trade only."

Yes! Some sailors would have given their right arm for one of those.

The strike lasted for seven weeks and ended at the beginning of July and suddenly all of my mates returned to the sea. However, my leave was also coming to an end, so I returned to the Pool with my letter from Dr Massey to see what my next ship would be.

PART FOUR – BIG BOATS AND LITTLE SHIPS.

Chapter 19. Able Seaman.

It was surprisingly quiet down at the Pool office when it came to looking for my next ship. The seamen's strike had been over for nearly three weeks so most of the ships were back at sea and the seamen glad of the work, so I didn't expect to find anything quickly especially as I was now 'home trade only'. So it was with surprise when on July 20th, 1966, I was offered and accepted a job on the Associated Humber Line ferry mv 'Melrose Abbey'.

The 'Melrose Abbey' and her sister ship the 'Bolton Abbey' were two small ferries that operated a "city centre to city centre" service from Riverside Quay in Hull to Parkhaven in Rotterdam. The ships carried about ninety passengers for the overnight passage and the passengers' cars and vans were lifted on and off by derricks or cranes. The cars where lashed down by hand in the tween decks or on the open decks. It was an old-fashioned system which would soon be superseded by the roll-on roll-off ferries that had just started operating in the form of the 'Norwave' and 'Norwind' from King George Dock in Hull and went to the new Europort on the outskirts of Rotterdam.

The 'Melrose Abbey' had been built in 1959, had a gross tonnage of 2,741 and was propelled by twin screws that gave her a speed of about fifteen knots. The ship had steel hatches over two holds with six derricks, two for the forward hold and the other four for the other double hold.

The main routine for the ship was to sail on a Saturday from Hull, always at about five o'clock in the evening, and then cross the North Sea to arrive at our destination in Rotterdam on Sunday morning, usually about eight o'clock. Then sail from Rotterdam on Tuesday afternoon, arriving in Hull on Wednesday morning and sailing again the same evening (after a quick turn round) to arrive in Rotterdam on Thursday morning, and sailing from Rotterdam on Saturday afternoon to arrive in Hull on Sunday morning and so on, always sailing on Saturday, Tuesday and Wednesday evenings.

For a few months in winter the sailings were reduced to Saturdays and Wednesdays. In the spring and summer many of the passengers stayed on board using the ship as an hotel while they enjoyed a mini holiday going on coach trips to see the bulb fields, when in season, and other beauty spots and places of interest in Holland.

The deck crew had very little contact with the passengers as we would be lashing the cars and preparing for sea as they came on board for the five o'clock sailing. Then we'd cast off and the watches would begin as we headed down river. This routine was the same on the Rotterdam side as instead of the Humber we would have to navigate the river Maas. Now the saloon on the Abbey boats was not very big so the passengers had to have their dinner in two sittings, so the first sitting was always as we headed down river in relatively calm waters. The North Sea however, is noted for being unpredictable and even the Humber estuary could get very rough. If this was the case, then the diners from the first sitting were often depositing their meals over the side while the second sitting saloon would be half empty, as only the sea-hardened or intrepid travellers risked eating a heavy meal, whilst even fewer would find their way to the small bar. In saying that the food on the 'Melrose' was very good and we could choose whatever we wanted from whatever the cook and second cook were preparing.

If the passengers were staying on the ship for the day trips in Holland they'd often ask the stewards where they could go for a good night out and, particularly the female ones, would be directed to a club, known as the Casino, situated under a building called the Euromast in the park next to Parkhaven. Any passengers taking this advice would find that they would be soon joined by a group of the younger and single crew members suitably scrubbed up and suited. The Casino in fact was very good and a much better night out than some of the local bars that we also used to use. But one of the things that I enjoyed most about Rotterdam was eating fried mussels and bags of crispy chips with a big dollop of mayonnaise on top as we walked back to the ship after a night out.

There were seven of us on deck which included the boatswain and six EDH/ABs split into two watches. As the ship did not have an automatic pilot it had to be hand-steered, so on the overnight passage we worked four on - four off with all hands out for mooring, lashing and unlashing the cargo and opening and closing the hatches. On a Sunday in Hull, as the dockers didn't work that day, we also had to discharge the passengers' vehicles using the ship's derricks. It also meant that because we were moored on the river that was tidal, one watch had to stay on board on a Sunday for the rest of the day until relieved by the shore-based night watchmen. This wasn't too bad as we could bring our wives, families or girlfriends aboard if we wanted to, or not, as the case may be. On days when we were not sailing or docking we would be expected to turn-to on normal day work. This meant that as well as being home regularly there was also plenty of overtime.

As you'd expect on a regular trader like this it was very attractive to married seamen and there was a hard core crew of Associated Humber Line men.

On deck the regulars were the boatswain called Eric Matson, who had been in the company for years, as had two much older seamen, Old Harry, who lived in Hornsea, and Paddy Sullivan who lived in the Avenues. Then there were two younger seamen in their thirties called Gary Puckering and Charlie Reid, and then there was me, the youngster of the lot, and one other, a position that seemed to change regularly until an amiable middle-aged fellow called Eddie Vint joined the crew.

The captain when I joined was Jack Collier and the other regular captain was Captain Blackburn. The chief officer for most of the time I worked on the 'Melrose Abbey' was Fred Rowden. The second officer - there was no third officer - position changed several times but the one I remember most was Alan Markham who fancied himself as a bit of a ladies' man. I got on well with these two as they didn't take themselves too seriously and had a good sense of humour.

I soon got into the routine of the sailing schedule of the 'Melrose Abbey' and the fact that we got some nights at home on a regular basis, never Saturday nights, but Thursday, Friday and Sunday nights were good nights out in Hull. Unfortunately it all looked short-lived as within three weeks, on August 7th, a radio message came through that the hospital wanted me in that afternoon. It was just after midnight when Fred Rowden received the message and I happened to be on the wheel at the time. He asked me how long I expected to be off but I had no idea. In the morning, it was a Sunday, we docked at Riverside Quay and after I'd helped discharge the cars I then packed my bags. My shipmates told me to come back and see them when I got better and that they'd sort me out with a bit of tobacco, and with that I left the ship.

That afternoon I found myself in the men's surgical ward of the Hull Royal Infirmary that was then located in Prospect Street. It was a big ward with lots of beds and the walls lined with ceramic tiles like a Victorian urinal. It resembled an illustration of a military hospital in the Crimean War. I was shown to my bed and told that I wasn't allowed anything to eat as I would be operated on the next day. Being starved was bad but worse was the humiliation of an enema where a brute of a nurse put a tube up my arse and then poured a jug of what looked like Fairy Liquid into the funnel at the other end, waited a minute and then said, "Now run!" I legged it to the toilets where I thought my insides would shoot out as I blasted away making noises that sounded like I was blowing for a tug. Embarrassingly I could hear some of the nurses chatting in the sluice room next door but they must have heard it all before as they just carried on. I understand that people pay a lot of money for this type of torture, er treatment, that they now call 'colonic irrigation'.

During the course of the Sunday evening the consultant came around, accompanied by his entourage of junior and trainee surgeons, to review their victims for the next day. He only briefly stopped at by my bed saying, or should I say shouting, as the consultant only seemed to have one setting on his voice level - LOUD, that he'd be conducting an exploratory operation on me to try to release my undescended left testicle. He then moved on to the next bed that was occupied by an elderly man who'd been a docker. The entourage stopped and the consultant asked a fresh-faced, young man what he would do if he was conducting the operation. After looking at the patient's notes and leg the young doctor said, "In this case sir, I would amputate the big toe."

The consultant was aghast.

"THE BIG TOE! THE BIG TOE! NO! NO! NO! FOOT OFF! BIG TOE NOW – FOOT OFF NEXT YEAR! DO IT ALL AT ONCE!"

And then they moved off to the next bed.

I looked at the old man, just lying there. They'd spoken as if he didn't exist or was just a piece of meat. I asked him what he thought about what we'd just heard. "They know what's best," was all he said.

Not much time was wasted in getting me to the operating theatre and on the Monday afternoon I came out of the anaesthetic and was in dreadful pain, mainly due to wind circulation inside my body. I'd expected a little nick in my scrotum and to be able to feel my newly descended testicle but was surprised to find that I had a wound about thirteen inches long, from my scrotum to above my hip, held together with fifteen stitches. Well, I say stitches but at sea we'd have called them 'homeward bounders', as they were not far off an inch apart. That night my sister and her husband came to see me and I complained about the food and that I was starving, so my sister went off to buy me a sandwich. While she was gone Jack asked how many stitches I'd had and I told him fifteen.

"Fifteen! That's nowt! I had fifteen when I cut my eyebrow when I fell down the stairs in Jackson's Ballroom," he said pointing to a small scar above his eye.

I pulled down the covers and showed him my red and gaping wound.

"Fucking hell," he said, looking at it with horror.

The next morning the consultant appeared again with his entourage to survey the damage that they'd inflicted the day before. They stopped by my bed to look at the wound and the consultant said that he hadn't been able to save my testicle as it had been starved of blood and had withered. He'd thrown it away along with the connecting tubes as there was a risk of cancer, but I had not to worry because the other testicle was big and healthy and that would be all I would need. Then he turned and went. Nowadays they would have implanted a prosthetic one but I don't think they had them in those days, so I was left not much better off - but with less of a cancer risk - than I was before, except for a big ugly scar. I couldn't see exactly what had been done because of the bandages, nor could I feel anything because of the swelling but my main thought was how long would it be before I could try it out.

If you go into hospital nowadays they sling you out as soon as possible but this was not the case then. I'd been in the Infirmary about two or three days after the operation when I was approached by a senior nurse who asked me if I'd mind if they took me to a convalescent home in Withernsea to complete my recovery. I had no objections to this although it would mean that I'd get fewer visitors. I was duly put in an ambulance and shipped out to what used to be a very large residential house next to the railway station in Withernsea. The house had nice big gardens and the ward I was in, although there were quite a few of us in it, was spacious and comfortable. I was still in a lot of pain but some of the other fellows in there told me that once they'd taken half of your stitches out they would let you out "in the grounds" in the afternoon for a couple of hours. A goal. Something to work towards. After a few days of hobbling about I began to nag the nurses about when they'd be taking some of my stitches out and eventually the day came.

"Can I go out now?" I asked.

"Yes, after the after lunch nap (we were forced to do this) but only in the grounds." The nap finished at two o'clock and at ten past I was having my first pint in the Spread Eagle.

It was mid-summer, the weather was lovely and as Withernsea was a popular seaside resort, there were plenty of people about. A couple of student nurses from the Hull Infirmary came for a day out and to see me and I remember spending a nice afternoon walking along the seafront and drinking coffee in a café with them. The only other visitors I saw was when my dad came through from Halifax with my step-mother one Sunday and brought my sister and brother-in-law and their kids as well, so that was nice. Then, after about two weeks, they took the rest of my stitches out and sent me home.

I was still not yet ready to go back to sea but when I felt fit enough I went down to see my mates on the 'Melrose Abbey' to take them up on the promise of a packet or two of tobacco. They seemed pleased to see me when I got back on board and asked me when I was coming back. I hadn't really thought of this, the bloke who had taken my place had by now been on the ship longer than I had so I told them that I didn't think it would be fair on him.

"Please come back, he's driving us barmy as he never stops talking," they said. I replied that I'd think about it and then as I was going down the gangway I was stopped by the mate, Fred Rowden, who asked me how I was and again when I'd be coming back. Once again I said it wouldn't be fair on my relief and he said if I didn't come back it would be unfair to everyone else on the ship as he was driving everyone up the wall with his constant chat. So that made up my mind and on September 9th I rejoined the 'Melrose Abbey'.

Getting back into the routine was no problem even though I still felt a little sore at first. The good thing about being on the 'Melrose' was that I felt that I was making up for the time lost on the 'Verconella' in that I was getting ashore regularly. Every Saturday, Tuesday and Wednesday nights were spent at sea but the other nights were free to be enjoyed, although Mondays were a bit dead in either Hull or Rotterdam. It was almost like having a shore job without losing the buzz of going to sea with every voyage in some way different. In the winter months we got an extra night ashore as the quick turn round on Wednesdays didn't apply.

Shortly after my return to the 'Melrose' in September I met up again with my pre-'Verconella' girlfriend. She must have thought I was suitably skint and, to be fair, I had done my best. This was the swinging sixties so some money had gone on clothes and records but most had gone on having a good time: pubs, parties and dance halls if they had a bar, and I wasted the rest.

For the first time since leaving school I was having a Christmas at home which was quite a novelty as the shipping company decided to tie up the two ferries in Albert Dock over the Christmas period. Unfortunately there were no shore watchmen so this duty had to be shared between the deck crews of the two ferries. Only one man was required at a time and the Christmas Day watches were for only a few hours each so that the crews got the maximum time off. I had one of the longest watches as mine started at midnight on Boxing Day and lasted until eight the next morning but that didn't bother me as I spent that evening with my girlfriend before getting a taxi to Albert Dock for the night shift.

There is nothing more eerie than a ship in total darkness with no engines throbbing, not even a generator. The wind was blowing that night and was rattling the plastic sheeting on the roofs of the warehouses on the dock-side that were being refurbished which made it even more eerie. As there was no power all I had to patrol the two ships with were an oil lamp and a torch, so I had a quick mooch around the 'Bolton Abbey', then the same around the 'Melrose' before going to my cabin, downing a couple of glasses of whisky and dozing off on the seat locker. I awoke about five in the morning and noticed that the lights were on and the generators were thumping on the 'Bolton' which was preparing to go back out to load on Riverside Quay that morning. We wouldn't be sailing for another couple of days.

On January 18th we were paid off the 'Melrose' in Immingham while she went into dry dock for her annual survey. This meant that I had three weeks to kill so I thought I'd put the time to good use and take my Lifeboatman Certificate, which would take me two weeks at college in Grimsby. I wasn't getting paid for this but by signing on I got my Unemployment Benefit and the Pool paid for my course and transport. It also kept me out of the pubs during the day, especially after the unexpected collapse of my romance.

All had been going well when suddenly my girlfriend told me it was over and that she "Didn't want to go out with me anymore." I asked her why and again on several occasions later, but all I got was a shrug of the shoulders, a shake of the head and a bite of the bottom lip, but no explanation. I'd been smitten the first time that I saw her at the top of Whitefriargate when I'd just turned sixteen and thought that she would be everything that I would ever want, but it was not to be.

In retrospect though we weren't that compatible as she said she didn't like bald men, so if she had seen my dad that would have been the end of it there and then, never mind when my own hair fell out (grass doesn't grow on a busy street). Also, she preferred soggy chips and I liked crispy ones.

Anyway I thought I needed a distraction: I couldn't think of anywhere more distracting than Grimsby in January.

There were only a few of us on the course and only two of us were from Hull and, as the course started at nine every morning, it was a very early start on every day of the fortnight starting with the paddle steamer Humber ferry to New Holland and a train to Grimsby. Some of the course was held in the classroom where we learned about lifeboat structure, rigging, stores and survival techniques, but a lot of it also involved boat work, rowing and sailing around Grimsby dock. This reminded me of being back at Trinity House except instead of once a week for a couple of hours this was nearly every day in a bleak cold January. It was obvious that our instructor really loved sailing and expected his students to share his enthusiasm. Some days we were joined by some Grimsby fishermen who were doing their mate's or skipper's tickets. One day they were clearly fed up of sailing up and down the dock.

"You can't do things under sail like you can with an engine," said one of the fishermen.

"Yes you can," replied the instructor.

"No way," insisted the fisherman, "You couldn't put this boat alongside those steps over there unless the wind was in the right direction."

"No problem, just watch this," said the instructor as we all ducked our heads to avoid the swinging sail boom as he turned the tiller and headed for the steps. He put the boat alongside with no effort but his next words were, "Come back," as half a dozen fishermen scrambled up the steps and were gone.

On the final day of the course a man from the Board of Trade came to give us a test on our knowledge and I passed.

The next thing that I had to do was take my certificate to the Board of Trade office in Posterngate to get my discharge book stamped. I knew that with an EDH Certificate and a Lifeboat Certificate if you had thirty-six month's sea time (under articles) you qualified for the rating of Able Seaman and got a bit more money but I felt that I may have to wait a little longer for that. I presented my discharge book and new Lifeboat Certificate to the uniformed man on the desk and he duly registered it and stamped and signed my discharge book, it was January 31st 1967. He then said that he'd check my sea time to see how long it would be before I could be given the AB rating, so he got a note pad and pen and started reckoning it up. He then reckoned it up again before calling across a colleague who also checked the numbers. They then called over another more elderly officer with a bit more gold braid than them and showed him the note pad. Again, he added up the numbers before saying that there was evidence that I'd had more than thirty-six months at sea under articles and therefore was entitled to the AB rating now. He then went on to say I was the youngest that they could recall ever being given the full AB rating in Hull at the age of only nineteen. He then stamped my book again, this time with the AB Certificate Number 68004.

On February 6th I signed back on the 'Melrose' in Immingham as an A.B. and we started on the Hull to Rotterdam routine again. While we were at sea on the first voyage after the dry dock I was at the wheel chatting to the mate Fred Rowden when he said, "I see you used the time ashore to get your Lifeboat and AB Certificate, what made you do that?"

"I just wanted to," I replied.

"Yes, get your AB Certificate if you want to, get your Second Mate's Certificate next if you want to."

I didn't reply to this but Fred's words did register and got me thinking.

At that moment though my aim was to have as good a time as I could. I didn't socialise much with my crew mates in Hull as most of them were married with family commitments. A few of them, particularly the younger ones, would venture ashore in Rotterdam although there wasn't that much to do there in the wintertime. Although we sometimes still used the club in the park we would also use the two seamen's missions which were warm and comfortable and occasionally put on dances. However, one of them didn't have a bar so we used to take our own booze in, leaving the empty bottles in the aspidistras. The padre's wife in this one thought that she would be able to teach me to ballroom dance and although it was fun for me, her

211

bruised feet were evidence that I lacked the co-ordination to be successful in this venture.

Once spring came and we started with more passengers on mini breaks the missions were abandoned for the bars and the club in the park.

In Hull things were different. If I were free during the day I'd frequent the pubs around the Pool used by seamen to see who was home and up for a night out. The pubs that I used mostly were the 'Monument' in Whitefriargate, 'Bonny Boat', 'Kingston' and 'Malt Shovel' near the indoor market, 'King Billy' in Market Place and sometimes 'Green Bricks' on Humber Dock side. What also became popular was the 'White Horse' in Carr Lane, which became like an alternative Pool for non-pool seamen and off-shore workers for, the about to open up, North Sea gas and oil industry. On the other side of the road to the 'White Horse', in the same block as the Cecil cinema was the 'King Edward', that apart from being an afternoon haunt was also an evening meeting place. Evenings very rarely involved the Old Town pubs as nights out might start at the 'King Edward' and then move to the 'White Horse', maybe the bar in the Portland Hotel, the 'Star of the West', and ending up at the 'Spencer's Arms, particularly if it was a dance night at the Locarno.

On some nights I'd maybe go in 'The Burlington' near the Guildhall, as I knew some young people who always used it, and, if I was really skint, I might just use my local, 'The Swan', on Beverley Road. Failing any of those there was always the bar in Merchant Navy House.

One of the comforts on 'The Melrose' was a television in the mess-room although the problems with televisions on ships in those days was that you needed to be fairly close to land to get a good signal. You also had to continually turn the aerial in the right direction every time you changed course or moved from one transmission area to another. This meant that if you were watching a programme you couldn't guarantee seeing the end of it as the ship sailed out of one transmission area, say Yorkshire, into another, say Anglia, which could be a real pain. On a Sunday in Hull when one watch had to stay on board to watch the moorings, the television was quite useful for passing the time although there were only two channels then.

In addition, on a Sunday one of us would go ashore and buy the Sunday papers that we'd all devour and enjoy. Sometimes we had visitors who we'd invited to share our day that also helped to pass the time and made the day more of a party. I used to carry a Phillips portable, battery operated record player (not much good at sea when the ship was rolling but fine in port) and a box of LPs with me to help pass the time, that was also useful on the odd times a girlfriend came down to see me. I had a good selection of records: rock, folk and also some good middle of the road music like Johnny Mathis and the Walker Brothers, which always seemed to go down well with the girls. I liked them all myself and I particularly liked, and still rate him as my favourite singer, Scott Walker, especially after he went solo. However, you can always have too much of a good thing, and a few mates and I were forced to leave a pub in Hessle Road after a lovesick, sentimental fisherman decided to continuously play "My Ship Is Coming In" on the juke-box to impress his girlfriend.

Almost every trip on the return to Hull custom officers would pay us a visit, sometimes bringing a black gang (rummagers) to search the ship looking for contraband watches (which were an expensive commodity in the UK at this time) alcohol, tobacco and cigarettes, and checking to see that we hadn't gone over our personal use allowance. Going over the allowance meant either a fine or having the cigarettes or alcohol put back in the bond. Anyone caught smuggling could face a heavy fine or imprisonment, as well as losing their job, so it was a big risk. The ferries and short sea traders had a reputation for smuggling, mainly, in those days, watches and tobacco (drugs didn't figure then), and the customs knew it. There were rumours that the big money from smuggling had been made just after the war with contraband bicycle tyres (a big demand apparently) to Belgium and Holland, and this explained why some of the older seamen had managed to buy nice houses on their relatively low pay, but those days had now gone.

Occasionally the rummagers would find a few packets of hidden tobacco and maybe a few watches but never, during my time, caught anybody smuggling.

While on the 'Melrose' because I was home regularly I made a number of shore-based friends who I'd meet up with now and again, as well as other seamen when they were home. One of my friends at that time was Mick Harrison who was a few years older than me but was a great laugh and we remained friends until he died. Mick always had a plan or scheme but rarely did they pay off. His dad was a tug skipper with United Towing and Mick used to skip from the merchant navy to tugs as the whim took him. Along with Mick were people like George Collins, also a friend of Mick's as well as being my brother-in-law's brother, and a lad who had been on a tramp with George and Mick called Bob Mahoney who was also the brother of an schoolmate of mine, Stuart Mahoney.

Generally we were out for a good time and maybe find a girl and make arrangements for a date for the next night. Usually this meant meeting the girl at the 'kiosk' in the bus station. This little yellow lock-up kiosk sold newspapers and magazines and was situated on the pavement opposite the bus station behind the ABC cinema next to the side entrance of Paragon Station. Every town and city has its equivalent of the kiosk as a meeting place where every night young men and women would stand waiting for their dates, hoping that they wouldn't be stood up. It was worse than that for me because I admit that I had been so drunk on a couple of occasions when making a date that I couldn't remember what she looked like. I just stood there and waited for someone to come up to me with a smile on her face, hoping that smile would show that she had her own teeth.

Inevitably there were times when the date didn't show at all. How long should you wait? Five minutes? Ten minutes? Twenty? Until the arrival of the next bus from where you thought she lived? Then the nonchalant, 'I don't really care' embarrassed walk of shame towards… where?

On one occasion though when my chosen date hadn't turned up, I noticed a girl who used the King Edward. She also looked fed up of waiting and about to start the 'walk of shame'. We said hello, got chatting and decided that rather than waste the evening, we'd go on a date together.

In those days a man couldn't get into a club or dancehall if he was wearing jeans and it was also a requirement to wear a tie. This meant that most blokes wore suits for going out at night. There wasn't that much selection off the peg so most were made to measure or bespoke. The popular tailors were Burtons, Jackson, John Collier and Alexander. These manufactured made to measure suits which meant you were measured in the shop and then the suit was made in a factory in the West Riding and you picked it up a couple of weeks later or when you next got home from sea. My favourite of these was Jackson's, which seemed to care for more individual needs, particularly when I started to go for three piece suits with a four button jacket. If I had the money for a bespoke suit I'd go to a small tailor popular with merchant seaman called Browns opposite the King Edward pub. Here, they would require you to go for a fitting before the suit was finished, to make sure it was just right. Also coming in though, was a more smart and casual look of bright blazers, hipster trousers and flowery shirts etc., that reflected the swinging sixties.

The girls at the time were beginning to wear very short miniskirts which were quite exciting for us lads, especially as tights were only just coming in and were very expensive, so that the girls continued to wear suspenders and stockings, or if it was warm, no stockings at all.

Early in 1967 the council decided to demolish most of the houses in Fountain Road and, after previous criticism about destroying communities during their urban development programme of slum clearance, came up with a plan to relocate whole streets so that neighbours stayed together and retained the community spirit. Streets like Holmes Street, which also was a dead-end, had many terraces with face to face houses coming off the main street, so that there were lots of defensible spaces where, because there was always someone close and watching, children could play safely, old and infirm people monitored, and there was also plenty of opportunity for social interaction to maintain that elusive community spirit.

The replacement that my sister received was a house in Jenthorpe on the new Orchard Park estate. This house had three bedrooms, two toilets, a bathroom, and central heating so no frozen windows in winter. The house was in a terrace but instead of looking at the street and the fronts of other houses it looked out over a footpath and the dustbins and back garden of the terrace in front. True most of Holmes Street moved there as well but you didn't see anyone unless you met them at the bus stop, or if by chance, they'd chosen to use the footpath in front of the house and you happened to be in the kitchen and saw them passing. There were also no defensible spaces so within a few years the estate would suffer from vandalism and other anti-social behaviour. For me it wasn't too bad in that I had a bed in a room that I shared with my toddler nephew, rather than sleeping on a single sofa bed in the front room, and my mate Dave Turner from Holmes Street, also lived nearby.

It was a longer journey to get to the city centre for nights out from Orchard Park though as it also was to the ship on Riverside Quay (nearly in the city centre), so if I was out late and had to be at work in the morning I'd often choose to sleep on the ship rather than go home.

A couple of the crew of the 'Melrose Abbey' had cars and while the main mode of transport in Hull then seemed to be the bicycle, it was not the most convenient, so I decided to take driving lessons with the 'Quick Pass School of Motoring'. On my second attempt I passed my driving test. I asked my dad who knew about that type of thing, to find me a cheap car and in May he said that he'd found just what I was looking for but I'd have to go to Halifax, where he lived, to collect it and drive it back to Hull and he'd follow. Now Halifax is on the edge of the Pennines and very hilly as is most of the West Riding, whereas Hull is very flat, so much so that when learning to drive and on the test, you had to use a railway bridge, usually T. Bridge near Albert Dock, to demonstrate a hill start, so using the clutch and the right gears for going up and down hills were skills that I hadn't, as yet, fully mastered.

We'd arranged to come back to Hull via my stepmother's parents' house in Pontefract by which time my terrible hill driving has ensured that I'd burnt the clutch out and my dad had to repair it before we could go any further. But apart from that I loved it.

The car was a four-door Austin A30 painted grey like most of the other Austin motors on the road at that time. It had a pull-out choke and starter knobs, a starting handle in case the starter knob didn't work or the battery was flat, no radio, and instead of indicator lights it had these ear type things that shot out of a slot on the door posts. My mates immediately christened it 'The Grey Coupé', although in literal terms it was a saloon and not a coupé, but it had a nice ring about it. Anyway I was here, there and everywhere in it that spring and summer; Hornsea, Withernsea,

Bridlington and Scarborough were all now within easy driving reach. It also meant that I no longer had to use the kiosk as a meeting place and could use the car to take girls home and pick them up if we agreed on another date.

I was really enjoying my life now, with a car, a regular job on the 'Melrose' and a good social life. I had also got interested in union activities, particularly in regard to improving working conditions. However, all good things come to an end and this started to go wrong when Fred Rowden left to become a Humber pilot and was replaced by the Shore Superintendent who I didn't like much.

We also learned that the 'Melrose' was due to go back into dry dock to be lengthened so that she could take more containers because of the competition from the roll-on roll-off ferries. It would also be the end of the city centre to city centre service, so things would not be the same, so on September 13th, 1967, I left the 'Melrose Abbey'.

I was now back on the Pool and looking for another ship but there wasn't much doing until Claude Lock offered me a job on the last voyage of the 'Queen Mary' to New York, with the possibility of taking her around to her last resting place of Long Beach, but I didn't fancy it and reminded Claude that I was 'home trade' only.

I had to wait a few more days on the Pool but finally, on September 22nd, I was sent by Claude to Alexandra Dock to sign on a small coaster.

What a contrast it was from one of Britain's largest ships to one of its smallest and as it turned out, one of the grottiest...

Above. The "Melrose Abbey".

Below right. Mick Harrison with Ben the boatswain on the "Silver Falcon".

Below left. "Silver Falcon" shipping seas.

Chapter 20. Home Trade and Beyond.

The ship was the mv 'Lerwick', a typical, grey-painted small coaster of 372.35 gross tons, 166.33 net. Apart from me the crew consisted of the captain, mate, two engineers, an AB/cook (he wasn't much of a cook - or an AB for that matter) who was the captain's nephew, and a deck-boy. I was told the ship was in Alexandra Dock so drove down there in the grey coupé to put my gear on board and find out when she was sailing. I was told that she'd be sailing on that evening's tide for Antwerp and that she wouldn't be returning to Hull so I'd need to take the car back home. I arrived back on board early and took a stroll around the ship, which I'd already judged as being crap, to get my bearings. While I was doing so I noticed that the mooring wires, particularly the spring, were in poor condition, full of kinks and snags that could have caused a nasty injury. As I was examining this wire one of the engineers appeared and introduced himself and started chatting. I pointed out that I didn't think much to the mooring wire and asked him what all the white and red stuff was, that looked like mashed up corned beef, scattered on the deck and embedded in the strands of the wire.

"Oh that," he said. "That was the bag of flour that I threw to stop the bleeding when the bloke whose place you're taking lost his leg when we came through the lock pits the other night."

What! No wonder he lost his leg with wires like that and working in a confined space! It was a Friday afternoon about 4 o'clock when I was informed about this accident and I was straight on the telephone to the Union. But the representative who was supposed to be out somewhere on the docks couldn't be contacted, no mobile phones in those days remember, and there wasn't anyone else who could come out to see me. Instead they said there was a Union officer in Antwerp so I should contact him when we arrived there. So, that night we sailed.

At sea watches were five hours on with five hours off and then we would be expected to work through while in port – so there was lots of overtime to make up for the lack of comforts. A day or so after we'd sailed, it was a slow ship, I was sitting in the mess-room with the deck-boy when he asked me what I was doing, "I'm keeping a record of my overtime," I said.

"We don't get overtime," he replied.

"What do you mean, we don't get overtime?"

"We get paid a standard rate as part of our wages."

"Nobody told me that when I signed on."

"We also get money stopped for our food," the deck-boy said.

"Nobody told me that either so it's news to me," I replied. "But it should all be written in the articles.

I went in search of the articles, which by law should have been on display, but all I found was the empty lockable display case so I went in search of the captain and asked him, "What's this about us not getting paid overtime, just a standard rate?"

"That's right, it's in the articles you signed," he said.

"No one pointed that out to me or that we had to pay for our food, and the articles are not even in the display cabinet, so show me."

He rummaged about a bit and produced the printed articles that had some scraps of paper taped to them containing the statements about the overtime and quoting a disparaging amount in compensation. I knew that on home trade agreements deductions could be made for food and it didn't seem a lot so I didn't dispute that amount. But in regards to the overtime I said, "This was not pointed out to me when I signed on and the articles were not displayed for me to read, therefore, I don't accept them and I just want to be paid for the overtime that I complete, nothing more, nothing less," and walked away.

In Antwerp we worked most of the time that we were handling cargo, both discharging and loading. I did manage to get ashore for a couple of hours and contact the National Union of Seamen official based there but he was "too busy" to come and deal with my complaints. Instead, he gave me the name and address of the union man in our next port, Methol, so that I could contact him. Not wanting to let this slip I quickly wrote a letter to our man in Methol outlining all my concerns and complaints but particularly about the poor maintenance and cost-cutting that possibly lead to a sailor losing a leg, and questioning the legality of the articles and the overtime situation.

After a couple of days we left Antwerp and headed towards Methol. I'd had a couple of run-ins with the mate already during the voyage as he seemed to object to any suggestions in regard to doing a job more efficiently and preferred the "this is how we've done it for years, so this how we'll always do it," method of working. Anyway, I didn't think he was a bad old stick, so one day when I saw him unlashing a cylinder on the boat deck I decided I'd have a little chat with him to make things up. The cylinder had been lashed by using several turns and hitches around the hand rail, a half turn around the cylinder, several turns and hitches around the hand rail on the other side, another turn half around the cylinder, several turns and hitches around the handrail and so on. There were certainly far too many turns and hitches around the handrail and most of them not doing anything. I watched him unwinding some turns and undoing some hitches from around the handrail and said, "Blimey Chief, there's a lot of turns and hitches there."

There was no answer.

"Bloody hell, a right cowboy must have lashed that there."

Still no answer, just a sidelong glare, so I continued.

"What a waste of rope, those turns and hitches are not doing any good whatsoever, fancy doing a job like that?"

Now, with a snarl, he replied, "If you don't mind, I lashed this here three months ago and it hasn't moved an inch."

Whoops.

Before we got to Methol I watched as the mate and the AB-cook replaced the stern spring wire with a brand new one and stowed the old snagged and kinked one forward.

The AB-cook wasn't that good at either job, although his cooking was limited by the catering budget and the stores on board which he replenished by going ashore shopping and returning with several full carrier bags of groceries.

Apart from frying bacon for breakfast his only two dishes seemed to be roast chicken and stew, but mostly roast chicken. This dinner, for the deck-boy and me, consisted of a chicken leg, carrots, peas, potatoes and gravy. Now that sounds all right but it was the same nearly every meal and we always got a leg.

I asked the deck-boy if he'd ever had the chicken breast and he said no, so I asked the cook, "These chickens that you use, have they been crossed with a centipede?"

"What do you mean?" he asked.

"They seem to have an awful lot of legs, what happens to the breast?"

"It goes in there," he replied and nodded towards the little saloon used by the captain, mate and engineers.

"Do they pay more for their food than we do?"

"No they pay the same."

"In that case then it's their turn for the legs, send some breast in here!"

To be fair, from that point on, the food was the same for both mess-rooms as it should have been.

We docked in Methol on September 29th; I'd been on the ship only a week and couldn't wait to get off it. I'd handed in my notice in Antwerp so it was expected that I'd leave as soon as we arrived. However I had a job to do first. I rang the union man from a call box on the quay.

"Hello, I'm on the mv 'Lerwick' that's just docked in Methol, did you receive my letter?"

"Yes I did and this is what I want you to do. Go back on board the ship and the captain will ask you to sign off. Refuse and tell him that you will not sign off until a shipping master (an official of the Board of Trade) is present. On no account sign off, have you got that?"

"Yes."

"Don't worry about the shipping master, I will take care of that and we'll see you about ten o'clock in the morning."

Just as the union man had said the captain asked me to sign off as soon as I returned to the vessel, and just as I'd been advised, I said I would not sign off until a shipping master was present.

The captain just muttered, "I thought as much," and walked off.

The next morning I packed my bags and got ready for the journey home. I had to hang around a bit but was amused by the owner of the ship, a big stout Scotsman, who had appeared that morning and was fussing about turning off any lights that had been left on while asking the question, "Would you leave the lights on at home?" Was he saving electricity or the light bulbs? This about summed up the economics of the ship really.

I'd discovered that the union man in Methol was an ex-seaman who had also lost a leg which had added to his interest in my letter. And sure enough at just before ten that morning two gentlemen, one with a pronounced limp, came around one of the dockside sheds and walked towards the ship. Once on board the union man introduced himself to me while the other gentleman went in search of the captain. I went through the letter with the union official for a short while and then we were called into the captain's cabin. The owner was also in attendance but didn't say a word.

The shipping master said to the captain, "I understand that there has been some dispute with this young man over his overtime, is that right?"

"No, there's no dispute as it's written in the articles that he agreed to when he signed on."

221

"That was explained to him before he signed on, was it?"

"Er, no, not exactly."

"So the answer is no then."

"Yes."

"Were the articles on display?"

"Yes."

"Really, or did you put them on display after this young man had questioned you?"

"Er, yes."

"Can you show me the articles and the passage referring to "standard overtime?"

The captain produced the printed document with the taped on additions and pointed to one, saying, "That's the clause there."

The shipping master looked at the articles and then ripped off the disputed clause.

"That is not legal and neither are these," he said, tearing off some other slips that had been added. The captain looked shocked as did the ship's owner. "Now," said the shipping master turning to me, "Have you kept a record of your overtime?"

I replied that I had and gave him the notebook that I kept. He then showed the total to the captain and asked, "Do you agree that he has worked these hours?" The captain looked at the notebook and nodded.

"Then pay him," said the shipping master. I can't remember how much it was but it was a fair amount for a week's work.

The shipping master then said, "Before you leave there is the matter of the dangerous mooring wire that led to a serious accident. Is the wire still on board?"

"Yes, it's hidden in the fore peak," I said.

"Thank you, and have a safe journey home," said the shipping master.

To give the captain his due he said goodbye and shook my hand as I was going down the gangway, then added, "It was good to have you on board but one thing's for sure, I won't be employing a Pool man again if I can help it. Your wages this week were more than mine."

I didn't have much leave so it was more or less straight back on the Pool and on October 5th I was sent down to Saltend to join a small tanker called the 'Silver

Falcon' owned by the Silver Line of London. I wasn't that excited to be joining another tanker and it wasn't strictly home trade but on a six months' foreign going running agreement, which meant that you could sign off at any UK port if you wished, so it was the next best thing to home trade.

I had also been told to take my gear with me as the ship would be sailing almost straight away. I arrived on board and went straight up to the captain's cabin to sign on. We recognised each other immediately, it was the Moonman himself, Captain Morrison, son of Skye, and ex of the 'Pass of Glenclunie' who had awarded me a VNC (Voyage Not Completed) in my discharge book.

"Oh it's you again is it? Are we going to have the same trouble with you that we had before?" he said.

"Who knows, but if you don't want me I can soon get a taxi back to Hull," I replied.

"Oh no, there's no need for that, lets just forget about it shall we?" said the captain and in fairness it was never mentioned again.

The 'Silver Falcon' was a new ship with stainless steel pipes and tanks designed to carry dangerous and corrosive chemicals, mainly acids. The ship was small, only 1,301.24 gross tons, 661.41 net. She was described as being "automated" which, later experience told me, meant less crew and more work. All bridge controlled, with all the labour-saving devices available at that time, she would be described as 'State of the art' in shipbuilding terms. While the ship was small the accommodation and single cabins were spacious and comfortable, and the white bedding was the same for everybody. She had a very small crew, just three ABs and a boatswain on deck, two engineers, captain, chief officer, second officer, third officer, cook, steward and a catering boy.

Everyone on this ship seemed to get on, which was essential given the small number of us on board. The boatswain was called Ben and came from Market Weighton, and we got on really well. There was also an AB from Grimsby called John and another lad from Hull who left the next time we returned to Hull. The mate was called Mike Barratt, another good man to work with and for, the second mate was a really pleasant Indian gentleman, and the third officer, who I got on really well with, came from the Orkney Islands, even Captain Morrison was fine in his own way. On top of that there was an excellent cook – what more could you want?

The ship was not strictly a home trade vessel and we sailed under a six months' foreign going running agreement, renewed every six months but you could still give in your notice and be paid off at any UK port if you wished. Captain Morrison only had a home trade master's certificate so had to sail under what was known as a dispensation using the foreign going master's certificate of the chief officer, Mike Barratt.

At sea the ship was fine in good weather but in bad weather it seemed to have a mind of its own, not just pitching and rolling but going round in circles as well. Fully loaded the ship was also very low in the water, so that it sometimes felt that we were on a submarine as the foredeck always seemed to be awash with one rolling wave after another. The ship also had to be battened down tightly which meant that fumes from the engine room and galley circulated around the accommodation. I hadn't been seasick for a long time but boy was I seasick the first time we hit bad weather in this ship.

The ship wasn't on a regular run and our first runs took in Rotterdam, Grangemouth, Copenhagen and Aberdeen, before returning to Hull. On our return the other lad from Hull wanted to pay off but as he'd not given enough notice Captain Morrison said he could only do so if we could find a replacement. I offered to find one knowing that my mate Mick Harrison was out of a ship after just coming out of working on deep sea tugs. Mick was a bit of a raconteur, lothario and a jack the lad, and always had a master plan that never came to fruition but he was always good for laugh.

I found Mick in the unofficial Pool office, the White Horse, and he jumped at the chance and dashed off to pack a bag before we returned to the ship at Saltend. I told him on the way that the ship had a peculiar motion and he would probably be seasick but he scoffed at this as he'd just come off a deep-sea tug so it wouldn't effect him. We sailed that evening and were soon shipping green water in a pretty wild North Sea. Next morning at breakfast a very 'green looking' Mick was feeling quite sorry for himself as he conceded that he'd never experienced anything like it, but he soon got used to it.

Mick soon settled into the routine of the ship and we had a good laugh while working hard. I was surprised though that Mick, although six years older than me, wasn't that handy when it came to some of the jobs that we had to do. During my time on the ship the boatswain had given me a number of jobs like splicing mooring ropes and wires, and obviously had been happy with my work as he kept giving me those types of jobs, and I was happy because I liked doing them.

One day he told Mick and me to make some new lifelines for the lifeboats. This involved putting a series of figure of eight knots in the rope at about a fathom apart. These were meant for hand and footholds should a person have to lower themselves into the boats. Now on the 'Verconella', I'd been shown a trick so that you didn't have to tie each individual knot, which was a long drawn out process. So, after we had our ropes prepared, Mick with one me with another, I measured where I wanted my first figure of eight knot and held my rope at that point in my left hand with arm outstretched, measured the fathom by running the rope through my right hand until both my arms were outstretched, and then gripped the rope in my right hand and twisted it twice clockwise while bringing the created bight over to my left arm, measured another fathom in the same way and repeated the process until I had the right number of bights on my left hand to reflect the number of figure of eight knots needed.

I then threaded the end of the rope through the bights and then, hey presto, pulled out the ready made figure of eight knots ready for tightening and adjusting. Finished. Mick was still wrestling with his first knot and looked amazed.

" How did you do that?" he asked.

"Magic," was the reply.

Around this time Ben the boatswain told me that he planned to go on leave soon and said that he would put me forward as his relief, much to Mick's chagrin. Unfortunately the mate and captain thought I was too young to take on the role. Why is it in life that you always seem to find yourself either too young or too old?

One Sunday we were docked in Grangemouth in Scotland where they had strange licensing laws that meant that only hotels were allowed to serve alcohol on a Sunday, so we all ended up in a hotel bar that evening for few drinks. During the course of the evening, John from Grimsby, 'disappeared' so we returned to the ship without him. He was all right John but he tended to brag a bit and was always trying, and failing, to impress us.

The banter on the ship had gone up a notch since Mick had joined and everyone was fair game but this time John really put himself in the firing line. The next morning we were all sitting in the mess-room having a smoko when Mick said to John, "Where did you get to last night John? You were with us in the bar and then disappeared."

"I'm sorry, can't tell you that," said John.

"What do you mean, you can't tell us?" asked Mick

"No, not allowed to say," said John mysteriously.

"Was it a woman?" asked Mick.

"No, I'm not allowed to say," was John's evasive reply.

"So it was a man then?" said Mick mischievously.

"No, it certainly wasn't a man!" exclaimed John.

"You protest too much," said Mick before turning to us and saying, "It was a man."

"No it wasn't a man, if you must know it was a fellow Buff!"

"Why didn't you say you met a fellow puff?"

"No! Buff! Not puff! I met a fellow Buff!"

"We heard you, you met a fellow puff."

Everyone in the mess-room was now in hysterics.

"No, no, no, you don't understand! I'm a member of the Grand Order of Buffaloes and go to Buff Lodge."

"Oh, there is such a thing as a puff lodge?"

"It's the Order of the Buffaloes and I was invited to the local lodge."

"Really, we didn't see you talking to anyone, how did you get there?"

"There was another Buff in the bar."

"How did you know he was a Buff?"

"We have our secret signs."

"Oh, and we know what those signs are," said Mick as he held up a limp wrist and blew John a kiss.

"I give up," said John as we all stood up still laughing to go out on deck.

We grabbed the odd chance that we got for a run ashore as the turn rounds on this ship were very quick and, on top of that, we were always having to clean the tanks.

The 'Silver Falcon' was purpose built to carry dangerous acids and other chemicals that could be contaminated by the smallest amount of water or foreign matter. This meant that the tanks had to be washed out and thoroughly dried before they could be used. Each time the tanks were cleaned they would be inspected and any contamination meant we had to clean them again, so time was money. In addition the powerful acids could burn through the normal steel plate on the deck if spilt and would eat at the welds that held the stainless steel tanks and pipes together. All this meant a lot of work and it was not unusual to go days without sleep. I remember one time when we had done about three ports in Holland and Belgium. We hadn't slept for about three days when we finally tied up about midnight waiting to load the next morning for a slightly longer trip. I was absolutely exhausted and could only think, - bunk, bunk, bunk - when the mate tapped me on the shoulder and said, "You're night watchman Bob." Everybody immediately turned in but I sat in the mess-room awhile and then went for a walk about checking the moorings. I was too tired to read so kept on the move and then about four in the morning I sat again in the mess-room with a mug of tea.

The clang of pans in the galley woke me!

What time is it? Half past seven!

I hadn't called anyone!

Oh no, I could be in trouble!

The second mate then popped his head around the mess-room door and said, "There you are. I told them not to wake you as you were absolutely knackered. Don't worry I called everybody."

That was why this was such a happy ship.

When we were carrying anything really dangerous or unusual the mate would brief us on 'safe working practices' before we would be let loose on deck. One of these involved a chemical called phenol, which came on board in a liquid state and had to be kept at the correct temperature, otherwise it would solidify. It was particularly dangerous as the skin could absorb it. It didn't burn so you wouldn't initially feel it like an acid, but once absorbed it would begin to destroy your blood corpuscles and if untreated, you would eventually die. An armful meant you could be dead in forty minutes, a legful in twenty, the mate cheerfully told us after also telling us that the driver of a road tanker had died after falling into it up to his ankles the week before. It was even dangerous when it had been diluted so we had to be extra careful and not take any chances and to go straight to the mate who had an antidote if we got any splashes.

All went well until we had cleaned the tanks and were putting the flanges back on the tank tops. Around each tank top was a trough to catch any spillages. Mick and I were busy putting the flanges back, which meant putting our hands in the trough, now full of water, poking the bolts up through the bolt holes and then tightening the nut on top.

I looked at Mick and said, "Have you got any holes in your gloves?"

"Yes, why?" he replied.

"Phenol in here," I said. And he was gone, leaping over pipes and up the ladders to the accommodation, shouting for the mate. Some time later when we had finished on deck we went into the mess-room to find Mick with his hand bandaged and in a sling.

"What happened, Mick?"

"The mate thinks the phenol got on my finger and thumb and put some of the antidote on, it's turned white."

I whistled through my teeth and then turned to the others and said, "What did the mate say, forty minutes armful, twenty minutes legful, what do you say finger and thumb? Do you give him two hours?"

"Fuck off!"

I cannot remember the exact sequence of ports that we visited but I remember going up the Norwegian fjords to Odda. Odda is about thirty miles inland from the Norwegian coast but to get there we had to navigate over sixty miles through narrow fjords. The fjords are always a spectacular run and this was no exception.

Another port of call was Gothenburg. I had the idea that I'd like a leather jacket and wrongly thought that they may be cheaper in Sweden, so Mick and I ventured forth to see what we could find amongst the main shops in the city centre. We didn't have much luck even though we'd been given a leaflet and a map to direct us to a department store where I was more likely to find what I wanted. But shopping was thirsty work and we were also getting a bit hungry so we went into a large café for refreshments. After paying an arm and a leg for a drink and an open sandwich we looked for somewhere to sit and could only find a table that was already occupied so had to sit side by side and face an elderly couple. After a short while the couple finished their coffees and left but before we could move their place was taken by an attractive young woman who plonked down her coffee and bun and started to read a book.

Mick nudged me and said, "Cor, she's gorgeous, what do you think Bob?"

I had to agree. Mick then carried on praising her virtues while expressing his wish that we didn't have to be back on board later that afternoon. After a short while I produced the leaflet and map and despite Mick's reluctance drew his attention to our task of finding the shop and we started debating whether we turned left or right after leaving the café. We debated for a couple of minutes and then the young lady carefully put down her book and, in perfect English, said, "You need to turn right out of here, walk up to the next junction, turn right again and you will see the store across the street."

We stuttered our thanks to her and then headed, in red-faced embarrassment, for the exit. I looked back and noticed the self satisfied smile on her face.

Our next port was Wismar in, the then, East Germany. My search for a leather jacket in Gothenburg had been fruitless so I thought maybe Wismar had the answer and once again Mick decided to accompany me in my quest. Wismar was amazing. It was like going back in time, almost to medieval days. It was the type of town that you would imagine as the setting for a Grimm's fairytale. The main reason was that the town was completely devoid of advertising hoardings and flashing neon so that we could see the buildings just as they'd been built and without any modern day signage. Eventually we found a store that seemed to sell almost everything, everything that is except leather jackets. But what we did notice was that they sold spirits at incredibly low prices. Always looking to make a bit of extra cash on the side Mick mentioned that we'd been told that we were going back to Gothenburg and that while we'd been there previously we'd been continually asked if we had any booze to sell.

"We could make a killing," he said. I agreed and as I had already given up on the leather jacket we pooled some money and bought a fair number of bottles.

We sailed from Wismar and headed north back towards Sweden as planned. But then, our worst nightmare happened. A change of orders told us to proceed to Billingham on Tees instead.

Billingham! Noted for its enthusiastic customs officers! What were we going to do?

We were in shock but Mick got an even bigger shock when he received a radio message from his girlfriend telling him to get home quickly as she was pregnant.

Mick now would have to leave the ship in Billingham so we got rid of as much of the booze as we could amongst the crew and Mick decided to risk taking the rest home. As soon as we tied up in Billingham, he ordered a taxi and when it arrived disappeared down the jetty carrying his bags, one clinking suspiciously, and drove off to sort out his domestic concerns. As we watched Mick's taxi turn out of sight we were amazed to see several black cars pulling up and discharging their cargo of black-clad rummagers. A near run thing.

The next time that the 'Silver Falcon' returned to Saltend I asked if I could leave as well. I would have stayed I think if I'd been given the relief boatswain's job but it was getting near Christmas and the chance of returning to Hull before then was not certain. As before Captain Morrison said I could pay off if I could find a replacement at short notice. In fact I needed two as Mick had not, as yet, been replaced. I dashed down again to the unofficial Pool, the White Horse, and found two volunteers, Pete Fowler and his mate Ernie Russell, who were both out of a ship and needed the money. Captain Morrison was happy with these two so, on December 12th 1967, I said my goodbyes and went. I'd had a good time on the 'Silver Falcon' mainly because of the excellent officers and crew. In fact the third mate, who said he also planned to leave, invited me up to Kirkwall for New Year but unfortunately I didn't take up his offer, as I'm sure it would have been more exciting than where I ended up spending New Year's Day.

Being home for Christmas left me a bit skint again so I was soon looking for another ship and on December 28th I signed on the m.v. 'Baltic Express', sailing the next day for Helsinki in Finland.

The 'Baltic Express' belonged to the United Baltic Corporation and had been built in Germany in 1957, 2,940.7 gross tons, 1,424.52 net. Like most of the Baltic boats she was still quite modern even though she was over ten years old. Our accommodation was aft with two to a cabin, my cabin mate was Cyril Norman who I hadn't met before but one of his brothers, Ahmed, had been an engine man on the 'Melrose Abbey'. The boatswain was Pete Grady, a member of another well-known seafaring family in Hull and one of his brothers was also a member of the crew. Pete was a great boatswain and good for a laugh provided that you pulled your weight. There were also a couple of younger members of the crew, Trevor Daley and Mick Templeman, who I also got on with. But like all these ships there were crew changes virtually every time we returned to the UK, mainly because the Baltic in winter is not the most pleasant place to be and more often than not it was too cold to go ashore.

I remember in one port, it may have been Kotka, we were watching the TV and we noticed that the temperature on the weather forecast had risen to −25C. Warm! So we went ashore but came back less than an hour later with our clothes frozen stiff after not finding anything open. The only other time I remember going ashore was in Helsinki looking for fur hats, but that was it.

Anyway the prices of drinks in Finland were prohibitively high, which made it much more sensible to buy our booze on the ship and enjoy a drink in our cabins. My little Phillips record player was also useful for these social events and, particularly in Helsinki, we would often be joined by some local young ladies looking out for a cheap good time.

After a couple of, to be fair, enjoyable trips on the 'Baltic Express' I also decided that I'd had enough and paid off in Hull on February 5th 1968.

Chapter 21. The New Zealand Shipping Company.

Back in Hull in a cold, but not as cold as Finland, February I decided that I needed a change. I'd heard a lot about New Zealand and what a wonderful country it was but how could I guarantee getting there as the ships trading there didn't seem to crop up on the Hull Pool very often. Then someone told me that you could send your discharge book directly to the shipping company offices on the speculation that there may be a ship in the offing. So, as there didn't seem to be much happening on the Hull Pool, I sent my discharge book by registered post to the New Zealand Shipping Company offices on the Royal Albert Dock, London and waited for a reply.

As it happened I didn't have to wait long as the very next day, a Tuesday about lunchtime, the telephone rang and it was a Mr Moxley, the appointments' manager for the New Zealand Shipping Company. Mr Moxley said that they had received my discharge book and noticed that I'd had passenger experience - the discharges from the 'Melrose Abbey' were marked home trade/passenger - and that he'd like to offer me a job as a quartermaster on one of their passenger ships the RMS 'Rangitoto'. He went on to say that this was a petty officer role and the company would provide a uniform but I would need to get down to London quickly as the ship was due to a sail on the Friday.

His next question was, "Do you want the job?" You bet I did and I told him so. He then said that he'd contact the Pool in Hull to arrange my rail warrant and looked forward to seeing me the next day.

I immediately jumped in the grey coupé and headed down to the Pool office, which was always quiet in the afternoon. I approached the desk and asked Claude Locke if he'd had a call about the 'Rangitoto' and he said that he had and started to write the warrant. He then checked something else and said, "There's a problem. You are down for home trade only."

I explained that this was because I'd been waiting for a hospital appointment for an operation but I was all right now but he insisted that I got clearance from Dr Massey. I dashed down to Dr Massey's surgery but had to wait while he finished his liquid lunch and meandered his way across the zebra crossing from the Merchant Navy House Hotel opposite. I told him the problem so he examined me in his usual way asking, "Do you feel all right?" and showing me the card with the number 27 on it, made up of coloured dots that he used for checking for colour-blindness. Then it was back to the Pool for the warrant.

The shipping company wanted me down in London as soon as possible and the next morning I was directed to the early Pullman train direct from Hull to King's Cross. I'd never been on a Pullman before so didn't know the routine and I searched up and down for the normal second class carriage that I'd been used to, only to find that all carriages consisted of what looked like posh dining cars with tables set out with white tablecloths. I found an empty table and sat down to enjoy the journey. After the train left I looked up and down the carriages again to see if there was a buffet but this appeared to be closed although I could hear some activity from the galley, so I gave up and went back to my seat. After a while a steward appeared and asked if I wanted any breakfast. I didn't fancy paying British Rail prices for a full cooked breakfast so I just asked for a cup of coffee and a slice of toast and thought no more about it. As we approached London the steward appeared again with the bill. I couldn't believe the price as I had been charged for a full breakfast! When I pointed out that I'd only had a coffee and a slice of toast the steward told me that it was a set price for breakfast no matter what you had! I asked him why he didn't tell me that before but he just shrugged his shoulders and said, "You didn't ask." Begrudgingly I paid up but this made a considerable hole in my already meagre funds.

My next problem was getting from King's Cross to the Royal Docks. I was familiar with the West India and Surrey docks but I had no idea about the Royal Docks other than that they were further east than the West India docks. I studied the map of the tube but that was no help as it did not show the level of detail that I required. So I ended up making a guess and caught the tube to Whitechapel, where I asked a taxi driver how far it was and how much would the fare be to the Royal Docks. It turned out to be more than what British Rail had left me but less than what they had charged me for breakfast. Anyway, I was in luck as the taxi driver said he was on his way home for lunch and would drop me off at the dock gates for a nominal fee, so I've had a great deal of respect for London taxi drivers ever since.

I signed on that morning and was sent with a chitty to a marine outfitter to get my uniform. It wasn't that much of a uniform, just navy blue trousers, navy blue jumper with the New Zealand Shipping Company logo on it, a couple of the white, Royal Navy sailor type shirts with the square necks, and a white topped sailor hat, again with the NZ badge on it. I soon found that the only time you were required to wear the full rig was when on passenger gangway duty. For normal watch keeping you could get away with clean jeans and the sailor shirt.

The RMS 'Rangitoto' seemed to me to be massive after the small ships that I had become used to. She wasn't as big in tonnage and length as the 'Verconella' but this was a cargo passenger liner of 21,808.3 gross tons with a length of 609 feet. The main difference with the 'Verconella' was the number of decks which made the ship seem much larger, although I now realise that she would have looked like a lifeboat compared to today's monster cruise ships. But she wasn't built as a cruise ship, more as a functional passenger ship taking migrants out to New Zealand with the added practicality of being able to carry refrigerated cargo. And although fairly old, as she'd been built in 1949, she could still tramp along at a fair speed of 17 knots.

The ship carried over 400 passengers, again not a lot by today's standards, and over 600 crew including: the captain, chief officer, second officer, three third officers (two seniors and a junior); several radio officers, umpteen engineers of various types (general, refrigeration and electrical) and engine ratings; a purser, writers, printer, hairdresser, shop keeper, laundry workers and an army of stewards of different types (bedroom, topside, barmen and swimming pool attendants); nursery nurses, doctor, nurse, hospital attendant, chief cook, general cooks, pastry cooks, butchers, soup cooks, butchers, crew cooks and scullions; and on the deck there was a boatswain, boatswain's mate, lamp trimmer, and a troop of deck-hands, and let's not forget the six quartermasters.

I boarded the ship by way of a gangway that led to a doorway in one of the lower decks and immediately felt that I'd entered some form of maze with a bewildering number of corridors. Soon however, I found my cabin and introduced myself to my cabin and watch mate, Neil Johnson, who informed me that I'd find the ship big at first but it would soon 'get smaller' as I found my way around. Neil, who was in his thirties, had been on the ship for a few trips so knew his way around and said that he'd show me the ropes. He told me that he originally came from the Isle of Barra, which was a surprise as most of the people I'd met from Barra had been called MacNeil, but he now lived in Glasgow with his Canadian wife. It turned out that there were six of us quartermasters on the ship: Taffy Hayes, an 'elderly' seaman in his fifties from South Wales, Big Jim (in his forties) from Blackburn, an Australian known as 'Aussie', also in his fifties who, according to his tales, had been quartermaster on nearly every passenger ship going and had kept all of the uniforms, which he wore on this voyage at least once in an attempt to upstage the rest of us. But this maritime fashion parade only led to Taffy loudly speculating where Aussie kept his trunk.

Aussie was the complete professional quartermaster, if there was such a being, as he also had a wayward eye that allowed him, when he was on the wheel, to keep one eye on the compass while the other scanned the horizon. The last member of our little team was a young New Zealander in his late twenties of Maori descent from the Ninety Mile Beach area of New Zealand called Bob Clark. He was a really nice bloke but would remind anyone who appeared to be going too far in any good-natured banter that the Maoris were the last cannibals of the South Pacific.

Our voyage out would be from London to Auckland, calling at Curacao, Panama, and Tahiti, no wonder I got the buzz of excitement as we nosed our way out of the oily black water of the Royal Albert Dock and headed out into the Thames.

I soon discovered that our accommodation was on 'E' deck and that was criss-crossed with alleyways and small squares for the crew to sit in if they didn't want to sit in the, always hot, mess-rooms. The quartermasters had their own small mess-room with a deck-boy assigned as 'Peggy' to bring us our food and keep the place clean. That took some doing as the ship was alive with cockroaches that preferred the extra warmth of a hot press - a type of oven for keeping food warm - as their nesting place. Even though the ship was regularly fumigated the cockroaches always won in the end. Also on 'E' deck was the 'Pig and Whistle', the crew bar that didn't serve much else other than beer but at least it was cheap. For the quartermasters the accommodation was a shared double cabin while the regular deck crew had cabins of four or more. The stewards were just as badly off with many sharing six berth cabins.

Above 'E' deck was 'D' deck, where the passenger's dining room, the galleys, pantries and the cheaper passenger accommodation could be found. The claim was that the passengers were all one class and this was true as far as the food and facilities were concerned. But there was no doubt that the passenger cabins on 'C' deck, and even more so on 'B' deck were much better than the four or more berth cabins on 'D' deck. Also on 'D' deck was a baggage room, part of the hold where the passengers could leave larger trunks and baggage that they may need access to on the voyage. 'C' deck was the main passenger deck and the location of the ship's shop, hair salon and purser's office. Another baggage room, for the more affluent passengers, was accessed from 'B' deck where you would also find the nursery. 'A' deck had the main public rooms, bars, promenade deck and passengers' swimming pool. (The crew's pool was a temporary affair constructed out of wood and tarpaulin and erected on the foredeck.) At the forward end of 'A' deck above the passengers' saloon and below the bridge, were a couple of decks of officers' accommodation, making it a long climb up (about eight flights of stairs) from 'E' deck to the bridge for our watch keeping.

The job of quartermaster was a doddle. It was the easiest job I've ever had on any ship. Two of us on a watch, an hour about on the bridge, and the only steering we did was coming in and out of port. All we had to do was keep an eye on the automatic pilot, keep a good lookout, and maintain the bridge. We would also get daily overtime doing whatever the chief officer asked us to do like check and maintain the lifeboats. As the requirement for being a quartermaster was being an able seaman and holding a lifeboat certificate we were also given command of a lifeboat each for drills and should there ever be an emergency. I was even lucky in that allocation as my boat had an engine. In port we were responsible for the gangways and accommodation ladders and kept watch over those to make sure that they were safe and that no undesirables came on board. Because of this we were the only members of the deck crew who had regular contact with the passengers.

Neil turned out to be an excellent guide when showing me the ropes and introducing me to the workings of the ship and the key people on board, for example, if you needed any American jeans or other clothes you could get these from one of the unofficial outfitters on board like 'Jim the Butcher', who kept his store in the meat handling room and 'Bill the Pill', the hospital attendant who kept his store who knows where. Bill's cabin was near the hospital at the after end of the ship and was also handy as a call in spot for a mug of tea or a beer if time allowed. Bill looked a bit like Phil Silvers but it was Neil who sometimes acted like Sergeant Bilko by always having a scam.

If we were working overtime our instructions came from the chief officer, a New Zealander by the name of Highfield, who looked like the comedian Benny Hill but was over six feet tall and one of the best officers that I sailed with.

On the first day out from London Mr Highfield stopped Neil and me as we came off the bridge after being relieved from the morning 8 to 12 watch. He gave us a list of baggage requests and said that our overtime that afternoon would be tracing and delivering wrongly labelled passenger baggage. Apparently passengers could only take a limited amount of baggage into their cabins, but other items wanted on the voyage could be stored in the baggage rooms, which were opened for one hour each day, and the rest went down into one of the main holds. Inevitably some passengers labelled the baggage wrongly and what was wanted on the voyage had ended up down the hold, so our job was to sort some of these out. As soon as we were out of sight of the mate Neil turned to me and told me to book a broken meal hour as the mate had spoken to us during our lunch hour. I thought this was a bit over the top but that was apparently how the ship worked.

After our lunch hour we set to work following Mr Highfield's instructions. Most of the items were pretty straightforward although it took some rummaging in the hold before being delivered to the relevant baggage room. One, however, was a little different, as the passenger wanted a missing trunk delivered to her cabin. We found the trunk and hauled it up out of the hatch before loading it on to a trolley and wheeling it to the designated cabin. As we approached the short alley that led to the cabin Neil said, "Hold your horses. Where do you think you are going?"

"The cabin's just down here," I replied.

"Yes but we'll take it off the trolley here and we will drag it the rest of the way," said Neil.

"Why not use the trolley?"

"You'll see," said Neil as he took the trolley away and with much banging, dragged the trunk to the cabin. He knocked loudly on the door and an elderly lady opened it.

"I think this is your trunk madam?" said Neil gasping for air and mopping imaginary sweat from his brow, "It was a bit of a job (gasp) but we got it here in the end (gasp), where would you like it?"

"Just down here please and please take this (handing him a note) for your trouble."

We thanked her and left the cabin.

"That's the way to do it," said Neil.

Neil's enterprise took another twist on the night that subs were given out to the crew for the first time. I was lying in my bunk when Neil came in and started rummaging about underneath the drawers.

"What are you up to," I enquired.

"You'll see," said Neil.

A little later I decided to go to the 'Pig and Whistle' for a beer and the first thing I saw was Neil with a crown and anchor board (a gambling game using a spinning arrow on a marked board) shouting, "Place your bets!" From that point on Neil's crown and anchor board was a regular feature in the Pig as he attempted to relieve gullible crew members of their hard-earned cash before they could squander it on booze and, should they get the opportunity, wild women.

Our first port, however, was Willemstad in Curacao. This was really a bunkering port, so while there was shore leave to allow the passengers to stretch their legs the crew were not given a sub so, unless you'd brought money with you, you were stuck. Curacao was also where we'd change watches, so from the eight to twelve Neil and I would move to the four to eight.

I was sitting in the mess-room on the day of our arrival chatting to Bob Clark when he asked me if I was going to have a run ashore that night. I told him that I didn't have any money so would stay on board.

"Well Yorky", (that was my nickname) "I've got some Yankee dollars. You can have some of them if you like?"

Would I like? You bet I would, I nearly grabbed his hand off.

So after my early evening watch I was showered, changed and down the gangway with a couple of the lads. As we headed for the bars of Willemstad we tried to dodge the huge cockroaches that appeared with the nightfall and crunched under our feet as we walked along the road. A few of the crew had headed to sample the delights of 'Happy Valley' (a notorious red light district) but this was not for me as I just wanted a good night out. Soon we were downing a local variation of the spirit anisette that seemed to go down very well. After a fairly raucous and enjoyable evening I headed back to the ship about midnight to get a few hours sleep before taking watch on the passengers' gangway at four in the morning.

I was awakened for my watch and thought I was dying. I had a hangover to end all hangovers. One of those hangovers that's never forgotten. I also had an incredible thirst and just wanted to drink cold water. This seemed to have the effect of activating the anisette all over again and I struggled, suffered and staggered through my watch but I persevered and although the time dragged and at times the clock seemed to be going backwards, finished my stint at eight. I couldn't face breakfast but managed to sit in the mess-room nursing a mug of tea looking pale, grey and feeling very sorry for myself. Taffy Hayes was in there having his breakfast and when he'd finished he pushed his plate away, stood up, looked me up and down, shook his head and said, "First port tells, first port tells," and walked out.

Our next stop was Colon where we picked up the pilot for the Panama Canal. There is a trick pub-quiz question about the Panama Canal linking the Atlantic to the Pacific Ocean. Those who do not know the geography of the canal assume that a ship would pass through it east to west but, due to the angle that the canal builders cut across the isthmus, the ship actually passes west to east, or more specifically north-west to south-east. The canal, although built in an area that always seems hot and humid, is spectacular and gave the passengers something to look at before we stopped again at the port of Panama.

The Panama Canal at that time was run by the U.S.A., which administered an area of the country of Panama known as the Canal Zone, through which the canal passed so all the canal pilots were American. The 'Rangitoto' had a Tannoy system that allowed announcements to be made from the bridge and a few of the American pilots made full use of this by giving a kind of running commentary outlining the history of the canal and the difficulties in building it through tropical jungle. The canal had three sets of magnificently large locks that linked the man-made cuts and artificial lakes that formed the basis of the navigation, so there was a lot to see and talk about as well as the possibility of spotting local wildlife.

On one occasion while I was steering through the canal one of the pilots dashed into the wheelhouse, grabbed the microphone and announced to the passengers, "If you're quick and look over the starboard side, you'll be able to see a local alligator basking on the bank of the canal!"

He may have said right side knowing Americans, but whatever it was I swear I heard a rumble as over four hundred pairs of feet ran across the decks and the ship took a small but noticeable list to starboard.

Soon, however, we reached Panama City and the end of our outward canal journey. This was where the crew could have a sub for the first time so consequently where Neil appeared with his crown and anchor board. It was also a place where the passengers could also have a run ashore although they were always issued with a warning notice in their cabins about the dangers of Panama, and on our homeward voyage, Colon, due to street thieves and pickpockets. One trick the pickpockets used was to work in pairs, sandwich an unsuspecting victim, and then slash the victim's trouser pockets to gain access to their cash and wallet. Handbags were even easier for a thief with a sharp knife. Nevertheless, despite the warning, there were always passengers who returned to the ship shocked, distraught and devoid of their personal belongings, complaining to us as we on the passenger gangway were the first of the ship's crew they'd come across, that we should warn people about this. We would then show them the notice that had been distributed to all the cabins.

"Did you see this notice in your cabin?"

"Yes."

"Did you read it?"

"No."

The passengers also complained that the local police hadn't been any help. They'd just shrugged their shoulders and said, "The people have to earn a living somehow."

I know I had lucky escape on the following voyage when I'd arranged to meet some of my shipmates in a bar in the centre of Panama. They'd gone on ahead of me as I had to finish my watch. It was a hot afternoon when I left the ship to head for the centre and I was unsure of which direction to go when I reached a crossroads, should I go left or straight on? Straight on looked busier, so I assumed that must be towards the city centre and set off walking in that direction. Coming the other way was a big black guy who stopped me. He obviously couldn't speak any English, but he turned me around and pointed to the left hand turning that I'd rejected. He then pointed in the direction that I'd been walking in, shook his head, dragged his finger across his throat in the cut-throat manner, and then walked off.

Usually in Panama or Colon I'd just go ashore for a few beers with my mates but we were always wary and kept together as life there seemed cheap. Even so various sleazy characters would still accost us trying to peddle sex shows, most of which seemed to involve the pleasuring of a donkey. This was not my scene, nor thankfully, was it for the lads I'd palled up with although there were inevitably other members of the crew, and quite a few passengers, who did follow up on these types of attractions and then wondered why they'd been ripped off.

Back at sea we started our passage across the Pacific towards Tahiti. On the four to eight watch we'd come off the bridge at eight in the morning and then do a few hours overtime, ending up by opening the baggage rooms for an hour to allow the a passengers access to their belongings. This was another doddle, which simply involved unlocking the hatch doors, switching on the lights, and chatting to whoever appeared. The rest of our overtime would be perhaps checking and overhauling the lifeboats and safety equipment.

Generally it was interesting and clean work and, to be fair, stretched out a bit to make the work fit the time. On watch on the bridge, our job was to make sure that the ship stayed on course, so we kept a good look out (although we seemed to spend as much time looking aft as we did forward due to the location of the swimming pool) and followed any instructions that the officer of the watch asked.

In carrying out these duties we naturally had access to the whole of the bridge and chart room so I was able to familiarise myself with some of the other equipment as well as the, what had been until then, the mysteries of the chartroom. I got on well with all the navigation officers but particularly the junior third officer, a young man only a couple of years older than me by the name of Hutchinson who came from Nottingham. This close proximity to the navigational workings of the ship led me to think that perhaps I should have stuck at it harder at Trinity House and not been so hasty in leaving to go deep sea fishing.

I looked at these officers and thought, I could do that. At the first opportunity I'd invest some money and buy my own copies of the books I remembered from Trinity House: Norie's Nautical Tables, Nicholls's Concise Guide (Navigation) and Nicholls's Seamanship and Nautical Knowledge (All Grades). I was on the bridge, I'd got Hutch if I got stuck with the calculations, and I'd got the time during long sea passages to start working towards a second officer certificate. But that would apply more during my second voyage on the Rangitoto, at the moment I was still learning and revelling in my job as quartermaster.

Apart from the Pig there was little entertainment for the crew so it was no surprise that any visit to the Caribbean meant that another pungent herbal odour was added to the cocktail of smells that included, stale food, sweat, farts, feet, cheap aftershave, tobacco - remember at that time nearly everybody smoked - that hung in the air in the crew's accommodation. There were so called air blowers in the crew's cabins but they were ineffective and it got so hot in the tropics that many crew members, especially those in four or six berth cabins, chose to sleep out on the open deck on the forward hatches. I was lucky in that I was in a two-berth cabin with portholes but even so it got pretty uncomfortable at times.

There was not that much entertainment for the passengers either on the 'Rangitoto' although the main meals of breakfast, lunch and evening dinner must have passed some time for them. Apart from the usual deck games, reading and cards, the main entertainment seemed to be the head waiter, who sometimes played the piano for the passengers in the evening. His two claims to fame were that he'd played the piano at some time for Johnny Mathis and that he'd once sacked a young catering boy called Tomas Hicks who went on to be known as Tommy Steele – but I've no idea if these stories were true.

The lack of entertainment must have been a bit boring for the passengers but the passage from Panama to Tahiti meant that we would cross the equator. This gave the officers and some of the catering staff the opportunity to do some showing off and have a bit of fun, mainly for their own benefit by having a 'crossing the line ceremony' with a visit from King Neptune. They made this last a good couple of hours in the afternoon to break up the day and made it a good-natured spectacle that the passengers would remember, generally for good reasons, as a highlight of the voyage.

I know that some people on general cargo ships and tankers suffered indignities as this form of 'initiation ceremony' could easily get out of hand with young sailors being made to suffer what would now be described as physical, or even sexual abuse, with the excuse that "it was only a bit of fun". I can say that I was never subjected to the 'ceremony' because by the time I crossed the line for the first time I'd been at sea for a few trips and it was assumed I'd been 'done'. Nor did I ever participate in a 'ceremony' because I wouldn't want my genitals shaved, painted with fish oil and red lead or some other concoction and I certainly wouldn't get any pleasure by putting anyone else through it. Just as there is a fine line between banter and verbal bullying, there is also a fine line between this type of initiation ceremony and physical abuse.

Following on from the above it would be a boring voyage on any ship if there was not some form of good-natured banter which is fine so long as it stays good-natured and no one takes offence. Generally I gave as much as I got as I was always up for a laugh. However, there were one or two of the deck crew who seemed to resent the fact that I, a young twenty-year-old, was a quartermaster and they hadn't been chosen for the role. They would make sarcastic asides as I passed by the sailor's square outside their mess-room on the way to our mess or the stairway that led to the passenger accommodation and the bridge. One of them in particular, an EDH from Hartlepool was more vocal and resentful than the others, even though he couldn't have been quartermaster anyway as you needed to be an AB with a lifeboat certificate.

As I said earlier usually I gave as good as I got but old Taffy Hayes must have picked up that this EDH was bothering me, as one day in the mess he raised the issue.

"Don't let them get to you because of your age," he said. "You're qualified and entitled to do the job, don't rise to their petty jealousy. Is it that one from Hartlepool who bothers you?"

"Yes," I replied.

"The next time he makes a comment just ask him who hanged the monkey? That'll cure him."

Taffy then went on to remind me of the story of a monkey that was washed up on the beach at Hartlepool during the Napoleonic Wars and as the locals had never seen a monkey before, or Frenchman, they hanged the monkey for being a French spy. I stored that useful titbit from Taffy and waited until the sailors' square was full after the evening meal and I overheard another of the EDH's sarcastic remarks.

I stopped walking past and said to him, "Do you mind answering a question for me?"

"No," he replied with a smirk.

"Who hanged the fucking monkey?" I asked.

The square erupted in laughter and the EDH from Hartlepool blushed but, to give him his due, he also smiled as if in acknowledgement and that was the end of the comments.

Chapter 22. A Medical Emergency.

A short stay in Papeete, the capital of Tahiti, broke the voyage across the Pacific. This again gave the passengers time to go ashore and stretch their legs or perhaps go on a sightseeing tour of the island or on a trip on a glass bottomed boat to look at the wonders to be found on a coral reef. Most of the crew who could be bothered headed for Papeete. I say could be bothered as it looked a pretty run down place with many of the natives in a sad state due to drink or drugs. This was a case of a tropical paradise that had been ruined by European, particularly French, administration. The main, and still developing industry was tourism, with the inevitable gift shops selling local wares, mainly tikis – small, carved wooden replicas of Polynesian warriors. While claiming to be genuine hand-carved statuettes the shelves were full of identical models. We all bought 'genuine' hand-carved tikis to take home as gifts, just like the passengers.

What did I do in Tahiti? Well I had a fascinating time as Bob Clarke asked me if I wanted to accompany him while he sought out some long lost relatives. Apparently most Polynesians are related in some way even though their communities are spread out far and wide across the Pacific.

The island only seemed to have one main road, a coast road that went right around the island with smaller roads coming off it at right angles. So we set off and caught a bus. I say bus but it was more like a lorry with benches down each side. The bus just went round in circles around the island picking up people on the way. Some of the people on the bus had been to a market in Papeete and carried big baskets full of their purchases, mainly food but also some livestock, which I suppose was food as well.

Eventually Bob and I got off the bus and headed inland looking for the village where his relatives lived. There didn't seem to be any street names or house numbers and I don't think Bob knew exactly where we were going anyway, as we kept stopping to ask directions. This involved a kind of ritual of smiles and handshakes all round, a twenty minute chat about nothing much at all, but as if we had been known in the area for years, and then finally we'd be asked our business and Bob would tell them what or who we were looking for. This led to much nodding and pointing before we had handshaking and smiles again and we carried on our way. Thus we spent the rest of the afternoon until Bob finally gave up looking for his relatives and suggested that we should head back. I think Bob was a bit disappointed but I wasn't, as I'd seen some of the real Tahiti and experienced the friendliness of the Tahitian people. I've no doubt that this was because I was with Bob as they treated me the same way as him but it was an experience I wouldn't forget.

We didn't know where the bus stopped but had no need to worry as when we were walking down a hill towards the main coast road we saw the bus stop and the people on board shout and wave for us to run and catch it.

Back on board ship I decided to go for a quick drink in the Pig. A ship called the 'Southern Cross' was also in the port and some of the crew had come aboard the 'Rangitoto' for a drink and a yarn, so the Pig was quite full and noisy. But above the noise I could hear a singing voice that I thought I'd heard before and sure enough, on the end of it, giving his well known rendition of "Maggie May" to a bunch of the waiters was Jimmy Cain, steward and boozing partner from the 'Verconella'. Jimmy, who was in his normal state, drunk, immediately recognised me.

"Bob! Me old mate, from the 'Verconella'."

Jimmy then went on to start telling the waiters, who were mostly from Liverpool and Glasgow and had spent most of their sea career on the Cunard Atlantic passenger ships, known disparagingly as the 'Big Ferries' as they were only ever away for a couple of weeks, about our voyage on the 'Verconella'.

He ended the story with, 'You bastards don't know what a proper trip to sea is like! See this bloke (hic), see this bloke (hic). We were away on a trip when we never knew when we were getting home! A full year! A full year we were away, and you bastards are bleating after a few weeks!'

It was good to see Jimmy again and share a laugh. However, the seriousness and significance of his words would soon become apparent and take on a more sinister turn as the discord that was developing amongst the waiters started to escalate into violent confrontations as the voyage progressed.

Watches again changed in Tahiti and the next stint for Neil and me on the last leg of the outward voyage was the graveyard watch, the twelve to four. The only good thing about the twelve to four on this ship was that the cooks left out a black pan - a fry up - so that we didn't have to get up for breakfast if we didn't want to, although as we always worked a few hours overtime we got up for breakfast anyway. Another part of being on the twelve to four was that if there were any clock changes for that night we would have to inform the various heads of departments early in the afternoon so that they could make the necessary adjustments.

I liked doing this as I got to parts of the ship and met people that I normally wouldn't have had much contact with such as the doctor, the hospital staff, the printer, the engineers, cooks, chief steward, head waiter, nursery nurses and purser. Visiting the galley was the best part as I was often offered delicacies that were only served to the passengers and officers and would never grace the insides of our cockroach-infested hot press in our little mess-room.

The nursery nurses were always good for a laugh although the comments I received would be considered sexual harassment nowadays. When you think about nursery nurses the image tends to involve young ladies but this lot were quite different as they were all of, shall we say, mature years with most of them as high as kites on the amphetamines that they took as slimming aids, which obviously didn't work, well not for slimming anyway. Usually they would be sitting drinking bottles of Guinness in their day room when I appeared to inform them of the time change as quickly as I could before making a hasty exit from their comments. Taffy reckoned that he'd been watching the head nursery nurse walking down a corridor when she stopped and lifted her leg and farted. I don't know if this was true but it sounded right at the time.

It was very hot in the Pacific and early one evening I decided the best way to cool off was with a dip in the crew's swimming pool, which was situated on the port side of the foredeck just below the bridge. I'd chosen a time when the pool was not being used by others and enjoyed a lengthy, quiet, cooling dip. After a while I decided to get out of the pool but as I climbed out I felt a dull pain in my scrotum area. As I made my way to my cabin the pain got worse so as soon as I reached my cabin I tried to lie down. Neil must have been in the Pig fleecing the crew with his crown and anchor board as he was nowhere to be seen. No matter how I tried to get comfortable in my bunk the pain increased even more, like someone had my scrotum in a vice and were twisting it. The pain became unbearable. Indescribable.

This was a Spinal Tap moment like when one of the band members in the film explains that his amplifier is more powerful than any others as it has been especially made with a volume control that goes all the way up to eleven rather than the normal ten. This pain went all the way to eleven. I decided that I needed medical help and made my way to the ship's hospital using alleys and stairs where I hoped I wouldn't bump into people. Eventually I found the hospital attendant, Bill the Pill, who put me in the hospital while he went off to find the ship's doctor. The doctor was an elderly, retired Harley Street surgeon who was assisted on board by Bill and a nurse. Both the doctor and the nurse were in the dining room where the main dining event of the voyage, 'The Gala Dinner', was being held. The nurse had been looking forward to this dressing-up saga when Bill approached the doctor and told him that I was in the hospital in extreme pain. The nurse apparently asked if it was necessary for her to leave the dinner to attend to one of the crew and was quickly told by the doctor that they were there to attend to the sick no matter who they were.

A young New Zealand surgeon who had been working in the UK and was heading home overheard the conversation and asked if he could accompany the medics to offer assistance if required (the Gala dinner must have been really boring) and the doctor agreed.

I was writhing in agony when they arrived in the hospital and the doctors took a look at what could be the source of the pain. The doctor quickly decided that my one remaining testicle had somehow got twisted and needed to be 'untangled and secured', which would mean an operation. The young NZ doctor immediately offered to carry out the procedure and the surgery was prepared. In the meantime I was given an injection of morphine to dull the pain until they were ready to give an anaesthetic and perform the operation. The operation, I'm pleased to say, was a success. They untwisted the testicle and put a permanent stitch in to reduce the possibility of it happening again and I'm happy to report that it has worked okay ever since. After the operation I was kept in the hospital for a couple of days where I got to know the nurse, who was really a nice person, even if she was disappointed about missing the Gala dinner, and Bill the Pill who both became my friends on the ship. Of course I was sore for a while afterwards but as my job was not really physical, and I could sit down more or less when I wanted, I was soon back at work on the bridge. One thing that I'm certain about though is that I was extremely lucky that I was on a ship with a doctor and a surgery. I hate to think what it would have been like if I'd had a similar accident on a foreign going cargo ship or tanker.

The largest crew group on the 'Rangitoto' were the catering staff, where there seemed to be a steward for every occasion. They even had a kind of hierarchy. I don't mean the hierarchy of the purser, chief steward, head waiter etc. but the rank and file hierarchy that started with the captain's batman and officers' steward, topside stewards and barmen who worked mainly on A deck, the bedroom stewards who looked after the passengers' cabins, and the waiters who worked in the dining saloon. There was a whole other hierarchy in the kitchens and I used to feel sorry for the scullions who spent their days up to their armpits in greasy water as the cooks slid their dirty roasting trays and pans down towards the scullion's sinks. Despite this however, the scullions seemed to be the happiest people on the ship with singing and banter coming from their direction all day. The waiters on the other hand were less happy and, as said previously, most on this voyage came from Liverpool and Glasgow and had spent most of their time on short sea voyages. So, after weeks at sea, a small number of them were finding it difficult and were hell bent on causing as much trouble as possible. This would peak on the homeward journey when the chief officer, Mr Highfield, had to put together a 'heavy gang' to keep law and order.

One day I was ambling through the passengers' accommodation when a rather lively young woman passenger complained loudly to me that she'd just heard that one of the crew had had his balls cut off, and if that wasn't bad enough, all the best looking men on the ship were gay!

I was in turn shocked, pleased and insulted by this outburst as I quickly realised that the member of crew having his balls cut off that she referred to was me but before I could put her right, and maybe offer her proof, she had disappeared and I consoled myself that at least she hadn't put me in the gay category. But then again I realised that I obviously didn't figure in her perception of being one of the best looking men either.

The lady had been correct about one thing though and that was the large number of obviously gay men on the ship, mostly among the bedroom and topside stewards and waiters, with some having their own feminine alter egos were they'd given themselves names like Cynthia, Maria and Toni. Generally they were flamboyant and entertaining with their chat and banter and were popular with the passengers. I know I had a surprise late one night while on gangway duty when I thought that there were a group of young girls about to try and gain access to the ship, before realising it was a bunch of the stewards returning from a night out in full drag.

Boat drills were a big thing on the 'Rangitoto' and every week we'd have a drill when we'd lower the boats from their davits to the embarkation deck. While we had boat drills on other ships they were rarely as regular as this and I think this was to add reassurance to the passengers that we were on the ball. In addition we'd also have a drill in Auckland when we'd lower some of the boats into the water. Being a quartermaster I was allocated a boat of my own, which meant that I had to supervise the preparing and lowering of a boat and also organise the lifting and re-cradling after the event. This lowering was fine because gravity took care of that but getting it back was much more like hard work and required a number of hands on the crank handles. This always caused a bit of banter if I'd allocated any of the more obvious gay stewards the task of winding the boat falls.

"Oh, look at my poor hands," and "Oh, he always chooses us on purpose," and so on but all good-natured. The deck crew never complained and just got the job done as quickly as possible.

Not all the stewards were gay though by any means and some used their close proximity to the passengers to their full advantage, particularly some of the topside stewards, barmen and the swimming pool attendants. It was of course a serious offence for crew members to fraternise with the passengers but inevitably nature took its course and things happened. The younger officers certainly took full advantage of this as part of their role was to socialise at mealtimes and during the evening entertainment. The deck crew had little or no chances of any form of interaction with the passengers while on the ship, however the quartermasters did have to move about through the passenger decks and had direct contact while on gangway duty in port.

I witnessed an interesting discussion once while queuing for a pint in the pig one evening. Sitting down nearby was a group of the Glaswegian and Liverpudlian waiters; a bit of a rough bunch who became the ringleaders of later trouble. Just in front of me was another waiter who, shall we say, in terms of butchness was the opposite to his Glaswegian and Scouse colleagues.

"What's yer name," said the biggest of the Glaswegians.

"My name?" questioned the young steward.

"Yer, yer name, who do yer think I was talking to?"

"It's Tony," said the young man with a shrug.

"No! What's yer fucking name!"

"I said it's Tony."

"Not your real name! Your other name!"

"I don't have another name."

"Yes you do! All you people have other names, like a girl's name!"

"Well I don't, its Toni with an I," said the young steward with a bigger shrug and a sigh.

Anyway it shut the Glaswegian waiter up.

Eventually we docked in Auckland and the passengers left the ship. New Zealand turned out to be as good as everyone had said. A green country with everything: long sandy beaches, fiords, mountains, plains and a climate that ranged from almost tropical in the north to one resembling that found in the south of the UK. The Maoris, who discovered the islands, referred to them as the "land of the long white cloud", which explains why the land is so green and lush as, along with some beautiful sunny weather, there was also the possibility of tropical torrential rain at certain times of the year, particularly on the North Island, while the south coast of the South Island was subjected to cold grey mists and drizzle, and, in winter, was cold enough for snow.

Our berth in Auckland turned out to be almost at the bottom of the main street, Queen Street, which, further away from the dock area, contained the shops and bars that you'd expect in a city centre. But Auckland didn't seem very big then, although there were sprawling suburbs made up of large bungalows, built mainly of wood. Nearer the dock end of Queen Street were a number of takeaways and restaurants specialising in fast food like fried oysters and "fush an chups" as the Kiwis would say. Fried oysters were oysters dipped in batter and deep-fried and were absolutely delicious, tastier even than the fried mussels that I'd feast on after a few beers in

Rotterdam. The bars in New Zealand served beer in a similar way to that found in Australia, through pipes with a gun on the end like a small petrol pump. They pumped the beer into glasses or big jugs that you could put on the table and pour what you needed into smaller glasses. The ice-cold beer was quite good and very welcome on hot days but the pubs shut about ten o'clock and didn't open at all on Sundays.

A major difference between Australia and New Zealand at that time was that the population of New Zealand was much more racially integrated than Australia which maintained a form of apartheid that applied to the indigenous Aborigines and kept out any overseas immigrants of the wrong colour or race. In New Zealand, the indigenous inhabitants, the Maoris, were themselves the original immigrants on the islands having landed there about a thousand years ago from other parts of Polynesia. Although there had been some violent exchanges between the Maoris and the European settlers in the past, generally they had decided to live together on the islands in social harmony and racial tolerance. However, it was still possible to pick up some racial tensions between the New Zealand Maoris and the Cook Island Maoris and the European settlers. For example, if there was any crime and any Maoris were suspected the New Zealand Maoris would blame the Cook Islanders, who they apparently considered a different race, as being the source of the trouble even though they had descended from the same Polynesian ethnic group.

Like in all seaports there were a few bars close to the quays that were pure drinking joints catering for a certain class of local clientele as well as the dockworkers and sailors. However, most of the dockworkers would have gone home by the evening when these places really livened up. Auckland was noted for 'Ma Gleeson's' and the 'Snake Pit' and it's best to say that these were for the intrepid only. The clientele was a mixture of the roughest elements of the local ethnic groups, hard drinking and tough looking wearing tight, T-shirts to show off their tattoos, muscles and beer bellies. You certainly wouldn't have chosen to tangle with this lot – and some of the men were just as fearsome! The girls though had a lot to offer and offer it they did, with added value if the queues outside the Bill the Pill's surgery every morning were any indication.

During the run out to New Zealand I'd made pals with the captain's batman, a young steward by the name of Joe who came from Luton. In the past he'd been a topside steward so had made a number of contacts in New Zealand with ex-passengers, so it was him and another couple of topside stewards, Fred de Cosse from Colchester and Little Danny from Derry, and a few others, that I chose as my shore mates. This meant that there was always something going on that usually ended in a party somewhere involving young local people with music, often guitars, cool beers, beaches and stars, no matter which port we were in. This was a much better way of enjoying New Zealand than drunken nights ending up in a brawl at the Snake Pit.

The 'Rangitoto' normally would spend some time in Auckland before moving down to the capital Wellington and then Lyttleton in the South Island, before returning to Auckland to load the passengers for the voyage back to London. One change of this routing was made to accommodate the Easter break when everything shut down. Ships don't earn money in port so the company arranged for the "Rangitoto" to sail on a mini cruise from Auckland in the North Island to the west-coast of the South Island, calling at Picton in the Queen Charlotte Sound. This added a nice distraction as it enabled us to see parts of New Zealand like the fiord area that wouldn't normally be visited by this ship.

It was also interesting that the passengers for this trip were nearly all locals from the Auckland area and included a number of the dockers who worked on the ship and their wives. Now I said earlier that the officers were expected to socialise with the passengers and for this purpose were expected to furnish themselves with a number of different uniforms for the various functions and the captain would order the 'dress of the day'. The 'dress of the day' for one evening on this cruise was for, I believe they are called 'number elevens', an all white uniform with a high, buttoned-up jacket very similar to the one worn by the topside stewards although bedecked with gold braid to show their officer status. And wearing this outfit, one of the third mates came bounding on the bridge in an obviously agitated state saying, "The bastards! They know who I am but every time I walked passed one of those dockers they shouted, "Waiter! More coffee please!"

Picton was a very small town in those days but we stopped there while the passengers went off on some trip or other. We of course ventured ashore to see what was going on and discovered that there was precisely nothing happening because it was Sunday and the pubs closed on a Sunday. So we ambled up the main street but passing a boarded-up and locked pub we could hear the sounds of a piano and laughing. On closer investigation and venturing around to the back door, we found that the pub was full with the beer flowing and soon we joined in. We asked what the police would do if they raided the place and a portly man with a glass of beer sitting in the corner was pointed to with the comment, "That's him there!" I think this was our only stop on the mini cruise before we returned to our routine in Auckland.

During our stay in New Zealand the quartermasters were required to maintain watches at the top of the accommodation ladder to log visitors on board and for safety reasons. The watch consisted of one quartermaster assisted by a deck-boy or ordinary seaman, my assistant was a deck-boy. Boy? He was over six feet tall! - from the East End of London called Dave Wall. Dave was a real nice lad and a good laugh so our watches went fairly quickly. With the log book for recording visitors was a list of standing instructions, which stated the times when visitors would have to leave the ship: 10pm for crew members' visitors; 10.30 for petty officers' visitors; and 11pm for officers' visitors. This to me was another example of the unacceptable class structure on a merchant ship. Not content with having your status emphasised by the height of your bunk above sea level or the colour of your bedding you had to suffer the indignity of having your visitors shooed off an hour before those of the officers. An injustice if I ever saw one but when I raised it with one of the officers he just said that if I wanted I could always apply for an extension – which wasn't really the point. I asked would it be fair if we (the officer and I) met up ashore with a pair of sisters and when invited back on board 'my sister' would have to leave half an our earlier than the other one. Giving me a look that said this would never happen he said the sisters could be his guests or I could again apply for an extension – still not the point.

When we were not on duty on the accommodation ladder in port we were given jobs by the mate, usually overhauling the lifeboats and lifeboat equipment, or occasionally the boatswain would give us odd jobs to do like wire splicing. The 'Rangitoto' had a little workshop in one of the winch houses with a bench and vice that made this easier and I always enjoyed jobs that involved rope or wire.

The boatswain incidently was a really good bloke called John McClure who led a fairly large deck crew. John had been on the ship for some time and followed a maintenance schedule that was so routine that the officers used to say that they didn't need to work out the ship's position as they could tell where we were by looking out of the bridge window and checking what the boatswain had the crew doing.

After Auckland the ship would go down to Wellington to discharge and load cargo before returning to Auckland to finish loading cargo and to take on board the homeward bound passengers. However, just before we were due to leave Auckland for Wellington a massive gale started to blow causing the captain to delay our departure. This was unusual because it cost a lot of money to keep a ship the size of the 'Rangitoto' in harbour but the wind was ferocious.

The next day, April 10th 1968, we learned that a large roll-on, roll-off ferry, called the "Wahine", on passage from Lyttleton to Wellington, had got into difficulties that led to the ship being wrecked in the approaches to Wellington harbour. People apparently watched helplessly from the shore as the ship was pounded and eventually turned on its side with a loss of fifty-one people – and another was to die in hospital later. It was a major tragedy, possibly the worst that had been experienced in that country and was more shocking because the "Wahine" was a state of the art vessel, only two years old. A couple of days later we passed the wreck of the stricken ship that was a sobering sight for us all. We had come down from Auckland experiencing the tail end of the gale so we also had a pretty rough passage but were thankful that Captain Guyler had not been prepared to risk sailing into the height of the storm.

Wellington was as pleasant a city as Auckland and I, along with Joe, Danny, Fred and a few others tested the bars of the city centre. Somehow early in our visit we ended up in a strip club. I don't know whose idea this was, certainly not mine, but as it happened it turned out to be a very tame affair as the regulations in New Zealand regarding nudity were practically puritanical. The girls were allowed to go topless very briefly but that was it. The lead dancer went under the name of "Fifi Lamour from Paris", although she probably had spent as much time in Paris as I had, which at that time was no time at all, and her exotic good looks were due more likely to being part Polynesian rather than Parisian. We watched the show for a short while and then carried on with our pub-crawl.

A few days later I was walking through the city centre when I bumped into Fred who was with a young lady and we popped into a bar for drink. Fred introduced me to the young lady, who I vaguely recognised but couldn't quite place, and then told me that they'd got married that morning. I was a bit taken aback by this as Fred had not mentioned a regular girlfriend, never mind a potential wife, but it was obvious he was smitten and I wished them well.

Now in the UK we all knew the "News of the World" and other Sunday tabloids as purveyors of scandal but the equivalent in New Zealand was another Sunday publication called the "Truth". Of course we all used to read this rag and as it happened, on our next trip on the 'Rangitoto' it was the first thing that we bought on arrival in Auckland. The headlines related to a bust of a strip club in Wellington where some of the dancers had been charged and convicted of gross indecency by over stepping the strict rules on which parts of the body could be shown. The main offender apparently was named as Carol de Cosse, otherwise known as "Fifi Lamour from Paris".

Unfortunately Fred found his wife's new fame difficult to cope with and the marriage was abruptly ended. I can't say that it was the shortest marriage on record but in actual time spent together – from meeting, wedding and sailing – it must have been close.

Above. The "Rangitoto".

Right. Author in Fort Lauderdale.

Below left. Bill (the Pill) and the ship's nurse.

Below right. Neil Johnson.

Chapter 23. A Burial at Sea.

Anyway, back to this voyage. The 'Rangitoto' left Auckland with a new bunch of passengers to retrace our path across the Pacific. We knew that the ship had a limited time left as the ship, and her sister ship the 'Rangitane', were due to be put up for sale as the long haul passenger ship as a form of travel was being rapidly replaced by the speed and convenience of airliners. If there was a future it was in the floating casino palaces and holiday camps known as cruise ships and a number of shipping companies were already moving in this direction. The emigrant ships like the 'Rangitoto' and 'Rangitane' were doomed.

Our passengers were a mixed bunch of young and old. On the outward journey many would be immigrants looking for a new life and on the voyage back we got a few of these who didn't like the new life and wanted the old one back. In addition to this it seemed that it was also a right of passage for young New Zealand people to return to the European countries of their parentage for a few years. We also had people who'd settled in New Zealand and were returning for a holiday, visit relatives or for other personal reasons.

Our return voyage involved a return to Tahiti: a short detour around the Galapagos Islands - to waste some time and allow the passengers to do some wildlife spotting, mainly sea lions as I recall; the Panama Canal - this time stopping in Colon; then to Kingston Jamaica, Port Lauderdale, Florida; and Hamilton, Bermuda before heading home.

Generally, on most ships, the long sea passages could become a bit boring but not on the 'Rangitioto' as there always seemed to be something happening and our crossing from Tahiti to Panama was no exception.

I was looking forward to the end of my watch on the eight to twelve with less than half and hour to go when the bridge telephone went and was answered by Hutch the third officer who then turned to me and said, "Just pop down to A deck there seems to be some commotion going on." So off I popped. Down on A deck I discovered a small group of people surrounding one of the bedroom stewards known as Cynthia. Cynthia was standing by the ship's rails dramatically gesturing with his hands while saying words to the effect that he'd had enough. 'Don't anyone stop me, I'm going to end it all, I shall jump," he shouted.

I'd heard that this had happened before with Cynthia and that he liked an audience, so he was really making the most of it and responding with increasing drama when the people watching tried to console him or talk him out of it. He was only leaning against the ship's rail and not sitting on it or even on the outboard side of it so, after listening to this nonsense for a few minutes I decided another approach was necessary so I said, "Cynthia, will you do me a favour?"

This seemed to stun him a bit and he said, "What?"

"Will you just hang on with your jumping for about fifteen minutes?" I said.

"Why?" asked the puzzled Cynthia.

" I go off watch at midnight and it will save me the hassle of being stuck on the wheel if we have to turn the ship round!"

There was a moment's silence as the people watching must have thought what a heartless bastard I was and then the silence was broken by Cynthia saying, "Typical! Typical! That's all the care you get on this ship!" and then flounced his way back to his cabin. My ploy had worked but in retrospect it could have so easily gone wrong.

Some of the waiters had begun to start playing up again during the Pacific crossing by being abusive to the passengers and on a couple of occasions disguising themselves and throwing bread rolls at them during the evening dinner. There were also violent incidents amongst the waiters themselves that forced Mr Highfield to bring into force his handpicked heavy gang to break up any trouble that flared up. Sometimes it wasn't possible to recruit the heavy gang in time as when the rebellious waiters chose to attack the passengers in the saloon during dinner. However, the offenders misjudged Mr Highfield as during one of these bread roll attacks he personally grabbed a couple of offenders and exposed their faces so that the ringleaders were quickly identified. Rumours started to circulate that three of the ringleaders were going to be put ashore in Panama. This got the mess-room lawyers speculating that "they" were not allowed to do this so it would never happen. How wrong they were. The Panama Canal Zone at that time was a protectorate of the USA and therefore they policed the area. When we arrived in Panama two American policemen came on board and the three ringleaders were taken to their cabin and told to pack their bags. They started to protest until one of the policemen pulled out a gun, pointed it in their direction and said, "Pack your bags!" They packed their bags and left the ship under an escort and were taken to some waiting police cars.

After this drama we passed through the Panama Canal and docked in Colon for a short stay. Inevitably some of the passengers, like on the outward bound journey in Panama City, had ignored the news-sheets produced by the ship's printer and posted in their cabins warning them of street thieves in Colon and returned shocked and mugged. Colon also gave us a chance to stretch our legs and visit a few bars.

Our next port was Kingston, Jamaica and we took on board a number of extra passengers for this short passage. Most of these were Jamaican people who worked in the Canal Zone returning for some home leave and, as it was just a fairly short passage, their luggage, made up of bags and baskets, was stored in the gangway recesses. There was a strict regulation that no livestock should be carried on board but I swear some of those baskets moved and clucked.

From Kingston we headed to Fort Lauderdale, close to Miami in Florida. Florida was only just becoming a major tourist destination in those days and one of the first attractions to open was a park called Ocean World. So, for a change to looking for the first bar and with having some daytime hours free, a couple of us decided to give it a visit. It was worth it because we'd never seen anything like it. Now, sea-life centres are all over the place as are theme and wildlife parks but this must have been a pioneer in the genre. You would have thought that we'd have seen enough sea lions, dolphins, sharks and killer whales in the wild without paying to see them. The Americans however really knew how to put on a show, even though in hindsight we know that the animals really are better off in their own habitat and left alone by man. Still it's not often that you see someone wrestling with alligators at sea.

After Fort Lauderdale the next call was Hamilton, Bermuda where, unfortunately, only the passengers had shore leave. However, now we were on the final leg of the voyage. I was pottering around on the bridge one morning when the junior third officer, Mr Hutchinson, known as Hutch, answered the bridge telephone and, in a matter of fact way, said to me, "Just pop down to A deck Bob, someone's just died."

What! Down the ladder I dashed to find an elderly gentleman collapsed in a deck chair next to a weeping wife and a couple of topside stewards. I immediately sent for a stretcher and was relieved to see Bill the Pill and the ship's doctor hurrying along the deck. Sadly it was too late to save the old gentlemen who, we later learned, had a heart condition which he knew was terminal. His wish had been to die in England; but unfortunately he hadn't made it. His wife was given the choice of having his body transported to London that would incur some considerable expense, or for him to be buried at sea. In P and O apparently this would have also incurred a cost but on the 'Rangitoto' the service was free. She opted for the latter.

His body was taken down to the ship's hospital but unfortunately there was no way of doing this without carrying it along the crowded A deck. This meant that some of the other elderly passengers looked at us as though we were the 'Angels of Death' selecting our latest victim, as they desperately crossed themselves as we passed by with our laden stretcher. This was a new experience for me, so with the macabre curiosity of youth, I asked Mr Highfield if I could witness the proceedings of preparing the body to which request he readily agreed.

That night, under cover of darkness, so that the passengers could not see, the carpenter brought the wooden board and a canvas bag used for sea burials to the hospital. Here, the boatswain, boatswain's mate, lamp trimmer, a couple of others, me and some cans of beer, were waiting. The body was placed in the bag along with a couple of fire bars, which were lashed to his feet so that the body would sink. The bag was then sewn up tightly around the body like a mummy. During this process Mr Highfield appeared with the traditional bottle of rum that he poured out while making a few toasts, replenishing our glasses as he did so, ensuring that the evening ended on high note for us if not for the gentleman in the bag.

The funeral was planned for six the next morning before the passengers got up. Usually the service was conducted by the captain but on this occasion we had an archdeacon amongst the passengers who offered to conduct the service, probably to keep his hand in so to speak.

The next morning we mustered outside the hospital and manoeuvred the body onto the launching board. The funeral would take place on the starboard quarter where a section of rail could be removed in order to slide the body into the sea. The hospital however was on the port side so that the body had to be carried around the stern. No passengers were allowed to witness the funeral and the man's wife had elected not to attend as she was too upset, so only a representative group of the ship's officers, in line, in uniform, with doffed caps, and the quartermasters were present. Two quartermasters were charged with keeping any onlookers away while four of us were required to carry the body on the board around the stern to the point where it would be dispatched and the archdeacon conducted the service. As we picked up the laden board from the bollards outside the hospital the archdeacon decided that it should be a proper funeral procession and he would lead it at a respectful, slow – no very slow, pace. Unfortunately the hand holes in the board were quite small making it difficult to hold as we could only just hook the ends of our fingers through the holes. And this bloke weighed over sixteen stones, so the load was heavy. Then it got heavier and heavier still, and our fingers were hurting, so we increased our pace. But it got heavier, so we moved a little faster, and our fingers were really hurting, so the speed increased to the point that the archdeacon had to jump out of the way as we made the final few yards a mad dash for fear of dropping the body. The bloke got his own back in a way, however, as when we finally lifted the board and slid the body into the sea he made an enormous splash that left us drenched and dripping.

The funeral had taken place close to the Azores so that the unfortunate passenger was only a few days away from achieving his wish to die in his old country. But for us the voyage continued and now we were all looking forward to getting home.

As it happened my twenty-first birthday occurred during this final leg of the passage, just three days before we finally docked in London. Normally I wasn't bothered by birthdays but in those days a twenty-first was considered special and some of my shipmates were not going to let a good excuse for a piss-up to pass by. Neil and I were on the twelve to four watch so had to be back on watch for midnight but we decided to have a few beers in the sailor's square after tea. Soon though the beer began flowing freely as others joined in to wish me all the best. They'd even planned it as they produced a wooden key, made from a mosaic of New Zealand woods, that most of them had signed, and a barometer that they'd clubbed together to buy from the ship's shop. I hadn't expected any of this and I still have the barometer in my hall and the key in my kitchen, although most of the signatures and messages have now faded to illegibility.

The party ended when Neil and I had to go on watch. Neil went on to the bridge first and it was immediately apparent to the third officer, one of the senior ones, that he was in no fit state to be on watch and called me up as I was first standby, only to find that I was just as bad. In fairness he could have reported us and we'd have been in big trouble but instead he made us take the automatic pilot off and steer by hand. This, he said was to "Stop us falling about", so that was how we spent the watch, either on the wheel or staggering about on the wing of the bridge with the third mate telling us to keep moving if it looked like we were flagging.

One of the perks of the twelve to four on this ship was that our peggy would collect a 'black pan' from the galley so that we could cook our own breakfast. This was so that we didn't have to get up for breakfast if we didn't want to but as we always worked overtime in the mornings the 'black pan' was not really necessary. But it was a treat, as the cooks were quite generous, leaving eggs, sausages, bacon, black pudding, chops and other goodies for us to indulge. The routine was that the final hour standby, which should have been Neil, would cook the 'black pan' after he called the next watch. At 3am Neil asked the third mate if he could go down to cook the 'black pan' and call the next watch and was told a definite, "No!"

I then heard him chuntering on the wing of the bridge, "He's fucking starving me now!"

I don't know why but the third officer seemed to want to punish Neil more than me but eventually, when it was time to call the next watch, he sent him down and told me to switch the automatic pilot back on. The next watch he took me into the chart room and showed me the printed graph of our hand steerage. The line was nice and steady until we turned off the automatic pilot and started to steer by hand, from then on the line resembled a jagged mountain range as we zigzagged our way through the Atlantic for the next four hours. Talk about drunken drivers! But, thanks to the third mate, we were lucky to get away with it.

We were now close to home and I'd already decided that I'd return for a second trip on the 'Rangitoto' as I'd thoroughly enjoyed myself. Neil, however, decided that he'd be leaving to spend more time with his wife. Neil lived in Glasgow although he originated from the Isle of Barra and had told me that his wife was Canadian. He'd also told me that he lived in a street called Mclean Street near the docks. I mentioned to Bill the Pill, who also came from near Glasgow, that I wouldn't be happy leaving my wife, if I had one, in an area like that while I went off to sea for months at a time.

Bill raised his eyebrows and said, " You haven't seen Neil's wife!" The image that immediately crossed my mind was that of a strapping lumberjack in drag but I may have been putting her down. Later, I'd come across Mclean Street when I was on a ship that docked at Plantation Quay in Glasgow and to me the tenement lined street looked even grimmer than the terraced streets I knew so well in Hull. There was a bar on the corner of Mclean Street opposite our berth and I remember a Saturday lunchtime going with a couple of shipmates for a beer. As we entered the bar it was like one of those scenes from an old Western movie when the stranger enters the saloon and the piano stops and everyone watches in silence as he walks to the bar. The men in the bar sported scars, black eyes, broken noses, wall-eyes, missing eyes and torn ears. We walked in silence to the bar as the local clientele watched us - some of them even had two eyes. They were drinking some form of spirit in shot glasses washed down with pints of heavy. We decided just to have a pint of heavy and retired to what we hoped was a safe corner, while still being eyed by the regulars. I'd been in some of Hull's notorious dockland pubs like the Sportsman and the Earl de Grey, which were considered rough but were strictly second division compared to this bar. Without saying a word, but exchanging a few knowing looks, we decided to drink up and get out as quickly as possible. Then suddenly the door burst open and another gentleman staggered in, covered in blood and with a wall-eye and a torn ear. We supped up and left. Crossing the road back to Plantation Quay we noticed a cat crossing from the other side. Its face was caked in blood, it had a wall eye and a torn ear. Even the local cats fitted the stereotype.

Back to the 'Rangitoto' and the last leg of the voyage. Finally we moored at the Tilbury Passenger Terminal for our passengers to disembark. Normally the ship would be allowed to remain there until it was time to proceed on the next rising tide up river to the Royal Albert Docks, giving those crew with free time a chance to have a pint in a local pub. However, because of all the trouble on board, which had continued despite getting rid of the ringleaders in Panama, the ship was ordered to leave the terminal and anchor in the river, with a police launch standing by, until we could dock and the crew paid off. We paid off on May 31st 1968.

It was always good to get home to Hull and get back into the social swing up there, enjoying the pubs and clubs, the Locarno, and another twenty-first birthday party. The grey coupé unfortunately was not liking being left for months on end and had shown its displeasure by refusing to start or breaking down on a regular basis, so it made sense to get rid of it. Anyway, being twenty-one I could now hire a car when I needed one.

I had about three weeks at home before returning to London to 'work-by', before signing on for another voyage on the 'Rangitoto'. Working-by was a bit like being on leave really as some of my mates Joe, Fred and Danny were also working-by, prior to the next voyage. These lads had contact with some young Kiwi passengers who were now living in Chiswick in West London so we were able to visit them for a bit of a party, which made a change to our usual visits to the pubs and cinemas in the West End.

I know that I managed to get to the Palladium during this time to see Sammy Davis Junior in a musical called 'Golden Boy'. All boxing films, books, plays and, in this case, musicals seem to tell the same story but nevertheless it was an amazing show. The icing on the cake, however, was the show that Sammy put on as an encore to the main one when he stayed on and entertained us for nearly another hour. He was a true all round, multi-talented entertainer or alternately the world's biggest show off depending on how you looked at it.

On July 2nd I signed on for my second voyage on the 'Rangitoto'. There were a few changes but not that many. Our first concern was from where the waiters had been recruited. Belfast! What! It had been bad enough with the blood bath of hatred that had materialised from the ex-Cunarders of Liverpool and Glasgow with their Blues verses Reds, Celtic verses Rangers nonsense, which was far worse than the Airlie Birds versus the Robins rivalry that we had in Hull. At least in Hull it wasn't complete sectarian violence based on religion. But now Belfast. The Orange versus the Green – what would happen? Nothing. They were as good as gold and surprised everybody by the way that they operated as a team, helping each other out as needed.

The rivalry did surface though on the homeward journey when the laundryman organised a boxing match supposedly for the entertainment of the passengers. The hatch immediately in front of the bridge was converted into a boxing ring and the tournament commenced under amateur boxing rules with Bill the Pill and the ship's doctor in attendance in case of a mishap. Attempts had been made to make sure that the combatants were evenly matched but what became obvious was that, for the majority of the bouts, in one corner would be a member of the Green followers while in the other you'd find an Orangeman. Still, it was better than carving each other up in the dining saloon.

Another change for me was that Neil had left the ship and had been replaced by an older quartermaster from Withernsea near Hull called Tommy Hanley. His arrival got Taffy saying, "Shall I do you now, Sir?" every time he left the mess-room. Apparently another Tommy Hanley had been a popular radio comedian and used this as his catchphrase. I vaguely remembered it but Taffy thought it funny. Tommy I think was in his late fifties and while we got on all right, the age gap was a bit of a problem and I don't think he always approved of my rather erratic social life at the time. He also liked to turn in early and made it clear that he wasn't too happy if I was up and about or even sitting at the desk in our cabin trying to study my Nicholls's and Norie's. Mr Highfield also informed us that he would be leaving when the ship returned to New Zealand and we also had a new captain. Things were definitely changing.

This voyage didn't seem to have quite the drama of the first voyage although I had a better time, as I was now familiar with the routine and the good times to be had in New Zealand. However, after Mr Highfield left, the ship for me was not quite the same as the new mate and captain were a little more officious. The new captain even introduced a new safety drill, on top of the boat and fire drills, only this time it only involved the officer of the watch and the quartermaster on duty.

This new drill revolved around the potential failure of the steering gear. We were all briefed on this drill and about what to do if this happened. The officer of the watch had to inform the quartermaster that the steering gear had failed, tell him to switch off the automatic pilot and proceed with him to the steering flat to link the manual steering gear, and bring the ship back on course from the spare wheel on the top of the poop deck. Probably because we were the youngest, the captain chose a time when the junior third, Hutch, and I were on watch. The captain came up on the bridge with the mate and told Hutch the steering was broken. Hutch turned to me and gave me the spiel about coming with him to the steering flat but forgot to mention turning off the automatic pilot, which I did anyway, and then we legged it off the bridge, down the ladder, along A deck where the passengers wondered what the hell was happening and down again until we reached the steering flat. There, we did the business and then climbed onto the poop deck and brought the ship back on course. It had all taken only a few minutes. We were then told to put everything back and return to the bridge where the captain said that we'd done very well before turning to Hutch and giving him a bollocking for forgetting to tell me to turn off the automatic pilot. That was the first and only time I was ever required to carry out that drill.

It was a pity that Hutch got a bollocking for this as I really liked him and if I got stuck with my studies he was the one I could turn to and he never failed to help. I had now had enough of the 'Rangitoto' and decided to leave even though the vessel only had one more voyage to do before being sold on. Air travel had done for the long haul passenger ships. Why spend weeks at sea when you could reach your destination in days or hours? Although the ships would be replaced by cruise ships carrying passengers for pleasure in ships that resembled a combination of theme park, shopping mall, casino, nightclub and hotel – a posh Butlins at sea! So on October

23rd I signed off the 'Rangitoto'. Mr Moxley, the New Zealand Shipping Company recruitment officer asked me why I was leaving so I told him that I wanted to study for my second mate's certificate and that there were too many distractions on the 'Rangitoto' and that I also needed my own cabin to study quietly.

"Don't worry about that, I'll sort you a berth on another one of our ships if you like. Go home and take your leave and I'll be in touch," he said.

Say no more.

Back in Hull on leave I met up with one of my old mates, Mick Harrison. Mick and Bob Mahoney had both married and settled down with girls who lived down the same street off Beverley Road. The girls had been friends since childhood and Mick told me about a third girl who was also a friend of his and Bob's wives who also lived on the same street. The girl was single and Mick arranged for us to meet on a blind date. It worked. Her name was Madeleine and soon a romance developed. Her dad, Norman (Nobby) Clark, was a trawler engineer on the St Dominic, so she was used to her dad being away at sea for three weeks at a time but would she be happy with absences of several months? Time would tell. In the meantime, with me with a hired car and every night being Saturday night while I was on leave, we just had a good time and enjoyed each other's company enough for us to decide to get married. I was only home for three week's leave so this seemed fairly quick, not as quick as Fred de Cosse though as a white wedding was planned for the following year depending on when I'd be home again.

When my leave was up I received a call from Mr Moxley asking me to return to London. He explained that he'd found me a berth as quartermaster on the cadet training ship the RMS 'Otaio', which he said would suit me down to the ground as I'd have my own cabin and have access to the cadets' tutors should I need it. However, the 'Otaio' wasn't sailing until December so in the meantime he wanted me to join a new ship called the mv 'Manapouri', which was going around the land before leaving on its maiden voyage. So, leaving Madeleine to her wedding plans, I returned to London.

I joined the 'Manapouri' on November 14th in the Royal Docks in London. The 'Rangitoto' was still in port so I managed to link up with some of my old mates, Joe, Fred and Danny for a few days before sailing on my new ship. The 'Manapouri' was a slick new ship described as a refrigerated freighter but designed for the container trade with cranes, derricks and hatches operated by hydraulics. Containers were an up and coming thing in freight transport with the big metal containers being lifted straight from the ship onto the back of a lorry or railway wagon. They meant quick turn rounds in purpose built ports away from the main dockland areas. The container trade was in its infancy in the 1960s and no one could have envisaged the huge container ships that would dominate and revolutionise world trade in the 21st Century. The 'Manapouri, built to the best specifications of the day in 1968 in Japan, would, at only 9,505 gross tons, 4,457 net, be tiny by comparison.

Captain Guyler, who I knew from the 'Rangitoto', seemed more at home on the general freighter, the 'Manapouri'. The accommodation on the ship was quite luxurious, as you'd expect on a new ship, and I quite enjoyed the month spent taking her around the land. This also meant that I could continue my courtship by regular telephone calls but unfortunately I didn't get a chance to return to Hull. We paid off in Newport, Wales, on December 11th and had to travel directly to London to join the RMS 'Otaio'. A young AB from Deal tried to persuade me to go with him on the Houlder Brothers' meat boats, where you could earn a lot of money but, as wedding arrangements were being made, I felt it best to stay with the New Zealand Shipping Company rather than risk the unknown.

Above top. The "Otaio boys - Ted, Paddy, Fred and Joe.

Above and left. The "Otaio".

Chapter 24. Around the World.

I signed on the RMS 'Otaio' the next day, December 12th 1968. The "Otaio" was the company's cadet training ship built in the John Brown yard in 1957. The ship carried refrigerated cargo and was fairly large at 13,314 gross tons, 6,875 net. The 'Otaio' carried about 40 deck and 20 engineer cadets, which meant that the only deck crew were five quartermasters, a boatswain - Angus from Skye, a lamp trimmer - an old seaman from Shetland who had something against "Papists" which he voiced at any opportunity, a carpenter and two deck-boys. We were called quartermasters but in fact we never had to take a watch, never mind steer. Instead we were on day work with instructions to help train the cadets in practical seamanship. In addition to those mentioned above there were also a seamanship instructor and a doctor. The ship also carried a PTI - Physical Training Instructor - but was unable to recruit one for the first voyage.

Work on the 'Otaio' meant getting back to grips with the real work of a seaman rather than the cushy life of a quartermaster on the 'Rangitoto'. Leaving our last port for the main sea voyage meant stripping the derricks, overhauling and greasing the blocks, oiling the wires and stowing the lot down in the hatches. When nearing our first port this whole procedure was reversed and being the youngest of the ABs meant that I spent a lot of this time up aloft unshackling or shackling the big topping lift blocks. I never minded working up aloft, in fact I didn't mind most of the jobs involved in the general ship maintenance that we were asked to do, except chipping. I hated chipping! I hated the noise, the smell, the metallic dust that clogged your throat and the shear monotony of the task.

As promised by Mr Moxley I had my own cabin next door to Ted the mess-steward's, so that I had the privacy and quiet that I needed to carry on my own studies. I was also quite comfortable and I'd go on to do two voyages in the ship, and in a way, the 'Otaio' was going to change my life.

I've already mentioned the Seafarers' Education Service that also ran the College of the Sea. This organisation was noted for putting libraries on ships and arranging correspondence courses for seafarers wishing to further their education, but in addition to this they also employed ship-board tutors. One of these tutors, a young artist called Peter Knox, joined the 'Otaio' for the trip out to New Zealand.

Peter soon got to know most of the people on board and based himself for his classes in the cadets' recreation room. We were all invited if we wished to observe his demonstrations and try us ing the art materials ourselves under his supervision. He delivered a number of lectures on art using slides, which I found quite fascinating. He also encouraged me to try painting myself, something that I hadn't done since

Boulevard School before Trinity House, and although I wasn't brilliant, the results were not bad and I enjoyed the process. This meant that most nights after we'd finished our overtime, which was usually painting a cabin or something like that, I'd join Peter's class and a lifelong interest in art developed. Peter introduced me to the works of Chagall, Giotto, Gauguin and many others which stirred my curiosity and made me realise how limited my nautical education at Trinity House had been and I wanted to learn more.

The first voyage was on a similar run to the 'Rangitoto' without the stops in Tahiti, so it was a long passage across the Pacific from the Panama Canal to Auckland. On the New Zealand coast we visited Auckland, Gisborne, Napier, Wellington and Lyttleton before heading the same way back. In Auckland Peter asked me about the 'Snake Pit' and if I could take him there. I explained that it was a pretty rough joint and not one that I'd normally visit but as a one-off I'd risk it. In fact the night went very well, as for once, there wasn't a fight, just good-natured drinking and joking ending with a big Maori woman stuffing my head up her T-shirt; briefly disorientating but I survived. I thought that would have been enough to quench Peter's curiosity but no he had enjoyed himself so much that he went back alone the following night.

The next morning a visibly shocked Peter turned up at my cabin to tell me how he'd gone to the bar and had been sitting enjoying the ambience when suddenly the whole bar had erupted into a bloodbath with bottles and chairs flying everywhere, and punches being thrown. He felt lucky to get out alive.

Also in Auckland, with Peter's advice, I bought a few bits of art equipment to continue my new hobby and a few books on the artists that interested me. Peter left the 'Otaio' to join another ship and spent a few years travelling like this for the Seafarers' Education Services before settling down in the North East to become a full-time artist, what a great way to earn a living. I was very lucky to have met him, very lucky to have been on that ship for that voyage, as his stimulation would, in part, shape my future career choices.

The 'Otaio' visited smaller ports that had not been part of the 'Rangitoto' schedule, like Gisborne, a small and friendly port on the east coast of the North Island in an area known as Poverty Bay. This was where Captain Cook first landed in New Zealand and he gave the area the name of Poverty Bay because he failed to collect fresh water and rations due to the less than friendly reception from the local Maori people. The resulting skirmishes left several of the local Maoris dead from musket shots.

The main export from Gisborne was, as you may imagine, New Zealand lamb, and to facilitate this there was an abattoir and meat processing plant on the quayside, which we were allowed to visit. What I noticed first was that the plant was almost entirely manned by Maoris and that the process was like an assembly line in reverse. Waiting outside the factory were flocks of wide-eyed and innocent sheep that were gently corralled into a fenced off area and a queuing system for the checkout. Once a sheep became the first in the queue, or last in line depending on how you looked at it, it arrived at a kind of wooden cradle where a large Maori pushed it into the cradle, pulled a lever, and the sheep landed on its back on a table. Here, there were another three jovial and singing Maori gentlemen waiting to dispatch it on its way. One held it down, one slit its throat, and the other wrapped a strop around its rear feet and hooked it onto an overhead rail and sent the body, gushing blood, on its way. The blood had a nauseating smell and was everywhere and at the sight of this carnage two of the cadets in our party immediately fainted and had to be taken outside.

Now on its way, the sheep was then split down the middle of its stomach and its insides flopped out onto a conveyor belt. A few yards further on, with a few deft cuts the sheepskin was peeled from the carcase and again added to another conveyor. Finally the carcase was trimmed and put in a muslin bag and sent to the freezers. Within minutes it had gone from a cuddly, woolly animal to what you would see hanging at the back of the butcher's shop.

After a pleasant stay in Gisborne our next port of call was Napier on Hawke Bay. Cook had a better reception in this area just having to warn the locals off with a few musket shots and the odd blast of a friendly cannon. Napier, as well as being a port was also a seaside resort but it seemed stuck in another era, and very reserved and quiet compared to what we'd expect in the UK. The beaches seemed nice though and there were attractive park areas on the sea front, one with a statue of Pania of the Reef, a sea nymph who legend had it lured sailors to their death on Napier's off shore reef. She didn't manage to lure us though and we sailed safely on to Wellington, and then Lyttleton.

From Lyttleton our voyage home was via Panama and Curacoa, although instead of shore leave in Curacoa we were required to help the engineers change a piston liner, which had to be done quickly during the few hours we were in port bunkering, so that we could continue our homeward passage on all cylinders.

The 'Otaio' paid off on March 31st 1969 in London and I returned to Hull after agreeing to return for a second voyage. In Hull, plans were well on the way for the wedding and house hunting was also on the agenda. Madeleine's mother wanted her to have a big white wedding as the eldest daughter had got married at the register office and she felt that she, the mother, had missed out. So the wedding was arranged to take place at St Mary's in Sculcoates, with a reception at the Dorchester Hotel on Beverley Road on May 2nd. I thought this was cutting it a bit fine given that I'd need to rejoin the 'Otaio' about then but it was out of my control.

On the house-hunting front we soon found a house for sale opposite where Madeleine lived in Cromer Street that would suit us as a starter home. I didn't mind living close to her parents as I got on well with them and I'd be at sea a lot anyway. It was just a small house in a terrace with a front room, living room, kitchen, three bedrooms, but one had been fitted out with a bath, and the lavatory was in the back yard next to the coal-house. At the front was a tiny garden. The house cost £1,200. Yes. £1,200! I've had monthly Visa bills bigger than that! But it still seemed a fortune at the time and we had to get a mortgage! Unfortunately the sale had not gone through by the time of the wedding but it would be completed while I was away at sea.

The wedding took place on May 2nd. My brother-in-law Jack, who was my best man, instructed the taxi to drive past the church and go to the nearest pub that turned out to be the aptly named for me, the Golden Ball, where we had a couple of pints before heading back to the church. Unfortunately, although it was May, the church was very cold so it meant that I spent most of the service dying for a pee.

After the wedding we went to stay in an apartment in Bridlington, mainly out of necessity rather than for a honeymoon, as we had nowhere else to stay until our house became vacant. It was only for a few days anyway because I had to return to London to sign back on the 'Otaio' on May 8th – married for five days and then away for five months – such was the life for a sailor and his wife.

I did manage to get home once for a day or two while we were going around the land before the main voyage but our main communication was by telephone during this period and then by mail once the voyage commenced proper as there was no mobile phones, satellite or internet in those days.

Joining me for this second voyage was a nice chap called Fred Hurd from Hull, a large jovial Irishman from Cork called, you've guessed it, Paddy, an AB from Stornaway called Murdoch who was going out to New Zealand to settle as he'd married there, and an ex-Royal Navy AB called Clive. Going around the land we didn't have a full complement of cadets so with only having five ABs and two deck-boys it was essential that everyone pulled their weight but it seemed we had a weak link. Clive, who despite being a really pleasant bloke and shipmate, did not seem to have much of an idea of what was going on and did his best to avoid showing his lack of knowledge by volunteering to fetch any tools or equipment that we needed when carrying out a job. For example if someone said, "We need a big stillson (wrench) for this job."

"I'll fetch it," would be Clive's response.

We quickly realised that after leaving the Navy, Clive would be about forty, he'd only been on ships with large crews and from our conversations we also discovered that his job in the Navy had been as a PTI. I suggested to him that the 'Otaio' might need a PTI as the company had been unable to recruit one the previous trip but Clive scoffed at this suggestion, saying that he'd "finished with all that business" when he left the Navy.

One day I was chatting to the mate and I asked him if we had recruited a PTI and he said that they hadn't been able to find one, so just in passing, I mentioned that Clive had been a PTI in the Royal Navy. The mate suddenly showed interest and asked if I thought that he would be interested in taking on the role and I answered that of course he would. Of course Clive said that he wouldn't take on the role when I told him about the conversation with the mate but as soon as he was told that a uniform came with the job he accepted. The mate said that he was relieved to have been able to fill the position but not as relieved as we were to get rid of Clive.

The five quartermasters were now Fred, Paddy, Murdoch, myself and Joe Armitage, a Liverpudlian who supported Everton to the point that I think that everything he owned was Royal blue, including his work boots. The voyage this time would be a bit different, as we were to sail around the world eastwards. This meant that because the Suez Canal was closed due to warfare, we sailed south through the Atlantic, had a short stop at Cape Town for mail, then across the Indian Ocean through the Southern Ocean and Great Australian Bite, until we reached our first port of call, Melbourne.

One day I was sitting in my cabin when the door burst open and Ted the mess-steward asked me to come quickly next door to his cabin. One of our deck-boys, a big strapping six-footer of a sixteen-year-old, was on Ted's day bed with his eyes rolling and his limbs flaying about. Ted said he was just sitting there chatting when he went into these spasms. I got Ted to help me lift him onto the deck and then sent him for the doctor while I held the deck-boy's head to stop him hurting himself. The doctor, who came just as the lad was quietening down, said he'd had an epileptic fit and we'd done the right thing in looking after him and all we could now was wait until he came around. When he recovered the deck-boy said that this had been the first time that this had happened and didn't know what had triggered it. Sadly we knew that this young lad's dream of becoming a seaman was now over. The captain tried to arrange for the lad to continue at sea as a catering boy but this was also refused and we all felt for him.

We had a good crew on the ship and we all got on well together. The cadets were a good bunch of lads and were happy to share in our banter. Unfortunately I can only remember one by name and that was because he was subjected to a bit more banter than the others. His name was Darling. The conversation usually went something along the lines off, "The mate must really like you."

"What do you mean?"

"The mate must really like you a lot."

"Why?"

"He always calls you darling."

On the outward bound journey we carried a deck cargo of dogs. There were several different breeds and were kept in kennels on the boat deck. The cadets would sometimes take them for walks around the decks but generally they were kept on ropes attached to the kennels. Occasionally we would visit them and watch them fussing about. One day I was watching them and chatting to the mate when he asked me which dog was my favourite. I pointed to small brown dog and said,"That one". He asked me why and I told him that it was because it was quieter than the others and wasn't barking and yapping all the time. He looked, and then we both laughed when he said that no wonder it was quiet, it was a special breed of African hunting dog called a basenje and they didn't bark!

We had a pleasant stay in Melbourne that I remember as being a very nice city in a kind of green, European way. On a sunny Sunday local people would take a leisurely walk along the quayside looking at the ships while I also remember spending a warm afternoon sitting outside a bar on a marina. From Melbourne we sailed up the coast to Sydney.

I'd previously been to Sydney on a tanker, which meant that we'd berthed miles from anywhere as was usual on those ships, but the 'Otaio' docked in a much more convenient position almost in the city centre.

We tied up late in the afternoon of our arrival and Joe and Paddy asked me if I wanted to go ashore for a cold beer. I didn't need asking twice and we set off to find a bar, which meant crossing a bridge known as Pyrmont Bridge. It was rush hour and people were making their way home after a hard day's work and as most lived in the suburbs they were crossing the bridge in the opposite direction to us. I was busy yapping to Joe and Paddy when a guy casually walked by us and as he passed said, "Good day, Bob."

We stopped and looked to see who it was and looking around smiling and carrying his lunch box was Mick Parkinson from Hull who I had last seen sitting on the quayside in La Spezia after he jumped ship there. When you have travelled over 12,000 miles to the other side of the world the last person you expect to bump into is an old mate from your home town. Joe and Paddy's faces were a picture of disbelief.

While we were in Sydney, Murdoch and I decided to look up a couple of other mutual friends. During the second voyage I did on the 'Rangitoto' the swimming pool attendant and another topside steward had jumped ship in Auckland, travelled by train to Wellington and then caught a ferry to Sydney, therefore entering Australia legally. The journey had been well planned in advance and they had even kept their plan secret from their closest mates. Murdoch had been on the 'Rangitoto' before me so he also knew them. We arranged to meet them in the King's Cross area of Sydney where they were living. They were working as window cleaners and making big money. This doesn't mean that they were going around the streets balancing a ladder while riding a bicycle; these guys were working from cradles on the Sydney skyscrapers. Apparently the Aussies weren't keen on the job but our friends liked it because they could start early in the morning and finish at lunchtime before the sun got too hot, and they were very well paid in the process.

From Sydney we sailed to Auckland and continued down the New Zealand coast, stopping at the same ports as the previous voyage. In one of these there was a shortage of dockers so we were asked to make up their numbers and we would be paid at 'New Zealand docker rate', which was considerably more than our normal pay. We were set to work unloading boxes of butter from railway wagons. This meant either picking the box up in the railway wagon and putting it on a kind of conveyor belt made of steel rollers or picking the boxes off the conveyor and stacking then onto a pallet, ready to be lifted aboard the ship. The boxes seemed small and light and we felt we had really cracked it as we totted up in our heads what we'd do with the extra money for so little effort. But after an hour the boxes seemed to get a little heavier, and then heavier still, then even heavier. By the afternoon they felt like they were filled with lead and we wanted the day to end as our arms and backs ached but the work continued. It was the same the next day and we were relieved when we finally emptied the last wagon and then waited with anticipation for our wages. We had all expected to be paid in addition to our normal wages for helping out like this to make sure the ship kept to its schedule. But in true shipping company fashion, our ship's wages were deducted from our 'docker earnings' and we were just given the difference. It hardly seemed worth the effort.

Our final port in New Zealand was Dunedin, deep down in the south of the South Island. While on the New Zealand coast one of our jobs had been painting the ship's side and in Dunedin we just had to finish it off by re-painting the white line around the ship's hull using a painter's punt. We were painting around the stern of the ship when there was sudden splash in the water so we looked expecting to perhaps see a fish. But then there were more splashes as the punt was surrounded by a group of small penguins that put on a marvellous display of their swimming skills for us. The penguins also reminded us that we were in the Southern Hemisphere and that our homeward voyage would take us further south to even colder waters.

During my time on the 'Otaio' I was elected as shipboard convenor. This arrangement, a sort of floating shop steward, had been negotiated by the National Union of Seamen following the strike and the idea was that if there was a grievance aboard ship, then the convenor would act as the spokesperson and take it up with the captain and officers concerned. Generally there was little to convene on the 'Otaio' as it was a pretty happy ship but I did learn a lesson that stood me in good stead, when in later life, I became more involved in more important disputes and negotiations. The lesson I learned was to never respond immediately to an issue and wait until all the facts of a case were apparent. An example of this was when the boatswain complained about the food. Now the food on the ship was not brilliant but there was always plenty of it and no one else had complained so what was the real problem? Answer, the boatswain had had an argument with the cook two days before the complaint.

I always found the captain and the mate to be very amenable, however I did take one instance very personally and it was that old class-consciousness thing again.

The problem arose because of a chair. Just an ordinary wooden chair with arms. The chair had been in my cabin from the day I joined the ship and to me it was just a chair that I used to sit at my writing desk or just to relax and read. Everyone had a chair in their cabin and while they may have been of different designs, I didn't think that mine was in any way extraordinary. Then one day, returning to my cabin after one of the captain's inspections, I found my chair gone! I asked the boatswain who had been around while the inspection was going on what had happened to my chair and he said that the mate had taken it.

I went straight up to see the mate and said, "Why have you taken my chair?"

"It's an officer's chair and it shouldn't have been there," he replied.

"It's been there since I joined the ship last trip, you had no right to take it."

"It's an officer's chair," he said again.

"What do you mean it's an officer's chair, are your arses different to ours?"

"No, it's because it's made of wood and has arms, the crew should have metal chairs."

"I don't think I've ever come across anything so trivial and pathetic before. The chair hadn't been stolen, nobody missed it, no one even noticed except you."

"It's not that big a deal is it?"

"Can I have it back?"

"No."

"Then yes, it is a big deal for me."

Up until this time I'd been happy on this ship but this was, in my opinion, blatant class distinction and I didn't like it. It soured the way I felt, and the mate who I'd previously liked, went down a long way in my estimation.

The voyage home from Dunedin involved some pretty nasty weather: fog, mist, snow, heavy rainstorms, squalls and gales. We experienced all of these during our voyage through the most southern part of the Pacific and then the Drake Passage and around Cape Horn into the Atlantic. Even the Falklands Islands were swathed in murky mist so it was a relief to head north in the Atlantic to meet the warmth of the tropics. Our only stop was at La Palmas in the Canary Islands and although there was no shore leave, we did have a couple of bum-boats vying for trade. Finally we docked in Liverpool and paid off on October 2nd 1969. Joe came to Lime Street station with me for a few beers before I caught the train to Hull Paragon. I'd been married for five days and away for five months, and, although I didn't know it, I'd just completed my last deep-sea voyage.

PART FIVE – CHANGING COURSE.

Chapter 25. Middle Water.

I returned to Hull and my new home in Cromer Street. Friends and family had donated several bits of furniture and other household items and, although second hand, everything worked and the house was comfortable giving us a good start until we could get ourselves together. My brother-in-law Jack helped me to do some decorating and all seemed well. Madeleine and I even went to the dog's home and got a cute little champagne coloured kitten that eventually grew into a mean and lean killing machine of a ginger tomcat that ruled the neighbourhood. A roaring fire, a cat on the mat; the image of domesticity.

I was home for just over five weeks before joining my next ship. Bear in mind that the total time we'd actually spent together, when I'd not been away at sea, which included our meeting, courting and getting married, was about thirteen weeks in just over a year. How well did we know each other? It didn't seem to matter as we were both taken by the novelty of the learning experience and every night was still Saturday night for a silly sailor. Madeleine had made it clear though that she did not want me to do another long voyage. This made it difficult for me as being a Pool man I could only turn down three job offers so I kept a low profile while watching the jobs board in the Pool office. This accounts for my extended leave but eventually I had to make a choice. The next best thing other than a ferry or a home trade vessel would be one on a six month's running agreement, which meant that you could give your notice in when you liked prior to docking in any UK port. I was running out of choices when I noticed a six-month's running agreement job on a ship called the mv 'Camarina'. I'd never heard of this ship but thought it worth a try as at least I'd be able to get off it if I didn't like it. On top of that running agreement ships were often on regular runs which would again be an advantage. However, the 'Camarina' turned out more to be a middle water tramp ship, trading anywhere between the Baltic and the Mediterranean, but I still liked it.

The ship was a new ship of only 1,473.23 gross tons, 852.82 net, so she was much smaller than what I'd been used to. She was described as being fully automated with her engines being bridge controlled, with hydraulic hatches and cranes on deck. Being automated meant that she carried only a small crew of twelve, which included the captain, chief officer, second officer, cook, steward, two engineers, motorman, boatswain and three ABs. The captain's name was William Urquhart according to my discharge book, who turned out to be a good captain although he did like a drink and was a bit accident prone. It was a good job then that we had a very efficient and pleasant chief officer to keep things running. I always felt that the atmosphere on a ship was determined by the attitude of the captain and the chief mate and I discovered that this was a very happy ship. The idea behind automation was to reduce labour, as was the case on this ship, but what became apparent was that this certainly didn't reduce the work load of those left to sail the ship. Teamwork and pulling your weight was therefore absolutely essential hence the need to maintain good working relationships.

The ship was owned by the Hadley Shipping Company, and showed the company's colours on the funnel, but it was actually managed by Houlder Brothers. The mate was a Houlder Brothers' man and the company had been involved in the design of the ship from the off and it showed. Our accommodation was very comfortable with single cabins fitted out with wood-lined bunk beds and wardrobes that I had only seen in officers' cabins on other ships. Between the cabins were showers and toilets for our convenience. The mess-room had a hot water geyser that kept itself topped up and boiling, and there was an international television for our entertainment should we need it. The food was excellent with no expense spared and in addition everybody had the same bed linen and bedding. This, to me, was luxury at sea.

The rest of my deck crew mates were a good bunch. There was a young AB, just a bit older than me from Swansea called, yep, you guessed it, Taffy. Then there was Jock who in fact lived in Leicester, and the gruff voiced boatswain with a scraggly beard and the tendency to hit the booze hard with his mates, Jock and the motorman.

My memory is a bit vague on the actual ports that we visited on the 'Camarina' but it would be six weeks before we returned to the UK. Our first port I believe was Copenhagen before going through the Kiel Canal to Ventspils and Riga. My first indication that Captain Urquhart was accident prone was on our return through the Kiel Canal. I was on the wheel when we entered the lock pit prior to entering the Elbe and it was dense fog. The Captain said to the German pilot that he wished to anchor on leaving the canal until the fog lifted but the pilot said there wasn't a safe anchorage in the vicinity and the ship would have to move further down river to anchor. This lead to a an argument between the two with the captain ending it by saying, "I'm the captain, I'll anchor where I want!"

I didn't hear anymore as Taffy relieved me. I was supposed to go directly on deck but felt that I deserved a warm up first so went to the mess-room for a quick mouthful of coffee. I could tell by the engines that the ship was now leaving the lock pit to head out into the river. Then the engines stopped and as I lifted my mug to my lips I heard the rattle of the anchor cable followed by an almighty bang as the ship lurched to starboard and the coffee flew out of my mug across the mess-room, with me following it.

I ran up on deck to see the bow of another ship backing off away from our stern. The captain had come down off the bridge as we watched the ship disappear into the fog leaving, thankfully well above the waterline, a dent and a small hole in our stern. The next thing we heard were cries from down below so the captain and I made our way down the steep ladder to find that the cries were coming from the galley. Where the ship had hit us and caused the hole was in the pantry just off the galley. Lying injured on the galley deck moaning was the cook being attended to by the steward.

"Save yourselves. Leave me, I'm an old man," he was saying with some drama.

After we had reassured the cook that we were not sinking and were not now in danger things calmed down a bit. The cook however had suffered a serious back injury, which meant that he had to be put ashore and a replacement sent out to our next port. The cook on a ship is an important job in terms of being a key in keeping everyone happy and during my time at sea, on trawlers as well as the merchant navy, I witnessed two main types: those that rushed around everywhere in a last minute panic with grubby checks and dripping sweat into the soup, and those that always seemed to have immaculate checks and T-shirts, never seemed rushed and always had time to lean on the galley door for a chat. Needless to say the latter type always produced the best food and the replacement for our injured chef, who would have just been in the former stereotype, was firmly in the latter category and the food got even better. Every cloud don't they say.

The second incident that made me feel I was almost in an episode of 'The Navy Lark' was when we'd been to Rochefort in France. I was up on the bridge to escort the French pilot down to the pilot ladder when I overheard him say to the captain that the only thing he had to avoid now was a light-bouy that he pointed out some distance away. We dropped the pilot and the captain put the ship on automatic pilot and took charge. The light-bouy was the only visible thing ahead of us in the whole of the Bay of Biscay, it would have been much harder to hit this small target than to miss it, but hit it we did, only this time there was no damage.

Rochefort was a nice little inland port incidentally, approached by navigating up a winding river. We were there for a few days and the boatswain and his drinking partners soon familiarised themselves with a local hostelry. I'd taken to carrying a few acrylic paints and a painting pad with me to pass the time when I was not reading and the boatswain asked me if I'd "knock him up" a picture of the ship to give to the landlord of the bar before we left.

I hadn't tried "ship portraiture" before but I had a go and the boatswain was happy with my efforts and took it to the landlord who, apparently, was delighted with it. Also some of the local patrons were interested in where the boatswain had got the picture from and asked if I had any more. I didn't have any more ship pictures but I did have a few paintings that I'd done in my pad so the boatswain said to bring them to the bar that night. I was a bit shocked when the locals liked them and asked me how much they were. I hadn't a clue so just said a figure that covered my material costs and a little extra and they bought the lot. With the money I ventured into Rochefort the next day, found an art shop, and used it to buy more materials.

The 'Camarina' carried mainly general cargo but she had also been built to transport bulk loads, although this had not been requested until we were told to prepare the holds for carrying bulk grain. This meant constructing shifting boards in the holds. The shifting boards had been supplied when the ship was built but needed assembling, which was complicated by the fact that no one could find the plans for fitting them together. In addition to this the boatswain and Jock, with their mate the motorman, were on a bender and were in no fit state to help so the work had to be carried out by Taffy, the mate and me. I've said before that the mate was a terrific bloke from Houlder Brothers and the three of us worked together as a small team to work out how the stanchions and boards fitted together. We were working against time as well, so we just carried on until we finished. It was exhausting but we got there in the end and the mate was delighted with our efforts.

The next day, when he was sober, the boatswain was called to the captain's cabin to receive a good rollicking for his inebriated lapse. Taffy and I were sitting in my cabin having a yarn when the chastised and sheepish looking boatswain appeared in the doorway with a bottle of rum saying that the captain had given it to him to give to the lads who'd done all the work. Nice one. Of course we shared our bottle with Jock and the boatswain because as I have said before, this was a very happy ship.

Other ports that we visited on the 'Camarina' were Santander in northern Spain, Oporto and Lisbon in Portugal and Malaga in southern Spain. In Santander the boatswain and the motorman convinced the officers that they could repair the hole in the stern. The ship was equipped with welding and burning gear that could be fed from the gas canisters in the engine room to anywhere on the ship. The master plan was to weld a plate across the top of the dent and hole and then braze the plate and hammer it to the shape of the dent and then weld all around it. I said I didn't think it would work but nevertheless Taffy and myself were told to rig a stage over the stern and to then pass the gear over when they needed it. The boatswain and the motorman climbed over the stern and onto the stage but before they could start they needed to chip away the paint where the first weld was to be and measure the plate. For these two this meant stopping every twenty minutes or so for a drink, so by the time they'd got to the point when the welding gear was needed they were both a bit merry. They started the weld with the boatswain holding the plate in place while the motorman did the welding and soon they were engrossed.

Bang! One of the pipes flew off the welding gun, the motorman dropped it and it then set fire to the boatswain's trousers. While they were beating out the flames they forgot about the welding gun, which by then had set the stage ropes on fire. The boatswain was shouting for us to do something but Taffy and I were just creased up laughing. Eventually, it would have only lasted seconds; the dynamic duo put out the flames and then fuming in every sense, climbed up on deck. They did try again but it was a waste of time and it needed a professional dockyard job.

Malaga was our last port before heading home to the UK with our destination port being Manchester. We knew that we would be arriving about Christmas and some of us gave our notice in. The mate said he was also leaving to go back on the Houlder Brothers' meat boats running to Argentina and told Taffy and me that if we wanted a job with him we would be welcome, a nice touch but I'd made the decision to try life shore side.

When we were a few days from Manchester the mate said to me, "Good News, Bob, we will be arriving at the Manchester Ship Canal about five o'clock on Christmas Eve."

I immediately told him that wasn't much good as it could take six or seven hours through the canal and we'd be too late to catch our trains home and would be stuck in Manchester over Christmas. He replied that he hadn't thought of that but to leave it to him but in the meantime find out where people were hoping to travel. I returned to the bridge with the destinations. Sometime later I was called back to the bridge and the mate said, "Right Bob, we've arranged for a shipping master to board at the second set of locks on the canal to pay off those of you who are leaving. At the next locks there will be a taxi waiting to take you all to the station. Taffy's train for Swansea leaves at 9.10, Jock's to Leicester at 9.20 and your train to Hull leaves at 9.35."

I asked him who was going to do the mooring when the ship docked in Manchester and he said not to worry as whoever was left would muck in. What a ship! I think this was the best ship I was ever on.

As we headed north on the final leg of our homeward journey we hit a severe gale. I was on watch with the second mate when I noticed that the foremast navigation light was out. I pointed this out but we were shipping heavy seas and the second mate considered it too rough for me to go forward to replace the bulb. About twenty minutes later the mainmast light went out.

"We can't have both navigation lights out Bob," said the second mate handing me a bulb. "Do you mind seeing if you can put a new bulb in the mainmast light?"

I wasn't too keen to be honest as it really was blowing a gale but it had to be done. The second mate left me on the wing of the bridge looking up while he made his way back to the shelter of the wheelhouse.

"Where are you going?" I asked. "At least you could stand by and watch so that you can accurately log my death if I fall."

It was cold and wet as I climbed the mast to reach the lamp and I had to wrap my legs around the cross trees as I undid the wing nuts in the lamp housing to be able to change the bulb. Looking down I could see the second mate on the bridge wing looking up but more disturbing was the amplified roll of the ship at this altitude. First I was looking down at the boiling sea on the starboard side while clinging on for dear life, then up and over and I was looking at the boiling sea on the port side and even more clinging on for dear life. I changed the bulb as quickly as I could and made my way down, which seemed more difficult than going up as each wave seemed to be trying to shake me off the mast. It was a relief to get down safely and it was not an experience that I'd like to repeat.

Finally we reached the Manchester Ship Canal a little later than expected due to the weather we'd experienced but the mate's plans worked just as well. The captain came down to shake our hands as we left the ship in the designated lock pits and said that it had been a pleasure to have us on board and he'd take us back anytime, again a nice touch. I caught my train on time and I arrived home in Hull at just before midnight on Christmas Eve.

Merry Christmas.

Above. The Upper Whitton Lightship anchored in the Humber to mark the channel between Brough and Winteringham. (By kind permission of John H. Bratton).

Below. Location of the Upper Whitton Lightship.

Chapter 26. Shoreside and the Upper Whitton Lightship.

There were a million people unemployed in 1970 that, according to the newspapers, was a national disgrace after twenty-five years of full employment, but nevertheless I had no alternative other than to join the queue at the dole office.

Financially it wasn't too bad as the employment benefit at the time was called 'earnings related benefit', which meant that you were paid a percentage of your previous wage for a short period of time before falling back to the basic dole money. However, I soon got bored so started applying for jobs almost immediately. And I was soon disillusioned. What is an ex-seaman with no academic qualifications qualified for? What good is an AB's certificate? Who on shore wants a certificated lifeboat man? I had also left school without any formal qualifications and I soon learned that when being interviewed and asked, "What is your background?" they didn't mean eight years as a silly sailor. They wanted academic qualifications.

In the unofficial Pool and dole office of the White Horse pub I discovered that a lot of ex-seamen were getting jobs on oil rigs or oil rig supply ships. Someone would come in the pub and say that a company was recruiting in Aberdeen and then those interested would dash to the telephone in the corner. But that meant going away again which was no good for me so I had to look nearer home. Eventually I saw a job advertised in the Hull Daily Mail that looked – wrongly - interesting. The job was as a printer's labourer with a company called Hull Premier Printers. I got the job.

I think I took this job because I was bored as it certainly wasn't for the money. I'd been getting £11 a week on the dole and my new weekly wage was £13 per week, only two pounds more, although I was told at the interview that it would go up to £16 after a few months when they felt I was suitably trained and able. They must have been employing monkeys previously as I was on £16 within three weeks. I was told that I had to join the union, the Society of Graphical and Allied Trades (SOGAT) and that the union was very militant. My first thought was that it couldn't be that militant otherwise I would be on a much higher wage. I was also made aware that other unions operated within the printing industry and that the qualified printers were represented by the NGA. My job was to work with the foreman of the works, a really great bloke called George Boynton. George was down to earth but knew more about the business than the general manager, who also was a nice bloke, and was continuously called to the office to help the manager when dealing with customer's queries.

The main work meant operating a massive letterpress machine. The company's main work was printing cardboard boxes for her sister company, Hull Box, situated above the printing works. When we didn't have a job in, I was required to assist on the much smaller Heidelberg machines doing more general printing.

The factory was in Cumberland Street off Wincomlee, too far to walk from Cromer Street and not on a direct bus route, so I bought a bike. This meant riding down Sculcoates Lane, down the misnamed Air Street (and the Golden Ball pub) and then along Wincomlee, savouring the cocktail of odours churned out by the sickly, sweet smell of a confectionery factory, intermingled with the fragrances of tan-yards, oil mills, soap manufacturers, the glue factory and the fumes from a thousand chimneys. The stench of Wincolmee drowned out even the dominant Hull smell of the fish farm. A trip down Wincolmlee in those days was a real treat for the senses.

Working in the factory, apart from George and me, were a male compositor/machine operator called Alan and three young women. Next door was another workshop with a large lithography machine operated by George's son and another printer's labourer. All women, except for the foreman, operated the box factory upstairs. In addition to the general manager there were also a couple of office clerks so it was relatively a small organisation and we all got on pretty well.

The routine was first thing in the morning put the rollers in the machine, check the runners for the passage of the sheets of cardboard and stack the feed tray at the back of the machine with sheets of cardboard, while George filled the ink tray. Filling the ink tray could only be done by a member of the NGA. Once the machine started that determined my work pace for the day, completely run by the machine. The only time the machine stopped was when more cardboard was needed or there was a problem with the colour. As the machine spewed out its coloured sheets I had to stack them so that they dried before they were put through the machine again if it was a multicoloured print run, or taken upstairs to the box factory. If the ink started to fade I was supposed to call George or another printer in our workshop who was a compositor and operated the Heidelbergs as well as being the NGA representative. But George soon told me to stir the ink if it was fading but don't let anyone see. At the end of the day one of the girls who worked on the Heidelbergs would come across to help me clean the machine. This meant taking out the rollers and putting them on a stand. Women apparently were not allowed to do this, which was why they got paid even less than me, and then I'd clean the rollers while the girl leaned into the machine and cleaned the plate. We all then had to watch the clock until the bell went dead on five o'clock and the door was opened to let us out.

The seriousness of the inter-union demarcation became apparent one morning when the general manager came to me and told me that George would be in late and had told him to ask me to set the machine up without him. Fair enough.

It was a Fenner's, (a local engineering company's) job that only required one colour of ink as the boxes just had the word Fenner repeated in diagonal lines printed on them in a shade of orange. I duly put the rollers in, set the runners, filled the feed with the required size of cardboard and opened a tin of the orange ink. I had just put the first trowel of ink into the trough on the machine when the compositor Alan, who must have been watching from behind a machine, came rushing and shouting across the workshop.

"Stop!' he yelled. "Put that ink down at once, you're not allowed! That's an NGA job!"

Everyone looked around to see what was wrong. I was embarrassed and angry and quickly retorted with, "You speak to me like that again and you'll be wearing this fucking tin of ink on your fucking head. Now take it and stick it up your arse, sideways!"

He took the tin and then went to tell the manager that I'd threatened him. I just waited to see what would happen and if I got the sack I got the sack. Then, while Alan filled the machine trough with ink, the manager had a word with me. Basically he was sorry for putting me in such a position but I shouldn't have threatened Alan. I said he should tell Alan to speak to people properly in future and after a few words with Alan he returned to his office.

With them both out of the way I started the print run. Now while the print run was only one colour the colour had to be consistent across the whole of the printed surface otherwise the boxes would be rejected and, at times an area would appear faded which would mean either stirring the ink or adding some more. George would leave this to me most of the time, otherwise he'd have had to stand watching and waiting. But of course George wasn't there on this particular morning and Alan had made it clear that I was in the wrong union to touch the ink. After a few minutes the ink faded so I hit the stop button and called Alan over and he stirred the ink. A few minutes later the ink faded again so I called Alan over again and he stirred the ink once more. This happened about four or five times before Alan said, "I'm busy why can't you stir the ink?"

"Because it's an NGA job," I replied.

"Alright you've made your point, I won't bother you again," he said and then left me to get on with it.

George came in a bit later with the general manager and apologised again for dropping me in it while offering the opinion that Alan was a complete prat. This should have been the end of it but it was the beginning of the end for me.

The funniest thing that happened while I worked in the factory was one day when we didn't have a job for the Letterpress machine so I was doing some machine minding on the Heidelbergs. We were printing agenda cards for the Freemasons and during the course of monitoring the print run we had to pick a sample and check for print quality. Reading one of the cards I asked George a question.

"George, look at this a minute, what does this mean?" I pointed out that after each of the names there was a number like, seven, eight, nine, eleven, etc., followed by a degree sign, the type used for angles or temperature.

George looked at the card quizzically for a few minutes and then said, "I don't know Bob, maybe it's the angle of their cocks when they're pissed?"

Generally my workmates were okay but the job was pretty boring. Occasionally, when it was a new job, George would send me up to the box factory with the first print proof so that the foreman up there could check that it matched the cutting plate that he'd prepared. This was fine if the foreman was in sight when I got up there but if he had been called away to the office I was fair game for the ladies who worked there. Talk about political correctness! This was pure incorrectness with me as the victim. Their comments were far ruder, cruder and more obscene than any that men could make and I'm sure I blushed to my hair roots as I inwardly wished for the foreman to appear quickly. Of course as soon as he appeared all heads went down and all looked pure innocence.

On the home front things were settling in but not in the way that both parties envisaged. Bored by the programmes on television, there were only three channels then, I'd joined the library so spent a lot of time reading. I also did a bit of painting and spent a lot of time listening to music. Saturday nights were now just one Saturday night a week, not every night as had been the case when Madeleine and I had first met.

"You've changed. I didn't know you read," was one statement that she made so I pointed out that there wasn't much else to do at sea other than read and it was better than what was on the television. It was obvious though that she was a bit disappointed and we needed to get out more but most of our friends lived in other parts of Hull. When we'd first met, and until we married, I'd usually hired a car during my leave. Obviously hiring was out of the question now but as winter turned to spring we managed to save up to buy a 'banger'.

We bought a very cheap mini van, painted a horrible shade of green, that had belonged to a local decorating firm called 'Lightowler's'. You could just make out the faded name on the side panels and it still had the horns on top for the ladders. One owner and several not very careful drivers, would have been a fair description. The first thing I did was remove the ladder horns and then paint the van blue. The van seemed really economical when we first bought it as it didn't seem to need petrol, that was until I broke down on Beverley Road and discovered that the fuel gauge was broken and was permanently stuck on half full. I liked it though and minis were noted for being nippy and having a relatively low suspension so with the van having only two seats I could imagine I was driving a sports car with a, very large, boot.

At work I became more and more unsettled, or should I say bored, in what was obviously a dead end job at the printing factory. I then saw a job advertised at the Ideal Standard factory for a 'Trainee litho machine operator', which looked like it offered more prospects, so I applied and was called for interview.

It was easy to get to the Ideal Standard factory from Cromer Street as at the top of the street in St Leonard's Road was the terminus of the bus service that went directly to the factory gates at the bottom of National Avenue. I got smartened up for the interview in a collar, tie and a three-piece suit, even though it was a warm and sunny day. Allowing myself half an hour to get there I hopped on the bus and asked for a ticket to the factory. I was told however that the bus only went to the factory during times between seven and nine in the morning and four and six in the afternoon, the nearest dropping point at other times was at the top of National Avenue. I paid my fare and watched the minutes tick by until I got off the bus at the top of National Avenue with only five minutes to spare to get to the factory and find the office where I'd be interviewed. So I legged it. I arrived at the interview on time but gasping for breath and pouring with sweat, not a good look. Needless to say I didn't get the job but learned a good lesson about prior planning and punctuality.

Back at Hull Premier Printers I found myself longing for an outdoor job again, especially now that the summer was setting in. Then in June I saw that the Humber Conservancy was advertising for lightship keepers so I put in an application. This time when asked about my 'background' I fitted the specification perfectly and I was offered the job. The conservancy operated several lightships at that time: the Spurn and Bull lightships marking the approaches to the Humber, and the Middle and Upper Whitton lightships up river near Brough.

I gave my notice in at the printers in anticipation of starting my new job as relief deck-hand on the Upper Whitton Lightship.

My instructions were to catch a train from Hull to Brough and then go down to Brough Haven where a conservancy launch would take me out to the Upper Whitton Lightship, which would be my home for the next two weeks. Following that I would be home for two weeks, one week off and the other working in the buoy shed at Sammy's Point. The pay was better than the factory but I was also required to take out my own food and drinks to last me the fortnight, which I hadn't bargained for. So armed with an extra bag containing mostly baked beans and bacon, I set off allowing myself time for a farewell drink in the White Horse before catching the train.

In Hull it was quite common for sailors to bring back exotic pets like monkeys and parrots from their far away trips to West Africa or South America and these would often change hands in pubs. Indeed my dad had returned from one of his regular, every evening jaunts to the pub with a monkey when I was a toddler which, for a brief period, became part of the family despite its tendency for violence should anyone approach my mother. "Kindred kind," my dad used to mutter. Anyway a number of seamen were in the White Horse when I arrived so I sat with them for a couple of drinks until it was time for me to go to the station.

I stood up and started to pick up my bags when one of them, I'm not sure whether it was Bob Foster or Pete Grady, said, "Where are you going?"

"I'm going to join the Upper Whitton Lightship," I replied.

"Upper Whitton? How do you get out there?"

"A train to Brough and a boat from Brough Haven."

"Brough Haven! Bring us a monkey back!

With the laughter ringing around my ears I was in a good mood for what I hoped would be an adventure ahead of me. I even got the buzz as the launch nosed out of the Haven and into the river; but not for long.

It started off badly when my shipmate - there were only two of us on this lightship whereas there were about five on the ones out at sea - said that I shouldn't get disturbed but he didn't normally speak much after the first couple of days. So was I to spend two weeks in silence? Not quite, because he had to 'show me the ropes' before he lapsed into his silence, and anyway we had to radio Hull Radio with the weather report every two hours, as well as inform the radio operators of any ships that passed on their way to and from Goole and the Trent ports. Also occasionally the conservancy launch would drop by for a pot of tea and a chat. My colleague John, who was a middle aged ex-fisherman, did become quite taciturn, which was a bit disconcerting but as we didn't have much in common, it was not worth worrying about.

Our job was to maintain the lights and make sure the ship stayed on its station. This meant working a four on, four off, watch system with some overlap during the day when we would do any general chores, mostly cleaning, that needed doing; the ship was spotless. The only entertainment on board was a radio that John owned that I wasn't allowed to touch and which he kept permanently tuned to Radio Four - or was it still the Home Service then? This was good for the news and the odd comedy show but not for the pop and rock music that I enjoyed. If I had known I would have brought my own radio, preferably one louder than his.

Everything, apart from the light housing, was below decks and split into three sections. John and I shared a cabin in the after end of the ship accessed by a steep ladder. At the forward end of the cabin was a solid fuel stove. A table held the central position in the cabin and on either side of this were our bunks. The central hold of the ship held the bunkers for the solid fuel and water tanks and the final forward section was used for storage and cables etc. That was it.

Sometimes I felt the cleaning was just for the sake of it or an area was deliberately made dirty to justify cleaning it, as was the case with the central hold. Our bunkers, water, etc were delivered by a larger conservancy launch from Hull called the 'Hutchinson' and the solid fuel was tipped from sacks down a chute into the bunkers in the hold. As the bunkers were open this meant that the dust from the coal and coke went everywhere so we set about cleaning it as was, apparently, the routine.

I thought that this was a lot of work created by not very good planning so I said to John, "Anyone ever thought about putting up curtains to stop all this dust during a delivery? It would save a lot of work."

John looked at me with contempt as he obviously had no time for a new boy with fancy ideas and replied, "No, this is how we do it and this is how we will always do it." And that was the end of another scintillating conversation.

One day John did find his voice though. He'd left me on deck while he went down below to the cabin where he switched on his beloved radio to listen to Radio Four. Screaming out of the speaker came the voice of Aretha Franklin belting out one of her soul classics. John shouted while clambering up the cabin ladder, "You've been messing with my radio!"

"I haven't been anywhere near your radio," I replied.

"It's playing music! I don't play music! You've been at my radio!"

"I haven't touched your fucking radio," I repeated.

"Yes you …"

"After Aretha Franklin, what would be your next choice to take with you to your desert island?" The honeyed tone of the voice of Roy Plomley, the host of the radio programme "Desert Island Discs", hushed John to silence and, with a grunt, which may or may not have been an apology, he disappeared back down below.

The worse thing for me on the lightship was that I was on a ship going nowhere. It was like being at anchor, only without the incentive of knowing that you would be on the move again eventually. I always hated being at anchor, not moving and looking longingly at the bright shore lights of the nearest town or city. Not that there was much evidence of Brough advertising its raucous nightlife by flashing multi-coloured neon signs, but I could see the lights of domestic civilisation clear enough. I hated it.

The day after we landed ashore after our two weeks stint, I went down to the office to give my notice in. The office was in Queen's Gardens to the rear of the Dock Offices and the manager who had interviewed me for the job asked me why I was leaving? I told him how I found the experience on the Upper Whitton to be boring and uninspiring, made worse by sharing my time with someone who, for most of the time, was not objectionable but certainly unsociable.

"A ha! I thought so. I didn't think that the Upper Whitton would be a good place for a young man but it was only a one-off and next trip I'd like you to go on the Spurn Lightship. That has a bigger crew and you may like that better."

"And maybe I won't. Please give me my cards."

That was the end of my time on the lightships but when I met up with Madeleine that evening she was not best pleased.

"You've what? You've given your notice in? You've left?"

"Yes."

"You're unemployed? Again," she said, as if I made a habit of it.

"What are you going to do? Live off me?"

Oh dear. She shouldn't have said that. I was angry but I said nothing, as I knew exactly what I was going to do. The very next day I was straight down to the Pool office and said to Claude Locke that I wanted to go back to sea.

"Where have you been the last six months?" he asked.

"Working ashore," I replied.

"I will need references from your employers," said Claude.

I hadn't thought about this so just said. "You don't need references Claude. All the references you need are in that filing cabinet over there."

He looked where I'd pointed, thought for a minute and then said, "Okay, I've got a collier sailing tonight from Immingham, will that do you?"

"It certainly will."

I went home that afternoon and packed my bags. When Madeleine came home from work, she worked for a fish merchant from an office in Dunswell called Woods Fish Supply, I told her that I'd got a job.

"Already. What's the job?"

"The Hudson Deep."

"The Hudson Deep? Is that a ship?"

"Yes, a collier. I'm sailing from Immingham tonight."

"You're going back to sea?"

"Yes, don't ever say that I can't get a job while I've got a discharge book."

With that I left the house and caught the bus to the city centre and then walked to the pier to catch the ferry from Hull to New Holland and then a train to Immingham. There were three ferries that used to run across the Humber at that time: the 'Tattershall Castle', 'Lincoln Castle' and 'Wingfield Castle' with two on the run at a time so that as one would leave New Holland the other would leave Hull, passing each other in the middle of the river on the twenty minute passage.

I liked travelling on them because my grandma used to work on them but gradually they were phased out. They were steam paddle steamers and as their boilers needed replacing it became too expensive for them to be repaired so they were laid up. Eventually they were replaced by a motor-propelled paddle-boat, the 'Farringford', until the service ended with the opening of the Humber Bridge in 1981. But that was all for the future; right now on a bright summer's evening as the paddle steamer left the floating pontoon of Hull's Victoria Pier, I felt the old buzz again.

Above. The "Baltic Swift".

Left and below. Ice in the Baltic.

Chapter 27. Back to Sea.

The mv 'Hudson Deep', a large collier, was berthed at Immingham Coal Terminal when I joined her on the evening of July 6th 1970 on a home trade agreement. I say large collier, she was more of a small bulk carrier of 6,197 gross tons, 3,401 net, built in 1952 at South Shields for the Hudson Steamship Company. I introduced myself to the boatswain, a chap from South Shields, and he asked me if I wanted to be the "back watchman". I'd never heard that expression before but when he explained that it would be day work, mainly working alongside him while the ship was loading or unloading, it seemed a good job.

The ship left Immingham to discharge at Gravesend. There were a few other Hull lads on the ship so we decided to go ashore in Gravesend in the evening for a pint, on what I remember as, 'The night of the dogs'. First we were in the pub generally swinging the lamp and talking nonsense like blokes do, when a couple of the lads started talking about dogs and how to train them. One of them said that if you masturbated a dog it would never leave you. What! We all said we had heard of dog whisperers but not dog wankers and anyway surely it was illegal. Most of us said he was talking bollocks, although that word was probably too near the mark. The bloke however said he'd prove all us doubters wrong if he could find a willing dog. So after we left the pub at closing time this bloke insisted that we went on a kind of urban safari to find an innocent stray dog for him to seduce. However, the stray dogs of Gravesend must have got wind of a northern pervert on the loose and kept safely out of sight.

We did manage to find a chip shop that was still open and feeling peckish after our few drinks and enforced walk about went inside. It was obvious that the shop was winding down for the night and there didn't seem an awful lot left.

"What have you got left?" someone asked.

"We've plenty of chips and a few pieces of fish left," said the girl behind the counter.

"Haddock and chips then, please."

"We haven't any haddock."

"Got any cod?"

"No."

"What have you got?"

"We've got some rock salmon."

"Oh, dogfish."

"No, it's rock salmon."

"They've only got dogfish lads."

"I said it's not dogfish, it's rock salmon!"

With that the owner of the shop who had been cleaning his fryers with his back towards us turned around and said, "Where are you lads from?"

"Hull," we replied.

"You're right it's dogfish. You won't kid these lads when it comes to fish Mavis."

So it was dogfish and chips all round to eat as we made our way back to the ship with our potential dog molester still on the lookout for a victim.

I was hoping that after Gravesend the ship would return to Immingham and do the run on a regular basis but this was not to be as we got orders to proceed to the Tyne. I wasn't too pleased with this and neither was Madeleine who was saying she wanted me home again so I had to leave the ship after only ten days and came home on July 16th from South Shields.

It must have been hard being a sailor's wife and I was lucky in that mine had some idea of what it was like to face long absences. Some women coped better than others and some, allegedly, took full advantage of the absences as there were tales of some women having two or three fishermen or seamen on the go at a time, just hoping that they never got home together. Again I was lucky because Madeleine just wanted me at home and regretted saying anything about me being unemployed after leaving the lightship. The problem was that I still wanted a job to do with ships and the sea.

I was once told that you never see the best jobs advertised in the Hull Daily Mail and there seemed some truth in that. Jobs on the docks for example were out of the question as dockers' books were handed down from father to son. At school I'd watched the pilot boat operating from Minerva Pier and I'd never seen those jobs advertised either. Madeleine was friendly with my mate Mick Harrison's wife and we used to visit them fairly regularly. Mick had retrained from being a seaman to being a welder so he could get jobs on gas pipelines and oil rigs but while he was waiting for his training course he'd worked on the pilot boats. Not on the Hull station but on the new pilot boats that served the large super tankers and bulk carriers that were boarded out in the North Sea. True, he'd got the job because of his dad who was now a skipper on the pilot boats, but it seemed like a good job and, despite not having the advantage of nepotism, I decided it was worth a try.

Mick told me that the best thing for me to do was just pop into the Pilot Office near the pier from time to time to see if they had any vacancies and with luck I may get a job. I tried several times but I didn't have any luck so it was back to sea.

My next ship was the 'Pacific Stronghold' on a foreign going agreement but I was only on it for a week as I paid off in Glasgow on August 5th after joining the ship on July 29th. To be honest, I didn't like this ship as the accommodation was crap but I did fancy the voyage, which was to the west coast of the U.S.A and Canada. The ship was 9,439.49 gross tons, 5,571.67 net and carried general cargo but she was not for me.

Three days later on August 8th I joined an ore carrier called the 'Orepton' in Immingham. The ship was fairly small in bulk carrier terms, being only 6,859 gross tons, 2,801,81 net. The 'Orepton' belonged to Houlder Brothers and I remember her as being a very comfortable ship with single berth cabins and good food, as expected in ships of that shipping line, but I was only on her for a month before paying off on September 3rd in Workington. The thing I remember most about this ship was the wiry built boatswain who only seemed to wear a white nylon shirt no matter what the weather. I know we went up beyond the North Cape of Norway to Kirkenes to load iron ore and the weather, although it was still the summer, was still chilly and the ship was shipping spray. But there was the boatswain in his white nylon shirt while everyone else was in oilskins.

The train journey from Workington back to Hull was epic. We left Workington early in the evening on a slow rattler across the Lake District to reach a mainline railway that would take us to Manchester. As it was getting dark we didn't even have the benefit of the magnificent scenery of the Lakes to pass the time. It was late at night when we arrived in Manchester where we were told that not only did we have to change trains but stations as well, which was even more of a pain. Finally we boarded our train to Hull, which turned out to be the milk train. If we thought the train across Cumbria had been slow it was like an express compared to this one that stopped at every station and went in a roundabout route that took in Sheffield and Doncaster before arriving in Hull just in time for breakfast.

Each time when my leave was up I hoped to find a job on one of the Rotterdam or Zeebrugge ferries but I was never lucky enough; those jobs rarely appeared in the Pool office. I would also visit the Pilot Office to see if there were any vacancies there, going up the stairs to the office of the company secretary, John Singleton, and asking if there were any jobs going and getting the usual answer, "Sorry, not at the moment."

My next ship was another bulk carrier called the 'Welsh Herald'. This was a larger ship than the 'Orepton' at 19,542.95 gross tons, 9,858.95 net. It had been built in 1963 for Welsh Ore Carriers and, although she was nine years younger than the 'Orepton', the accommodation was not quite as comfortable although we all had single berth cabins. The crew was a bit like a League of Nations with Asians down below and Chinese catering staff. One of the ABs was an elderly Estonian. The only time he took leave was when the ship was in dry dock when he'd move into a seamen's mission or hotel. I never did find out his full story but I suspect that he was a refugee following the war and had lost his home and family and the ship and the merchant navy now had replaced these.

The merchant navy was the ideal place for misfits and those without a permanent home. My sister had even asked me just before I got married if I was doing it to get a home of my own but I had assured her this was not the case although I confess that it did make me think. "Good life merchant navy, Sunday dinner everyday," was a saying that I'd heard many times but it was much more than that. It was three good meals a day, clean bedding and towels every week, cheap cigarettes and booze, and increasingly on many ships, good cabins and leisure facilities. Then there was the camaraderie of your shipmates, and seafarers were as far as I was concerned, the best you could hope for; to say that no one locked their cabin doors at sea, only when in port, says it all. In fact with good accommodation it was almost like being on a cruise and with the additional benefit of getting paid for it. Sorry, I forgot that we had to work as well, which spoils the image a bit but brings me back to the 'Welsh Herald' and the bringer of much work, the boatswain.

The boatswain was a big Geordie and we didn't quite hit it off at first. A number of us had signed on in Hull on September 25th and turned up in Immingham the next morning to find that the ship was still discharging and wouldn't be sailing for a day or two but we were still required to work. After sorting out our cabins and such like, we made our way to the mess-room and were enjoying a mug of tea and a bit of banter when the boatswain appeared.

"Right lads time to turn to. We are going to be painting the ship's side so I want you to rig a couple of stages on the starboard quarter."

We all looked up and I must have fancied myself as a mess-room lawyer as I said, "What?"

"I want you to rig stages over the starboard quarter; have you got a problem with that?"

"Stages? Painting? We don't do that in our home port. Besides it's against port rules."

I'd no idea if this latter statement was true, I was just trying it on with the "home port" bit.

"So you're refusing to do it are you?" replied the boatswain.

"Yes, because like I said it's against port rules," I said. With that the boatswain left the mess-room to return about ten minutes later.

"You're right it is against port rules to work over the side so we will have to do some painting somewhere else."

I'd tried not to look surprised when told about the port rules but still decided to press on. "It's still not right to do any painting in our own port when we have just joined the ship." I said. The others, who until then had said very little, stated their agreement that it wasn't the normal procedure.

The boatswain who by now was getting a bit exasperated said, "You won't do this, you won't do that, what do you do for fuck sake?"

"Standby," I replied.

"Standby! Standby for what?"

"Opening and closing the hatches. Shifting ship and things like that."

"All right," said the boatswain after some thought, "I'm glad you said that because we are shifting ship tonight about eight o'clock."

"Eight o'clock! You've got no chance. We've got a train and a ferry to catch back to Hull so we have to leave at half past five at the latest."

A not very happy boatswain left us in the mess-room until he needed us to open or close the hatches and then early in the afternoon said that we'd be shifting ship about four so we'd have plenty of time to catch our train.

Now on this ship we discovered that we could have whatever was in the bond locker, which meant that as well as the unlimited cigarettes, tobacco and beer we could also have bottles of spirits. The captain's only condition was that if anyone turned up on watch drunk they'd have their alcoholic drinks stopped and anyone providing the guilty party with drink after that would also have their alcohol stopped.

The deck crew were split up into watch keepers and day workers and I was a day man. One by one, however, my watch-keeping colleagues slipped by the wayside as they succumbed to the temptation of the booze. I liked a beer or a dram as much as anyone and always had a bottle of rum in my cabin, but at sea I was quite contented to sit in my cabin and read or work on a few exercises in studying for a ticket. I read so much that one of my mates from Hull on the ship, Paul Murtagh, described me thus, "You're a fucking bookworm you are; always got your head in a book." It was true and I would read anything, even the books that had been put aboard the ship on a previous visit to the Soviet Union like English translations of, "The Communist Manifesto" and "Das Kapital". These could not be described as light reading but I found some parts interesting and I was reading one of these books in my cabin one night when the boatswain called just as I was about to pour myself a dram of Four Bells rum.

"Sorry Bob, but from tomorrow morning you will have to go on the eight to twelve watch as another one has let us down and got pissed," he said.

I was disappointed with this because I liked being on days but knew I couldn't do anything about it so replied, "That's fine. Matter of fact I was just about to have a dram myself, will you join me?" The boatswain sat down and I poured two drinks.

After a bit of a chat about changing over to go on watch the boatswain said quite out of the blue, "You know Bob, I was dreading this trip after that first day when you came aboard in Immingham. I even said to the mate that we had a right mess-room lawyer on board, which could mean trouble. But, I have to say this, and the mate says the same, we got it completely wrong because of all the new signings you've turned out to be the most, reliable, efficient and (as I took a swig of my rum) sober of the bunch."

The boatswain then noticed my navigation and seamanship books and asked me about them. So I told him that I'd like eventually to become an officer and use what I'd learned about how or how not to behave, to make sure that the crew always got dealt with in a polite and fair way. The boatswain, rather than scoffing at this, said it was commendable and was what the merchant navy needed. He then asked me about my other reading noticing the books written by Karl Marx. So I explained that I'd started reading them because they were there and I didn't have anything else at the time, and although I found them tough going, I could identify with some of the concepts and ideas as they reflected some of my own beliefs. He then went on to talk about other politicians and thinkers like Keir Hardie and Thomas Paine. It was like getting a master class in socialism. The man was a natural scholar. I've come across several people like this. They may not have had a brilliant, formal education but they made up for it later and could present their case as well as any academic.

I felt I'd had a personal tutorial and came away with a recommended reading list that I was able to follow up at the library when I got home. The man was inspirational and his encouragement would not be forgotten.

Life on an ore carrier was not quite as bad as a tanker but not far off. Mostly we loaded in out of the way places like Seven Islands in Canada or Kirkenes in Norway where there was little point or little reason to go ashore. On top of that loading took place quite quickly using conveyor belts and chutes. The iron ore was so heavy that the holds never looked full as even when we were fully loaded the ore looked like small mounds in the bottom of the hold. The effect of this weight low down meant that when we were loaded if there was any swell the ship would roll constantly. Sometimes it felt that we were rolling from one beam end to the other, like being on a massive see-saw. I know that because my bunk was thwart-ships I had to sometimes hook my feet under the bottom of the mattress to stop myself sliding up and down.

Discharging was usually in a port closer to civilisation, Newport, Immingham, Middlesbrough, Workington, and took longer than loading because it was done by grabs so that was when we'd have a chance to get some shore leave.

My final trip on the 'Welsh Herald' involved taking a cargo of iron ore from Seven Islands in Canada to Middlesbrough where a few of us paid off on October 22nd, so I'd been away for about a month.

After a few days' leave I joined my next ship the m.v. 'Baltic Trader' on October 28th. The 'Baltic Trader' belonged to the United Baltic Corporation on a regular run between Hull and the Baltic countries like Finland, Latvia and Poland so was as good as a ten-day boat as far as I was concerned. A sister ship of the 'Baltic Merchant' she had been built in Germany in 1954 and was of 1,596.3 gross tons, 701.9 net, and like all of the Baltic boats in this class had three steel hatches and ten derricks served by electric winches. Two hatches were before the centre castle and one aft. The deck crew's accommodation was aft but because my job on this ship was AB/handyman, a replacement post for a carpenter, I was given the old, now disused, hospital as my cabin. So I had the privacy of a single berth with the added luxury of an en suite, well a sit-in bath and toilet.

As AB/handyman, I found myself working with the boatswain most of the time so that meant no watches. Every morning my day started with taking and recording the soundings in the ballast tanks and bilges before carrying out any other general duties. Other than that it was pottering about doing general maintenance like replacing leaking porthole seals. I developed a remarkable skill in hearing the pop of a beer can before knocking on a cabin door and asking the occupant if their porthole was leaking. Like any other chippie I was required to drive the windlass and drop the anchor when required. I was also expected to act as boatswain when he took leave and went back to his home in Doncaster while we worked cargo in Hull. This worked well for a couple of trips but then for some reason we were diverted to London and told that the regular run would now be London to Finland. This was no good for me so on December 14th 1970 I paid off the 'Baltic Trader' and once again returned to Hull.

Somehow I managed to avoid getting another ship until after Christmas. I'd made a few futile trips to the Pilot Office hoping for an opening there and had received the same negative story but I needed work, so on December 30th I signed on the m.v. 'Baltic Swift' which was sailing almost straight away. I wasn't bothered about this as the 'Baltic Swift' was also a regular runner between Hull and Gydnia in Poland. This ship was a bit different to the 'Merchant' and 'Trader' being built in 1957 and being slightly smaller at 1,224.28 gross tons, 457.75 net. The ship had three steel hatches, one forward and two aft, served by electric winches and six derricks. All of the Baltic boats I sailed on had steering mechanisms different to the traditional wheel, some had press button steering and some a kind of aircraft wheel which worked in a similar way to the press button steering. I think the 'Swift' had the aircraft style.

Just before we left our berth in Hull I was told that I was on watch so I went up to the bridge to take the wheel. Waiting up there was the third mate and the captain. I recognised the captain immediately, it was Captain Foss who'd sacked me from the 'Baltic Merchant' for insubordination when I'd been an ordinary seaman. He also recognised me.

"I've had you before haven't I?" said the captain.

"Yes, on the 'Baltic Merchant'," I replied.

"That's right. I remember now, what was your name again?"

"Addey captain."

"Ah yes, Addey."

The captain was stopped saying anymore by an interruption from the third mate who asked me if I was familiar with the steering on the ship and I was assuring him that I was when captain Foss started speaking again.

"Steering! Don't worry about the steering, Mr Addey knows all about how these ships steer, he's been with me before!"

I'd expected a comment on the incident that led to me leaving the 'Baltic Merchant' but the captain never mentioned it and the slate seemed to have been wiped clean.

In those days Poland was behind the Iron Curtain and had similar, if not quite as severe, restrictions as I'd found in Russia. The area had recently experienced some rebelling against the Soviet dominated regime but it was still a shock to look down what was considered a normal residential street there and see a military tank parked at the end. Like in most Iron Curtain countries there was a flourishing black market in western clothes, mainly ladies, and foreign currency so this meant that we only got a token sub in zlotys and changed our English pounds for double the rate on shore. The currency was easily concealed but the only way to get clothing ashore was to either wear it or stuff it around your body. This meant that it looked like we lost weight at a considerable rate, going down the gangway looking like Oliver Hardy and returning looking like Stan Laurel. It certainly wasn't anything to do with any vigorous dancing that may have been on offer at the one nightclub that seemed to be open for our entertainment in Gydnia.

There were a lot of local girls using this club and their primary aim was to earn enough foreign currency to be able to leave the country. Many of them lived in small flats in faceless concrete blocks, that were very clean but sparsely furnished, but all with the obligatory crucifix hanging over the bed to signify their Roman Catholic religion. They were always on the lookout for the English pound and for western clothing, particularly Marks and Spencer clothes.

Most of the girls were very attractive but it was dangerous for a married sailor to partake in any carnal delights on offer due to the fact that some of the girls were noted for giving unwanted gifts in return for the pleasures they offered a sailor, leaving many to play the game of genital bingo on the short journey home – eyes down and look in for a full house. I knew one married seaman from Hull who had to feign a groin strain to explain to his wife his lack of sexual drive while he surreptitiously received treatment at the Mill Street clinic - not an easy thing to do when the girls from the nearby Woolworth's store would monitor the patients going in and coming out. One of the ship's stewards, who had been on the ship for some time, seemed to know all the girls and their STD history and I remember one day sitting in the mess-room talking to one of the crew called Jim, who had been ashore the night before, when the steward entered and joined in the conversation.

"Where did you get to last night, Jim?" asked the steward.

"I met up with a girl called Marie," replied Jim.

"Marie? Marie? Rather small with short, curly dark hair?"

"Yes, that's the one," said Jim.

The steward noisily sucked air through his teeth before saying; "A bloke got soft chancres off her a few trips ago!"

Jim looked shocked for a moment. Sitting in the corner was an old motorman, sweat rag around his neck, greasy flat cap and (you never saw him with a full cigarette) a tiny stub of a roll-up in his mouth which he removed as he stood up to walk out and said, "Never mind Jim, those soft chancres are a fucking sight better than the hard bastards!"

Most of us married sailors, if we ventured ashore at all, were happy to just have a few drinks and crack a few jokes in the warmth of the club. Most of the locals were friendly and we usually had a good time but knew it was over when we heard the singer with the band start crooning, "I 'ad zee lass voltz mit chew... two lonny peopulz toge-eh-zzer..."

I was on the wheel again some time on the homeward voyage, it may have been leaving Gydnia or approaching the Kiel Canal, but we didn't have a pilot on board. Captain Foss was on the bridge dressed in a silk dressing gown and pontificating like a maritime Noel Coward. Once again the third mate was on watch and captain Foss's subject was comparing Gracie Fields, on whom he considered himself some type of expert, to modern day entertainers and their longevity. The third mate just kept saying, "Yes sir," and "No sir," but didn't enter into the conversation. But suffering from the boredom of steering when not in a tricky pilotage, I decided to interject.

"Gracie Fields may have been of her time and useful to lift people's morale during wartime but you can hardly compare her talents to those of the Beatles," I said.

There was an immediate silence and the look of shock on the third mate's face was a picture. Captain Foss was also caught off guard but he immediately smiled and came back with another comment about the greatness of Gracie Fields in comparison to the Beatles and a debate started. I said that the only real comparison between Fields and the Beatles was that they both originated from Lancashire and a better comparison would involve a contemporary of Fields, George Formby, because not only did he come from Lancashire but also he was a singer-songwriter like the Beatles. I went on to say that there were other similarities between a couple of Beatles' songs and the tongue in cheek ditties of Formby but anyway, because Beatles' songs were being recorded by other established figures, their legacy would be bigger and last longer than that of Gracie Fields. The smile on the captain's face told me that he was enjoying being challenged rather than having someone say "Yes sir," all the time. My spell on the wheel seemed to fly by and the captain thanked me for an interesting discussion when I was finally relieved although he did get the last word in on the greatness of Gracie Fields as I walked out of the wheelhouse.

Once again this ship didn't return to Hull as we were given orders to go to Ipswich where I paid off on January 24th 1971 as again Madeleine was asking me to come home. The train journey from Ipswich to Hull seemed as long as the journey from Workington to Hull but at least it was daylight.

On arrival back in Hull I was only entitled to a couple of days' leave before returning to the Pool looking for a job on that elusive ferry.

It was obvious on that first day back looking for a ship that there was nothing happening, so I took my usual stroll down to the Pilot Office near the pier, climbed the stairs to the first floor office and tapped on the window. The company secretary, John Singleton, opened the window and I asked if there were any vacancies for a deck-hand. John was used by now to seeing me and usually the answer would be "No," but this time he asked me to wait a minute. He came out of the office and crossed the landing to another office with the words 'Commodore of Pilots' on the door. A couple of minutes later he asked me to come into the commodore's office where I was introduced to the commodore himself, a man named Bill Perry. Mr Perry gave me, I suppose it was an interview, and then asked me if I could start straight away. I said of course I could and was told to start the next day on a pilot launch based in Grimsby.

Madeleine was pleased, I was pleased and the next morning I was again at the Pilot Office to get my tickets for the ferry and the train to Grimsby. And when those big paddle wheels started to churn up the muddy waters of the Humber I got that old buzz of excitement once more.

Above. The Farringford at the floating pontoon. The Farringford was brought in to replace the steam paddle steamers while the Humber Bridge was being built. Below. A Humber ferry on its way from New Holland to Hull.l

Chapter 28. The Humber Pilots' Steam Cutter Company.

On arrival in Grimsby I found my way to the lock basin where I was to join the launch the 'John Good'. This was easy to find as the main, possibly only, landmark is the tall, Venetian style, water tower under which I saw the steps leading to the 'John Good'. The vessel turned out to be one of the smaller launches operated by my new employer, the Humber Pilots' Steam Cutter Company, a wholly owned subsidiary of the British Transport Docks Board, which meant I needed to join a new union, the National Union of Railwaymen. This was because historically the docks in Hull had been built by railway companies, so employees of these companies working on the dock like rail shunters, crane drivers and dredger men, but not dockers, were considered railwaymen. The British Transport Docks Board, a nationalised company like British Rail, had taken over the docks and the responsibilities of the Humber Conservancy Board as well as the Pilot Cutter Company, which had originally been set up by the Humber pilots themselves in 1894.

In 1971 there were several different types of pilot: Humber pilots, who served the lower Humber and the ports of Hull, Grimsby, Immingham, Killingholme, Saltend, Barton and New Holland; Goole pilots, who served Goole and a small port on the Ouse called Blacktoft; and Trent pilots, who served the Trent ports of Flixborough, Keadby, Gunness and Gainsborough.

Ships for Goole and the Trent would change pilots in Hull Roads, which meant that there was a pilot boat based there permanently for this purpose. The lower Humber pilots were taken off or boarded in the vicinity of Spurn or the Spurn Lightship, except for the exceptionally large ships that were boarded or landed further out to sea around the Humber Lightship.

The pilots were all classed as self-employed although a pilot master in the Pilot Office gave them their work. The largest number of pilots were employed on the lower Humber service where you'd find three classes: junior, senior and ten-year plus pilots, which determined the type of ship they were allowed to pilot based on tonnage and experience. The large super tankers and bulk carriers carried two pilots, one senior and a ten-year man in charge. Our job was to make sure that the pilots got on and off the ships safely.

Two large cutters called the 'Frank Atkinson' and the 'William Fenton' served the pilots at Spurn with one cutter on station at all times. Each cutter had accommodation and catering facilities on board for the pilots while they waited to board their ships. The boarding was done by using small motorised boats, like ship's lifeboats, manned by pilot apprentices. This worked fine when most of the ships could make their way close to Spurn Point but as ships got bigger and the ports on the Humber, Trent and Ouse got busier, it became more difficult to provide the service needed. These cutters were then supplemented by a launch based at Grimsby to ferry pilots back and forth as required, and larger launches used to take pilots to and from the super tankers and bulk carriers that needed to be attended to much further out, up to twenty miles beyond Spurn, at sea.

Inside the Humber was a specially dredged channel, the Sunk Dredged Channel, to make sure that there was sufficient water to allow the deep-draughted vessels to proceed to the new jetties at Killingholme and Immingham. In addition to this, there was also a mono buoy for tankers serving a refinery at Tetney in North Lincolnshire. Like the one I'd come into contact with at Miri, the tanker moored to the buoy at the forward end only, and the pipelines for the discharge or load were floated around to the ship for connection.

The first thing I found out was that I was a kind of spare deck-hand required to provide cover as and where needed, whether it was the boats doing the super tankers which worked twenty-four hour shifts, the Grimsby station which also worked twenty-four hours on (starting and ending at mid-day) with the regular crews getting seventy-two hours off, or Hull Roads, which worked rotating shifts: an eight hour day shift (08.00 until 16.00) followed by 24 hours off, then a sixteen hour night shift (16.00 until 08.00 the next morning) followed by 48 hours off.

When not required for cover I'd be on day work, as organised by the shore foreman, based in the old lock-keeper's office on Humber Dock. I also learned that there were big changes planned to take place with the main one being the phasing out of the large cutters to be replaced by a base at Spurn Point with the boarding and landing done by high speed launches. The first phase of this was that all the Grimsby crews were being made redundant. They were offered the opportunity to relocate to Hull but the only one to take this up was a skipper who had already moved from Hull to Grimsby when originally offered the job based in Grimsby.

The launches in service when I joined were the 'John Good' and 'Dracaena' – small, fast, forty-foot or so launches mainly used on the Grimsby service. The 'Vala Nos Deus', later renamed 'Captain Holmes', and the 'Captain Sibree, which were larger, being between sixty and seventy feet long with a beam of about seventeen feet, and the much slower 'Captain Newlove', which looked like it had been built as a fishing boat before being fitted out as a pilot boat with a wooden hull and a length just over sixty feet and a beam of about eighteen feet.

On Hull Roads you'd find the 'Commander Snowden' and the 'T.W.Prickett'. The 'Commander Snowden' was the smallest of the fleet being just short of forty feet.

This boat was built for salmon fishing in Scotland and was quite slow especially when punching the tide, which made us speculate when she was eventually fitted with radar, which happened two or three years after I started, that the boat would start spinning rather than the scanner.

The 'T.W. Prickett' was another wooden-hulled fishing boat fitted out for the pilot service and was slightly bigger at forty-seven feet by fifteen feet, slightly faster and certainly more comfortable than the 'Snowden'. Gradually the fast fibreglass launches would also be used on Hull Roads when the 'Snowden' and 'Prickett' were out of service, or if the 'Prickett', which was a good sea-boat, was required to support the service at Spurn Point. All the launches could carry up to twelve pilots.

The crews of the pilot boats working from Grimsby and Spurn consisted of a skipper (coxswain), engineer and deck-hand. Hull Roads' pilot boats only carried a skipper and an engineer/mate, which sounded grander than deck-hand but the only engineering involved was starting and checking the engines, running the generator when the engines were not running, pumping out the bilges and occasionally changing an impeller or packing a leaking stern gland. All other jobs would be done by the more qualified engineers. Eventually, when the service consisted of launches only, the engineer/mate job title would be dropped and all the launches would carry just a skipper and a deck-hand and only take an engineer if going further out to sea than the Spurn Lightship.

The crews came from a variety of maritime occupations with the skippers being mainly ex-trawler, tug or barge skippers, but some had also come through from being deck-hands as the job demanded local knowledge of the river and small boat handling skills that could only be learned by experience. The engineers, except for the engineer/mates on Hull Roads, were nearly all qualified marine engineers who'd served their time in local shipyards and marine engineering companies, but a couple had also been trained in the Royal Navy. The deck-hands came mainly from fishing and the merchant navy when I started but as the personnel became larger some came from barges, the Royal Navy, and even a couple from the Humber ferries.

I can't remember all of the names of the crew members when I started but some of the main Hull based ones that I can remember were the deck-hands: Mike Piper, Ray Frear and Jock; Spurn based skippers: Bert Harrison - ex United Towing, (there was another ex-tug skipper but his name escapes me), Bill Thundercliffe and Arthur Fletcher (both ex-trawler skippers) and Bernard Gillyon Snr. (ex-barges and hovercraft), with the engineers Don Simms, Jim Hoodless (the brother of Charlie Hoodless who I'd sailed with on the 'Verconella'), the Christie brothers, Pete Spencer and Ted Sagar. Other engineers who joined later included an ex-Boulevard schoolmate, Mike Simpson, who had just come out of the Royal Navy and a really jovial chap called Dave.

On Hull Roads were the skippers Keith Woods, Bernard Gillyon Jnr., Mick Smith and Eric Hopcraft with engineer/mates Mike Clancey, Tommy Ellis and 'Foppo'. There were others but unfortunately I have forgotten their names and some of those that I've mentioned were to leave or retire within a year or two of me starting but were replaced by a larger team as the service developed as the large pilot cutters were phased out to be replaced by a fleet of fast launches.

At first my work was very varied as I was required to cover for people if they went sick or on holiday. So in one week I could find myself as engineer/mate on Hull Roads, working on the Grimsby station or doing a few days at Spurn on the Humber Lightship runs. Generally I got on well with all the crews and I knew a couple of them before I started. One of these was Bert Harrison, Mick's dad, who was an ex-tug skipper and I did a number of watches with him. I remember being on the 'Newlove' with Bert and an engineer called Pete Spencer. Pete was a very big bloke and liked his food. We all used to take food with us to cook on the galley stove on the 'Newlove' which we would then share. Mostly this was a fry-up, which Bert used to orchestrate using the biggest frying pan I had even seen. Into this frying pan would first go a lump of lard, followed by sausages, bacon, chops, and even baked beans. Each time something was added the fat in the pan would rise until it was about an inch deep at which point Pete would come along and drop a pork pie into the fat and immediately the fat level would drop as it was sucked up inside the pie. He must have had a strong stomach as it was wintertime and we were often bobbing about in pretty foul weather. I never tried the pies but Bert's fry-ups were always very good.

Another story involving Bert concerned an engineer who had the habit of slipping into trance like silences for long periods while sitting in the corner of the mess-room on the 'Newlove' and sucking on a pipe. Bert had once been told to watch this engineer's behaviour as he had served time in prison for murdering his wife with an axe. During quiet periods, between jobs and after all the cleaning and maintenance chores had been completed, it was usual for the crew to have a nap, provided someone kept an ear open for calls on the VHF. No worries about missing a call when this engineer was on watch with Bert as Bert made sure he was always awake to keep a watchful eye on the potential mad axeman of Spurn. I don't think there was one grain of truth in the story about the engineer but nobody chose to put Bert right.

I liked the variation of the work and all the time I was learning and watching about the river, the tides and boat handling. When not working on the launches I could be sent to do any number of jobs, which could involve working with the engineers one day or carrying out general maintenance on the large cutters or any of the pilot boats in dock on another day. On day-work those available would turn up at the lock-keeper's office on Humber Dock lock head for our instructions from either the shore foreman, Billy Larder, or the engineering foreman, Ernie Lornie. Both of these two were good blokes but I particularly liked Bill as he was close to retiring age and quite laid back. The job was well paid and never boring so I was quite happy, and settled in to what, in part, resembled a shore job. Often I would be working on a boat in one of the docks during the day and then receive a call that I was wanted to do a night shift on Hull Roads or make up the crew for a Humber Lightship run during the night so there was quite a lot of overtime.

On one occasion both Bill Larder and I were required to do the night shift on the Hull Roads station. The main work on Hull Roads involved boarding and landing the Goole and Trent pilots, which usually took place about three hours before and two hours after high water. Many of the ships going up river would have come up to Hull Roads in between tides and anchored while others would have picked up a Humber pilot at Spurn a couple of hours earlier and come up the river on the flood tide. So while we were expected to serve all the ships at anchor, we would also do the other up river ships on the run, putting the Trent or Goole pilot on board and landing the Humber pilot. It could therefore get hectic for a couple of hours while this was going on. Similarly, a couple of hours after the tide turned, we would get the ships coming down from the Ouse and Trent wanting to change pilots for the passage to the open sea. In between these tidal activities the Hull Roads boat would transport pilots to and from New Holland if no ferries were running. Occasionally we would also be asked to pick up pilots from Barton or New Holland haven.

It was a clear but cold, winter night when Bill and I were working the 'T.W. Prickett' on Hull Roads. The 'Prickett' had been built as a fishing boat with a wooden hull and single screw powered by a big Gardner engine. The vessel had a wheelhouse that contained the wheel, throttle, gear mechanism - a sort of hurdy-gurdy affair that you wound one way for the forward gear and the other way for astern - a compass, radar, VHF radio and a cooker. A hatch and a ladder from the wheelhouse led to the forward cabin that had a table with big seat lockers on both sides and a coke-burning stove for heating. Outside, behind the wheelhouse, were a lavatory and the engine room housing, with the engine room accessed by a hatch and ladder near the stern.

It was approaching midnight when the ships from Goole and the Trent started to arrive in Hull Roads for us to change the pilots. Usually we would try and pick up and land the pilots between ships but often this was not possible when the ships arrived in line. On this night we had been quite busy when the last few ships appeared and slowed down for the change over. My routine was to escort the Humber pilot to the pilot ladder and standby while he boarded and then wait for the Trent or Goole pilot to descend the ladder and help him on board. Bill would then peel our boat off the side of the ship and turn to port to make the approach for the next one or return to shore. In the meantime I would note the name of the ship, time of boarding and the names of the pilots, to be entered later in the logbook. We successfully changed the pilots on one ship and then peeled away to port. Bill's intention was to turn full circle and drop alongside the next ship. However, one ship must have been going slightly faster than the others and had come inside the ship being boarded. I filled in the details of the previous ship and then opened the port side wheelhouse door to see towering above me the bow of a ship that almost immediately crashed into us amidships with a sickening crash. The 'Prickett' then took a massive list before righting herself as we were flung clear of the ship's bow. Our lights had also gone out. It was one of those events when you are not frightened until afterwards and without thinking or waiting instructions I dived down the engine room to start the generator and switch the lighting back on. Our main engine was still working but I noticed that we were taking water just below the waterline, so I started the bilge pumps. Luckily the 'Prickett' was a strongly built wooden boat and although badly damaged, the pumps managed to contain the water and we carried on until all the boardings were completed. We then assessed the damage and arranged for a replacement boat while the 'Prickett' was repaired. It was only then that I think we realised what a close call the accident had been and how lucky we were to get off so lightly.

A couple of weeks later Bill and I had to go to a solicitors in the Land of Green Ginger, a street in the old town of Hull, where he had us demonstrating what happened using small wooden model boats. This was to facilitate the insurance claim. I don't think Bill recovered from this incident as he retired soon afterwards.

I carried on as before doing whatever was required but now my instructions came from Ernie Lornie. One day I was sent to work with a couple of the engineers on the 'Prickett' which was on one of the fish dock slips being given an overhaul. We cleaned out the bilges and worked for a while on the main engine until Ernie appeared and asked me if I could cover the nightshift on Hull Roads.

It was close to the four o'clock relieving time for the shift so I wouldn't have time to go home and get packing up and any other stuff I needed but he said I might get chance to do this during a quiet period. I was pleased to do this shift as it meant more overtime and therefore more pay.

The launch on duty was the 'Commander Snowden' skippered by a young man called Bernard Gillyon. I'd done a couple of shifts with Bernard previously and we got on well together. The 'Commander Snowden' was an ex-salmon fishing boat but a bit smaller than the 'Prickett' but with a similar layout except that you had to come out of the wheelhouse to access the forward cabin, which was still fitted out with four bunks, a table and a coke stove. There was no heating in the wheelhouse but there was a calor gas stove. The wheel and gearing system were similar to the 'Prickett' and the single screw 'Snowden' was also powered by a Gardner engine although a smaller version to the one on the 'Prickett'. Some of the regular crews on Hull Roads hated the 'Snowden' because it was very slow, the wheelhouse could get very cold and it was only comfortable when using the forward cabin with a good fire going. It was now spring however, so there were no real issues about being cold.

On taking over the shift we did a couple of jobs and then Bernard said it looked quiet so I could pop home to go and get my stuff for the night. I returned about an hour later when it was still fairly quiet with only the odd ship to attend to. During one of the runs I happened to mention that the exhaust seemed to be getting hot and the engine sounded a bit rough. Bernard was originally an engineer before becoming a coxswain and went to take a look. When he returned he said that it was hard to tell if there was anything wrong with the engine as the 'Snowden' always sounded rough and some lagging had come off the exhaust pipe so it did feel hotter than normal. But during the next hour Bernard thought that the engine was starting to sound rougher so he decided to call up the engineering foreman, Ernie, for his opinion.

Ernie came down and didn't like the sound of the engine. Bernard then mentioned in conversation with him that he had heard one of the other crew members complaining about the 'Snowden' and that they would get rid of it by putting sand in the engine. Now a box of sand was kept in the engine room for the purpose of putting sand down on the slope on Minerva Pier to stop the pilots slipping on the wet and muddy timber, inevitably some of the sand spilled on to the engine room floor so it was not unusual to see and feel sand down there. Ernie felt around the oil filler cap and thought it felt gritty but he couldn't tell if any sand had got in the engine. Ernie then went ashore and telephoned the commodore of pilots. Mr Perry was at home suffering from a cold when Ernie told him that we needed to replace the 'Snowden' with the 'John Good' as sand may have been put in the 'Snowden's' engine. Perry immediately called the police.

A short while later two detectives from the British Transport Police appeared, looked over the boat, checked the engine room with Ernie and asked some general questions while drinking our tea. Eventually they went ashore then came back a few minutes later and said that they needed to take some statements and asked me if I would go to their car and give a statement, so I agreed.

In the car they asked me a few general questions, which I answered, and then one of them turned to me and said, "We think you did it so we are taking you to the police station."

I was shocked.

They took me to an office on the first floor of Monument Buildings above Maurice Lipman's and the wet fish shop in Victoria Square. I've seen plenty of comedy duos playing detectives in my time but none of them matched these two comedians although at the time my appreciation of their policing skills was more tragic than comic. The more I protested my innocence the more they found a way to twist the words that I said. I think they tried to play the "good cop, bad cop" but their performance was mostly "bad cop" in all senses of the word bad because they were not very good detectives. I don't recall a spotlight in my eyes but the interrogation went something like this:

"Why did you do it?"

"I didn't do it."

"Oh yes you did."

"Why would I do it?"

"That's what I asked you. You did it because you have got a grudge against the company."

"No I haven't, I enjoy my job."

"You did it because you don't like that boat."

"I'm only relieving on the boat so it makes no odds to me."

"That's it! You've a grudge against the company because you've not got a regular job."

"I like relieving because it gives me variation and I'm learning the job."

"If you are relieving, what were you doing today?"

"I was working on the 'Prickett' on the fish dock slip."

"The 'Prickett'? What's that?"

"It's another launch."

"That's it! You were working on a better boat and you resented being taken off it to work on the 'Snowden'."

"No, the day was nearly over and a relief shift would be overtime."

"That's it! You had been working all day and you resented having to work a night shift as well."

"I didn't resent it – I volunteered and it is more money."

"What were you doing on the 'Prickett'?"

"Working with the engineers doing general stuff like cleaning the bilges and helping them clean the engine."

"That's it! Cleaning bilges that's a dirty job as is cleaning the engines, you had a grudge against the company for giving you a dirty job."

"I've had dirtier jobs and I was learning about the engines."

"You did it because you had a grudge against the company and you objected to have to work all night on an old boat."

"That's ridiculous. Why would I put my own life at risk by deliberately damaging the engine? Why would I put my job at risk? It doesn't make sense."

"We'll decide if it makes sense or not. Anyway, it doesn't matter if you didn't do it, we'll make it look like you did, so you may as well plead guilty and get a lighter sentence rather than not guilty and go to jail!"

I couldn't believe my ears. It didn't matter if I was innocent or not provided they got a conviction. With that they took me to the main police station in Queen's Gardens where they asked the desk sergeant to put me in a cell. The desk sergeant, after taking my personal details, asked them what the charge would be? It was obvious that they hadn't thought about this so we were subjected to a kind of Chuckle Brothers' "to me, to you" exercise, as they passed ideas between themselves before one of them blurted, "Sabotage! That's it. Industrial Sabotage."

The desk sergeant looked at me and raised his eyebrows as if to say what a pair of clowns, before writing down the charge and taking me to a cell. If he thought that these two clowns were funny, I certainly didn't.

I was left in the cell with a plastic covered mattress and a blanket that I had no intentions of using. So I just sat on the mattress thinking. This is just what they wanted me to do I later realised, as thoughts were swimming around my head while I pondered over the detective's words, "It doesn't matter if you didn't do it, we'll make it look like you did, so you may as well plead guilty and get a lighter sentence rather than not guilty and go to jail!"

I thought about how my wife would feel, how my family would feel, how this would be the end of my sea career, and how they, the police, thought they could get away with this. I convinced myself that there were innocent people who'd been convicted of serious offences because they'd given in to police psychological pressure: and I was determined that I wouldn't become one of them.

The Tweedle Dum and Tweedle Dee of the detective world, after making sure I was safely locked-up, returned to the riverside where the 'John Good' had replaced the 'Snowden'.

A couple of hours later, still sitting in the cell in disbelief, my thoughts were disturbed by the reappearance of the dynamic duo who once again asked me what I knew about the alleged offence. But then to my amazement they said, "We're taking you back to the boat and letting you go because the foreman and the skipper said it couldn't possibly be you and that you were one of the most reliable and conscientious workers of the lot."

Apparently when they'd returned to the launch in triumph after locking me up they asked Ernie and Bernard more questions and background information, and when my name was mentioned Ernie said, "By the way, where is Bob?"

"Ah, we've got him where he can't do anymore damage," said one of the self-satisfied detectives.

"What do you mean?"

"We think he did it, so we've locked him up."

"Well you had better unlock him quick because he certainly didn't have anything to do with it, as he didn't have the time or the inclination and he is one of our most conscientious, obliging and efficient crew members."

Eventually I received a full apology from the policemen but as far as I was concerned the damage had been done and I still believe that innocent people are pressured into admitting to crimes that they didn't commit.

When the detectives brought me back to the launch to finish my shift they asked Ernie and Bernard about any other potential suspects.

They answered that most of the regular crews didn't like the 'Snowden' and there had been jokes about "spiking the engine", but no one took these remarks very seriously.

The detectives did take them very seriously though and asked if the previous engineer/mate had made any such comments and they were told that he had but that he seemed to be joking. It was no joke for the detectives though, as at six in the morning they were hammering on the young man's door before arresting and charging him. Anyone could see that this was on the flimsiest of evidence, circumstantial and hearsay at best. The arrested man was a young Dutchman by the name of Foppo who'd married a girl from Hull. The fact that he was foreign meant that in the eyes of some he was already guilty before even a trial.

The commodore immediately suspended Foppo without pay. The launch crews just as quickly came out on strike on the grounds that the company had no right to suspend anyone without a fair trial, hearing or investigation. Needless to say the strike didn't last long before the company agreed to Foppo's suspension on full pay.

Eventually the case came to trial so a number of us had to appear in court. This was a nerve-racking experience but my evidence consisted of one of the barristers reading out my statement and occasionally asking me for confirmation and to clarify specific points. After my evidence the judge told me I could go and would no longer be needed.

Bernard got much more of a grilling when the defence lawyer employed by the NUR seemed to imply that he could have been the culprit as he'd been left on the boat alone for a period of time and that he had personal reasons for trying to implicate someone else.

It looked as though the jury was going to have a difficult job until a forensic engineer was called. The union had insisted that the engine of the 'Snowden' was subjected to independent examination and analysis. The results turned the case on its head. The expert concluded that no sand or other foreign body had been put in the engine. An analysis of the sump oil had shown that the level of grit found there was what would be expected in any engine of that age and usage. There was no evidence of sabotage just a normal old and overused engine in need of a thorough overhaul. Foppo was acquitted.

No one came out well from this incident. Foppo returned to work but after a short while decided to relocate his family to Holland. Bernard was given a hard time by some of his colleagues and even the management for a while but managed to keep going. While these two suffered the most from the incident, no one questioned the management's decision to call the police so hastily. They had responded to hearsay rather than conducting a proper investigation and the result had been very costly indeed.

Anyway Ernie was also to leave within a short time and the commodore would follow him in a couple of years to be replaced by a Humber pilot called Frank Berry. He, as a representative of the pilots in their professional association, had been one of the main campaigners to change the service to one serviced by high speed, fibreglass launches, but more of him later.

For me the experience had once again shown how important the role of a trade union could be in protecting its members. I started to become more interested in the NUR and also politics by attending the union meetings that were held once a fortnight at the Railway Club on Anlaby Road. It was also a good excuse to go for a pint with some of the lads afterwards.

The rest of the summer of 1971 I spent doing mainly holiday cover. A lot of this was on Hull Roads, which was quite handy. The Hull Roads launch generally tied up at Minerva Pier close to the Minerva pub, but would also use the ferry and floating pontoon if convenient, or, if the tide permitted, the Horse Wash opposite the Pilot Office and close to the mouth of the river Hull. The Horse Wash was a concrete slope that had been used, as the name suggests, by carters and draymen to wash their horses when the tide was up high enough to cover the slope. Those days had long since passed so now it didn't really have a use except by us for a couple of hours each tide and for bystanders to watch the activities on the river. Cars would also sometimes park there although there was a risk as one unfortunate driver found out when he parked to eat his lunch with the front of his car just sticking out slightly over the edge of the concrete at the top of the slope. Mick Smith was the skipper of the 'Snowden' when he came in to do a rapid changeover of pilots. Mick just misjudged his approach a fraction and the 'Snowden' failed to stop in time before crashing into the front grill of the car and leaving a big bow-shaped dent. As he backed off Mick dropped the wheelhouse window and shouted, "Now try to tell that to your insurance!"

T.W. Prickett approaching Minerva Pier.

Captain Newlove at Minerva Pier.

Chapter 29. Coxswain – Hull Roads.

I was working on Hull Roads with Keith Woods when I heard that the company was looking for another skipper. I didn't think I'd much of a chance as I knew that there were a couple of other employees who'd been there much longer than my seven or eight months but I banged in a letter of application anyway as I had nothing to lose.

I was surprised then when I was called to the office and told that my application had been successful and I was given a start date for a day shift on Hull Roads. I still had one more shift to do as engineer/mate and when I joined the 'Prickett' for that shift Keith said, "She's all yours then, I'll be mate tonight."

So my last shift as engineer/mate was an intense training exercise supervised by Keith, but I knew I still had a lot to learn.

Hull Roads was considered the easier of the pilot boat stations because it didn't involve the open sea but it had its own hazards. The Humber is known for shifting sandbanks with a large tidal range, which exposed some of the sandbanks at low tide while others were just covered. The tide was also fast running between five and seven knots, so apart from times of slack water, was a factor that always needed consideration particularly when we were required to venture out of the marked channel to go to New Holland. The fast tide against a strong wind could also mean that the Humber, about two miles across at Hull, could get quite rough. Our job was to get the pilots on and off the moving ships quickly and safely, which meant judging the speed and timing for dropping alongside the pilot ladder. It also meant rapid changeovers on the pier or Horse Wash with no time for dallying so the skill was to be able to drop alongside and be off again as quickly as possible. With the twin screw launches we would use the throttles to do this making sure that we didn't get caught in our own backwash. On the single screw boats the trick on the flood tide was to approach the landing head to tide, cut the engine to neutral, come in on the port shoulder, and then wind the gear full astern so that the action of the propeller turned the stern into the quay and alongside. Normally the screw of a ship turns clockwise so you got used to this manoeuvre but the 'Captain Newlove' had a propeller that turned the other way that could catch you out until you got used to it.

So now I was a captain of sorts, what next? Would this be my job for the next forty-one years? I was happy now but would that always be the case? I still read a lot and was interested in art and history and I was well aware that I didn't have any academic qualifications, not even an O level, but perhaps that could be rectified. I knew that there were night classes available and correspondence courses but I needed a bit of advice. I'd got to know a new neighbour in Cromer Street who I knew was a just married teacher at the local college as well as a student at Hull University, so I decided to ask him for some advice. His name was Ron Fairfax who came from Sheffield and had trained as a teacher but now needed a degree, hence his move to Hull. I told him that I wanted to do some O levels to broaden my education and he asked me how old I was. He then surprised me by saying I didn't need to do O levels or A levels as a new thing called the Open University had just started up which was designed for people like me; adults without qualifications. I said that I didn't think I was ready for that but he convinced me that I should make enquiries and give it a try and that he'd help me if needed. So I applied to the Open University, which had started formally that year, and was told that I could start the following year in February 1972.

The Open University had been supported and encouraged by Harold Wilson with the aim of offering a university standard education service for those who lacked formal qualifications. However, while every student was required to complete a foundation course, a kind of sampler course where you were given the basics in several different disciplines before making specialist choices, those with no qualifications had to do two foundation courses. You could do up to two full courses a year but as I had other commitments I opted for one at a time so for my first year I chose the Arts Foundation Course which would give me an introduction to history, literature, theatre, art history and philosophy. Every student was allocated a counsellor for advice and a tutor to provide subject support and to mark and give feedback on written assignments and essays. The courses were delivered through a series of handbooks written by academics, supported by set books, radio programmes, TV programmes, summer schools (a residential week at a university for intense study and drinking) and, where possible, tutorials and seminars. Assessments included computer-marked assignments, written assignments - usually essays - and an end of course examination. So it was pretty intensive and quite daunting for someone whose only real writing since leaving school were letters home when at sea, and I don't think (although I may be wrong) that anyone judged those on my spelling and grammar.

When I expressed my concerns to Ron he told me not to worry as it was just like learning to ride a bike, you may fall off a few times but eventually you get the hang of it. He then offered to check my essays before I sent them in for formal marking, which he did for the first couple until I got the hang of the type of content and structure they were looking for. This certainly helped ease my way through the first year.

New students at the Open University were given the first three months on trial so that if they felt it was not right for them they could drop out with minimal cost. There was a cost that involved a long list of set books as well as the tuition fees and the summer school fee. I don't remember how much this all came to but it was a considerable sum so I applied for a grant from Hull City Council. This was worth a try because while the council said it would not give me a grant up front, it would reimburse me of all fees and expenses if I passed the course. Well that was an incentive and while I had to fund my first year's education up front, I was able to use the grant, when it was paid, to fund my next year, a Social Sciences Foundation Course introducing me to the subjects of sociology, psychology, social psychology, economics and politics.

One of the interesting things about the Social Sciences Foundation course was that one of the set books was "The Fishermen" by Jeremy Tunstall. This was a sociological study of the fishing community of the Hessle Road deep sea trawling industry in Hull of which I had first hand experience, so this helped make the course much more interesting for me.

Tutorials in those early years were held in Hull University were my tutors were lecturers. My counsellor, who I also found very supportive, came from the College of Education and was called Patrick Doyle who later became involved in local politics as a city councillor. While the written work was daunting in one sense, talking in tutorials and seminars was daunting in another, as I was very conscious of my local Hull accent. Most of the people taking up the Open University in those early years seemed to be teachers who needed a degree, people who'd dropped out of university, and professional people who needed an extra or more up to date qualification. In short, the middle classes dominated. It took me some time to pluck up the courage to speak during a tutorial and the first time I did I felt extreme embarrassment. I was sure that all the heads in the room turned to look at me to see if one of the caretakers had abandoned his brush and fag end, and was about to say hurry up as it was time to lock up. As it happened my fears were unfounded and my fellow students were as encouraging as my tutors.

After the foundation courses I started to specialise in sociology, social psychology and history subjects that supported my interest in working class history, trade unions and politics. It took me five years to build up sufficient credits to be awarded a Bachelor of Arts degree and a further two years to convert that into an honours degree, so it was a long-term process. During that time though I attended summer schools at York, Keele, East Anglia, Warwick and Sussex universities and attended numerous lectures at Hull University. While most of my studying took place at home, Open University students were allowed to use some of the facilities at Hull University. For example we were allowed to use the library but the chief librarian, the always miserable looking Phillip Larkin, wouldn't allow us to borrow any books. I had used the Central Library in Hull a lot but when I first entered the Hull University Library I confess I was a overawed by the size and number of books and had a bit of a panic attack and had to leave before returning later. As it happens I knew a lecturer at the university, Nick Worrall, so I went for a pint with him in the students' union bar.

My interest in left wing politics and trade union activity drew me towards the Communist Party of Great Britain which I joined for a couple of years before deciding it wasn't for me. I remembered my experiences when visiting the totalitarian regimes of the Soviet Union, East Germany, Poland, Latvia and China, while in the merchant navy and realised that the words of Marx were open to many interpretations, not all of them good. However, I was influenced by the alternative viewpoints offered by many Marxist academics particularly in the areas of history and art history.

I also bought the Morning Star for many years. In fact I also sold it when I was available to do so, outside the Co-op in Hull on Saturday mornings. I remember that W.H.Smith across the road wouldn't sell the Morning Star at that time so when I got bored I'd venture across the road and slot a couple of copies into their newspaper display. I never did find out what happened at the checkout when someone wanted to buy one.

Ron Fairfax and I also set ourselves up as local reporters for the Morning Star with Ron writing the copy and me taking the pictures, all in black and white, on my Russian Zenit E camera. In this way we would cover industrial disputes like the closure of Imperial Typewriters, crime stories such as the alleged arson attack that killed a number of people in an old folks' home, and of course the cod wars. When we'd finished our articles we'd send them down to London by the appropriately named 'Red Star' on British Rail and wait to see if they were published. As we were not members of the NUJ our names could not be used so they were always printed under the "Our Correspondent" banner but it was still satisfying to see my photographs in print.

About this time we heard that the council wanted to demolish our houses. While there were examples of very poor housing in parts of Sculcoates Lane we felt that the houses in our little area, Cromer Street and St Leonard's Road, were worth saving. Many of the residents had cared for their homes and had added bathrooms and kitchens, so we decided to fight the blanket redevelopment of the area. It was a bit like a Cromer Street Commune as we gathered support from other residents and after much argument got the council to reprieve its demolition plans. Not only that but we got the council to further improve the area by clearing some bomb sites and planting trees and grass, to not only improve the aesthetics of the area but provide grassy play areas for the children. Of course there were people who said it was a waste of time and the areas would be vandalised but this proved not to be the case and members of the local community appreciated the improvements.

Ron, as well as being a mature student at Hull University, also worked at Hull College teaching general studies and English and after I'd settled down into my second year of Open University studies he said to me, "Have you ever thought about teaching? You'd go down a treat with the apprentices on day release at college. They'd love you and your background." But I replied that I couldn't see myself ever doing that.

"Of course you could do it," Ron insisted but I didn't think any more about it... until I got the telephone call.

We didn't have a telephone at that time but the call came through at my in-laws' house across the terrace. The caller introduced himself as the Head of Department of General Studies at Hull College and said that Ron Fairfax had given him my name and number and that I was available for part-time work as a college lecturer. He then asked if I would be available to cover a class the next evening?

I replied, "Yes," and he gave me the class and room details.

What had I done? What was I supposed to teach? Ron gave me some advice and provided a short film that I could use to stimulate a discussion and set some written work but I still wasn't sure I'd done the right thing.

I was even less sure when I was faced with the class. Many times I'd passed the college building in Queen's Gardens and wondered about the marvels that went on within. A nice new building with classes filled with expectant students' faces as the lecturers created an environment to encourage and develop their learning. My first class destroyed that image.

It was a group of third year welders who didn't want to be in the college late in the evening, especially when they could not see any relevance in an hour and half of general studies. It was obvious that the lecturer who I was replacing had let anarchy reign if only for a quiet life. It was like being in a monkey enclosure at Twycross Zoo as the students took absolutely no notice of me as some walked about the room chatting, some climbed onto the window ledges and a few others just sat around looking bored or worse, hostile. Anyone who has read any of Tom Sharpe's 'Wilt' novels will get the picture. It was a long, stressful hour and half for me and it was a relief when it was all over. It had been a disaster. When I told Ron he just said that not all the classes were like that.

I thought that might be the end of my brief teaching career but the telephone went again and I was offered classes to cover at the Park Street College buildings. Reluctantly I agreed but resolved that I was not going to be beaten and I would be prepared for any insurgency.

The classes this time were both mechanical engineering apprentices. I hyped myself up and entered the classroom ready to lay the law down straight away. But I needn't have bothered, they were as good as gold, interested, responsive and polite. This was more like my original image and as I was offered more and more classes, although I confess I was flying by the seat of my pants, it got better and better as my confidence developed. It is quite a nerve-racking experience to enter a classroom and develop material to deliver a planned hour, hour and half, or two-hour class and I realised that I needed a lot more experience if I was to be successful.

These early classes had been offered to me as one-offs at the end of the academic year and I'd been able to take them as the times offered fitted in with my shifts on the pilot boats. My introduction to teaching had therefore been short but it had sparked an interest in what could, with a bit of hard work and luck, become an alternative career should I get fed up of the sea. However, to gain experience I needed to be teaching regularly, which was difficult given the rotating shifts that the pilot boats worked. Then I saw an advertisement in the Hull Daily Mail for a course leading to a certificate for part-time teachers in adult and further education validated by the Yorkshire and Humberside Council for Adult and Further Education; so I made enquiries.

I was told that the course, delivered mainly in evenings but with some Saturday attendance, was based around instructing part-time teachers in the basics of lesson plans, schemes of work, producing materials, and delivery methods, just the things I needed. But the course was only open to those regularly teaching three hours a week. How could I do that with my shift work commitments?

The first thing I did was contact the Head of Department at Hull College who had given me the few hours cover and told him that I'd been offered a place on the training course but needed to be teaching for at least three hours a week. This was a bit of a lie but it worked and he offered me two, hour and a half classes, 17.15 to 18.45, on Thursday and Friday afternoons. I then applied for the course and told them that yes I did teach three hours regularly at Hull College and I was given a place fully funded by Hull City Council. The problem now was how could I get time off the pilot boats to deliver my teaching commitments?

At that time I was working on the Hull Roads station. I'd settled into the skipper role and everything seemed to be going smoothly. It was now 1974 and I'd been skipper for three years. The other skippers on Hull Roads at that time were Keith Woods, Eric Hopcraft and Bernard Gillyon. Mick Smith had left and so would Eric in due course. The shift system on Hull Roads worked on a rotating shift pattern of a day shift, 08.00 until 16.00, so no problems there, a night shift, 16.00 to 08.00 the next morning, and then a day off. My problem was the evening shift when I was always relieved by Bernard, so I approached him to see if he was prepared to cover for me on the odd days that I'd be late taking over, provided that I paid him at the appropriate overtime rate. Bernard without hesitation agreed to this arrangement, so my plan had worked.

I was now studying with the Open University, doing my teaching course, teaching my three hours a week - plus some daytime cover from time to time, doing my shifts on the pilot boats, and, as I'd now been elected as a union representative, carrying out my union activities. Did I mention that I also still pursued my hobby of painting?

My sister and brother-in-law were also going through some changes as Jack had taken voluntary redundancy from the docks and used his severance pay to buy the tenancy of a pub called the Providence in St Stephen's Square behind the bus station. At first this was very much a family affair with his dad working as odd job man and gardener, and my mum helping with her bar and pub management experience. Jack made the Providence a success by running darts teams and gaining a reputation for good beer, a feat he repeated when he moved, after he and my sister divorced, to a bigger pub called the Robin.

Finally he ended up running the 'New York' bar and 'Jack's Place' nightclub in the city centre. However, before these developments the Providence became the place to meet or end up if out on the town, which for some of the pilot boat lads and me was the Wednesday night union meeting routine. The drawback to this was that they'd chat to my mum who, as mums do, let out a family secret. When I was a toddler I had long, curly, blond hair and people called me Bubbles after the popular Gainsborough painting that was used to advertise soap. She told this to my deck-hand, Bernard Keating, who immediately told the rest of the lads, so my nickname became Bubbles. At that time, but not now sadly, I still had curly hair combed in an Afro style and one night I even heard him telling one of the pilots, who'd asked him why I was called Bubbles, that in fact it was my stage name as I also doubled as a male stripper. The pilot then asked me if this was true and rather than disappoint him I told him it was.

The job on the pilot boats paid quite well due to the bonuses for working around the clock, 365 days a year. We were paid fortnightly in cash, which we collected from a Docks Board office in Bond Street. The nearest pub was the Dram Shop otherwise known as Wilson's Corner so it was here that you'd find a lot of the crew members on their day off enjoying a drink and a laugh. Some of the lads would then go on to the Hoffbrauhaus bar where the management were trying to boost lunch-time trade by hiring strippers and topless dancers with an entry fee of five pence.

Five pence! One shilling in old money! I found this sad and degrading and I bet the girls felt just as bad. I only went once and left early feeling embarrassed but not half as embarrassed as the girls may have felt. Imagine having to put that you were a 'five pence, lunchtime stripper' in a Hull pub on your CV?

On the domestic front Madeleine seemed to put up with this list of time consuming activities and we still managed to maintain a pretty good social life. We'd also decided that we'd like to start a family but so far nothing had come of this. We kept on trying but nothing happened. Madeleine thought it could be because I'd experienced trouble in the 'tween decks' in the past and this may have caused problems with my fertility. The surgeon had assured me that one testicle was enough so I shouldn't have any problems in that department but her concerns did get me thinking. I offered to go for a test but she said she wouldn't put me through that ordeal. So we kept trying. I don't think that my wife wanted to rub my nose in it but she had taken up knitting as a hobby to use up the time when I was working or studying and the main things that she knitted were baby clothes. We also seemed to have collected a number of cats, which I think were her child substitutes except you wouldn't expect your children to invite all the waifs and strays in the neighbourhood to take advantage of the cat flap and trash the kitchen every night, although experience now tells me that children may also try this but by inviting their friends in through the front door rather than a cat flap.

Madeleine then said that we ought to move house so I thought a three-bedroomed house on the outskirts of the city would be nice but she set her heart on a five – yes, FIVE-bedroomed, terrace house in Grafton Street off Newland Avenue. So after a bit of debate we moved to Grafton Street.

Captain J.W. Evenden and Captain A.E. Newlove

The pier at Spurn.

Chapter 30. Working on the Humber.

Back on the pilot boats the service was undergoing a number of changes. The large pilot cutters crewed mainly by apprentices were being phased out to be replaced by a shore station and control tower on Spurn Point. The shore station would provide accommodation for the pilots who would board the ships by means of fast launches. A pier was to be built out into Spurn Bight to enable the launches to pick up the pilots and change crews. The pier would also be used for the Spurn lifeboat which was itself being replaced by a high-speed launch so would no longer need the traditional slipway. While the base was being built at Spurn one of the old cutters, the 'William Fenton', was moored in Spurn Bight to provide waiting accommodation and catering facilities for the pilots. Launches would then take them out or take them off their ships. A floating pipeline, with one end attached to the beach and a walkway on top, was a temporary solution to ensure that the pilots and launch crews had access to the shore at any state of the tide. When the pier was built the 'Fenton' was towed away before being scrapped.

The pilot service never stopped. Twenty-four hours a day, every day throughout the year, so at least three launches were needed at Spurn as well as the launch based on Hull Roads, which meant that more crews were needed. The main promoter of the new service using high-speed launches with a shore base on Spurn Point for the pilots was a man called Frank Berry. Frank was a representative of the Humber pilots in their professional association and his vision started to become reality when he became commodore of pilots after the retirement of Bill Perry. This meant that any negotiations we had about our working conditions were now with Frank Berry who himself came from a background of negotiating with his previous role as the pilots' representative. Our meetings with management became a bit more combative.

The elected union representatives within the pilot launch crews were Jim Dempster, Keith Woods, an engineering representative Ted Sagar, and me. Frank had a lot of good ideas and also tried to be fair given his own trade union background but he was also a bit of an autocrat and like all autocrats he hated his authority to be challenged.

One of the first things that Frank Berry wanted were fully interchangeable rotating crews so that we all worked Spurn and Hull Roads, which meant three months on the Spurn station followed by a month on Hull Roads. Frank thought this would be better for the company and also a fairer working system for the crews. Frank also wanted to get rid of the term engineer/mate and have only skippers, engineers and deck-hands. It was very hard to argue with this although some of the Hull Roads crew members who had only ever worked on that station were not happy with the idea to the point that some left when it became obvious that these changes would occur. The agreement in the end was that the Hull Roads shift routine would remain the same and the Spurn station would revolve around twelve hour shifts starting at 07.00 in the morning and 19.00 in the evening at Spurn. This meant having to be at the Pilot Office at 06.00 in the morning and 18.00 in the evening for the hour long drive to Spurn in a minibus. The company also purchased a fleet of six saloon cars that were used by the pilots and launch crews as necessary to get to and from Spurn Point.

I'd spent a few years on Hull Roads and it had been a good learning experience as well as allowing me to complete my teaching course and do some part-time teaching. This would not be possible if I was working at Spurn but luckily I'd finished by the time I was required to work there.

The main launches on Hull Roads during those first few years were the 'T.W. Prickett', 'Commander Snowden', 'John Good' and the 'Dracaena'. The 'Prickett' was a very comfortable wooden hulled boat with a good below deck cabin heated by a solid fuel stove. The wheelhouse contained the wheel, radar monitor, VHF radio, compass, calor gas stove, throttle and gearing mechanism. She was single screw but had a decent speed as well as a deep draught for a small vessel of about seven feet. She was a good sea-boat and would also be used at Spurn Point to provide cover for the launches there when needed. The only problem with the 'Prickett' was that with the deep draught there was always the chance of going aground when doing New Holland trips on falling spring tides. One experience I had on the 'Prickett' when returning from New Holland to Hull one night was that we got stuck in a hole on a sandbank. We didn't actually ground and remained afloat but couldn't get out of this hole until the tide turned and allowed us to proceed on our journey.

The 'Commander Snowden' was a much slower boat (about 8 knots) than the 'Prickett' (about 10 knots) and was slightly smaller. She also had a cosy forward cabin with a solid fuel stove which kept the place very warm in winter only there was not direct access to the wheelhouse from the cabin. The wheelhouse was unheated with drop-down windows (like old-fashioned train carriage windows with a leather sash), which you had to have open as the windows did not have wipers or clear views. There was a VHF radio transmitter and receiver, and a calor gas stove for making tea and heating food but no radar. The lack of radar made for some hairy times when operating in fog especially when Hull Roads was busy with anchored ships while others were moving. I remember picking a pilot up from New Holland one day in the 'Snowden' when thick fog came down. It was a real pea-souper but we set off for Hull anyway. It was not long to high tide but the flood was still running so I set my course making allowance for the run of the tide. I didn't have sandbanks to worry about because of the tide but I had to rely entirely on the boat's compass as no landmarks could be seen. The pilot and my deck-hand kept watch on deck and it seemed an age as we crossed over Hull Middle before we sighted the buoy with the same name and edged our way into the Horse Wash. My navigation had been spot on but not long after this the 'Snowden' was fitted with radar.

The Horse Wash and the 'Snowden' brings back another memory. During holidays like Christmas and New Year the pilot service still operated although shipping was often quieter and it was on one of those days when my deck-hand at the time, an elderly seaman called Ray Frear, told me that we were running short of coke for the stove. Ray was a bit of a character who'd been torpedoed five times while working on the Archangel conveys during the war. After the war he emigrated to Australia to work as a lorry driver and a prison warden before returning with his wife and family to Hull when she became ill. Anyway, Ray asked me if I could take the 'Snowden' into the Horse Wash while he went over to the Pilot Office to fill the coke bin. I said I could but he would have to be quick as the tide was falling. In we went and Ray jumped ashore and I waited with the engine ticking over, and waited, and waited. After about twenty minutes or so of agitated waiting Ray finally re-appeared.

"Where have you been?" I asked.

"Oh, I borrowed some matches from Charlie in Hull Radio - Hull Radio took up the top floor of the Pilot Office - the other day so I whipped them up to him."

"I told you the tide was falling and we didn't have much time, that could have waited," I replied as I wound the gear mechanism into astern and put on the revs.

Nothing happened! We were stuck fast. No matter what I tried the vessel was stuck on the mud by the bow.

"What shall we do now?" asked Ray.

"Just put out the ropes fore and aft while I tell the pilot master in the office."

With my head hung, I went across to the office and told the pilot master, the deputy commodore as it happened called Bill Shepherdson, that I'd some bad news that the 'Snowden' was aground in the Horse Wash. To my surprise he just said, "Don't worry there's nothing at all moving at the moment so just sit tight until the next tide."

I went back on board a bit happier but still annoyed with Ray and I ended up saying, "The only thing that could make my day worse would be for a Hull Daily Mail photographer to walk around the corner." I'd barely closed my mouth when a bloke appeared on the pier with a camera bag around his neck. He took one look at us and started snapping away. With no big news stories breaking, one of the pictures made the front page of the Mail the next day with the caption; "The pilot boat

'Commander Snowden' at Victoria Pier after going aground during a bunkering operation." Never believe what you read in the papers.

The 'Dracaena' and the 'John Good' were both twin screw, high-speed fibreglass launches. The 'Dracaena' was very, very noisy to the point that I campaigned to have the noise levels checked in the wheelhouse. The findings were that the decibel reading was far in excess of an acceptable safe level and could lead to permanent hearing damage. Again I campaigned for something to be done about this - so the company issued us with ear defenders. They then realised that if we wore the defenders we couldn't hear the VHF radio so couldn't give us instructions, which we of course exploited, so eventually they had to bring in experts who installed noise suppressing baffles under the deck boards of the wheelhouse which was situated directly over the engines. However, the engineers soon got fed up of having to lift the baffles as well as the deck boards to gain access to the engines so they soon disappeared, probably left on a dock side somewhere.

The 'John Good' was faster (about 18 knots) than the 'Dracaena' (about 16 knots) and nearly as noisy. The main problem with the twin screw launches in Hull Roads was that the tide would bring in semi-submerged logs and timber which could damage the propellers and, although we took great care, damage in this way was a fairly regular occurrence. However, apart from that the 'John Good' was the ideal launch for Hull Roads because of its speed and shallow draught, but I also have two, not very fond, memories of working on this boat.

The first involves an attempt, I firmly believe, for Frank Berry to assert himself as being the boss and not to be pushed. The launches on Hull Roads got their bunkers from tanks kept at the buoy shed on Sammy's Point and these could only be accessed around high water. It was about high tide when I'd taken over the 'John Good' in the Horse Wash at 16.00 one afternoon for a nightshift on Hull Roads and was immediately called upon to go out to a couple of ships entering the Roads. I did the first ship and then while approaching the second the engines spluttered to a halt. The fuel gauge said "empty" but I knew the 'John Good' well and knew that she had auxiliary fuel tanks that acted as ballast. These tanks were behind the seat lockers in the forward cabin so I just went down, turned the cocks to open, lifted the deck boards, primed the engines and started them up again. We were then able to complete the boardings, drop the pilots and proceed to the buoy shed to bunker. I made the necessary entries in the logbook and didn't think any more about it; until I got the letter.

The letter said that because the 'John Good' had run out of fuel I had failed to follow the standing instructions on taking over the vessel and I was going to be suspended for two weeks without pay. There were a number of standing instructions for coxswains relating to things like the use of the VHF and radar and responsibilities like crew discipline and keeping the launch clean etc., but what Frank Berry was referring to was a list of checks that we were supposed to carry out before taking over a launch. These included making sure the vessel was afloat, the bilges were clear, the radar, VHF etc. were all working and a number of others. It would normally take about twenty minutes or longer to carry out these checks in full but the necessities of the service meant that we usually put them off except the 'afloat' bit, until a more convenient time. In this case I had to take the launch out immediately after relieving the previous skipper otherwise some ships would have missed the tide if I'd insisted on taking on fuel first. On top of that, we hadn't actually run out of fuel as we had emergency tanks. To me this was a definite case of victimisation so I immediately contacted the branch secretary of the NUR, Tom Waddington, to assist me with my defence.

Tom Waddington was an experienced union official. He was a quietly spoken man who never seemed to get flustered even during the most heated union meeting discussions and observing him in negotiations was a master class. Tom arranged for a hearing with Frank Berry during which Frank presented his case, which he felt was unchallengeable and I presented my defence as stated above. Frank Berry came back saying no matter what the circumstances I should have followed the standing instructions as they were written for a purpose, and the rules should be followed at all times. On this point he was right of course even if the circumstances had been ignored but Tom suddenly took another tack.

"Have you had any complaints about Mr Addey previously?" he asked Mr Berry.

"No, none at all," Frank replied.

"Does he get on with the pilots and his other crew members?"

"Yes, I've never received any complaints and they all speak very highly of him."

" Does Mr Addey take a lot of time off?"

"No, his work record is very good and he has always been reliable."

"What about his time keeping, is he often late?"

"No, his time keeping as far as I know is very good."

"What about his ability, any complaints there?"

"No, he's a very efficient and conscientious coxswain."

"So he is a valued employee?"

"Oh yes, he is a very valued employee."

At this point I was starting to wonder who this model employee was, when Tom continued.

"So you have an employee who is popular, efficient, conscientious, keeps good time and is very reliable; if he is that good why do you want to suspend him?"

There followed a loud silence while Frank Berry contemplated this scenario before saying, "Er, hmm, I take your point, but in future Mr Addey must remember that all the rules must be followed."

I said that I would certainly be following the rules in future and we walked out of the office with the case dropped.

A couple of days later I took over a launch at Spurn Point and was asked to proceed urgently to the Spurn Lightship to pick a pilot off an outward-bound ship. My reply over the VHF was that I couldn't go until I'd carried out the checks.

"What checks skipper?" replied the master pilot in the control tower.

"The checks listed in the standing instructions," I replied.

"What standing instructions, what checks, how long will this take?"

"About half an hour to forty-five minutes," I said, sitting by the controls sipping a mug of tea.

"What! I'm telling you to forget the standing checks or instructions or whatever they are and take that launch out to sea as this is an urgent job!"

"Sorry, but only a few days ago Frank Berry tried to suspend me without pay for not carrying out these checks and I had to assure him that in the future I'd always carry out the company rules, so take it up with him if you have a problem," I said.

"All right skipper. I understand, but please leave straight away and I will take the responsibility if there are any comebacks."

"Okay, but please log this conversation."

I had proved that the rules were most of the time unworkable and noted this for future reference.

The second bad memory of the 'John Good' involved dense fog in Hull Roads. The fog should not have been a problem given that the launch had a perfectly good radar. I'd heard about radar induced collisions as when working from just the screen there was a tendency to steer closer to ships and obstacles than you would if using your eyes in good visibility, and working on the pilot boats we had to steer collision courses to come alongside moving ships and you don't get closer than that. The only problems were that in some weather conditions you could get a lot of clutter (interference), which meant extra care at close quarters as when you got very close to a ship the ship didn't show up on the radar at all, so it meant approaching very carefully until the ship came into vision.

On this day, it was a Sunday and fairly quiet, I was tied up on the floating pontoon used by the Humber ferries. We'd often tie up to the pontoon or ferries when the tide was low as Minerva pier would get very muddy on the ebb so this made access and egress much easier. I had a new launch skipper working with me as a deck-hand. All new skippers would do this so that they familiarised themselves with the service before taking their own command. This one was an ex-trawler skipper called Eddie and what an initiation I gave him on his first day.

The fog was dense and we were sitting, chatting and flicking through the Sunday papers when we heard the ferry, I think it was the Lincoln Castle, approaching. We let go, turned on the radar, and I edged the launch clear of the pontoon while keeping the Corporation Pier in sight as the radar took a few minutes to warm up. The tide had turned while we'd been tied up to the pontoon and a flood tide was starting to run. Suddenly the bow of the 'Lincoln Castle' appeared out of the fog as the captain had misjudged his approach and missed the pontoon and was now head on to Corporation Pier while the paddles were going astern. To avoid being run down by the ferry I took the 'John Good' around the ferry's bow and out into the river, well clear of the pier and waited until the radar warmed up. When we had a picture it was clear that we were on the outer edge of the channel but there was no sign of the ferry. The shore line and buoys were showing clear images and Eddie asked me where I thought the ferry was? I said that I expected it had used the tide to drop alongside the pontoon as no other image was showing and that I was going to tie up on Riverside Quay for a while until boarding time. I put the throttles ahead and turned the wheel to head for the shore.

Was it a bang? Was it a crunch?

No matter what it was, the sound was sickening as we came upstanding a couple of metres aft of the ferry's starboard paddle. The launch had gone under the sponson of the ferry and crunched and badly damaged the corner of our forward cabin and bent the safety rails. Eddie didn't bat an eyelid as I reported the incident to the Pilot Office and was told that the launch would be replaced as soon as possible.

I thought I'd get into big trouble for the mishap and was surprised when nothing was said. I bumped in to John Singleton, the company secretary, in the little kiosk on the pier and asked him if anything had been said and he surprised me by saying that some people were quite delighted as it meant that all the little bits of damage done to the launch over a period of time could now come under one insurance claim.

Eventually I was called to visit the solicitor handling the claim and once again I was subjected to showing what had happened by using little wooden models of ships while the solicitor took notes. Apparently the ferry had also put in a claim for damages but what for precisely I was not aware. Maybe it was for sweeping up our fibreglass chippings off the Lincoln Castle's sponson as there was no visible damage to that vessel at all.

When the results of the enquiry came through I was told that I was not considered at fault. The conclusion was that the ferry had acted, "in an unseamanlike manner" by reversing out into the channel rather than using the tide to drop alongside its berth.

T.W. Prickett on the fish dock slip.

Captain Sibree

Chapter 31. Life Changes and New Directions.

Around 1975 a number of changes took place in my life. On the domestic front we had moved from Cromer Street to the large house in Grafton Street, which meant that I had to reduce my Open University studies while I decorated the house and did other DIY stuff. On the work front we were now all working a rota system that involved a month on Hull Roads and three months at Spurn which meant that I also had to give up my part-time teaching. The shifts at Spurn were for twelve hours at a time but because we had to be at the office an hour before the watch turn over for the long drive to Spurn Point and at the end of the shift having a similar drive back to the office, the shifts were really for fourteen hours. Even then there was no guarantee that you'd be relieved on time because if the launch had been sent out on a Humber Lightship run it could be a couple more hours before you could be relieved. In those cases we would take one of the company cars or a taxi would be provided to take us back to Hull.

Spurn Point is a narrow spit of sand, about three and half miles long protruding from the Holderness coast of East Yorkshire at Kilnsea, dividing the North Sea from the Humber estuary. It starts out very narrow and then widens towards the seaward end. The Point shifts in time due to the effects of the tide and the weather but the main part is held together by the remains of a warren of concrete military buildings developed during the First and Second World Wars as part of Britain's sea defences built, along with the Bull Sand Fort and Haile Sand Fort, to protect the approaches to the estuary.

The military had also built a railway line that ran the length of Spurn Point to move stores and apparently, a large gun. Much of the railway line had disappeared but parts would occasionally be revealed after strong winds shifted some of the sand. Similarly the wind would, from time to time, reveal a concrete building where once there had been an innocent looking sand dune. There are two lighthouses on the Point but only one is in use, the older one being used for research purposes by Hull University. The Point was also home to the only full-time manned lifeboat in the country whose crew lived with their families in a group of modern, purpose built houses like a small village. In addition to this were our new buildings: the control tower, pilots' waiting area and accommodation, and an engineering workshop and storeroom. The Point attracted a lot of visitors on day trips in the summer but in winter only bird watchers and sea anglers braved the journey. I remember one night starting a nightshift in blizzard conditions - it was before we were operating from the purpose built pier so were using the pipeline - and passing a group of men with their rods fishing I couldn't resist making a comment.

"By you must have fucking ugly wives," I said while wishing that I was at home safely tucked up in bed under the lee of bum island.

"If you'd been down t'pit all week son, you'd think this was paradise," was the reply in a West Yorkshire accent.

There were three crews and two or three engineers on each watch on the Spurn Station, which was usually very busy. The sea could also get rough at Spurn and as the pier we used was on the western side of Spurn Point it also faced the prevailing winds, which sometimes made it difficult to lie alongside this very exposed construction. As part of our union negotiations we had got the company to put a shelter on the end of the pier with an electric kettle and a telephone but they were the only comforts the pier offered.

The only other users of the pier were the Humber lifeboat crew to access the lifeboat, which was normally moored in Spurn Bight. However, one winter we also had an uninvited user, a very bad-tempered seal that made its home on one of the landing platforms on the pier. This animal attacked anyone that came near it so we kept well clear.

When I first went to Spurn the main launches used were the 'Captain Newlove', 'Captain Sibree', 'Captain Holmes', 'Dracaena' and 'John Good'. Later these would be joined by faster fibreglass launches like the forty-foot plus 'Gertude', 'Fox', (both 1975) and 'Mitchell' (1977), and the larger fifty-foot plus 'J.W. Evenden' (1975) and 'Tom Stanley' (1976).

My favourite launches in those early days were the larger 'Captain Sibree' and 'Captain Newlove'. The 'Sibree' (about 12 knots) was about seventy feet in length, with a large forward cabin and a pilots' lounge in the stern. The wheelhouse had the usual radar and radio but the wheel was like a small ship's wheel and the throttle handles looked like a proper telegraph. The 'Newlove' (about 10 knots) was the only pilot boat at the time that had a raised bridge. On the bridge apart from the usual equipment, there was also the facility to steer the boat by remote control or by using an automatic pilot. Not many used the automatic pilot as after one visit to the docks for a refit the automatic pilot didn't appear to work so no one bothered. However, I discovered that it did work but the compass reading was reversed so that, for example, if I wanted to set a course steering 100 I would set the automatic pilot to steer 280. A bit confusing but it worked and allowed me to sit in the wheelhouse with my feet up. The only problem with the Newlove was that the propeller turned to port rather than starboard which took some getting used to when coming alongside after being familiar with the more conventional single screw boats the 'Prickett' and 'Snowden'.

The 'Captain Holmes' (originally called the 'Vala Nos Deus') was, although fibreglass, one of the larger boats similar in layout to the 'Sibree'. The Holmes at about 15 knots was faster than the 'Sibree' with a nose that lifted when running at full speed but she was not as robust and prone to damage so seemed to spend a lot of time out of service.

The 'Evenden', 'Fox', 'Gertude' and 'Mitchell' were fast (capable of up to 25 knots but normally running at between 18 and 20 knots) comfortable and quiet after the ear damaging noise of the 'Dracaena'. All the fibreglass boats, except for the 'Tom Stanley', had the wheelhouse over the engine compartment so were prone to engine noise but the 'Dracaena' was the worst offender so she was used less and less as the new launches came into service until she was finally withdrawn and sold in 1976. The 'Tom Stanley' (1976) was built to a similar design to the then, also new, Spurn lifeboat, with a raised wheelhouse but there was a design fault with this launch which meant that it had to be withdrawn from service permanently the following year.

What all the pilot boats had in common was that they were very good sea-boats which was essential given that we operated 365 days a year in all weathers. Fog wasn't too bad and we could operate just by using the radar, and fog usually meant that there was little wind so the sea would be calm.

Snow was worse than fog because not only did you have poor visibility but it also seemed to create a lot of interference on the radar. Gales though were the worst of all and many days I listened with dread to the weather forecast on the radio as I sat at home prior to taking over a watch and heard that a gale was imminent or already blowing. The sea at Spurn and out into the North Sea could get very rough and there were times that Spurn Point would get breached by the sea and for a short period become an island until the road could be rebuilt.

One night it was blowing ferociously but we continued to take pilots off ships until we'd collected all that were due. One launch had already made its way to Grimsby as it was impossible to land on the pier at Spurn leaving the 'Evenden' and the launch I was operating, the 'Fox', to complete any stragglers. It was a terrible night, in fact it was the night that part of Skegness Pier got washed away and people were trapped on Cleethorpes Pier. I had about six or seven pilots on board as well as one of the engineers when the control called me and asked where I was going to land the pilots given that the pier at Spurn was not accessible. The choices were: go up to Hull, which would have taken ages against the tide and into the teeth of the gale; go to Immingham, not much better and not very good for shelter; or go to Grimsby, although there were major dangers as it was a falling tide and close to low water. I chose Grimsby and I could hear one of the pilots behind me give a big sigh of relief.

The best way to describe the trip into Grimsby was 'dry-mouthed'. The danger was not just the wild water but also the possibility of the props catching the bottom in a trough of the waves as we approached Grimsby dock basin. The other launch skipper had opted not to take any chances and head for Immingham but he later told me that they'd watched our progress into Grimsby and described how they could see our mast head light appear out of the waves, whip wildly from side to side and then disappear, only to reappear a minute later and repeat the exercise. It was a great relief to get into Grimsby and safely alongside the launch already there, knowing that there was no way that they would get me out of there again that night. We promptly sent one of the deck-hands ashore to find a fish and chip shop and then settled down for the night and waited to be relieved the next morning.

There were few perks on the pilot launches. On Hull Roads the main perk was that during slack periods you might have the chance to pop into the Minerva, a pub next to the pier of the same name that we used, for a quick pint. At Spurn we didn't have this luxury although if we were early and making good time on the journey from Hull we'd stop at a pub in one of the villages on the way.

While at work there were odd times when we'd be asked to deliver mail to ships at anchor and the bucket that was lowered to collect the mail would often contain a gift of a bottle of spirits and maybe some cigarettes and tobacco. We had to be careful as smuggling was a sackable offence and the customs would often raid the pilot station and the launches, although I have no recollection of them ever finding anything. Drunkenness was also a sackable offence so we had to be careful not to over indulge if we decided to drink anything that had come our way, so gifts were usually shared out.

During my time on the pilot boats no one was sacked for drunkenness but one skipper did leave before his disciplinary hearing and another was demoted after mistaking the lights on Cleethorpes pier for those of Grimsby and ending up high and dry on the beach there.

Another thing we used to do at Spurn was to take newspapers out to returning fishing boats that may have been out for several weeks and in return were given a basket of fish, which we'd share out amongst the crews and stewards in the pilots' accommodation. I think that on some days we'd collected enough fish to justify a landing at Grimsby ourselves.

When Frank Berry took over as commodore of pilots he wanted to instigate a number of changes, which included the merger of the Hull Roads and Spurn crews. He also wanted all the skippers to look presentable and smart, as they were representatives of the company. Up until this point nobody had bothered much although some skippers bought their own uniforms and one or two wore the battle dress style uniforms provided by the company. I just wore jeans and jumpers and felt a bit of pride when someone came down to the launch and looked at the scruffy individual, me, leaning against the wheelhouse door and said, "Can I have a word with the skipper?"

"You're talking to him," I'd reply.

Anyway, Frank wanted us all in a merchant navy style officer's uniform which, after some negotiation, he agreed the company would pay for and sent us all off to Sam Bass in King Edward Street to be fitted out.

Frank also used the merger of the Spurn and Hull Roads crews to argue that there needed to be new union representatives to reflect the new, extended service. We felt that he hoped by doing this he'd get rid of Jim Dempster, Keith Woods and me, and that others that were less likely to argue and make demands would replace us. An election was called and Jim, Keith and I were re-elected by a massive majority of about four-fifths of the entire vote, so while the management may not have liked us the workforce certainly did.

Frank had a lot of good points though. When I went to see him to ask for a week off without pay he asked why and when I told him it was for an Open University residential week he said that I could have it with pay, as he wanted to encourage that type of personal development.

He also was surprised when he found out that the company didn't do anything special for employees who worked on the pilot boats when they retired. It was compulsory to retire at the age of sixty-five and up until that point the company just let them walk away when their time was up. Frank made arrangements to change this by ensuring that in future anyone retiring would receive some form of recognition of their service from the company.

1977 was the year of the Queen's Silver Jubilee and she was due to arrive in the Humber on the Royal Yacht "Britannia" for a visit to Yorkshire and Lincolnshire on July 12th. The plan was that the "Britannia" would take the Queen and her party to Grimsby where she'd go ashore by royal barge, and then the "Britannia" would proceed up river to Hull to await the Queen's return for the next part of the round Britain tour. The arrangements for this visit were planned months ahead with meticulous detail. Steps and landings on the banks of the Humber were cleaned and painted, not because the royal party would use them, but "just in case". The forward planning went even so far as to name the pilot for the "Britannia", the launch that would be used to take the pilot out to the ship and the crew who would be doing it. When these details were posted in the Pilot Office some people were most surprised to see that the launch would be the "Mitchell", which had only recently been delivered from the builders, and the crew would be my deck-hand Bernard Keating and me.

We were to pick up the "Mitchell" from Hull first thing in the morning, rather than going down to Spurn, and then wait to be joined by Frank Berry and the pilot before going down river to the Spurn base. Then we were to head out to meet the "Britannia" somewhere beyond the Spurn Lightship, so that the pilot could guide her through a flotilla comprising of the dredgers owned by the port authority.

Arrangements were also made for the wives of crew members working that day to come down to Spurn and be taken out with the hope of catching a glimpse of the Queen.

The main question asked by some on the pilot boats was apparently, "Why have they chosen Bob Addey?" usually with added comments like, "He's a Red," and "He's a commie," or "He doesn't even like royalty, he wants a republic."

All of these comments had some elements of truth in that I was certainly left of centre, but I believed in democracy and equality. However, as far as I was concerned the royal visit was just another job but with the added buzz of doing something different. Anyway, the next time we had a crew's meeting to see if they had any grievances that we could take forward, I thought I could have some fun with these comments.

Our meetings would usually take place in a back room of the Oberon pub opposite the Pilot Office and usually there was a good turn out, although due to the shift system not everyone could attend. At the end of our business, when everyone was enjoying a pint and chatting, I managed to get the conversation round to the arrangements for the royal visit.

"Of course there's a good reason why I've been chosen to skipper the 'Mitchell' on that day," I said.

"And why would that be?" one of my colleagues asked.

"Apparently the 'Britannia' is so pristine the sailors have to polish its sides – I'd just made this up - so that it maintains its shine," I said.

"What's that got to do with it?" was the come back.

"Well its obvious, the civil servants making the arrangements were concerned that if a royalist was skipper of the launch he'd be so busy bowing that he wouldn't see where he was going and crash into it."

On the day we arrived at the Horse Wash and picked up Frank Berry as arranged. Frank was carrying a large parcel wrapped in yellow oilskin.

"What's in the parcel?" I asked.

"This Bob," said Frank pointing to the parcel, "contains all the daily newspapers for the Queen, and do you know she takes every newspaper except for the Sun and the Morning Star."

I quickly picked up my copy of that morning's Morning Star and said, "I can put half of that right if you want me to?"

It was a lovely, sunny day and our wives were able to join us for the run out to the "Britannia" and even the dredgers looked spectacular decked out in bunting. The boarding went without mishap, no bowing, and we were then allowed to follow the royal yacht to Grimsby Roads where we observed the Queen nearly going arse over tit as she stumbled while boarding the royal barge which ferried her into Grimsby.

Then we took the wives back to Spurn where they disappeared off to find a pub while we carried on working as normal. It was a good day, and it looked like it would be another good summer; but I was in for surprise.

Within a few days of the Spurn outing Madeleine told me that our marriage was over. She said we had drifted apart and she had found another man who she described as an 'antique' dealer. It would have been hypercritical of me to criticise her for straying, there had been a couple of times when I had given into temptation when the opportunity had arisen, and I certainly agreed that we had drifted apart. Working shifts and unsociable hours, using my spare time to study at least two courses a year, painting, some part-time teaching, spending time on union activities and the rest of the time I was probably drunk – obviously hadn't helped our relationship. The good thing was that because we didn't have any children we didn't have much to argue about so we went to the pub to sort things out to make it easier for the solicitors.

We agreed that we'd sell the house and split the proceeds and that I could keep the furniture as she said she wouldn't need it given that her boyfriend was an 'antique' dealer. So, with no hard feelings, I wished her well in her new life living above her boyfriend's junk shop on Newland Avenue.

The worse thing at first for me was coming home to an empty house and then rattling about in all five bedrooms and two receptions. Within a week my mate, Mick Harrison who had introduced me to Madeleine, came around and we spent the afternoon in the Grafton pub getting blathered. Unfortunately I was due to do a nightshift at Spurn and arrived at the Pilot Office in a taxi and, to be truthful, in no fit state to start work. My colleagues, who by this time knew I was going through a marriage break up, didn't say a word until I'd taken over my launch and the control tower called with a job. One of the other skippers, an ex-trawler skipper called Jim Williams, immediately picked up his radio and said, "We'll do that job Control." The next time they called me Keith Woods did the same and they kept doing this until I'd sobered up enough to complete my watch safely. These were good mates and I never forgot their thoughtfulness and support.

Soon though I had to attend an Open University summer school at Sussex University in Brighton that I thought would help me get back in focus. The course was called "Art and the Environment", which was run jointly by the Arts, Technology and Social Sciences departments and I found it one of the most interesting courses that I'd done. For a start the only set book was a thing called the "Last Whole Earth Catalog" and then the university provided a practical kit that included a Polaroid camera. The summer school turned out to be the best therapy I could have wished for where I was involved in practical projects involving interacting with people using earth-balls and parachutes based on a Californian idea, in fact it was led by a lecturer from a university out there, called New Games. I also got involved in a video project exploring how people maintain private space on a, gradually getting more crowded, beach.

The people on the course were great from a rather eccentric Punch and Judy man, to a lady called Diane Moylan who had the best folk singing voice I'd ever heard that would bring tears to your eyes. Everyone else were all friendly and supportive. At the end of the course a number of us agreed to meet up at the Open University headquarters in Milton Keynes for a promotional weekend later in the year. As it happened, later that summer the National Union of Railwaymen sent me on a shop steward's course at Frant House, their training centre in the village of Frant, close to Tunbridge Wells in Kent. The NUR had given me a travel warrant to get down to Kent, which allowed me to travel or break my journey as I wished. I travelled down to London on the Sunday and stayed over with some friends before continuing on to Kent the next morning. Similarly, on my way back I went via Milton Keynes for my Open University reunion weekend.

Tunbridge Wells is not the place that you'd expect to find anything to do with trade unions, as we'd soon find out. Frant House was an ivy-clad, country mansion that the NUR had bought to use as a training centre and it was very comfortable with large bedrooms, good food and a bar. However, after a couple of days we got a bit more adventurous and decided that instead of our own bar we'd try the nocturnal delights of the village of Frant itself so we set off to see what we could find; in other words the first pub.

The first that we saw appeared inviting with its car park full of sports cars and inside looked cosy in that mock, country pub style. The clientele seemed to be made up of cravat wearing twats nursing halves of bitter while they yapped about the merits of their cars parked outside. Undeterred we approached the bar and waited for the landlord's attention. And we waited. And waited. And waited a bit longer but still no attempt was made to serve us.

It was as if we weren't there, as if we were invisible. We looked at each other to see if we had, "working class - do not serve," tattooed on our foreheads, but no, to us we looked quite normal but obviously not to our friendly landlord. So we left and entered the village. Eventually we came to another pub, with no car park this time, so we'd no idea what the customers would be like or how we'd be welcomed. But it turned out that the pub was full of local agricultural workers, and the landlord had no qualms about taking our money, no matter where we were from.

These two courses and associated social events kept me occupied through most of the summer which helped keep my mind off things like getting back into the dating and chatting-up business. As it happened one of my mates on the pilot boats, Jim Dempster, was temporarily estranged from his wife and living in a bedsit in Albert Avenue, so we started to hit the town pubs and clubs to see what was what. What was what, was that the scene was pretty much how I'd left it when I got married, even some of the faces were the same except that now they were mostly married with children. The routine now was that the girls would go out with their mates on a Thursday – 'Grab a Granny Night.' at the Locarno - and the blokes went out with their mates on a Friday night, with both of them going out on a Saturday night if they could get a baby sitter.

If Jim and I were on the same shift, while the others were talking about football or rugby, we would be comparing the cost of baked beans so the other lads started calling us the "Odd Couple". Jim and I latched on to this by giving ourselves an alias so that we'd call each other on the radio to make our pubbing and clubbing arrangements, so he became Vivian and I became Gaylord. I'd got the idea from a story I'd heard from Ron Fairfax about a young man who made out he had the name Eugene as a chat up line. I thought that I would give this ruse a try but thankfully I only had to use it once when I approached an attractive girl with long dark hair standing on her own in a night club. While I didn't know her I did recognise her as our paths had crossed in the past so, after some introductory small talk, I asked her her name.

"Marilyn," she replied, followed naturally by, "What's yours?"

Hesitation and then I'd asked, "My real name?"

"Yes of course."

"I'd rather not say."

"Why not? I've told you mine."

More hesitation.

"No, I'd be embarrassed."

"Don't be embarrassed, tell me your name."

"No, you will laugh."

"No I won't."

"Yes you will, they always laugh."

"I promise you I won't laugh."

"All right then its, its, its... GAYLORD."

She laughed.

"There, I told you that you'd laugh."

"I'm sorry."

Pulled! And that was how I broke the ice with Marilyn, who'd later become my partner and future wife, when I met her in the Bali Hai club towards the end of the year. I did, of course, tell her my real name straight afterwards. However, we had actually met before when she had turned me down when, as a sixteen-year-old fisherman, I had asked her to dance at the local Locarno – who says you never get another chance?

I had fancied her then and I fancied her now, as the fresh-faced girl had turned into a beautiful woman. But this was no fleeting flirtation between two people from broken marriages, for me, I had finally found the love of my life. I was a lucky man.

The house now was up for sale but was not moving so I was stuck in it through the winter. The house would get very cold when I was out at work. The main heating was a coal fire in the lounge, which I eventually replaced with an electric fire and a gas fire in the dining room. This meant that I spent a lot of time in the dining room as the fire took a while to warm the large, it was two rooms knocked into one, lounge. My only company at home, except when Marilyn came around, was a little black cat that used to wait for me outside in Grafton Street and run up and down excitedly when it saw me coming home from work. I thought at first that the cat must really love me but the reality was that he only wanted his dinner.

On the work front in early 1978 Frank Berry presented his latest plan and we didn't like it. He'd somehow got it into his head that we were overpaid and as he couldn't just reduce our wages wanted to subject us to a job evaluation process. We were dead against this at first but then thought that this could work in our favour with a bit of luck. There wasn't another group of workers within those employed under the term "floating staff" by the Docks Board that worked like we did providing a twenty-four hour, three hundred and sixty-five days a year' service. The people they would be comparing us to would be the captains and engineers employed on the dredgers, buoy yacht and conservancy vessels, some of whom got paid more than we did, so we were fairly confident that the findings would be in our favour.

The next time Frank raised the issue we said that we'd co-operate provided that if the results were in our favour the company would honour the outcome.

"Of course we will honour the outcome," said Mr Berry.

The next thing that happened was that a number of men with clipboards started following us around while asking us questions prior to writing their report and recommendations. When the report was ready the recommendations were clear. We had been under-assessed and the recommendations were that we should be upgraded by two points.

We then of course asked Mr Berry when we could expect this to happen and we were told, "Never!"

He backed down on his promise.

We called a meeting of the crew members in the back room of the Oberon and told them that Mr Berry had refused to honour his commitment. At first the hard liners said that we should go on strike but I said no, by going on strike we wouldn't get paid and the company would just man the launches with junior pilots until we came back. The answer was a work to rule and overtime ban. I went on to explain about my previous run-in with Frank Berry, when he'd told me that we should all carry out the checks listed in the standing instructions, before moving a launch and that as we already worked an average two hours a week overtime due to the shift system, we should insist that we were relieved on time.

If we were sent out on a job just before relieving time, for example at six-thirty at Spurn we should steam out for fifteen minutes, turn round and come back again for our relief at seven, whether the job was done or not, then the relieving crew would refuse to move the launch until they'd carried out all the standing instructions which should take at least twenty minutes. The crews agreed to try my plan.

The next day I went into the office and asked Mr Berry again if he was going to honour his promise and again the answer was no, so I said, " As from sixteen hundred on Friday all the launch crews will be operating a work to rule and overtime ban."

"May I remind you Mr Addey that your members should be working to rule all the time and your contract says that you work a reasonable amount of overtime," replied Frank.

"We work a forty-eight hour week, every four weeks, which averages at two hours a week that we consider a reasonable amount of overtime," was my reply as I walked out of the office.

The plan worked and our work to rule didn't even last forty-eight hours. For an hour or so at each watch change over the ships and pilots were put through the inconvenience of having to wait for a launch without any of us breaking our contracts or losing any pay. On the Sunday I was on day shift at Spurn when during the afternoon I was called up by the control and asked to go up to the bus shelter on the pier as Mr Berry wanted to talk to me on the land line. His message was simple, call off the action and we will upgrade everyone as the evaluation recommended.

Pilot boats at work.

Below. Newlove at Spurn. Note the old lifeboat slipway and the girders for the, yet to be built, control tower.

Chapter 32. Last Voyage to Lincolnshire.

My own position was now changing as I'd completed my degree and Bob Addey A.B. was now Bob Addey B.A. I was also now in a position to evaluate what I'd do in the future, stay working on the pilot boats or chance a new career in education. I'd had to give up my part-time teaching because of the job but there was no doubt that I enjoyed it and there were also more longer term career prospects to consider.

Again I saw an advert from Hull College asking for part-time lecturers and I thought that if I couldn't do regular classes at least I could do some cover as there was only a few weeks left to the end of term. As soon as they received my application I was given some classes that fitted in with my full-time work schedules and I was also told that there was a full-time job at the college that would be advertised shortly. Jobs in further education at that time were advertised nationally in the Times Education Supplement on a Friday, and the Guardian on Tuesdays, so I bought these publications and waited for the Hull post to be advertised. I knew that the competition would be stiff for this job and that I lacked interview experience, so I thought it would be a good idea to apply for a few other jobs to get more confidence ahead of my Hull application. With this in mind I applied for about six lecturer jobs with the hope that the interview at Hull would be last. My plan went wrong. I was called for an interview for the job in Hull first; and it didn't go very well.

The set-up for the interview was in a boardroom with a massive table, in the middle of which sat the principal with me opposite. At the ends of the table were the head of department and a representative from the local council. The table was so big that it was impossible to maintain any eye contact with the interviewers without swinging my head from one side to the other and, on top of that the sun was shining right into my eyes through the large window behind the college principal. I knew I was on a loser when the principal asked me about the job I was doing on the pilot boats and I gave him a description.

"Oh, a sort of floating taxi driver," he sneered.

"In a way," I replied. "But I think that taxi drivers provide a valuable social service for the community in a similar way to how we provide an essential service to maintain the commercial validity of the ports that keep this country functioning."

It was down hill all the way from then on really and I was not surprised when I didn't get the job.

The way that the selection took place in those days in further education was to first submit an application form with a covering letter. Then, if you were lucky, you'd be called for interview that usually meant having to arrive in the morning to meet the principal and other key managers, then having a formal interview in the afternoon.

After the interview, instead of disappearing off, you were expected to stay in a room with the other candidates until everyone had been interviewed and the panel made its decision. This, to me, resembled the scenes backstage during a beauty pageant when the contestants are waiting and biting their nails before the winner to be announced, whereas in our case they'd be invited back in by the panel and offered the job.

Of the six jobs I applied for I was invited for interview for four: Scunthorpe, Chester and Boston, and of course Hull which had been a disaster. While Scunthorpe was commutable, although the Humber Bridge wouldn't be open for a few years, it looked like that if I wanted to further my ambitions I'd have to leave Hull. I spoke to Marilyn about this and she said I should go for it and we could set up home together even if it meant moving away.

This was a big step. A life changing decision and a much bigger gamble for Marilyn rather than me as she had two children to consider, Paul and Mark, and the move would be a major disruption for them as well as us. Anyway, there was the very likely possibility that I wouldn't get any of the jobs.

The first of the interviews was at Chester College. Here, one of the members of the panel had once worked for United Towing in Hull and knew the area, so the first part of the interview was mainly him reminiscing, before moving on to the main part that also went well. So well in fact that I thought I'd got the job when they called me back in after interviewing the others. However, the chair of the panel said that they had called me back in because I'd given a very good interview and that they had been fascinated by my background and they would have liked to have offered me the job but my teaching qualification was not nationally recognised. They advised me to get a nationally recognised qualification - which I did a few years later - and then reapply. I thanked them for their kindness and advice and left.

The next interview was at Scunthorpe College and again the interview went well. The problem here was that when talking to the other candidates I found that one was an internal candidate, usually the favourite, who'd already been doing the job on a part-time basis for about two years. He was young, married with a couple of children and I fully expected his name to be called when the panel made its decision. But it wasn't. They called me back in and offered me the job - and I turned it down.

"Why?" the chair of the panel asked.

"I can't take this job as there's a young man out there who's been doing it for two years," I replied. "I have a job that I can go back to. He hasn't and I would feel that I was taking the food out of his children's mouths if I were to accept."

The chair of the panel thought for a moment and then said, "Well, while I find your grounds for not taking the job commendable, I'll give you a piece of advice young man. If you want to get on in further education you need to get all those ideas of ethics and morality right out of your head."

That left only Boston. This was for a position of Lecturer in General Studies, Communications and Trade Union Studies. Basically they wanted someone to help deliver TUC courses for health and safety representatives and shop stewards and then fill up the rest of their timetable with general and communication studies – right up my street really. In the waiting area I discovered again that there was an internal candidate, so I suggested that he must be favourite.

The middle-aged gentleman concerned then turned to me and said, "Don't go in there thinking that, they've already turned me down twice."

And they turned him down again as I was offered the job. This time I accepted. The starting salary was similar to what I'd been getting on the pilot boats but no shift work and, of course, more holidays. In addition, apart from annual pay rises, I'd receive annual increments plus an increment if I added an honours grade to my degree (which I did within two years) and they would also give me an increment if I completed a Certificate in Education, on a day and block release basis at Nottingham Trent University, that the college would send me on. From A.B. to B.A. to B.A.(hons) Cert. Ed. – not bad for an ex-galley boy.

I'd attended the interview without having to take any time off. On the day I'd asked my relieving coxswain to cover for me if I was late and had taken an early morning ferry for the drive down to Boston. After the interview and a pint with the head of department, Colin Wilkins, I drove back again and was able to complete a night shift on Hull Roads.

It was still only late May and I was not due to start my new job until September so there was no hurry to give my notice in. But there was some urgency in sorting out accommodation. Marilyn, my new wife-to-be, had two young boys, Paul and Mark, so we just couldn't disappear down to Boston when we liked. We decided that the answer was to book into Butlins at Skegness, only twenty miles from Boston, and use it as a base. As it happened we found a house almost immediately in a cul-de-sac called Colindale, so things were falling into place.

One thing that was a concern though was my fertility. I needed to find out once and for all if everything was working. I went to my doctor and she said that normally they'd only send married people for a test but she thought that because my circumstances were special, in that I had a new partner, she could make an exception. I was given a phial and instructions to take the sample to Hull Kingston

General. Duly I collected a sample and the next morning took it to the clinic at the hospital. I was a bit embarrassed so tried to be as quick as possible in handing in the sample and making a dash to the door, when the nurse shouted, "Wait!"

I stopped dead in my tracks and looked back to see her holding the phial up to the light, "When did you take this sample?" she asked.

"La, la, la last night," I stuttered as I wanted the floor to swallow me up.

"Last night! Last night! That's no good! We want it fresh!"

Suitably humiliated, I was handed another phial and slunk off.

The next one was accepted without a hitch and I waited, with dread, for the results. However, the embarrassment and humiliation was worth it when I got the letter that said that the tests showed that I was "reasonably fertile" and we proved it by providing Paul and Mark with a sister, Jane, a few years later.

Eventually it was time to give my notice in to Frank who said that he was pleased for me and wished me all the best for the future. In the last week of August I left the pilot service and my sea career.

I'd enjoyed my time working on the pilot boats. My colleagues had been a great bunch of blokes and I also got on well with a number of the pilots, some of whom I'd sailed with in the merchant navy, like Fred Rowden and Mike Barratt, who both in their own ways had encouraged me to further myself.

The last ship that I attended on my final shift at Spurn was one of the large North Sea ferries, and at seven o'clock in the evening I stepped ashore for the last time as a paid sailor. I'd spent just under sixteen years at sea and the experience had defined me to a point that no matter what happened in the future, I'd always be a silly sailor. I knew that I'd always miss the sea although there would be many times especially in winter when I was glad that I wasn't out on the open water facing the elements.

Many years later, when I had my own warm office in a large college in Birmingham - about as far away from the sea as you could get if you don't count the Grand Union Canal – I'd have a picture of the 'Lord Jellicoe' on my wall. Then, if ever I started feeling sorry for myself because I was being worked too hard, I'd look at it and think: No, that was proper hard work.

At the end of that last shift as we jumped out of the minibus opposite the Pilot Office I said goodbye to all my mates and headed home to pack for the big move.

A couple of nights later I was at home in Grafton Street and Marilyn asked if I wanted to go out.

"I'm not sure," I replied and left it at that, then after a short while I said, "Maybe we could pop to the Providence for a couple?"

She said that would be all right if I really felt like it, so we set off. On entering the pub I noticed that there was something going on in the lounge so steered her towards the bar where Jack was standing by the door. Jack picked up a red book, I think it was his price list, turned me around towards the lounge and said, "Robert Addey, this is your life!"

And in the lounge were all the lads from the pilot boats who'd arranged this do in secret with Marilyn's help. It was one of the best things that had ever happened to me and they'd even had a collection to buy me a set of briefcases. The night didn't end at the Providence either as we all went back to Grafton Street for a party after closing time.

The following year we were able to invite them all again to the Providence to celebrate our wedding. I'd enjoyed my time on the pilot boats and would miss the camaraderie that I shared with the other crew members. They were a great bunch of blokes and we'd had many laughs and good times during that past seven years.

Finally it was time for the big home move. The removal van was loaded and we set off to board the Humber ferry, 'Farringford' for the trip over to New Holland and on to Boston.

A new job, a new house, a new town, a new family, a new wife and a new life; and as the ropes were cast and the big paddles churned up the muddy waters of the Humber, I got the buzz again.

The End.

Above, From the left: Louise Collins, John Thomas Henry Addey, Margaret Addey, Denise (Addey) Collins, Jack Collins, Paula Collins, Doris (Smith) Burke, Marilyn Addey, Bob Addey,   Marjorie Addey and Jim Dempster.

Below left. Three launch skippers: Bob (Gaylord) Addey, Jim (Vivian) Dempster and Keith (Woody) Woods.

Below right. Graduation day with Mark and Paul.

Above. The "Commander Snowden" aground in the Horse Wash.
Below. The Royal Yacht "Britannia" in the Humber during the
Queen's visit in 1977.

About the Author.

Bob Addey grew up in Hull in the 1950s and 60s when the city was the third major seaport in the country and the home of the largest deep-water fishing fleet in the world.

Bob left the Hull Trinity House Navigation School at age fifteen to join a deep-sea trawler as galley boy with a view to a career on the trawlers. As soon as he could he became a deckie learner (trainee deck-hand) but then soon realised that there were easier ways of making a living at sea other than being on the open deck gutting fish in all weathers, so he left the fishing fleet and the treacherous Arctic waters and joined the merchant navy in search of more exotic places and experiences.

He spent eight years in the merchant navy before joining the Humber Pilots' Steam Cutter Company and becoming a pilot launch coxswain, a role he held for another seven years. During this time Bob studied for an Open University degree and became a part-time lecturer at Hull College while continuing his job on the pilot boats. Eventually he decided that he would like to pursue a career in education and in 1978, after nearly sixteen years at sea, he became a full-time lecturer at Boston College in Lincolnshire.

Bob spent nine years in Boston starting as a lecturer and then moving into a management role as a Youth Training Scheme manager. He was then asked to introduce adult training schemes for the long-term unemployed into the college and after the success of this work was offered a job as Head of Department of Adult Training, Education and Community Development at East Birmingham College. Bob worked in education in Birmingham for the next twenty years serving in a number of roles both within the college and across the city of Birmingham. One of these roles was manager of the Birmingham and Solihull Widening Participation Project designed to get all of the education providers in those areas co-operating to encourage new adult learners to take up the opportunities on offer. Bob's final role before retiring was as Head of Campus of East Birmingham College which was then part of City College, Birmingham.

He contributed to a number of educational publications during his career but it was only in retirement that he decided to "swing the lamp" and write about his own education and his experiences during his time at sea.

Bob still lives in Solihull, a town about as far away from the sea as you can get if you don't count the Grand Union Canal, with his wife of over forty years, Marilyn.